Advance Praise for *Queer Th*

"*Queer Then and Now* is the balm we need to remind always stay vigilant against white supremacy, homophobia, transphobia, and fake moral panic. For as the lectures collected here index, every iterative "turn" in queer studies has emerged to address the multiple assaults on queer liberation. Chronicling the past twenty years of scholarship and activism, this volume is an essential addition to the queer studies archive."

—**E. PATRICK JOHNSON, author of**
Honeypot: Black Southern Women Who Love Women

"An evolving feast of insights and ideas, *Queer Then and Now* brings together some of the most brilliant minds in the academy, the arts, and community activism while tracking the most urgent issues in queer and trans studies over the past two decades. This stunning collection documents their evolution as barometers for social change, as signs without fixed political references, and as key concepts for the creation of a world yet to come."

—**DAVID L. ENG, author of *Racial Melancholia, Racial Dissociation:***
On the Social and Psychic Lives of Asian Americans

"*Queer Then and Now* collects nearly two decades of Kessler Lectures by queer luminaries, people of light and leading. Gathered here, and supplemented by authors' reflections written for this volume, these talks reveal and advance some of our most urgent conversations: about the value of CLAGS and other public queer intellectual and artistic spaces; about the changing nature of queer critique in its confrontation with racial capitalism; about the essential work of knowing the past and activating it anew; and about the commitment, by queers, to liberation. This is a book of indispensable and dear voices, a book to be heard, read, taught, shared, and spoken back to."

—**MATT BRIM, author of**
Poor Queer Studies: Confronting Elitism in the University

"A startlingly relevant collection of essays from cutting-edge queer thinkers and activists, *Queer Then and Now* combines a deep archive with trenchant reflections on what it means to seek justice, foster community, and shed the shackles of respectability in our unfolding present. By enlarging who and what constitutes queer, this series of diverse provocations invites us to fight for better ways of living."

—**AMBER JAMILLA MUSSER, author of**
Sensual Excess: Queer Femininity and Brown Jouissance

"Essential reading for anyone in queer and trans studies. The field's fundamental ethos is to crack open the knowledges governing disobedient bodies and desires. This volume does this and more, revisiting to glorious effect earlier iterations of the queer canon. Queer and trans theory was never thus, it was always this."

—**PAISLEY CURRAH, author of *Sex Is as Sex Does:***
Governing Transgender Identity

QUEER THEN AND NOW

The David R. Kessler Lectures
2002–2020

**FROM CLAGS:
CENTER FOR LGBTQ STUDIES**

**EDITED BY DEBANUJ DASGUPTA,
JOSEPH L. V. DONICA, AND MARGOT WEISS**

THE FEMINIST PRESS
AT THE CITY UNIVERSITY OF NEW YORK
NEW YORK CITY

Published in 2023 by the Feminist Press
at the City University of New York
The Graduate Center
365 Fifth Avenue, Suite 5406
New York, NY 10016

feministpress.org

First Feminist Press edition 2023

Compilation and introduction copyright © 2023 by Debanuj DasGupta, Joseph L. V. Donica, and
Margot Weiss

Copyright information for individual lectures appears on page 388, which constitutes a continuation
of this copyright page.

 This book was made possible thanks to a grant from the New York State
Council on the Arts with the support of Governor Kathy Hochul and the
New York State Legislature.

 This book is supported in part by an award from the National Endowment
for the Arts.

 This book is supported in part by public funds from the New York City
Department of Cultural Affairs in partnership with the City Council.

First printing August 2023

Cover design by Dana Li
Text design by Drew Stevens

Library of Congress Cataloging-in-Publication Data is available for this title.
ISBN 978-1-55861-245-7

PRINTED IN THE UNITED STATES OF AMERICA

Contents

Introduction: Queer Ideas, Messy Archives,   **1**
and the Then and Now of Queer Studies
Debanuj DasGupta, Joseph L. V. Donica, and Margot Weiss

2002   **Jonathan Ned Katz**   **15**
        Making Sex History:
        Obsessions of a Quarter Century

2003   **Gayle Rubin**   **33**
        Geologies of Queer Studies:
        It's Déjà Vu All Over Again

2004   **Isaac Julien**   **51**
        Cinematic Rearticulations

2006   **Adrienne Rich**   **67**
        "Candidates for My Love":
        Three Gay and Lesbian Poets

2007   **Douglas Crimp**   **87**
        Action around the Edges

2008   **Susan Stryker**   **111**
        Ghost Dances:
        A Trans-Movement Manifesto

2009   **Sarah Schulman**   **127**
        Ties That Bind:
        Familial Homophobia and Its Consequences

2010   Urvashi Vaid   147
         What Can Brown Do for You?
         Race, Sexuality, and the Future of LGBT Politics

Queer Then and Now **Roundtable:**   183
Histories of Queer and Trans Activism
Amber Hollibaugh, Dean Spade,
and Urvashi Vaid with Shanté Paradigm Smalls

2012   Martin Duberman   203
         Acceptance at What Price?
         The Gay Movement Reconsidered

2013   Cheryl Clarke   217
         Queer Black Trouble:
         In Life, Literature, and the Age of Obama

2014   Cathy J. Cohen   235
         #DoBlackLivesMatter?
         From Michael Brown to CeCe McDonald:
         On Black Death and LGBTQ Politics

2015   Richard Fung   255
         Re-Orientations:
         Shifts and Continuities in
         Asian Canadian Queer and Trans
         Identities and Activism

2016   Dean Spade   273
         When We Win We Lose:
         Mainstreaming and the Redistribution
         of Respectability

2017   Sara Ahmed   297
         Queer Use

2018   **Amber Hollibaugh**   325
           Hope and the Power of Desire:
           Our Vision for Changing the World

2019   **Jasbir K. Puar**   337
           A No-State "Solution":
           Inter/nationalism and the Question
           of Queer Theory

2020   **Roderick A. Ferguson**   353
           Queer and Trans Liberation
           and the Critique of Fascism,
           or When S.T.A.R. Met Césaire
           and the Frankfurt School

Queer Then and Now **Roundtable:**   371
Histories of Queer and Trans Scholarship
Roderick A. Ferguson, Jasbir K. Puar,
and Susan Stryker with Shaka McGlotten

Permissions Acknowledgments   388

Editors' Acknowledgments   390

Introduction: Queer Ideas, Messy Archives, and the Then and Now of Queer Studies

Debanuj DasGupta, Joseph L. V. Donica, and Margot Weiss

Queer Then, Queer Now. This volume represents twenty years of cutting-edge work in queer and trans studies from some of its most influential voices. As queer studies approaches its fourth (at least) decade, what's "now" in queer studies? Many approaches have come to define queer studies now: queer of color critique, transnational and diasporic queer studies, trans theory and the emergence of trans studies as its own field,[1] the affective turn, new materialisms, and razor-sharp critiques of the political and public sphere. Highlighting the intersections of race, ethnicity, nation, disability, gender, and sexuality, today's queer and trans studies works across activism, academia, art, and community practice. The scholars in this volume have been at the cutting edge of these transformations. In bringing together the past two decades of the Kessler Awards, we are in a sense returning to the past to think about what the future of queer and trans studies might hold.

Each year since 1992, the Center for LGBTQ Studies (CLAGS) has awarded the David R. Kessler Award to a distinguished scholar, activist, and/or artist whose work has had a significant influence on the field of LGBTQ studies. The seventeen scholars in this volume have shaped new directions in queer and trans studies by considering the synergy between theory and activism, the possibilities of queer art and media, the forma-tion and transnational circulation of queer of color critique, the challenges of transnationalizing queer theory, the lasting impact of Black feminisms, the multiple genealogies of activism and scholarship, and the challenges posed to queer studies by trans studies and activism. The winners include writers, poets, and filmmakers Isaac Julien, Adrienne Rich, Cheryl Clarke, Sarah Schulman, and Richard Fung; longtime activists Urvashi Vaid and Amber Hollibaugh; queer of color, trans, and transnational theorists Cathy J. Cohen, Roderick A. Ferguson, Sara Ahmed, Jasbir K. Puar, and Dean Spade; and historians and pioneers of queer/trans studies Jonathan Ned Katz, Gayle Rubin, Carole Vance, Douglas Crimp, Susan Stryker, and Martin Duberman, who chart some of the messy genealogies of queer and trans studies as it has become quasi-institutionalized in the academy and yet continues to serve as a site of panic and outrage in the political sphere.

We offer this volume as an archive of sorts: to preserve each Kessler Lecture as a snapshot of queer and trans thinking at a particular moment in time—the "then" of queer studies. But we have also sought a short reflection from each scholar to accompany their chapter, a "now" that takes up how queer and trans studies and activisms have changed since the lecture was given. And there has been change. The past two decades have seen the legalization of same-sex marriage in the United States, alongside new paradoxes of recognition after the "trans tipping point"—reopening the complexities of what David L. Eng, Jack Halberstam, and José Esteban Muñoz termed "queer liberalism" in 2005: "liberal inclusion" of some LGBTQ subjects in the form of rights, state recognition, and consumer citizenship.[2] We have seen the rise of the queer-led #BlackLivesMatter movement after 2013, coalitional trans-led anti-detention organizing, and, in recent years, a reinvigorated and bold white supremacist fascism in the United States. We have seen the rise of transnational queer and trans scholarship and activisms that challenge what Maya Mikdashi and Jasbir K. Puar framed as queer studies' US "parochialization"—the US/Western domination of queer studies: "queer theory as American studies"[3]—amid the ongoing wars of imperialism, settler-colonial genocides, and ecological disasters.

What do queer and trans studies offer now? How can we draw on the "then" to guide us into different futures? This volume offers some openings.

CLAGS and Kessler: Then and Now

The Center for Lesbian and Gay Studies (CLAGS) was founded in 1987 through conversations and dialogues led by gay historian Martin Duberman. CLAGS formally became a City University of New York (CUNY) institute in 1991.[4] The founding of CLAGS as the nation's first university-based "Gay and Lesbian" research institute offered an opening for the institutionalization of LGBTQ studies. CLAGS officially changed its name in 2014 to become the Center for LGBTQ Studies as a way of honoring the formation of queer and trans studies as thriving interdisciplinary fields that challenge assumptions about gender normativity, bodily capacity, and the privileging of white subjects in earlier iterations of "Lesbian and Gay Studies."[5] CLAGS has been part of CUNY—the largest urban public university system in the US—for over thirty-five years. The history of CLAGS signifies how the emergence of LGBTQ studies is entangled with struggles for funding and defending public education in the United States. CLAGS's history challenges the idea that queer and trans theory is nurtured in elite private and public universities. Many of CLAGS's staff, board members, and affiliated scholars have shown up to the picket lines to challenge the defunding of the CUNY system, resist the securitizing of CUNY campuses post–September 11, and more recently, to organize town halls that document the experiences of trans and gender nonconforming (TGNC) students, staff, and faculty within the CUNY system. CLAGS's current executive director, Justin Brown, is located at a community college, and doing significant teaching that integrates LGBTQ studies with coursework on leadership development and community and public health. The work of many CLAGS board and staff members is public-facing, significantly rooted in scholarly and activist traditions. The Kessler awardees, and their lectures assembled in this book, represent this dynamic interface between the street and the classroom.

Genealogies are political and contested. The emergence of queer and trans theory as a school of thought that extends cultural studies traditions such as those of the Birmingham School and French post-structuralist and postcolonial feminist theory has been told as originating from Teresa de Lauretis's introduction to the 1991 special issue of *differences* titled "Queer Theory: Lesbian and Gay Sexualities"[6]—alongside Judith Butler's *Gender Trouble: Feminism and the Subversion of Identity* (1990),[7] Eve Kosofsky Sedgwick's *Epistemology of the Closet* (1990),[8] and Michael Warner's special section of *Social Text*, "Fear of a Queer Planet" (1991).[9] And yet, as Michael Hames-García argues, this canonical origin story consolidates the whiteness of queer by positioning pre-1990s Black and women of color feminism, queer of color critique, and postcolonial queer/gender theory (the work of, for instance, intellectuals, poets, and activists like Kessler awardees Barbara Smith or Cherríe Moraga) as derivative or peripheral, rather than preceding and formative.[10] The emergence of queer and trans ideas also came from AIDS activism, interventions in art and film, and other cultural productions that shaped and were shaped in the dynamic exchange between academia, art, community, and activism.

Since then, the intimacy between academic institutions and LGBTQ studies has only deepened. Today there are robust departments, institutes, and programs in gender, women's, and sexuality studies, along with majors or minors in LGBTQ studies, in most academic institutions throughout the United States. This "progress," however, has brought its own challenges. Institutional recognition has brought demands for standardization of curriculum, as backlashes against gender and sexuality studies and critical ethnic studies impede our discussions of sex, desire, and sex work. The Kessler Awards resonate with these developments and yet can be thought of as a space that honors intellectual freedom. Many of the awardees are scholars whose work has been considered dangerous within academic settings, like Gayle Rubin, Carole Vance, and Jasbir K. Puar. Some are scholars who do not create knowledge primarily in or for academic settings; rather, they are public intellectuals, activists, and cultural workers like Amber Hollibaugh, Urvashi Vaid, Sarah Schulman, Cheryl Clarke, Adrienne Rich, Douglas Crimp, and Sara Ahmed. The Kessler awardees often signify major canons in the field: Susan Stryker and Dean Spade in trans studies; Cathy J. Cohen, Jasbir K. Puar, Sara Ahmed, and Roderick A. Ferguson in queer of color critique; Martin Duberman and Jonathan Ned Katz for gay and queer history; Isaac Julien and Richard Fung for queer art and film. However, as a field, LGBTQ studies has always resisted canonization. Queer is as queer does, then and now. Thus, we do not want to suggest the Kessler awardees as canonical, but rather as those who have left an imprint on our field. These are scholars who have advanced the field through provocations and incitement.

It has been nearly twenty years since the publication of *Queer Ideas: The David R. Kessler Lectures in Lesbian and Gay Studies*, featuring the first ten years of Kessler Lectures, 1992–2001.[11] That first volume provided an essential introduction to queer studies, featuring some of its most influential early thinkers, writers, and theorists: Joan Nestle, Edmund White, Barbara Smith, Monique Wittig, Esther Newton, Samuel R. Delany, Eve Kosofsky Sedgwick, John D'Emilio, Cherríe Moraga, and Judith Butler.

In the years that followed, the events of September 11, 2001, the subsequent George W. Bush regime and its War on Terror, and attacks on public education ushered in a different kind of geopolitical order. Simultaneously, we have seen the enrollment numbers in queer and trans studies classes increase. Movements such as #BlackLivesMatter and demands for immigration and climate justice are some of the critical issues addressed by recent

Kessler awardees. Changes in the art world, in transnational political organizing and feminist critique, in practices of archiving and making history have made possible new queer and trans worlds. And yet, white supremacy, virulent homophobia, transphobia, xenophobia, and racism as well as the rise of new authoritarian movements around the globe continue to threaten queer and trans communities in the early twenty-first century. In bringing together the past twenty years of Kessler Lectures, we highlight these contradictions and tensions among queer academics, cultural workers, and activists as well as the work queer and trans thought does today in multiple public and political spheres.

The volume also highlights the survival of CLAGS. CLAGS is housed in one of the largest urban public university systems, the City University of New York, which predominantly serves students of color, first-generation students, immigrant students, and poor students. At the time of writing this introduction, CUNY faculty, staff, and students are organizing to demand a $1.7 billion investment from the governor of New York and significantly more investment from the city. More than 60 percent of CUNY undergraduate students come from families with annual incomes of less than $30,000. The ongoing public programming at CLAGS, including hosting the annual Kessler Awards for free (supported through an endowment), gestures toward a queer reuse of public resources. In a 2008 interview, the man for whom the award is named, David R. Kessler [1930–2022], reflected that he had originally planned to donate to Yale University, with the idea that endowing a lectureship at prestigious Yale "would send a powerful positive public message" about homosexuality.[12] Yale was "not quite ready for the idea" of a public lecture on advancing gay and lesbian scholarship in the early 1990s, but CLAGS was—and indeed, CLAGS "was very happy to hear that somebody wanted to give them money . . . I don't think anybody had offered to give them any money before."[13] And thus, the Kessler Lecture Series became "the first of its kind at an academic institution."[14] We honor David Kessler in the year of his passing. The award that David Kessler endowed continues to highlight the best in queer and trans scholarship, building community and connecting scholars, activists, artists, and community members across generations. In this spirit, we hope this volume opens up new debates around queer and trans studies and their close proximity to settler colonialism, unending wars, and the ascendancy of whiteness as well as how queer studies then and now might offer resistance to such systems of oppression.

Overview of the Kessler Lectures and Speakers

Each chapter that follows includes the Kessler awardee's original lecture (lightly edited for clarity) in chronological order, alongside a new reflection on the key themes of their lecture in the context of queer and trans studies, politics, and communities today. The format of the Kessler Awards has traditionally included three testimonial speakers who attest to the impact of the Kessler awardee's scholarship. For reasons of space, we were unable to include all the testimonials from eminent and intimate CLAGS members and friends, but we provide a few highlights below. Given the fragility and incompleteness of queer archives, queer temporalities, and queer bodies, we were not able to include lectures and reflections for all our Kessler awardees. Two Kessler awardees, Adrienne Rich and Douglas Crimp, passed before this project began. Instead of reflections after their lectures, we have included tributes by those who knew their work well. We were not able to include Carole Vance's lecture; and reflections for Jonathan Ned Katz and Amber Hollibaugh are missing from the incomplete archive you hold in your hand. However, we have added a luminous quote from each of their testimonials as a way of situating each awardee within their field and highlighting their accomplishments. We have also provided a brief biographical note as well as some bibliographic information as a guide for the reader.

The volume starts in 2002 with Jonathan Ned Katz's "Making Sex History: Obsessions of a Quarter Century." An activist-scholar identifying and analyzing the experiences of gay and lesbian historical subjects, Katz has described his "documentary impulse" as "defensive, a compensatory reactive move against those who directly or indirectly denied the existence of our past." Gay and lesbian research required "detective work," a "tracing of history's missing persons." His 1976 book, *Gay American History,* is a foundational text in this tradition.[15]

In 2003, the fragility of the queer archive was addressed by anthropologist and queer/feminist theorist Gayle Rubin in her lecture "Geologies of Queer Studies: It's Déjà Vu All Over Again." Rubin describes the history of challenges queers have had in finding their own histories and their places within the scant documents that existed for much of the twentieth century. She describes her own uphill battle as she sought out a lesbian archive while in graduate school in the 1960s and 1970s. Using the metaphor of geological layers, Rubin notes that some eras have richer queer archives than others. It is our task, according to Rubin, "to ensure that such sedimentary formations are identified, excavated, catalogued, and utilized to produce new knowledge"—and to pass on collective queer knowledge to future generations.

Groundbreaking Black British filmmaker Isaac Julien's 2004 Kessler Lecture, "Cinematic Rearticulations," comes next. Julien's lecture focuses on how images shape our understanding of the world and possibly transform it. In his lecture, Julien historicizes queer art-making in the gallery and the cinema as raced and queered spaces, in order to develop visual vocabularies of critical transformation. Julien also reflects on his own legendary work, *Looking for Langston* (1989), *The Attendant* (1993), *Frantz Fanon: Black Skin, White Mask* (1995), and *Baltimore* (2003), as well as how cities like Philadelphia and Baltimore enabled his own visual awakening and served as sites important to the development of a distinctly queer urban aesthetic.

While we were unable to include the text of feminist anthropologist Carole Vance's 2005 lecture, "My Travels with Sex," the lecture can be viewed on the CLAGS YouTube channel.[16] In the lecture, Vance moves the biographical into the political sphere. She considers the institutionalization of antipornography feminism in the 1980s and 1990s, up to today's sex panic over sex "trafficking." Vance's expansive critique of sex as *only* danger, without pleasure,[17] is a queer critique of conservative moral panics that enshrine the private family as the zone of safety. She asks, "How do we address all ranges of sexual violations and rights abuses without inadvertently reasserting for women that purity is the most valuable thing they have?" Testimonial speaker Ann Snitow described Vance as a "discourse warrior" who fuses "precise and careful intellectual work" with "the political need to change the terms of public conversation."

The creation of new vocabularies is also the work of influential lesbian-feminist poet and essayist Adrienne Rich (1929–2012). In Rich's 2006 lecture, "'Candidates for My Love': Three Gay and Lesbian Poets," she turns her eye toward gay and lesbian poets, desire, community politics, love, and what she names as "a different kind of future." This is the theme of Rich's work and one she claims for queer studies—a "queer" that begins "not in academia but in spaces opened up by the movements of the 1960s and 1970s." Weaving together poetry and analysis, in this lecture Rich makes the still-relevant comment that "radical politics is a great confluent project of the human imagination, of which art and literature are indispensable tributaries." We include, after her lecture, a new tribute to Rich's work and her importance to the field of queer studies in the early 2000s written by her son, Pablo Conrad, and lesbian poet Julie R. Enszer.

Like Rich, AIDS activist and queer art historian and critic Douglas Crimp (1944–2019) looks for the radical possibilities on the margins and hunts for solitude in a cramped urban fabric. Crimp's 2007 lecture, "Action around the Edges," is a memoir of New York City queer and art spaces in the 1970s. Yet while centered in Greenwich Village and Tribeca, Crimp's work points to more universally emancipatory possibilities. Testimonial speaker Rosalyn Deutsche argued that Crimp "bound himself . . . to a course of action that places his work in the service of social emancipation"; his goal was to "change the way art functions in society." Feminist, queer, and affect studies scholar Ann Cvetkovich provides a tribute to Crimp and his influence on her own work thinking and feeling through the queer archive.

Historian, filmmaker, and trans studies visionary Susan Stryker's 2008 lecture, "Ghost Dances: A Trans-Movement Manifesto," is what she calls a "secular sermon." Stryker ponders the connections between trans studies and artistic responses to climate change, looking to trans affect as a site of transformation in relation to the Indigenous ceremony of Ghost Dance. Is it that "how we physically move our bodies, individually and collectively, has the power to transform both ourselves and the world"? she muses. Testimonial speaker Paisley Currah says that Stryker's work pushes against any attempt to allow trans studies "to be comfortably contained by familiar disciplinary tropes." Of her importance to the field, Currah says, "the advances that trans studies has made in the academy have been brought about to a huge degree by Susan."

Writer, activist, and AIDS historian Sarah Schulman's 2009 lecture, "Ties That Bind: Familial Homophobia and Its Consequences," also critiques larger structures, but through the lens of "systems of familial homophobia." She focuses her critique on the liberal "it gets better" political vision (of, for instance, same-sex marriage campaigns that imagine the privatized family unit as a foundation of US citizenship). "Being niche-marketed a product is not citizenship," she argues. "It's the end of autonomy, not the beginning." Schulman's lecture is a call for radically rethinking the queer's position in an unjust society, and she looks to lesbian experience as a site of possibility among the ruins. Testimonial speaker Sarah Chinn describes Schulman as offering "a vision of lesbian life that formed my dyke imagination. . . . In [Schulman's] writing, lesbians do not exist at the margins. We are the center of the universe. We are clever, sexy, politically astute."

The issue of niche marketization of identity also arises in LGBT/queer activist and writer Urvashi Vaid's 2010 lecture, "What Can Brown Do for

You? Race, Sexuality, and the Future of LGBT Politics." Vaid (1958–2022) explores in granular detail why matters of racial justice should matter to the LGBTQ movement. She argues that "race in our movement is seen primarily as an issue of diversity or outreach, not as an issue of equity or fundamental justice that it is our business as a movement to achieve." Vaid points to the empowered white nationalist movement and the theoretical bent of the field of queer studies, calling for us to "take up some new campaigns that actually put into practice our long-held theories that sexuality, race, economic status, disability status, gender, and gender identity and expression are all interconnected." We are honored to have been able to include Vaid's lecture and her reflections, as well as her discussion on our first roundtable. Vaid's passing during the assembling of this book is a huge loss for many in our communities. In her roundtable remarks, Vaid fondly recalls attending CLAGS events as a site of community-building. We are honored to have been in community with her throughout the history of CLAGS.

The state and future of queer studies is explored in the first of two roundtable discussions, "*Queer Then and Now*: Histories of Queer and Trans Activism," held virtually in 2021 and moderated by CLAGS board member Shanté Paradigm Smalls, a scholar, artist, and writer whose research focuses on Black popular culture in music, film, visual art, genre fiction, and other aesthetic forms. The roundtable features three Kessler awardees: Amber Hollibaugh, Dean Spade, and Urvashi Vaid, in conversation about the history of queer and trans activism. Honoring the scholar-activist ethos of CLAGS as well as the careers of Hollibaugh, Spade, and Vaid, the roundtable highlights CLAGS as a vital site of community formation, affirmation, and queer intellectual counterpublics—even during the pandemic. We hope to bring more attention to the "now" of queer and trans activism, scholarship, and scholar-activism in these reflective roundtables.

CLAGS founder Martin Duberman, historian, writer, and activist, wrestles with questions similar to Vaid's in his 2012 lecture, "Acceptance at What Price? The Gay Movement Reconsidered." Duberman is critical of the shift gay politics took from the 1980s to the 2010s, away from radicalism and toward (neo)liberalism. He asks, "How do we mobilize a large enough constituency for substantive change when most of [our] members prefer to focus on winning certain kinds of limited concessions?" Duberman points to the Human Rights Campaign's unwillingness to join "other dispossessed groups to press for a much broader social reconstruction." At the time of Duberman's lecture, Occupy Wall Street was just a year old, raising the "conundrum of how to sustain a radical commitment" to economic *and* cultural change.

Black lesbian poet, essayist, scholar, and feminist activist Cheryl Clarke also takes up radical queer politics in her 2013 lecture, "Queer Black Trouble: In Life, Literature, and the Age of Obama." Contemplating the vexing question of whether we must merely continue "to hope for a Democrat in the White House every four years so as not to lose all of our freedom," she asks, "What rituals, legacies, praxes give shape to our values?" Those values, for Clarke, found a home in the Black Arts Movement founded in the 1960s by Amiri Baraka and represented by eminent poets like Audre Lorde, Nikki Giovanni, Gwendolyn Brooks, Maya Angelou, Sonia Sanchez, and Clarke herself. Testimonial speaker Elizabeth Lorde-Rollins described how Clarke's work laid "the foundation for a new Black feminist criticism and is an essential part of what will be the canon of queer studies."

In political theorist and Black queer activist Cathy J. Cohen's 2014 lecture, "#DoBlackLivesMatter? From Michael Brown to CeCe McDonald: On Black Death and LGBTQ Politics," the values that queer studies as a field claims to hold are brought to account. Cohen explores the difference between performative and substantive solidarity, noting that the latter does little to save Black lives. In her lecture, Cohen references her canonical queer theory essay, arguing for "a politics where the *nonnormative* and *marginal* position of punks, bulldaggers, and welfare queens, for example, is the basis for progressive transformative political work."[18] Nearly twenty years later, Cohen finds hope for such a politics only in substantive solidarity that actively makes space for those most marginalized by queer studies and politics.

Canadian Chinese-Trinidadian filmmaker and writer Richard Fung's 2015 lecture, "Re-Orientations: Shifts and Continuities in Asian Canadian Queer and Trans Identities and Activism," takes us back to his first film, *Orientations: Lesbian and Gay Asians* (1984), in which he features "people [who] constituted themselves as queer in spaces such as bars, restaurants, saunas, washrooms, parks, and cultural events." Fung notes that, while these spaces were not always welcoming to racialized people, they were where one had to go to meet other queers across a variety of differences, including class. What haunts Fung is the question of "the usefulness and sustainability of the framework 'queer pan-Asian Canadian'" in the shifting transnational conditions of neoliberalism as gay activism—and media, art, and culture— is professionalized and institutionalized.

Trans activist, theorist, and law professor Dean Spade's 2016 lecture, "When We Win We Lose: Mainstreaming and the Redistribution of Respectability," turns these political questions to trans politics and criminal "justice." Spade argues that, in the context of our "long history of gender liberation work," the new "mainstreaming around trans issues . . . presents significant threats to our aims of actually winning trans survival, winning prison abolition, winning police abolition." Testimonial speaker Angela P. Harris described Spade's work as "intersectional to the core," while Craig Willse laid out Spade's potent "vision of justice," committed to "a politics of no exile."

What do we mean when we use the word "queer"? That is the question queer of color feminist independent scholar Sara Ahmed takes up in her 2017 lecture, "Queer Use." Ahmed explores the queerness of use as well as the uses of "queer." She offers an account of how institutional and sexual cultures are built to enable some uses more than others. Small "acts of use are the building blocks of habit": use can build walls as well as worlds. To bring out the queerness of use requires a world-dismantling effort; "to queer use is to make usage into a crisis." And the uses of queer have certainly ignited crisis after crisis.

Ahmed's usage of "queer" as a word and object is put to the test in long-time queer activist and writer Amber Hollibaugh's 2018 lecture, "Hope and the Power of Desire: Our Vision for Changing the World." Hollibaugh considers the imaginative powers and even more powerful effort it takes to change the world: "Before we can build something, we have to imagine it." She admits, "We are living in a terrifying time"—and, as the introduction to this volume is being written, we are still living in a terrifying time. Hollibaugh's lecture centers the power and vision brought by people who, like her, have "lived on the wrong side of sex"—"too queer, too poor, too strange, too POC or mixed-race"—whose very survival shows us how desire must remain at the center of our struggles.

Transnational queer theorist Jasbir K. Puar's 2019 lecture, "A No-State 'Solution': Inter/nationalism and the Question of Queer Theory," begins with an homage and reflection on the fields that have made her work possible. Highlighting the shift of the Kessler Awards from something marginal to mainstream, what, Puar asks, is the role of queer studies today? She links the mainstreaming of queer studies to the de-exceptionalization of Palestine, which "foregrounds links with Puerto Rico, with Flint, Michigan, with New Orleans, and with other locations where, as with Gaza, the natural disaster is not only the opportunity for a business plan; the natural disaster is the business plan." She argues, "If we understand the occupation as distributed, we once again hit the limits of a state solution, because the current status quo is the state solution. In this sense, the fight to free Palestine is the fight to liberate all of our futures. No one is exempt."

Queer of color theorist Roderick A. Ferguson's 2020 lecture, "Queer and Trans Liberation and the Critique of Fascism, or When S.T.A.R. Met Césaire and the Frankfurt School," like Puar's, focuses attention on the gaps in the liberal politics of identity. His lecture identifies the antifascism in the organization Street Transvestite Action Revolutionaries (S.T.A.R.). "As houseless and trans sex workers, S.T.A.R. conformed not to the notion of the proletariat but to that of the lumpenproletariat," he argues, so that trans sex workers and queers become potential revolutionaries. Testimonial speaker E. Patrick Johnson said that Ferguson's work "demystifies the operations of power so that we who inhabit minoritarian subjectivities might stave off being co-opted by the lure of neoliberalism's promiscuity—and you know I love a good lure—inside the Academy and outside of it."

We end the volume with a second roundtable discussion on *"Queer Then and Now*: Histories of Queer and Trans Scholarship," held virtually in 2021 and moderated by CLAGS board member Shaka McGlotten, a media studies and anthropology scholar of Black studies, queer theory, media, and art. The roundtable features Roderick A. Ferguson, Jasbir K. Puar, and Susan Stryker in conversation about the histories and current state of queer/trans scholarship and activist-scholarship. Ferguson, Puar, and Stryker address pressing questions of where queer studies is headed and what contributions queer and trans studies might provide in the context of a rise in conservative, authoritarian, anti-trans global politics. The roundtable gives a sense of new possibilities for queer and trans *now* while also reflecting on the multiple legacies of queer studies and politics we inherit.

Dreaming of Queer, Then and Now

The dreaming of this project started in the fall of 2019, just after Jasbir Puar's Kessler Lecture, at a cramped Korean karaoke bar in midtown Manhattan. In early 2020 we met only once in person after a CLAGS board meeting to discuss the volume, before the COVID-19 pandemic introduced spatial constraints, health challenges, and massive geopolitical shifts around the planet. Our work has been virtual, so has been the forged intimacy among us—taking place over countless Zoom meetings, shared Google Docs, and far too many emails. Some of us were displaced internationally, attending to aging parents, or grieving major losses, and all of us faced COVID-related challenges in our work and lives. The work of this volume has indeed been a kind of queer perseverance—as Katz and Rubin start off this volume, their words on the challenges of assembling and archiving queer history remain relevant today. In thinking about queer and trans studies in the future, we needed to reassemble a fragmentary archive by hunting down recordings of CLAGS lectures and transcribing them, and searching for images, flyers, and material for each of the awardees. We masked up and searched the bowels of the CLAGS office at the CUNY Graduate Center to find ancient VHS tapes we thought had been lost and then had them digitized. We deployed the Internet Archive's "Wayback Machine" to find excerpts of lectures previously published in CLAGS's old newsletters, and we cross-referenced lectures to track down citations and sources absent in the oral texts. Some awardees were able to find old lectures on ancient desktops, some were not—the work of assembling the lectures and producing this book has been the work of assembling an archive of a generation of trans/queer scholars. Such journeys are always incomplete.

Now, as we are wrapping up the project in the spring of 2022, we are dealing with a major leak of a draft decision from the US Supreme Court on the *Roe v. Wade* decision that proposes to overturn access to abortion. There are endless wars continuing in different parts of the globe, and racialized violence against BIPOC persons has intensified. Closer to home, we mourn the passing of queer and trans elders and leaders, including Kessler awardee Urvashi Vaid; queer Left public historian, and CLAGS board member from 1992–1995 and 2010–2013, Jeffrey Escoffier; queer and feminist theorist Lauren Berlant; queer activist Carmen Vázquez; and poet, HIV/AIDS activist, as well as one-time CLAGS board member and the cofounder of Gay Men of African Descent (GMAD) Colin Robinson. The struggle to create this archive, as so many deal with health challenges of all kinds, is an investment in the value of these words and worlds.

Holding on to our dream of bringing the Kessler awardees together through this anthology has been a site of queer pleasure and power, our investment in a queerer future. There is hope and hopelessness in this book, as well as the past, present, and future of queer and trans studies. We invite our readers to make their own meaning of *Queer Then and Now* as you read through the lectures and reflections—to consider what "queer" is coming to mean in our own moment, and in the world to come.

Notes

1. We made a choice to use "trans" theory or studies as a way of signifying the multiple life-worlds of gender diversity and gender identity that exist across time and place. Trans studies scholars such as Aniruddha Dutta and Raina Roy ask for decolonizing the anglophone term "transgender" in the context of India; similarly, scholars such as Howard Chiang use "Transtopia," as a way of highlighting diverse possibilities of gender, sexuality, and regionalities in their recent book, *Transtopia in the Sinophone Pacific*. "Trans" therefore signifies multiple possibilities of gender identities and expressions that defy the gender binary and Western understandings of somatotechnological processes—possibilities that remain central to the uses of "transgender." Aniruddha Dutta and Raina Roy, "Decolonizing Transgender in India: Some Reflections," *TSQ: Transgender Studies Quarterly* 1, no. 3 (2014): 320–37; and Howard Chiang, *Transtopia in the Sinophone Pacific* (New York: Columbia University Press, 2021).

2. David L. Eng, Jack Halberstam, and José Esteban Muñoz, "What's Queer about Queer Studies Now?," *Social Text* 23, nos. 3–4 (2005): 10.

3. Maya Mikdashi and Jasbir K. Puar, "Queer Theory and Permanent War," *GLQ: A Journal of Lesbian and Gay Studies* 22, no. 2 (2016): 215.

4. Martin Duberman, "The First Ten Years," *Women's Studies Quarterly* 44, nos. 3–4 (2016): 306–12.

5. Kevin L. Nadal, "The Intersection of Queer Theory and Empirical Methods: Visions for CLAGS, the Center for LGBTQ Studies," *Women's Studies Quarterly* 44, nos. 3–4: 301–5.

6. Teresa de Lauretis, "Queer Theory: Lesbian and Gay Sexualities: An Introduction," *differences* 3, no. 2 (1991): iii–xviii.

7. Judith Butler, *Gender Trouble: Feminism and the Subversion of Identity* (New York: Routledge, 1990).

8. Eve Kosofsky Sedgwick, *Epistemology of the Closet* (Berkeley: University of California Press, 1990).

9. Michael Warner, "Introduction: Fear of a Queer Planet," *Social Text*, no. 29 (1991): 3–17.

10. Michael Hames-García, "Queer Theory Revisited," in *Gay Latino Studies: A Critical Reader*, eds. Michael Roy Hames-García and Ernesto Javier Martínez (Durham, NC: Duke University Press, 2011), 19–45.

11. CLAGS: City University of New York, *Queer Ideas: The David R. Kessler Lectures in Lesbian and Gay Studies* (New York: Feminist Press at the City University of New York, 2003).

12. Mary E. Barber, "An Interview with David R. Kessler, MD," *Journal of Gay & Lesbian Mental Health* 12, no. 3 (2008): 254.

13. Barber, "Interview with David R. Kessler," 255.

14. Barber, "Interview with David R. Kessler," 245.

15. Jonathan Ned Katz, *Gay American History: Lesbians and Gay Men in the U.S.A.* (New York: Crowell, 1976).

16. Carole Vance's lecture is on the CLAGS YouTube channel at https://www.youtube.com/c/CLAGSTheCenterforLGBTQStudies/.

17. Carole S. Vance, *Pleasure and Danger: Exploring Female Sexuality* (Boston: Routledge, 1984).

18. Cathy J. Cohen, "Punks, Bulldaggers, and Welfare Queens: The Radical Potential of Queer Politics?," *GLQ: A Journal of Lesbian and Gay Studies* 3, no. 4 (1997): 437–65.

THE DAVID R. KESSLER LECTURES 2002–2020

2002   **JONATHAN NED KATZ**

2003   GAYLE RUBIN

2004   ISAAC JULIEN

2006   ADRIENNE RICH

2007   DOUGLAS CRIMP

2008   SUSAN STRYKER

2009   SARAH SCHULMAN

2010   URVASHI VAID

2012   MARTIN DUBERMAN

2013   CHERYL CLARKE

2014   CATHY J. COHEN

2015   RICHARD FUNG

2016   DEAN SPADE

2017   SARA AHMED

2018   AMBER HOLLIBAUGH

2019   JASBIR K. PUAR

2020   RODERICK A. FERGUSON

Jonathan Ned Katz

Historian activist and independent scholar Jonathan Ned Katz has spent his long career examining the social conditions under which sexuality and gender is constructed. In addition to being a founder of OutHistory.org (produced by CLAGS in its early years), Katz has published some of the key books in the canon of gay and lesbian history. Those include *The Invention of Heterosexuality* (1995) and *Gay American History: Lesbians and Gay Men in the U.S.A.* (1976). In addition to the Kessler Award, Katz was also awarded the Magnus Hirschfeld Medal, Yale's Brudner Prize, the Bill Whitehead Award for excellence in publishing, and the American Library Association's Gay Book Award.

Making Sex History:
Obsessions of a Quarter Century

DECEMBER 6, 2002

It was the winter of 1971 at a meeting of the media committee of New York City's Gay Activist Alliance in an apartment on West Sixteenth Street, in then-unfashionable Chelsea. We were discussing ways to publicize the existence of our new militant gay and lesbian liberation movement. I then made a vow to look for documents of gay and lesbian American history and to develop a theater piece based on the evidence I supposed I could find. I was inspired by Martin Duberman's documentary play *In White America* and my own earlier radio documentaries on Black American history. From the start, work on Black history and, later, women's history encouraged research on the gay and lesbian past. I stress that a political meeting led to my first research on homosexual history and the theater piece *Coming Out!*, presented at the Gay Activists Alliance Firehouse, in then-unfashionable SoHo, in June 1972. My and others' work on this history owes its existence directly to an organized sexual liberation movement, a fact that can be forgotten as this intellectual work is professionalized within academia and recedes in time from its political origins.

Looking back on the thirty-one years since that meeting, it is apparent that my work on sexual history has been driven by several related concerns, even "obsessions." They have powerfully haunted and focused the direction of my empirical research and analytical work.

Obsession 1: To Document

In 1971, my strong impulse to document was most obviously motivated by a desire to prove the existence of such a thing as "gay and lesbian history," and the possibility of doing serious responsible work to recapture it. My documentary impulse was defensive, a compensatory reactive move against those who directly or indirectly denied the existence of our past, or who denied the value of research to recover it. Collecting gay and lesbian history documents also seemed therapeutic. It worked against the feelings of inferiority experienced by a group told directly or indirectly that we had no past, or no past worth knowing; a group condemned to exist only in a diminished present.

In the 1970s, gay history evidence also seemed to prove our militant assertion that we, too, were a "minority group" subject to "discrimination" (a new, radical idea needing to be defended). The evidence that I began to discover in the early 1970s, and later published in 1976 in topical sections in *Gay American History*, appeared to prove the existence of "gay oppression" and "gay resistance." (Just a few years later, the term "gay" would be regularly supplemented by "lesbian" in works striving to be politically responsible, and still later "gay" and "lesbian" were regularly replaced by "queer." Then, all those present terms of ours came to seem problematic as ways of describing past worlds that differed in fundamental ways from those of modern America.)

In the 1970s, documents of early colonial American executions of men for sodomy seemed to show how long and acutely "homosexuals" had suffered. Early reports of Native American cross-dressing "berdaches" seemed to show how early and deeply "homosexuals" were ingrained in this country's culture, and how far back "anti-homosexual" prejudice had existed. Late nineteenth-century and early twentieth-century reports of psychiatric treatments newly demonstrated the culpability of mental health professionals in the creation of "homosexual" self-hate. Documents demonstrating the historical varieties of same-sex "love" and "intimacy" provided evidence of a central, "positive" aspect of our lives that was not well known. Documented tales of women who dressed and passed as men, and had sexual affairs with women, showed how women's history and feminism were illuminated by the documents of "lesbian" history. (One of those "passing women," Lucy Ann Lobdell, was the first to be labeled a "lesbian," in an 1882 American medical journal.)*

---

*Influenced by the transgender movement, Katz later radically revised his understanding of transgender history, stressing that we best understand and honor past transgender people by carefully studying how they named and conceptualized themselves and lived within specific social contexts.

In the early 1970s, document collecting and the presentation of documents in a theater piece and book also seemed appropriate to that early stage in the recovery of the gay and lesbian past. The documents gave ammunition to individuals just beginning to find our own voices and to speak publicly about our maligned loves, lusts, and lives. Certainly, my compilation of evidence into a documentary theater piece and book was an important first step in my own education in speaking publicly as a gay person, something I was just learning to do. Backed by documents, I also had the confidence to speak as a historian, even though as a college dropout in the 1960s I lacked the certification of any higher degrees. Speaking through documents, talking through other people's words, was a first step in learning how to speak for myself. My impulse to document was also from the start opposed to an earlier gay impulse to claim especially famous creative or noteworthy achievers as members of the tribe, often with little care about evidence and analysis.

In 1971, our new gay liberation politics asserted that it was okay to be gay and ordinary. You could even be uncreative. What a relief! No longer did homosexuals have to try to prove our worth by asserting our family link to extraordinary creators like Michelangelo and Shakespeare. My compulsion to document also countered another, different impulse: to fictionalize, to creatively make up past lives and worlds. Fiction had been the form taken by many earlier explorations of past same-sex intimacies. I think for example of several novels by Mary Renault, and of *Patience and Sarah*, the lovely fictional re-creation by Alma Routsong of the imagined lives of two women who actually lived together in Greene County, New York, in the nineteenth century.[1] (I heard, by the way, that Routsong researched her characters by questioning a Ouija board. That was not one of the techniques I used.)

I recall also *Song of the Loon* by Richard Amory: softcore porn set in an imagined nineteenth-century world of white pioneer studs and their Native American comrades.[2] In 1971, it seemed important to me to carefully distinguish between creatively imagined and carefully documented events and persons; but it was obvious even then that different types of documentation told very different tales about the "same" event. Not making it up—discovering fascinating and well-documented trials and tribulations—became a discipline that I fervently embraced. Finding tantalizing, ironic, and amazing evidence about past lives and lusts and love became a creative challenge. I loved the excitement of this detective work, this tracing of history's missing persons.

My documentary impulse was also from the first an effort to discover what drama, poetry, and humanity could be uncovered in the evidence and, importantly, made to live again for a popular, general audience in the present. From the get-go, the audience I imagined for gay and lesbian history was not exclusively or predominantly academic. Having begun my gay and lesbian history research for a movement theater piece, my leftist democratic politics urged me toward plain speaking to a general audience. My admiration for the apparent simplicity and emotional power of Bertolt Brecht's and Walt Whitman's poetry was another prod to plain talk. My focus on the human-interest value of the evidence was also encouraged by journalistic training under the tough tutelage of an editor mother, whose pretension detector went off at any hint of academic jargon.

My communist father's glowing recollection of the agitation-propaganda theater of the 1930s provided another incentive to capture history's drama. I recalled his description of a scene from *One Third of a Nation*, a play about poverty in the US in which a grass mat, passed from hand to hand, visually signified the transformation of Manhattan Island into property, transferred from Native Americans to Dutch colonists.[3]

That early 1970s moment in the recovery of gay and lesbian history documents was thrilling. My discoveries led to loud exclamations in quiet libraries, and quiet exclamations on noisy subways. I will never forget my first reading on the subway coming home from the Columbia University psychiatric library, where I remember the director seemed to be quite insane. I bowed and scraped and did anything I had to do to get in there, and I got this fabulous document. I was reading this detailed, novel-like case history of Alberta Lucille Hart, who had sexual affairs with a succession of women and settled down, passing as a man and marrying a wife, and later another wife after she got divorced. That medical journal report of 1920 about an anonymous subject gave so many clues to Hart's life that I was later able to track down her original name and college yearbook pictures. Still later, I discovered that Alberta took the name Alan, became a doctor, and published four social realist novels. One of those novels turned out, as I hoped it would, to include a sympathetic homosexual character. In the book, he is hounded to his death by a society unforgiving of sexual difference.

Another time, I was on the subway reading Henry Gerber's account of his founding in 1924 of the Society for Human Rights in Chicago, this country's earliest known homosexual rights organization. When Gerber mentioned in passing that "we even got a charter from the state," a document alarm went off in my head. I soon after wrote to the State of Illinois, and one day received in the mail a copy of the charter of that historic group, organized "to protect the interests of people who by reason of mental and physical abnormalities are abused and hindered in the legal pursuit of happiness which is guaranteed them by the Declaration of Independence, and to combat the public prejudice against them." There in my mailbox was the Magna Carta of the American homosexual rights movement, unknown and unread for some forty years.

It was on the subway that I first read that the Mattachine Society, the homosexual rights organization founded in 1950, had been preceded by a group called Bachelors Anonymous or Bachelors for Wallace. (That's a reference to Henry Wallace, running in 1948 as the Progressive Party candidate for US president, supported by American communists and liberals and leftists.) As a ten-year-old with my father, I had marched for Wallace in a New York City May Day parade. In the 1970s, on that subway car, it suddenly dawned on me that those Bachelors for Wallace, the Mattachine's founders, were probably pinko queers. That was surprising and moving to me, because as a homosexual and a leftist before gay liberation, I had met few others who combined both sexual and political persuasions. It was even more amazing to learn that the original Bachelor for Wallace, Harry Hay, the Mattachine Society founder, was then still alive and kicking—and to finally meet and interview him and learn more about his leftist past.

Expecting from the start to find a few gay history documents, I was soon finding a great abundance. I recall my surprise that no lack of evidence explained the lack of serious research on gay and lesbian history. It was the illegitimacy in academia of that research that kept this history from being better known. I was in the stacks of the New York University library, when I experienced a sci-fi moment: a revelation that my evidence discoveries were revealing a secret parallel universe, an invisible world of same-sex intimacies, existing side by side with a visible universe of male-female relationships. That mysterious shadow world was well documented and hidden in plain view.

In 1976, it seemed that the publication of *Gay American History* might be the one and only chance I or anyone might have to inform the visible world of the shadow world's existence. So I stuffed my fat book with every citation I had found. It's hard to carry it around, actually, it's so heavy. Today, though gay American history research is more commonly undertaken within academia, it has yet to provoke the wide-scale reevaluation of the American past that those first evidence discoveries suggest. One would think that the documentation of a same-sex eros in the lives of such canonical figures as Abe Lincoln, Walt Whitman, Herman Melville, Ralph Waldo Emerson, Margaret Fuller, Henry David Thoreau, Mark Twain, and Susan B. Anthony would force a major rethinking of nineteenth-century American history at least. Disappointingly, it has not.

Now a quarter century into the sex history trade, I am still thinking about how to publicize that shadow world, and I have two persistent unrealized grandiose fantasies. The first is to see my theater piece, *Comrades and Lovers*, about the conflicted relationship between Walt Whitman and John Addington Symonds, turned into a first-rate film.[4] The second fantasy is to put all the known data of gay, lesbian, bisexual, transgender, and heterosexual American history on an ever-expanding public website, in a form entertaining and educational for the general public as well as useful for scholars. Perhaps talking publicly about these dreams will help to realize them.

Obsession 2: To Understand Sexuality in Time

From the beginning of my evidence collecting, I knew that this archival work, however exciting, was not the same thing as understanding. And I desired, even yearned, to understand. I knew from the start that documents do not speak for themselves, that it takes a great deal of prodding by historians to reveal the meanings hidden in even the most obvious-seeming evidence.

I realized early on that to understand all the evidence I was finding would take years of collective, sustained struggle, and I despaired that I was just at the beginning of that long process. In the mid-1970s, as I finished the manuscript for *Gay American History*, I recall how hard it was to make sense of the documents in that book's "Love" section.[5] I realized it would take years of analysis to begin to understand the historical varieties of intimacy that my research had uncovered. Exactly twenty-five years after the first publication of those love documents, my most recent book, *Love Stories*, about sex and affection between men in the nineteenth century, continued the struggle to understand the historical varieties of intimacy.[6]

In 1983, in *Gay/Lesbian Almanac*, encouraged by Michel Foucault's thought-provoking thoughts on sexual history, I set out to be more analytical than I had been in my first gay history book.[7] I tried to understand gay and lesbian history in a wider political and economic context and presented a detailed analysis of sodomy within the reproductive system of the early American colonies. I began then to discern the difference between the colonial ordering of sodomy (the arrangement of "sexual inversion," as it was called in the late nineteenth century), the construction of homosexuality in the early twentieth century, and the reorganization of gay and lesbian life starting in 1969. I began to perceive that there were and are different historical ways of socially organizing sexuality—an insight that is now commonplace was once revelatory. I began to ask what it meant for phenomena called "homosexuality" and "sexuality" to be deeply, utterly enmeshed in time. I began to perceive that my study of homosexuality in history was substantially changing my understanding of my object of research. The quantitative addition of a historical perspective to the study of homosexuality was having an unexpected qualitative effect on my basic idea of what I was looking at.

I began to reject the idea that all of us had grown up with in the twentieth century: the hundred-year-old idea of homosexuality and heterosexuality, and sexuality in general, as timeless, essential, unchanging, universal things. I began to understand what we call homosexuality as one peculiar time-bound relationship of people and pleasure—conceived, named, socially ordered, and produced by human beings in a particular society in a particular historical moment. But if homosexuality was not universal, it had no continuous existence through time. As an object of historical research ranging widely over time, "homosexuality" began to dissolve. The problem of studying such an unstable, ever-changing object, is a difficulty that historians and all historically minded researchers are grappling with still. As I have come to understand this problem of sexual relativity, we can certainly look back on sodomy in the early American colonies and find evidence that lots of that activity involved what we today call "same-sex erotic acts" or "homosexuality." From our viewpoint in the present, homosexuality existed in the early American colonies. But from the perspective of colonial society itself, homosexuality did not exist.

That paradoxical theory of sexual relativity is a matter not only of words and ideas, but of the institutional shaping of particular kinds of pleasures. What is at stake is the different social and historical ordering of sodomy and homosexuality as distinct kinds of human acts and relationships. When we speak of colonial American sodomy as homosexuality, as if it is the same thing, we equate a past sexuality with a present one—we deny historical difference. Unlike homosexuality, for example, early colonial sodomy was not closely and centrally linked with gender deviance. It did not refer centrally to a same-sex act. Neither did it include oral-genital connections. Within early colonial America, sodomy was a theologically defined *reproductive* default and, as such, a serious challenge to the continuation of the state. Homosexuality, in contrast, has usually been considered according to a medical or scientific model as a default of erotic normality, a failure to conform to the best standard of proper pleasure.

My interest in understanding sexuality and its full historical complexity was aided and abetted by my earlier close, questioning reading of one of the world's most famous rebel thinkers, Karl Marx, along with numbers of Marxist writers. An early essay by the English Marxist Christopher Caldwell first opened my eyes to the historical varieties of love. The German Marxist Arnold Hauser, in *The Social History of Art*, first made me aware of the complex ways in which the changing historical organization of artistic production engaged with the economy to subtly influence the character of the art produced.[8] Discovering the work of the gay left historian Jeffrey Weeks in 1976 encouraged me to expand my analytical work on sexual history and changing sexual systems. As I look back on my extremely isolated, hermetic, pre–gay liberation self, I realize that the closet fostered reading—I sat in my closet and read Marx.

As I see it now, the study of Marx and Marxism, begun in my closet days, provided a good education in critical thinking, opening my eyes to the importance of a historical perspective and the value of theory and analysis disciplined by reference to practical, empirical research. When I started to analyze homosexual history, I recalled, in particular, Marx's talk of the rising bourgeoisie's use of the ideology of the natural to justify its own interests against the traditional rights of kings. Marx prepared me to question the use of the terms "natural" and "unnatural" as politically loaded constructs. Marx's presentation of capitalism as one time-bound way of organizing production, a system obscured by its ideologists as timeless, encouraged me to see claims to a historical, universal truth as rationales for particular economic systems and, later, sexual systems. From Marx and Marxists, I learned the importance of distinguishing relationships between people from relationships between people and things—things like technology, the human body, and sexuality.

From Marx, I learned that people with different access to the means of action and power produce the changing social world, including their pleasures—however obscured their acts are by deterministic ideas like "technology did it," "nature did it," "biology did it," "God did it," even "capitalism did it." With Jeffrey Weeks, Robert Padgug, and other gay leftist scholars, I began to develop the idea of different changing social and historical organizations of sexuality, and that concept became a basic analytical tool. Adapted in my usage from the Marxist analysis of different historical modes of production (feudalism, capitalism, communism), I began to think about the different historical ways of producing sexuality (ancient Greek pederasty, Judeo-Christian sodomy, twentieth-century homosexuality).

This conceptual tool led me to consider homosexuality and other sexualities as human inventions. In time, my attempt to understand the implications of studying homosexuality led gradually and unexpectedly to my considering the history of that most obscured, fetishized, universalized, essentialized thing of all: heterosexuality.

Obsession 3: To Explore Heterosexual History

In the mid-1970s—while first reading the late nineteenth-century medical documents referring to what was called "sexual inversion," "contrary sexual instinct," and later "homosexuality"—I began to notice a strange thing. Numbers of doctors referred to heterosexual relations as perverted and abnormal. In May 1892, for example, in the first documented reference to heterosexual relations published in the US, Dr. James G. Kiernan linked the word "heterosexual" to one of several "abnormal manifestations of the sexual appetite," in a list of sexual perversions proper, in an article on sexual perversion.

Later in my research, I came home one day to find a letter from the Merriam-Webster company revealing that, as late as 1923, "heterosexuality" made its first appearance in that company's unabridged dictionary. In its debut, "heterosexuality" was still a medical term meaning "morbid sexual passion for one of the opposite sex." But heterosexuality was moving on; it now referred to "opposite sex" relations. That was another documented discovery that made me shout aloud with glee.

"What's going on here?" I began to ask of those early references to heterosexuality as perversion. I began to understand that the definition of heterosexuality as perversion was not simply "misapplied," a mistake, as the *Oxford English Dictionary* claimed in 1933. The idea of heterosexuality as perversion was one logical, perfectly legitimate understanding based on a reproductive moral premise. According to that dominant nineteenth-century reproductive standard, any male-female sexual relationship not directed exclusively at procreation was perverted or abnormal.

From that moral perspective, heterosexuality, referring as it did simply to sexual relationships between different sexes, was perverted. Only in the 1920s and '30s, I realized, did a new pleasure ethic begin to widely legitimate male-female sexual acts not necessarily connected with reproduction. It was only in 1934 that Merriam-Webster's hefty *Second Edition Unabridged* first defined heterosexuality as a "manifestation of sexual passion for one of the opposite sex; normal sexuality." Only in the first third of the twentieth century did the term "heterosexual" and the heterosexual ideal come to normalize different-sex pleasures unlinked with reproduction.

Historical research on homosexuality had led to a startling new look at what in the 1980s, in numbers of public talks, I began to refer to as "the invention of heterosexuality." In the most literal, unmetaphorical way, we could trace the production of heterosexuality as one historically particular word, idea, object, and moral judgment; and as one specific sort of socially ordered relationship between men and women. In that relationship, sexuality was constituted as central to proper intimacy and love. Homosexuality served heterosexuality's invention by functioning as its nemesis.

Obsession 4: To Comprehend the Role of Language in the Making of Sexualities

In *The Invention of Heterosexuality*, I am sorry to say that I hedged a bit at the end about whether I thought heterosexual relationships existed apart from the word "heterosexual" and the idea. In that book's final pages, I said, "I *don't* think that the invention of the word *heterosexual*, and the concept, created a different-sex erotic."[9] I explained that in the early twentieth century, the word "heterosexual" and the idea had been appropriated by medical professionals to newly and publicly legitimate the previously existing, nonreproductive, different-sex pleasure acts of the middle class.

I now think that my intellectual caution underplayed the actual influential role of words and ideas in the social and historical production of heterosexuality, and all sexualities. Since 1995, I have thought more about the role of language in the construction of particular historical sexualities, and now grant language a more fundamental place. I now think that human beings use words as tools to create particular sexualities, as certain kinds of phenomena. So, the reality of a particular sexual relation is dependent on, and inseparable from, the different words used to socially describe it.

Looking back on my sexual history work, I realized that understanding the role of language in the historical construction of sexuality has been one of my continuing intellectual concerns. Naming was a source of personal trepidation in the mid-1970s, when I considered calling my first sexual studies book *Gay American History*. At that time, even this gay militant researcher trembled a bit before a title that so aggressively asserted the existence of a same-sex past that was then only barely visible, and a study just being brought tentatively into existence. In retrospect, it seems to me that naming a book *Gay American History* helped to create the past it referenced as a particular kind of object. Today's scholars are usually more careful about using "gay" or "homosexual" about past relationships that preceded those words. In today's ongoing struggle to pull an ahistorical sexuality into the realm of the historical, many of us now jump through convoluted verbal hoops to name and conceive that object quite differently. In 1976, naming a book *Gay American History* was a strategic move in the political word wars that define our perception of what is out there in the world. Today, the name *Gay American History* seems deeply problematic, except as a quick superficial glossing of a difficult-to-pin-down, ever-changing object of historical research.

The power of human beings to use language, to create sexualities of particular kinds, is also exemplified in the original invention in Germany in 1868 of the words "homosexual" and "heterosexual" by Károly Mária Benkert Kertbeny. Those coinages in the cause of sexual law reform were later co-opted by psychiatrists for the cause of nonreproductive normality. Those words helped the medical normalizers of the twentieth century create our society's firm belief that homosexuality and heterosexuality exist universally, outside of time. Those doctors' namings, I believe, helped to construct the social reality they posited.

In my last book, *Love Stories*, I traced the ways that Walt Whitman, John Addington Symonds, and other men waged nineteenth-century word wars to fundamentally reshape their society's concept of, response to, and social ordering of sex between men.[10] Whitman and Symonds labored to change their society's Judeo-Christian focus on the act of sodomy into a focus on erotic feeling and affection between men. Whitman called it "love of comrades" and "amativeness," helping to pioneer and legitimize the modern idea of sex-love.[11] Those examples demonstrate the ways in which human beings use words to create particular perceptions of the world, on which they then act. My revised judgment about the role of words and the creation of heterosexuality and homosexuality is that those specific phenomena did not exist, and could not have existed as such, before the words "heterosexual" and "homosexual" were available to describe them.

I thus reject the simple Marxist idea of language as a mere ideological element, secondary in influence to a determining material economic base. Instead, I believe that language is among the tools that human beings use to produce pleasures of particular historical kinds. In the case of "homosexuality" and "heterosexuality," the invention, use, and distribution of those words helped to produce the social existence and historical reality of the sexual relations so named.

Obsession 5: To Make the Past Live Again

Recently, my energies have turned in what may seem a surprising new direction. Inspired by the members of Alive, a grassroots revitalization group in Liberty, New York, I have been working with my partner, David Gibson, our friend, the historian Allan Bérubé, and numbers of wonderful new comrades to bring fresh life to this small town two hours north of Manhattan in the Catskill Mountains. In the heart of an economically depressed Sullivan County, Liberty is the former home of Grossinger's Hotel in the Jewish resort industry. Today, Liberty is a town at a turning point. The unique character of its main street can be destroyed by developers who care for nothing but the almighty dollar, as my dad might have phrased it. The town can be stripped of its old, quirky identifying features and end up looking like a nondescript mall—that has been done to one building. Or, building on Liberty's traditional existing assets, we can restore the best of its architecture, signs, and streetscape, bringing this depressed village back to life again as a charming example of a twentieth-century small town. Today, an energetic coalition of natives and newcomers, full-timers and weekenders, straight and gay, women and men, old and young, are working together in an amazing communal effort to restore Liberty to its best self.

Called by different names, our activities suggest very different political realities: real estate development, beautification, gentrification, rural redevelopment, revitalization, historic preservation, environmental conservation, community organizing. The reality, I think, is all of those, posing many big problems and a challenge to do it right. Sensing a link between my recent work in Liberty and my past sexual history research, a number of friends have urged me to talk here about that connection. I hesitated to do so unless I could figure out the interlink between my history work and Liberty labors. I finally understood that connection after finding an old fourteen-foot wooden sink in a dilapidated shed behind a former butcher shop in town. Restoring that dead sink to life as a counter in our new café on Liberty's Main Street, I understood the desire that linked my past and present work: to make the past live again. My work on sex history and my work in Liberty are both moves to preserve, cherish, and revivify.

Working on that old sink in Liberty, I realized how satisfying I find it to bring the past alive again. I experienced the same satisfaction in *Love Stories*, when presenting the forgotten detailed autobiography of a man who called himself Claude Hartland, and the touching love letters between Charles Warren Stoddard and the charming, winsome artist Francis Davis Millet. (Millet, by the way, died in the *Titanic*, a queer passing that got no publicity. In contrast, in one of the world's most popular movies, Leonardo DiCaprio played a fictional straight artist who died in the tragedy.)

My history work and my Liberty work are both restorative attempts. My making of sexual history and my helping to restore Liberty to its best self are intimately connected. Both efforts affirm life against death; both affirm the sensual pleasures of seeing, hearing, eating, drinking, and feeling against today's crabbed, right-wing, life-denying, death-dealing puritanism. Both affirm the beauty of old things and people against the American obsession with the young and new. Both affirm preservation against the senseless destruction of the past. Both affirm the power of human beings to collectively make our world a more joyful, lovely-looking, and pleasurable place.

Now, friends and comrades, let's honor the pleasure principle and party.

Notes

1. Isabel Miller (pen name of Alma Routsong), *A Place for Us* (republished as *Patience and Sarah*) (New York: Bleecker Street Press, 1969).

2. Richard Amory, *Song of the Loon* (Chicago: Greenleaf Classics, 1966).

3. Arthur Arent, *One Third of a Nation* (Federal Theatre Project, 1938).

4. Jonathan Ned Katz, *Comrades and Lovers* (Fund for Human Dignity, 1989).

5. Jonathan Ned Katz, *Gay American History* (New York: Thomas Y. Crowell Company, 1976).

6. Jonathan Ned Katz, *Love Stories: Sex between Men before Homosexuality* (Chicago: University of Chicago Press, 2001).

7. Jonathan Ned Katz, *Gay/Lesbian Almanac* (New York: Harper & Row, 1983).

8. Arnold Hauser, *The Social History of Art* (New York: Vintage, 1951).

9. Jonathan Ned Katz, *The Invention of Heterosexuality* (New York: Dutton, 1995), 181.

10. Katz, *Love Stories*.

11. Walt Whitman, *Leaves of Grass and Other Writings*, ed. Michael Moon, 2nd ed. (New York: W. W. Norton, 2002).

Bert Hansen on Jonathan Ned Katz

Along with bringing archival research into popular currency, Jonathan has brought with it his deep passion for social justice and made that history useful in our struggles for social and political change. When Jonathan began his gay history work around the time of Stonewall, "gay history" meant individual coming-out stories or a few queer English kings. His success in establishing the field was an inspiration to historians working in other countries. There was an eye-opening power to his work when it appeared. He edited a reprint series for Arno Press that offered sixty-nine volumes. This was in 1975, just a year before the publication of *Gay American History*. Often purchased by libraries, this treasure trove of our history became widely available to our community and firmly settled any question of whether traces of our history could be found, studied, and enjoyed. And just shortly before that enormous project came off the press, Jonathan's prodigious energy was being devoted to his innovative play, *Coming Out!: A Documentary on Gay Life and Liberation*.

A cast of ten in simple modern clothes, brought to life in about twenty vignettes, separated by blackouts of the stage. They had no period costumes and virtually no props to animate the historical scenes—only their acting and the words taken from original texts selected by Jonathan. These texts were not the polished works of great literature. They were court records and newspaper stories; diaries, debates, and private letters—but in Jonathan's editing, they were transformed, much as Walt Whitman had done, from ordinary language into light and beauty that brought shocks of horror and recognition, tears, and laughter. A minister's accusations of sodomy in 1629, the Boise witch hunt, the Snake Pit raid, and the Stonewall riots were set against the passions of Willa Cather and Gertrude Stein, the activism of the Lavender Menace, Allen Ginsberg in the Chicago conspiracy trial, and

David McReynolds debating Seymour Krim in 1959. A heady mix, scene after scene grabbing our emotions, pulling us in all directions, but always grounding us with the presence of real people who had lived these real lives. There was no fiction here, no fantasy. There was no avoiding the facts of our community's history, painful or pleasurable, and no one left the theater with the notion that many had arrived with: a feeling that somehow gay people had no history, or just a short homogeneous one.

Jonathan's books and his play are not explicitly philosophical, nor do they construct an ideology, but they clearly breathe life into the idea that identity politics by itself is not enough, and that working in coalitions across different identities is key to liberation. In his commitment to a leftist vision of struggling liberation, Jonathan dramatized our history and brought our past to life, making it energizing, entertaining, and politically engaged.

Bert Hansen is a professor of history at Baruch College, CUNY, and a past visitor at the Institute for Advanced Study at Princeton. His work focuses on the history of science and public health.

THE DAVID R. KESSLER LECTURES 2002–2020

2002 JONATHAN NED KATZ
2003 GAYLE RUBIN
2004 ISAAC JULIEN
2006 ADRIENNE RICH
2007 DOUGLAS CRIMP
2008 SUSAN STRYKER
2009 SARAH SCHULMAN
2010 URVASHI VAID
2012 MARTIN DUBERMAN
2013 CHERYL CLARKE
2014 CATHY J. COHEN
2015 RICHARD FUNG
2016 DEAN SPADE
2017 SARA AHMED
2018 AMBER HOLLIBAUGH
2019 JASBIR K. PUAR
2020 RODERICK A. FERGUSON

Gayle Rubin

Scholar and activist Gayle Rubin is the author of several foundational works in feminist and queer theory, including "The Traffic in Women: Notes on the 'Political Economy' of Sex" (1975) and the equally groundbreaking "Thinking Sex" (1984), perhaps the most reprinted and translated theoretical work in contemporary sexuality studies by an American author. Along with such foundational work, Rubin has written extensively on lesbian history, the feminist sex wars, the politics of sadomasochism, crusades against prostitution and pornography, and the historical development of sexual knowledge. Rubin is an associate professor of anthropology and women's studies at the University of Michigan.

Geologies of Queer Studies:
It's Déjà Vu All Over Again

DECEMBER 5, 2003

I thought I would use the occasion of this lecture to think about queer knowledges and the conditions of their production. I want to use an experience I keep having with GLBTQ (gay, lesbian, bisexual, transgender, and queer) knowledges to accentuate the continuing need to build stable institutional forms that can insure the ongoing development, preservation, and transmission of such knowledge. This is the déjà vu to which my title refers: the more I explore these queer knowledges, the more I find out how much we have already forgotten, rediscovered, and promptly forgotten again. I myself have attempted to reinvent the wheel on several occasions. I want to think about why this has happened with such annoying regularity. A major problem is that we still lack sufficient organizational resources to routinize the conservation of previously attained knowledges and their conveyance to new generations.

So if you will indulge me, I'll play Mr. Peabody and invite you into my personal Wayback Machine. It is around 1970, and I am a brand-new baby dyke. The first thing I want to do is to seduce the object of my desire; the second is to read a good lesbian novel. Having little luck with the former project, I head over to the graduate library at the University of Michigan and look up lesbianism in the card catalogue (this was before the advent of computerized catalogues). There were two entries under the subject heading of "lesbian." One was Radclyffe Hall's *The Well of Loneliness*. The other was a book by Jess Stearn called *The Grapevine*, a semi-sensational account of the Daughters of Bilitis (DOB), the San Francisco–based lesbian-rights organization founded in the early period of homophile activism in the mid-1950s.[1]

I did not yet know that DOB had produced a small journal called *The Ladder*, nor that *The Ladder* was still being published, albeit not by DOB.

Since the library at the University of Michigan was (and is) one of the greatest in North America, I concluded that there was very little written on the topic or else there was a screaming need for a lesbian bibliography. I decided to produce such a bibliography for my senior honors thesis, and spent the next few months of my life consumed with trying to locate any and all written sources on lesbianism.

The first step was to inquire at the reference desk why there was so little listed on lesbianism and ask if anyone had suggestions for finding more. I was met with blank stares. But over the next few weeks, as I was working in the card catalogue, I'd sense a presence at my shoulder. This would be some discreet reference librarian quietly whispering that I might be interested in the section on women philanthropists, or the books on women in prisons. The books on philanthropy were indeed full of accounts of wealthy bisexual women romancing their way through the distaff side of the social register. The literature on incarceration was full of reports of prison passion written by middle-class social workers scandalized by the erotic lives of the mostly poor and working-class women under their supervision (interracial liaisons provoking special consternation).

However, my big research breakthrough occurred accidentally on a visit to Boston. I stumbled across a copy of *The Ladder* in a small bookshop near Harvard Square. I immediately wrote a letter to *The Ladder*, explaining that I was working on a bibliography of lesbian literature and asking if anyone there could help. The editor was one Gene Damon, who was of course Barbara Grier. She replied with a sharp rebuke, informing me that such a bibliography already existed. This was *The Lesbian in Literature*, by Gene Damon (Grier's pseudonym) and Lee Stuart, published in 1967. I was also duly chastised for my ignorance of Jeannette Foster's even earlier book, *Sex Variant Women in Literature* (1956). Grier's mighty typewriter could have taken the hide off a rhino, and it certainly knocked some of the wind out of my youthful enthusiasm. I am happy to report that after this initially testy encounter, Barbara relented, generously sharing her extraordinarily detailed and vast knowledge of the hidden riches of lesbian texts. However, the point of this tale is how difficult it was circa 1970 to find such publications. The work had been done, but it was largely inaccessible. The mechanisms for systematic impartation and acquisition of lesbian knowledge were at best rudimentary.

After hearing that there were existing lesbian bibliographies, I returned to the reference desk to see if I could get them through interlibrary loan. A few days later, one of those probably queer reference librarians led me to another gateway into the hidden world of LGBTQ scholarship. He suggested I go up to Special Collections and ask for the Labadie Collection. Since the holdings of Labadie were catalogued separately, they did not appear in the main catalogue. But he thought some of the materials for which I was searching were up with the rest of the rare books on the seventh floor. I followed this breadcrumb trail upstairs to the desk of Ed Weber.

The Labadie Collection was founded in 1911 by a Detroit anarchist named Joseph Labadie. The collection was initially focused on anarchist writings, but had gradually expanded to include social-protest literatures, especially those considered "extremist." When Ed Weber was hired as curator in 1960, he began to collect homophile publications and gay materials. As a result, Labadie became one of the most extensive repositories of homosexual publications in the country at a time when most university and public libraries dismissed them as pornographic trash. It turned out that almost everything for which I had been searching was indeed upstairs in Labadie, a wonderland of homophile scholarship. The collection had it all: Damon and Stuart's *The Lesbian in Literature*, Foster's *Sex Variant Women in Literature*, some early bibliographies compiled by Marion Zimmer Bradley, and an almost complete run of *The Ladder*.

I pretty much moved into Labadie for the remainder of my undergraduate career in order to devour these documents. It still astonishes me how much these women knew about lesbian history and how difficult it was for me to find out what they knew. At the time I was fairly oblivious to gay male publications, so I did not explore Labadie's equally impressive collections of *Mattachine Review*, *One*, and the *One Institute Quarterly*. But I discovered later, when my interests broadened, that these too contained huge compilations of gay history, bibliography, social analysis, and political critique.

I was also unaware that my own interests were part of a large wave of scholarship emerging out of the gay-liberation movement. I have only understood in retrospect how much my cohort built on the trails charted by our homophile predecessors, even as we often dismissed them for ostensibly lacking theoretical sophistication or terminological precision. While I was preparing these remarks, I emailed several of my old friends who were also doing gay research at the time to ask how they found direction and source material. Everyone acknowledged significant debts to homophile scholarship, organizational records, and individual collections.

It is not surprising that much of the material for John D'Emilio's early book on the homophile movement came from publications such as *Mattachine Review*, *The Ladder*, and the records of the New York chapter of the Mattachine Society. But it is interesting where John found these periodicals and other documentary evidence. Many of the records he consulted had been amassed and preserved by individuals, mainly Jim Kepner in his Los Angeles apartment and Don Lucas in his San Francisco garage. John also consulted the vertical files at the Kinsey Institute, and he visited Ann Arbor to utilize Labadie's collection of periodicals. For his magisterial *Gay American History* (1976), Jonathan Ned Katz also relied heavily on the bibliographic largesse produced by the early homophile press. When I queried Jonathan about his treasure maps, he mentioned *The Lesbian in Literature*, *Mattachine Review*, *One*, and several gay male bibliographies, especially those of Noel Garde.

Jonathan's email made me want to take a closer look at Garde, and I had already decided in preparation for this lecture to spend some time with the old homophile publications. I was fortuitously back at Michigan and able to return to my undergraduate haunt to try to squeeze out more insight from the voices of queer scholars past. I had missed much of their significance thirty years ago because of a lack of context. I read these texts differently now, because I know so much more than I did then, and can filter them through the lens of work such as that of Jonathan Katz, John D'Emilio, Allan Bérubé, Jim Steakley, Estelle Freedman, and William Eskridge (among others). There are certain common themes and repetitive subjects. An individual who read through *The Ladder*, *One*, *Mattachine Review*, and the *One Institute Quarterly* would have had a pretty firm grasp of the important issues, legal cases, government reports, and polemics affecting gay life in the 1950s and 1960s.

Bibliography was a central shared obsession. In addition to Marion Zimmer Bradley's detailed and thoughtful review of Jeannette Foster in its May 1957 issue, *The Ladder* featured Bradley's regular bibliographic column called "Lesbiana." Barbara Grier eventually took on the "Lesbiana" column, the contents of which provided much of the material for *The Lesbian in Literature*. Similarly, in 1957 the *Mattachine Review* started a serial "Bibliography on Homosexual Subjects." In 1959 Noel Garde published *The Homosexual in Literature*, billed as a "chronological bibliography circa 700 B.C.–1958," and in 1964 Vantage Press brought out his book *Jonathan to Gide: The Homosexual in History*. At the time of their publication, the Garde and Damon/Stuart compendia were the state of the art in gay bibliography. While my younger self would have critiqued this kind of work for its failure to interrogate the category of "homosexual," I now understand such texts as a considerable achievement. Moreover, such compilations made possible the application of the theoretical armamentaria of late 1960s social history, cultural anthropology, and urban sociology to GLBTQ subject matter.

But what were their sources? How did researchers such as Garde and Grier find out what they knew? Both obviously were passionate in their bibliographic zeal, and both also were able to build on previous work. Grier and Bradley drew heavily on Jeannette Foster. Foster, in turn, was a reference librarian by trade who worked at the Kinsey Institute from 1948 to 1952.[2] She was thus able to utilize the incomparable collection amassed by Kinsey. Foster followed many leads, but it is clear from her own citations that she also carefully mined the sexological texts of Havelock Ellis and Magnus Hirschfeld, as well as the contemporaneous writings of John Addington Symonds and Edward Carpenter. In many respects, Foster's book is a kind of hinge text, linking the homophile generation to earlier accumulations of queer knowledge in the late nineteenth and early twentieth centuries.

Similarly, Donald Webster Cory's 1951 book, *The Homosexual in America*, is a major conduit of literature produced before the First World War to the post–Second World War cohort of homophile intellectuals. Noel Garde explicitly acknowledges Cory's references, as well as a bibliography produced by the New York chapter of the Mattachine Society. *The Homosexual in America* has many problematic aspects, but it also set an agenda for much of the homophile scholarship it preceded and prefigured.[3] Cory included every major US government document pertaining to homosexuality, including "The Employment of Homosexuals and Other Sex Perverts in Government" and the Veterans Administration regulations dealing with military personnel dishonorably discharged for homosexuality. *The Homosexual in America* also listed the legal statutes regulating homosexual activities in what were then all forty-eight states. Cory's own bibliography and list of sources is still remarkable, and he included as a special appendix a "Check List of Novels and Dramas" pertaining to homosexuality. Foster too had read, used, and cited Cory, and I suspect the bibliographies printed in *Mattachine Review* began by updating Cory's work.

Cory, in turn, drew a great deal of his material from another of the great sedimentary layers of queer knowledge, the one that accumulated in Britain and in continental Europe in the late nineteenth and early twentieth centuries. I often call this layer "late nineteenth-century sexology," but that shorthand does not do justice to the complex ways in which the medically credentialed sexologists, the stigmatized homosexual intellectuals, and the mostly anonymous but active members of the burgeoning queer communities engaged in a complicated tango of communication and publication, as detailed in Harry Oosterhuis's brilliant work on Richard von Krafft-Ebing.[4] It might be better to think of this large body of work as a fusion of medical texts with the writings of homosexual (or invert) intellectuals who assembled polemical resources with which to articulate early critiques of sexual injustice and persecution. These resources included biographies of famous homosexuals, material gleaned from the Greek and Latin classics, personal testimony about the effects of blackmail and sexual deprivation, ethnographic reports, data on animal behavior, observations about homosexual community life, and some of the earliest modern compilations of queer bibliography. Taken as a whole, the body of work we call sexology is an intensely collaborative enterprise between the doctors and the perverts. It resulted in a massive consolidation of a major stratum of queer knowledge— sometimes fruitfully mined, sometimes ignored, dismissed, or forgotten. But one thing has become abundantly clear: just as my gay-liberation cohort built on the publications and archival resources assembled by our immediate predecessors, homophile-era researchers drew on previous strata, particularly the "sexological" one.

Among the most important sexologists were Richard von Krafft-Ebing, Havelock Ellis, and Magnus Hirschfeld. The key polemics included the writings of Karl Heinrich Ulrichs, Edward Carpenter, and John Addington Symonds.[5] Magnus Hirschfeld was, like Ellis and Krafft-Ebing, a credentialed physician. He was also a brilliant polemicist, whose own homosexuality was sometimes used to undermine his medical authority. Ulrichs and Carpenter lacked medical credentials but were heavily cited in the medical texts. Symonds's role is especially complex. His name was removed from *Sexual Inversion* at the insistence of his estate, but he contributed a great deal of the historical information and much of the analysis that we attribute to Ellis.[6] Symonds's own work contains incisive reviews of the medical literature, in which he is cited in turn.[7]

Magnus Hirschfeld's thousand-page tome, *The Homosexuality of Men and Women* (1914), is emblematic of the attainments of this period. Hirschfeld intended a complete account of everything known on the topic of homo-sexuality. He incorporated the work of other medical sexologists, lay writers such as Symonds, Carpenter, and Ulrichs, and his own primary research. The second part of the book, called "The Homosexuality of Men and Women as Sociological Occurrence," is particularly compelling. It includes the results of one of the first statistical surveys of homosexuals, as well as chapters on homosexuality at different class levels and in different countries. Hirschfeld's book also contains an extraordinary report on urban gay life in the early twentieth century. John Addington Symonds noted that the homosexual passion "throbs in our huge cities. The pulse of it can be felt in London, Paris, Berlin, Vienna, no less than in Constantinople, Naples, Teheran, and Moscow."[8] Hirschfeld proceeded to detail the sociology of this heartbeat in the chapter on community life and meeting places of homosexual men and women (mainly in Berlin), including circles of friends, private clubs, political clubs, sports clubs, and a complicated network of bars catering to different subsets of the population. He documented the homosexual use of public theaters, a group of homosexual bathhouses, drag balls for both men and women, hotels and guest houses favored by homosexuals, cruis-ing in public parks and toilets, and the use of personal advertisements to find partners.[9] And the significance of this city-based subculture is shown, he noted, by the "many, who day after day have seldom been able to remove their masks, and feel here as if liberated. People have seen homosexuals from the provinces set foot in such bars for the first time and burst into violently emotional tears."[10] Hirschfeld also devoted considerable space to the legal and social victimization, persecution, and prosecution of homosexuals. He included a detailed history of the organized movement against this perse-cution as well as a list of anti-gay laws around the world.

Hirschfeld's intellectual significance has often been underestimated as a consequence of the paucity of reliable translations of his magnificent oeuvre.[11] A few excerpts of *The Homosexuality of Men and Women* were trans-lated by Henry Gerber and published in the *One Institute Quarterly* in the early 1960s, but a complete translation, by Michael Lombardi-Nash, has only been available since 2000. I had not read *The Homosexuality of Men and Women* when I first encountered *The Homosexual in America*. Now, having read both, I can see their kinship. Cory had read Hirschfeld in the German and was able to draw on Hirschfeld's bibliographic compilations, historical data, and rhetorical tactics. Cory discussed what he called the "Hirschfeld movement" and the "Carpenter movement" in the late nineteenth and early twentieth centuries, lamenting that there had been nothing similar since their decline. He probably could not know that a major revival of such activism was about to erupt, nor that his elaborations on the pre–First World War corpus of knowledge would be further embellished by an emerging group of homophile researchers.

The layer of queer knowledge generated from roughly the late 1880s to the 1920s, mostly in England and continental Europe, has continued to inspire new work as scholars excavate its resources in the service of more contemporary projects. For example, Jeffrey Weeks's early work, especially his *Coming Out: A History of Homosexual Politics in Britain* (1977), is in many ways an extended meditation on Havelock Ellis, Edward Carpenter, and John Addington Symonds, inflected with considerable knowledge of Krafft-Ebing. Foucault's *The History of Sexuality: Volume 1* is in large part a brilliant reading of Krafft-Ebing and late-nineteenth-century French psychiatry. Lisa Duggan's work on the Alice Mitchell case and Harry Oosterhuis's biography of Krafft-Ebing make whole new readings of sexology possible. Nonetheless, I believe both the sexological texts and the homophile corpus are underutilized and could still launch a thousand dissertations.

It is this sense of queer knowledges in sedimented layers that I hoped to convey with my title tonight. In the geologic record, certain strata are fossilrich, partly because of the conditions that produce luxuriant life forms and partly because of the conditions that favor their preservation in fossil form. Similarly, there seem to be periods in which social and political conditions have favored the abundant proliferation of queer knowledges, while other conditions dictate their preservation or destruction. And it is up to succeeding generations to ensure that such sedimentary formations are identified, excavated, catalogued, and utilized to produce new knowledge. Unfortunately, because of the lack of durable structural mechanisms to secure the reliable transfer of queer knowledges, they are often instead lost, buried, and forgotten.

For example, it is difficult to teach material that is only available in photocopied course packs or in special collections with limited access. Most of the books to which I referred tonight are out of print or hard to find. Many were briefly available in reprint editions during the 1970s as a consequence of the 1975 Arno Press series *Homosexuality: Lesbians and Gay Men in Society, History, and Literature.* These reprints of primary texts were among the most important achievements of the early wave of gay-liberation scholarship. The series consisted of fifty-four books and two periodicals, including the early homophile bibliographies by Damon, Stuart, Bradley, and Garde; several key US government documents relating to homosexuality; reprints of important books by Edward Carpenter, Xavier Mayne, Natalie Barney, Earl Lind, Mercedes de Acosta, Blair Niles, Renée Vivien, and Donald Webster Cory; lesbian classics and pulp novels; texts from the gay-rights movement in Germany; and reprints of complete runs of *The Ladder* and *Mattachine Review*.[12] This extraordinary series was three decades too early. Sadly, it, too, is now out of print, and the Arno editions are almost as rare as the originals. Both Krafft-Ebing's *Pychopathia Sexualis* and Havelock Ellis's *Sexual Inversion* were recently re-released in cheap paperback editions, but when I tried to order them as textbooks this year they were already once again unobtainable.

I want to use this brief review to make a few points. The first is the prevalence of amnesia about queer studies's past. I am continually shocked at the assumption that GLBTQ studies only got started sometime in the 1990s. I chose the metaphor of geology because it helps us think about longer time frames and pull our focus away from the present. In geologic time, the present is a blip. Our sense of what is important in queer scholarship should not be distorted by the glitter of the current, the trendy, and the new. I want us to think about longer processes that have shaped the present and in which the present is deeply rooted. Any scholarly project can benefit from an accumulation of knowledge that can be evaluated, validated, criticized, updated, polished, improved, or used to provide new trails to investigate. We need to be more conscious about including the older material in the contemporary canon of queer studies.

However, the causes of limited memory are more structural than stylistic, and are produced less by curricular decisions than by institutional impediments. My main point is that we need to do more to overcome the institutional deficiencies that constrict access to older knowledge. We must continue to develop organizational structures to guarantee the conservation, transmission, and development of queer knowledges. As a discipline, GLBTQ studies is still very rudimentarily institutionalized in the universities, and this is a challenge to its continued viability. Clearly, there is much greater institutionalization now than there was even a decade ago, as events such as this lecture series and the existence of institutions such as CLAGS demonstrate. But the number of departments of GLBTQ studies is minuscule in comparison to the number of, for example, departments of sociology or political science. The infrastructures of knowledge require physical space and durable organizational structures—offices, buildings, libraries, archives, departments, programs, centers, faculty lines, staff positions, and paychecks. We must work to accumulate more resources and build better bureaucracies.

Many of us instinctively recoil at the idea of bureaucratization and consider it distasteful. Bureaucracy has many drawbacks, including staleness, boredom, pointless procedures, and petty bureaucrats. Bureaucracies almost by nature lack excitement, glamour, or charisma. We often live for fleeting intensities and charged moments, and celebrate marginality as a kind of permanent desideratum. But if bureaucracy and routinization have their costs, so do marginality and charisma. Marginality and momentary excitements are intrinsically fragile, evanescent, and unstable. Part of the reason for our impaired memory of the older strata of queer knowledges is that the institutions and organizations that produced them are gone. Queer life is full of examples of fabulous explosions that left little or no detectable trace, or whose documentary and artifactual remains were never systematically assembled or adequately conserved.

Those of you who know me will understand the ambivalence with which I recall one such set of vanished institutions: the "women's community" that rose up out of feminism and radical lesbianism in the 1970s. By the late 1970s, there were dozens of feminist and lesbian newspapers, at least a dozen journals, several thriving feminist presses, and a network of local communities with significant public territory. In San Francisco, much of this women's territory was along Valencia Street where there were lesbian bars, feminist coffeehouses, the women's bookstore, and several women's collectives and businesses. There were similar settlements in western Massachusetts, in Iowa City, and across the San Francisco Bay in Oakland. Today, there is almost nothing left of that world. Most of the newspapers, journals, bookstores, coffeehouses, and businesses are gone, despite a few stubborn survivors such as *Lesbian Connection*. There are complicated reasons for the collapse of these communities, but one of them was their infrastructural fragility. In San Francisco, for example, most of the shops were in rented storefronts along a low-rent business corridor. When commercial rents began to skyrocket, these shops were driven out. The only remnant of this once vibrant women's neighborhood is the Women's Building, and the only reason it is still there is because it was purchased, not rented. But the built environment is expensive to obtain and challenging to maintain. Stability is resource intensive.

Queer populations have an overabundance of marginality and an insufficiency of stability. Max Weber noted that bureaucracy, once fully established, is among the hardest social structures to destroy.[13] That can be a curse. But we could use some of that stability, and the resources required to sustain it, in queer studies. New theoretical frameworks, new data, and new discoveries will always force rethinking of our premises and assumptions. We must count on periodic rebellions, reformations, and upheavals to bring refreshment and renewal. But to paraphrase Marx and Marshall Berman, all that seems solid can vanish in a heartbeat, and to mangle Santayana, those who fail to secure the transmission of their histories are doomed to lose them.

Notes

1. For more on the Daughters of Bilitis, see Marcia M. Gallo, *Different Daughters: A History of the Daughters of Bilitis and the Rise of the Lesbian Rights Movement* (New York: Carroll and Graf, 2006).

2. For Foster's biography, see Joanne Passet, S*ex Variant Woman: The Life of Jeannette Howard Foster* (Cambridge, MA: Da Capo Press, 2008).

3. Jeffrey Escoffier first alerted me to the significance of Cory's book.

4. Harry Oosterhuis, *Stepchildren of Nature: Krafft-Ebing, Psychiatry, and the Making of Sexual Identity* (Chicago: University of Chicago Press, 2000).

5. Richard von Krafft-Ebing, *Psychopathia Sexualis, with Special Reference to Contrary Sexual Instinct: A Medico-Legal Study* (Philadelphia: The F.A. Davis Company, 1894); Havelock Ellis, *Studies in the Psychology of Sex, Volume II: Sexual Inversion* (Philadelphia: Davis, 1915); Magnus Hirschfeld, *The Homosexuality of Men and Women*, trans. Michael A. Lombardi-Nash (1914, reprint, Amherst, NY: Prometheus, 2000); Karl Heinrich Ulrichs, *The Riddle of "Man-Manly" Love: The Pioneering Work on Male Homosexuality*, trans. Michael A. Lombardi-Nash (Amherst, NY: Prometheus Books, 1994); Edward Carpenter, *The Intermediate Sex: A Study of Some Transitional Types of Men and Women* (New York: Kennerly, 1912); John Addington Symonds, *A Problem in Greek Ethics: Being an Inquiry into the Phenomenon of Sexual Inversion: Addressed Especially to Medical Psychologists and Jurists* (London, 1901); and Symonds, *A Problem in Modern Ethics: Being an Inquiry into the Phenomenon of Sexual Inversion: Addressed Especially to Medical Psychologists and Jurists* (London, 1896). Excellent essays on Ulrichs, Krafft-Ebing, and Hirschfeld are included in the splendid collection edited by Rosario: Vernon A. Rosario, ed., *Science and Homosexualities* (New York: Rout ledge, 1997). Also see Crozier's critical edition of *Sexual Inversion* (Havelock Ellis and John Addington Symonds, *Sexual Inversion: A Critical Edition*, ed. Ivan Crozier [Houndsmills, UK: Palgrave Macmillan, 2008]); Lucy Bland and Laura Doan, eds., *Sexology in Culture: Labelling Bodies and Desires* (Chicago: University of Chicago Press, 1998); and Bland and Doan, eds., *Sexology Uncensored: The Documents of Sexual Science* (Chicago: University of Chicago Press, 1998). Biographies include Hubert C. Kennedy, *Ulrichs: The Life and Works of Karl Heinrich Ulrichs, Pioneer of the Modern Gay Movement* (Boston: Alyson Publications, 1988); Sheila Rowbotham, *Edward Carpenter: A Life of Liberty and Love* (London: Verso, 2008); Charlotte Wolff, *Magnus Hirschfeld: A Portrait of a Pioneer in Sexology* (London:

Quartet Books, 1986); Phyllis Grosskurth, *Havelock Ellis: A Biography* (New York: New York University Press, 1985); and Grosskurth, *The Woeful Victorian: A Biography of John Addington Symonds* (New York: Holt, Rinehart, and Winston, 1965). Additional work on Hirschfeld includes James Steakley, *The Homosexual Emancipation Movement in Germany* (Salem, NH: Ayer, 1993); and Elena Mancini, *Magnus Hirschfeld and the Quest for Sexual Freedom: A History of the First International Sexual Freedom Movement* (Basingstoke, UK: Palgrave Macmillan, 2015).

6. Edward J. Bristow, "Symond's History, Ellis's Heredity: Sexual Inversion," in *Sexology in Culture: Labelling Bodies and Desires*, eds. Laura Doan and Lucy Bland (Chicago: University of Chicago Press, 1998), 79–99.

7. See especially Symonds, *Problem in Modern Ethics*.

8. Symonds, *Problem in Modern Ethics*, 2.

9. Hirschfeld, *Homosexuality of Men and Women*, 776–803.

10. Hirschfeld, *Homosexuality of Men and Women*, 785.

11. James Steakley, "Per scientiam ad justitiam: Magnus Hirschfeld and the Sexual Politics of Innate Homosexuality," in *Science and Homosexualities*, ed. Vernon Rosario (New York: Routledge, 1997), 133–34.

12. The catalogue of the Arno series, *Homosexuality: Lesbians and Gay Men in Society, History, and Literature*, is itself a remarkable research document. Jonathan Katz was the general editor, Louis Crompton, Barbara Gittings, James Steakley, and Dolores Noll were the editorial board, and J. Michael Siegelaub was the research assistant. Jonathan Ned Katz, ed., *Homosexuality: Lesbians and Gay Men in Society, History, and Literature* (New York: Arno, 1975).

13. H. H. Gerth and C. Wright Mills, eds., *From Max Weber: Essays in Sociology* (New York: Oxford University Press, 1958), 228.

"Infrastructures and Queer Knowledges": Gayle Rubin Reflects on "Geologies of Queer Studies: It's Déjà Vu All Over Again"

Don't expect institutions to take care of you unless you take care of your institutions.

—TIMOTHY SNYDER

Institution:

An establishment, organization, or association, instituted for the promotion of some object, esp. one of public or general utility, religious, charitable, educational, etc., e.g., a church, school, college, hospital, asylum, reformatory, mission, or the like. . . . Something having the fixity or importance of a social institution . . .

—*OXFORD ENGLISH DICTIONARY*

I gave my Kessler Lecture in New York during the winter of 2003. I write these comments in the spring of 2022, in San Francisco, during a historic drought and with the expectation of another apocalyptic fire season. A great deal has changed in the interim. The not-quite-two decades that have passed have produced a social, political, and physical planet that differs markedly from the one in which I delivered those remarks. The intervening years have brought a vast intensification of wealth inequality. Escalating climate change threatens to make the earth uninhabitable for humans. The recent Russian invasion of Ukraine has challenged architectures of international relations that have, more or less, prevailed since the beginning of the twenty-first century. The COVID-19 epidemic has disrupted the routines of economic and social life. News coverage has shrunk dramatically with the demise of so many local and alternative newspapers. The disastrous presidency of Donald Trump, the Republican Party's ardent embrace of authoritarianism, and the worldwide resurgence of increasingly mobilized and heavily armed right-wing movements have all exposed heretofore unanticipated vulnerabilities in our political institutions.

My Kessler Lecture was concerned with the structural impediments to the production, preservation, and transmission of queer knowledges. I emphasized the need to build and sustain robust infrastructures of such knowledge: institutions such as archives, libraries, curricula, programs, and departments. I looked with wistful envy at the apparent stability and relative prosperity of the mainstream equivalents of such entities: research universities, major museums, and well-established archives and special collections. Compared to their vastly greater resources, funding, staffing, holdings, and physical space, queer institutions seemed frail and marginal.

At the time, I could be reasonably unconcerned about the survival and autonomy of major research universities, libraries, museums, and archives. That is no longer the case. Many of the mainstream institutions that seemed so durable in 2003 have turned out to be surprisingly fragile. This has been especially evident with respect to even major political structures in the United States, many of which require broad agreement about their legitimacy to function. In some quarters of our political spectrum, those agreements have been repudiated, or displaced by the ruthless pursuit of raw power. Many of the presumed "guardrails" of democracy are imperiled.

Education itself is under assault at many levels. Although much of the focus has been on public primary schooling, there is a long-simmering conservative crusade against higher education. While the characterization of universities as "liberal" is wildly overstated, the organized right is actively working to purge ideas and personnel it sees as liberal or progressive. The attacks on ostensibly "liberal" universities are often driven by special animus toward African American studies and all minority ethnic studies programs, labor studies, and women's, gender, and sexuality studies. LGBTQ studies are a particular target.

The "normal" against which many of us have railed seems unexpectedly tenuous, and much of what seems poised to replace it fills me with apprehension. In retrospect, the comfort with which one could critique so many existing institutions was in part a function of their apparent solidity, as well as the assumption that the likely alternatives would be better.

The evident instabilities of even seemingly adamantine institutions have made the project of sustaining queer ones even more challenging. It is difficult to pursue agendas that may become engulfed by developments that threaten much more than the future of queer scholarship. If climate change goes unchecked or nuclear conflicts erupt, there will be no libraries or archives, much less queer ones. The entire future as we tend to conceive of it may be in serious doubt.

Nevertheless, it is worth fighting for a future that is more just, less unequal, less destructive of both natural and human resources, and generally less lunatic. It is also worth fighting for a better world for future queers, and for queer knowledges. And that requires a determined defense of the institutions that produce and safeguard such knowledge.

Historian Timothy Snyder has focused closely on modern Eastern Europe, and the totalitarian political systems that have dominated much of it in the twentieth and twenty-first centuries. In 2017, alarmed by parallel impulses in the United States during the Trump presidency, Snyder published *On Tyranny: Twenty Lessons from the Twentieth Century*. It is full of advice on how to contest looming authoritarianism and potential dictatorships, but I want to take special note of his comments on institutions. Snyder observes, "We tend to assume that institutions will automatically maintain themselves against even the most direct attacks," and warns that this is a potentially fatal mistake.[1] He further advises:

> It is institutions that help us to preserve decency. They need our help as well. Do not speak of "our institutions" unless you make them yours by acting on their behalf. Institutions do not protect themselves. . . . So choose an institution you care about—a court, a newspaper, a law, a labor union—and take its side.[2]

This advice applies to the institutions of queer knowledge as well. These need help, now more than ever. These rely on donations, memberships, volunteer labor, attendance at events, and general approbation. If you care about the future of queer knowledge, pick one of its institutions and support it. A partial list would include: your local queer studies curriculum, or the department or program in which it is housed; organizations such as CLAGS, the Lesbian Herstory Archives, the GLBT Historical Society, the Leather Archives & Museum, the Leslie-Lohman Museum, the Stonewall National Museum & Archives, the ArQuives: Canada's LGBTQ2+ archives, and Les Archives gaies du Québec; libraries and archives affiliated with universities, such as the ONE National Gay and Lesbian Archives at USC, the Cornell Human Sexuality Collection, the Labadie Collection at Michigan, and some very special collections such as those at Harvard (the Schlesinger), Brown, Duke, and Yale. And there are other organizations, libraries, and archives that accumulate, preserve, and make available the documentation of queer pasts, presents, and futures. Now is the time to do whatever we can to ensure their futures.

Notes

1. Timothy Snyder, *On Tyranny: Twenty Lessons from the Twentieth Century* (New York: Tim Duggan Books, 2017), 23.

2. Snyder, *On Tyranny*, 22.

THE DAVID R. KESSLER LECTURES 2002–2020

2002   JONATHAN NED KATZ

2003   GAYLE RUBIN

2004   ISAAC JULIEN

2006   ADRIENNE RICH

2007   DOUGLAS CRIMP

2008   SUSAN STRYKER

2009   SARAH SCHULMAN

2010   URVASHI VAID

2012   MARTIN DUBERMAN

2013   CHERYL CLARKE

2014   CATHY J. COHEN

2015   RICHARD FUNG

2016   DEAN SPADE

2017   SARA AHMED

2018   AMBER HOLLIBAUGH

2019   JASBIR K. PUAR

2020   RODERICK A. FERGUSON

Isaac Julien

Born in London in 1960, Isaac Julien CBE RA is an artist and filmmaker whose photographs and multichannel film installations feature fractured, multi-genre narratives on race, class, sexuality, and postcolonialism. His 1989 documentary-drama *Looking for Langston*, a meditation on the life, politics, and sexuality of Harlem Renaissance poet Langston Hughes, was a foundational work of queer cinema. Other groundbreaking work includes *Frantz Fanon: Black Skin, White Mask* (1995) and *Young Soul Rebels* (1991), which won the Semaine de la Critique prize at the Cannes Film Festival. Julien is distinguished professor of the arts at UC Santa Cruz, where he runs the Isaac Julien Lab, a platform for the innovation of visual and sonic languages for production and the critical reception of moving image, video art, and installation work by examining historical and contemporary art practice.

Cinematic Rearticulations

DECEMBER 10, 2004

I was in Philadelphia last week installing a double-screen film and video installation called *Frantz Fanon S. A.*, which was first shown at the Johannesburg Biennial in 1997. In the installation I abstracted a series of images from my feature film documentary *Frantz Fanon: Black Skin, White Mask* (1995) that corresponded to a lyrical register in psychiatrist and revolutionary Frantz Fanon's writing. The vibrancy and sensuality of the images abstracted from my earlier film are represented in a condensed form—presenting a spin or ironic quotation on Fanon's piece "There is no colour prejudice here," as the Fanon character in the film waves a South African ANC flag. The exhibition, curated by Mark Nash (my partner), is called "Experiments with Truth," a display of contemporary moving images intended to reassess the influence of cinema and documentary practice within contemporary visual art. In an increasingly troubled time of emergencies, war, and dis-information, the work represents an alternative view—one in which images can play a critical role in shaping our understanding of the world rather than merely being used as a tool for propaganda.

The gallery, rather than the cinema, is becoming an important space for making interventions to re-view the differing cultural and political perspectives that make up "moving image" culture from around the world. This shift brings with it a growing set of questions, including: How are we to consider the phenomena of contemporary artists working with film and video? How did a version of cinema become an increasingly common presence within the art gallery context?

This growing trend is marked in my own career as an artist and filmmaker who, after Derek Jarman's death, witnessed the end of an Independent (queer) film culture in the UK. Regrettably, what Ruby Rich once rightly crowned "New Queer Cinema" was lost. It can be argued that elements from the genre have reappeared, here and there, in advertising, in mainstream television, and in galleries. Through experimentations with film and video, the distinctions between narrative avant-garde and documentary practice have become blurred, along with shifts in viewers' experiences—whose viewing habits and subjectivities are influenced by new digital technologies. Distinctive experimental approaches to visual imagery, once the aesthetic hallmarks of the New Queer Cinema, have transcended into the space of the contemporary gallery. The documentary turn into video art was perhaps hinted at a decade ago in Derek Jarman's "imageless" feature film *Blue* (1993). With an anti-representational strategy, Jarman presented a blank screen of Yves Klein blue, which stood as a testament to a time now lost, by creating a blue frame where the spectator loses their sight into a sea of blue haze. The non-representational image retained poetic and factual information which Jarman sonically produced with precision—documenting his eventual blindness during his battle against AIDS. *Blue* premiered at the Venice Art Biennial as a video installation portraying the truth of his condition and, indeed, a part of our queer history.

Looking for Langston

Thinking about the representation of truth in the space of the city and notions of spatial temporality brings to mind my early research for *Looking for Langston*, which also led me to Philadelphia, the very place of the "Experiments with Truth" exhibition. A connection between the past and the present is clearly evident, haunting my every step. This city was home to two of the perhaps most important voices which created an impetus and interpolated my own art practice. I am, of course, referring to Joseph Beam, an activist and writer of the black gay anthology *Brother to Brother*, and to the poet Essex Hemphill. Indeed, Hemphill's poetic truth struck me again, as it did when I first read his poem in homage to Joseph Beam after his death, twenty years ago:

> When I stand
> on the front lines now,
> cussing the lack of truth,
> the absence of willful change
> and strategic coalitions,

I realize sewing quilts
will not bring you back
nor save us.

It's too soon
to make monuments
for all we are losing,
for the lack of truth . . .[1]

It was for the "lack of truth" that Bush recently won the American election—
as millions of voters lined up to vote against queer marriages it seems. But it
was only ten years ago that I first lived in New York to work on a four-part
television series titled *Question of Equality*, a history of the Lesbian and Gay
movement in the States, which chronicled the rise of religious-right funda-
mentalism. This project was commissioned by Channel Four and ITVS for
the program *Culture Wars* and in 2004 we are still deep in it.

In 1985 I first visited Joseph Beam in Philadelphia, and it was in the same
city where, in 1994, I last saw Essex Hemphill alive. Next year will mark a
decade since his death and it will also be the year *Looking for Langston* is
re-released on DVD. The updated DVD will contain many surprises to celebrate Hemphill's work. Looking back on the making of *Looking for Langston*
(1989) and *The Attendant* (1993), I can see the creation of a discursive space
for re-articulating the politics of queer difference. This was a response to
early developments in furthering what has now become known as "Queer
Studies" in the States, and in Britain "Cultural Studies" (an already named
and established discipline). I saw myself as a "cultural worker" who made
visual imagery that translated theoretical concerns—either through the
language of the cinema, or via progressive television programming, where
the cultural and media revolution was taking place through Channel Four
Television. Indeed it was Channel Four's lesbian and gay series *Out on Tues-
day*, in 1989, that commissioned and broadcast *Looking for Langston*. The
legacy of that intervention is a British version of *Queer Eye for the Straight
Guy*!—although I think that the American original is much better, but that's
where queer innovation has left us.

It is now left to artists and filmmakers to make utopic interventions into
spaces that seem to be more open and receptive to thematic and visual experimentation. Contemporary museums and galleries are certainly creative
spaces where a queer legacy of innovation continues and aesthetics interventions are not only possible, but also recognised. I don't want to claim

it is a triumph, but it is a site where "moving images" can explore "queer aesthetics" receptively. Several projects, which have successfully used the space of the gallery, come to mind, including *The Orange and Blue Feelings* (2003), a double-screen video piece by Glenn Ligon, who grapples with artistic creativity, growing up black and queer. The work invites the audience to explore the multiple significances of a "lost queer painting" of Malcolm X. Francesco Vezzoli's *The End of the Human Voice* is haunted by cinephilia, re-enacting key moments in art cinema through the camp performances of Bianca Jagger. The piece references Cocteau as Vezzoli casts himself, with iconic paper "eye-lids," on one side of a bed and Bianca Jagger on the other. Both pieces can be seen in the "Experiments of Truth" exhibition at the Fabric Workshop and Museum in Philly, not in cinema proper. The politics of the museum were ambivalently signalled in *Looking for Langston* and *The Attendant*. Both films explored spatial temporalities, queering history, transgressing racial boundaries and the space of the museum. In *Looking for Langston*, for example, sections of the black-and-white film show an art opening in New York from the 1930s. We see African American artists and their white patrons, while Stuart Hall reads a verse from Chaucer: "History, the smiler with the knife under the cloak" (*The Knight's Tale*). Here I was alluding to my suspicion of the art world and the possible dangers of patronage for black and for queer artists. In *The Attendant* a story of (imagined) interracial transgression occurs between a "closeted" middle-aged black guard, who works in a museum and after closing hours, and a younger white visitor.

Indeed the museum or gallery has become the site for my own rearticulations—an ironic relocation, I admit. Essex Hemphill was well aware of the contradictory nature of high cultural spaces, seeing them as sites for class and race wars ("Visiting Hours"):

> The government pays me
> nine thousand dollars a year
> to protect the East Wing.
> So I haunt it.
>
> Visiting hours are over.
> The silent sentry is on duty.
> An electric eye patrols the premises.
> I'm just here
> putting
> mouth on the place.

Modigliani whispers to Matisse.
Matisse whispers to Picasso.
I kiss the Rose in my pocket
and tip easy through this tomb of thieves.

I'm weighted down with keys,
flashlight, walkie-talkie, a gun.
I'm expected to die, if necessary,
protecting European artwork
that robbed color and movement
from my life.

I'm the ghost in the Capitol.
I did Vietnam.
My head is rigged with land mines,
but I keep cool,
waiting on every other Friday,
kissing the Rose,
catching some trim.

I'm not protecting any more Europeans
with my life.
I'll give this shit in here away
before I die for it.
Fuck a Remb-randt!

And if I ever go off,
you'd better look out, Mona Lisa.
I'll run through this gallery
with a can of red enamel paint
and spray everything in sight
like a cat in heat.[2]

This notion of treason and revenge of the multitude, hinted at by Hemphill, is a theme at work in *Paradise Omeros* (made for *Documenta11*, 2002) and *Baltimore* (2003). The latter was a multi-screen video installation that developed from a documentary called *Baadasssss Cinema* (made in 2002). *Baltimore* deals with the cinematisation of video art, on the one hand, and a "queering" and "racing" of the museum, on the other. I saw these video installations as interventions that attempted to address the "creolising vision" in the space of the gallery.

Isaac Julien, *Baltimore*. Third Berlin Biennale for Contemporary Art, 2004. 11'56", three-screen video installation, 16mm film transferred to digital, color, 5.1 sound. Photo by Werner Maschmann. Courtesy of the artist.

Baltimore

The aim of *Baltimore*, a large-scale three-screen video projection, was to try and create a re-reading across three distinct archives including that of Black action films from the 1970s. The installation aims to create a reflective "third space" using both "high" and "popular" cultural motifs such as black science fiction and Afro-futurism. The triptych component explores the aesthetics of the blaxploitation cinema genre and its contemporary references through a series of light-hearted citations from a number of movies. The work was shot in Baltimore—a city with a long history of black migration and settlement. Baltimore is also the home base of the NAACP in the States. The prime locations of *Baltimore* are the museums of Walters Art Museum, an important Renaissance art museum in downtown Baltimore, and the Great Blacks in Wax Museum (the equivalent of a Madame Tussauds gone wrong or a black Thomas Hirschhorn installation—and one of America's African American top ten history attractions). This is due to my own interest in archival spaces—including notions of power and memory and memorialisation.

The Blaxsploitation genres are profoundly imperfect, contaminated culturally, sexist yet queer. Certainly not everyone would call these films art, nor are many of them that compelling. I would argue this is irrelevant.

The films are valuable and provide a rich starting point for my own imagery. They are involved with the aesthetics of the vulgar. Video projection can draw attention to visual identifiers and codes, which I rework to produce a creolised vision of the museum. I hope the piece is received as a provocative and satirical intervention within the art world, critically re-arranging and un-tidying its curatorial endeavours.

The idea behind this first part of the *Baadasssss* project was to place the documentary in a pedagogical relationship to the spectator. I wanted to show the archival process and the power of visual iconography in relation to the aftereffects of the Black power movement, to people's lives—to their very representation. This attempt at queering Blaxsploitation imagery is an acknowledgment of its ability to influence other genres such as Hip-Hop, independent film, and so on. I also wanted to consider the misunderstandings and complexities of the genre through interviews with black queer icons, such as Pam Grier, engaged in debate and dissension. *Baadasssss Cinema* will merely enable the spectator to fully appreciate the spatio-temporality of Baltimore's multiple screens and sonic sound projections, allowing for a criticality that tackles the representational strategies inherent in blaxploitation films themselves and approximates these aesthetics for the space of video art.

The scenes in Baltimore are shot with deliberate diegetic effects that work to disrupt the narrative telos. The camera, tracking movements within the frame, makes use of the sculptural potential of cinematic space. In the triptych format the images are not merely representations of certain people but representations of "the spaces of representations." Here identities are spatialised by collocated images across all three screens. The highway scene, for example, mirrors the visual ideas on perspectivism from the school of Piero della Francesca's *The Ideal City*. This is achieved through pictorial montages in order to emphasise the politics of space.

The "Sweet sweet back Baadasssss song" is unique in allowing for a black fairy queen to skip along to it. And although Melvin Van Peebles did not intend to make a queer black film, it is indeed a very queer and strange black experimental art film. It was for this element of the unexpected that he was chosen to play the protagonist, along with Vanessa Myrie who plays the black femme fatale—part Angela Davis, part Foxy Brown, and part cyborg. Her character remains out of reach for Melvin—her sexuality is an enigma for some, but not for all. These characters are indeed haunted by the history of the spaces of the museum, and their own filmic iconography.

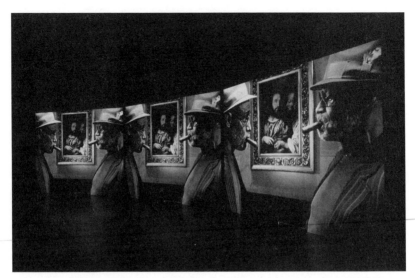

Isaac Julien, *Baltimore*. Third Berlin Biennale for Contemporary Art, 2004. 11'56", three-screen video installation, 16mm film transferred to digital, color, 5.1 sound. Photo by Werner Maschmann. Courtesy of the artist.

At the end of "Heavy Breathing," Essex Hemphill writes:

> At the end of heavy breathing
> the dream deferred
> is in a museum
> under glass and guard.
> It costs five dollars
> to see it on display.
> We spend the day
> viewing artifacts,
> breathing heavy
> on the glass
> to see—
> the skeletal remains
> of black panthers,
> pictures of bushes,
> canisters of tears.[3]

I imagine if he might have dreamt of a few frames of *Baltimore* or prophetically dreamt of my future.

Isaac Julien, *Baltimore.* Espace 315—Centre Georges Pompidou, Paris, 2005. 11'56", three-screen video installation, 16mm film transferred to digital, color, 5.1 sound. Photo by Georges Meguerditchian. Courtesy of the artist.

Paradise Omeros

In this piece, a homage to Derek Walcott, I explore an adolescent's perspective on the mixture of English and St. Lucian cultures within both countries. A young man prepares to come to terms with a loss of innocence and at the same time there is an Oedipal reading of postcolonial and intra-ethnic relations enacted between the protagonist and the tourist/rasta male character. In England, the young man and his family experience both happiness and racial tension—which is shown through scenes of enjoyment, juxtaposed to ones of anguish. Other sections of the film are set in St. Lucia, where the rasta character quotes Robert Mitchum's performance in *The Night of the Hunter* (directed by Charles Laughton in 1955) to the adolescent. Here the dynamics of love and hate are explored—Mitchum's tattoo replaced by gold rings worn by the rasta.

I wanted to consider the representation of the Caribbean as a site of mythic cultural fantasy. One of the principal scenes, for example, is the submersion of the boy in the sea, intercut with historical images of riots and immigration in the UK. On his journey through the sea and the archive, our protagonist encounters traumatic images. Memories, both personal and public, lead him to the metropolis, London. Yet he returns to St. Lucia, and then back to London again, through the visual looping of the film, which is projected on the gallery wall. The effect is one of oscillation—as though the character continually travels back and forth in time. He refuses to be located, preferring to occupy an/other space—somewhere between the sea, the city, and the gallery wall. Indeed, it is within the very walls of the contemporary gallery that artists remain free to explore such themes (which often sit outside mainstream interests). And, it is in this way that galleries are becoming an increasingly important critical and cultural site.

My emerging displacement of cinema, in an art context, can be seen as a continuation of some of my earlier independent cinema concerns. It could be seen as a reconfiguration of sorts—this mutation, from one technology to another, from celluloid to digital, makes new interventions possible. Along with this are changes in the nature of spectatorship and subjectivity. Deterritorialisation of the cinema into the gallery means that spectators who come to these spaces may have a different set of expectations, beyond the normative expectations of a general cinema audience. But, of course, that could be seen as a class difference as well, and that's why I like the idea of creating works that have an interdisciplinary approach. For example, *Baadasssss Cinema*, the documentary I made for the Independent Film Channel, was shown on Cable TV, but *Baltimore*, its sister project, was shown at Metro Pictures Gallery in New York.

These changes can also be viewed as a sign of the displacement of political demands, which once took centre stage in the cinema proper, but are now relegated to a "fine art" space. It is worth noting that many voices have been made absent in the cinema. It has been over ten years since Derek Jarman's death. His life is the subject of my next documentary—a project that is proving to be very difficult to raise funds for. To date, not one television station has agreed to support the documentary financially and I wonder, were Jarman alive, would he join me in the call for a rearticulated cinema? Or, for that matter, would the political video work of Marlon Riggs be shown in a gallery as video art?

Notes

1. Essex Hemphill, "When My Brother Fell (For Joseph Beam)," *Ceremonies: Prose and Poetry* (San Francisco: Cleis Press, 2000), 35–37.

2. Essex Hemphill, "Visiting Hours," *Ceremonies* (San Francisco: Cleis Press, 2000), 22–23.

3. Essex Hemphill, "Heavy Breathing," *Ceremonies* (San Francisco: Cleis Press, 2000), 4–21.

Isaac Julien Reflects on "Cinematic Rearticulations"

2004 was a pivotal year, two years after Okwui Enwezor's *Documenta11*. That year my partner, Mark Nash, curated an exhibition called *Experiments with Truth* at the Fabric Workshop in Philadelphia. This was a moment where the moving image in the gallery and museum context really came to fruition, in terms of its reception in a contemporary art context. There also were interventions being made around questions of race in an art-world context, which would have an avalanche effect by this time, twenty years later. I thought there were a number of queer cinema elements which were reoccurring in the moving-image practices of several artists working at that particular time.

I was also thinking about questions of art in a time of war and disinformation—then around the tremors or aftereffects of 9/11. It's interesting to reflect on these political moments and to see how these questions resonate. Because of course my introduction reads almost like it could have been written today: "In an increasingly troubled time of emergencies, war, and dis-information, the work represents an alternative view—one in which images can play a critical role in shaping our understanding of the world rather than merely being used as a tool for propaganda." In 2004, there was a sort of political atmosphere announcing itself, which is even more acute today.

One thing that has changed is that by 2010, if we think about analog film and technologies, new media platforms have kind of ripped apart the possibilities of aesthetic and political interventions. In 2004, video art—its experiments, and the ways it embraced independent film—was still in its infancy. Then there is a transition period where independent film culture is reigning to a certain degree. And then there is an explosion around digital technologies. Within that, we begin to see different voices develop, a proliferation of new voices.

When I think about contemporary artists and filmmakers who might be making thematic and visual experiments, I think of Black queer artists within pop music producing interventions where they are utilizing video art techniques and queering those in the mainstream. That is something we may not have thought could have developed as a kind of utopic intervention, and which transgresses the art world and film world into a popular culture arena. I think of Lil Nas X. Or, thinking about film, we had Barry Jenkins's *Moonlight* (2016), which was super important—even though he is straight—for queer cinema. Jenkins invited me last year to the Telluride Film Festival to show *Looking for Langston* (1989) as a film that influenced his work. In turn, I am working with André Holland, an actor who appeared in *Moonlight*, in the work I am currently making on Alain Locke. It is interesting to think of these recurring themes and connections in an intergenerational sense, in the context of the proliferation of works that appear on different media platforms, from gaming to independent film.

I have one student, Lívia Perez, who has made a short, queer, lesbian, experimental film from Brazil and is showing this work at Sundance. This is really exciting and marks a continuity with the panel "Barbed-Wire Kisses" that took place at Sundance in 1992—over ten years before my Kessler Lecture—where B. Ruby Rich produced a manifesto for new queer cinema. So we go from 1992 to 2004 to 2022. We can see that some things have been somewhat mainstreamed, some elements of their experimentation may have been a bit ironed out. Nonetheless, the specific interventions of seeing this work appear in different contexts—be it film, contemporary art, or different media platforms—are interesting. I can also point to the film installation in the Museum of Modern Art atrium at the moment by Adam Pendleton, *Who Is Queen?* Through the use of the collage effects of painting and moving image, it calls attention to the queering of these spaces in the contemporary art field by a younger generation.

At the moment, I am making a work that takes *Looking for Langston* as a visual reference. This new work, called *Statues Never Die*, features Alain Locke as a Black queer protagonist critic who is looking at questions around the repatriation of objects and African sculpture. The work looks at some of the seminal texts that he wrote at the same time as Albert C. Barnes, the great collector of the Barnes Museum. It is sort of a re-looking at these questions in modernism but recasting them in the visual iconography of *Looking for Langston* (black-and-white, four-by-three film). There are fairly explicit Langston references in the work. The project is called *Statues Never Die* because of this expanded relationship to art that has become a debate in the public sphere, calling into question the colonial legacy of statues and the question of violence in the museum itself: how these objects get to be re-situated as artworks from the African continent; how they enter into modernism; what that means for different gazes and subjectivities; how this engenders a certain creativity for Black artists in the diaspora; and how the objects are then utilized within art collections across the world. That's my newest project, which will come out in June 2022.

THE DAVID R. KESSLER LECTURES 2002–2020

2002	JONATHAN NED KATZ
2003	GAYLE RUBIN
2004	ISAAC JULIEN
2006	**ADRIENNE RICH**
2007	DOUGLAS CRIMP
2008	SUSAN STRYKER
2009	SARAH SCHULMAN
2010	URVASHI VAID
2012	MARTIN DUBERMAN
2013	CHERYL CLARKE
2014	CATHY J. COHEN
2015	RICHARD FUNG
2016	DEAN SPADE
2017	SARA AHMED
2018	AMBER HOLLIBAUGH
2019	JASBIR K. PUAR
2020	RODERICK A. FERGUSON

Adrienne Rich

Adrienne Rich (1929–2012) was an American poet, essayist, feminist, lesbian, and major public intellectual of the twentieth and twenty-first centuries. After receiving the Yale Younger Poets Prize in 1951 at the age of twenty-one, Rich never stopped writing in her distinct voice, with strength and conviction. In her own words, her poetry seeks to create a dialectical relationship between "the personal, or lyric voice, and the so-called political—really, the voice of the individual speaking not just to herself, or to a beloved friend, but to and from a collective, a social realm." Her essay "Compulsory Heterosexuality and Lesbian Existence," published in 1980, was foundational in theorizing lesbian existence as central to the work of feminism. Rich published more than fifteen volumes of poetry, including the National Book Award–winning *Diving into the Wreck* (1973), as well as four books of nonfiction prose, including *Of Woman Born: Motherhood as Experience and Institution* (1976) and *What Is Found There: Notebooks on Poetry and Politics* (1993). She was born in Baltimore, Maryland, and lived in Santa Cruz, California, until her death at eighty-two.

"Candidates for My Love":
Three Gay and Lesbian Poets

NOVEMBER 17, 2006

To speak here as the Kessler lecturer is a significant honor for me. I've pondered a good deal about what I could offer, to an audience of what I take to be intellectual subversives. Along the way I'll read some poetry by gay and lesbian poets of three generations and talk about desire, community, politics, and love, working through and around those poems.

The threads that grew into the texture of what's now known as "queer studies" began, of course, not in academia but in spaces opened up by the movements of the 1960s and 1970s, the breaking out from self-denial into self-definition, claiming agency, learning solidarity, arguing a different kind of future.

I've been thinking how behind every shelf of publications on gender and sexuality, every course offered in queer or gender studies, lie thousands of ghostly sheaves: leaflets, letters, pamphlets, mimeographed bibliographies, little magazines, posters, movement anthologies, some now preserved in archives, others reduced to landfill. Behind every academic program or lectureship under the rubric of queer studies stand lives that were participant in radical ideas about freedom and justice—movements that moved, in nonlinear ways, into and out of each other. In those movements, queer women and men, unknown at first unless to each other, invisible to their otherwise-comrades, emerged to declare a gay and lesbian politics, because the idea of inclusive justice is—was then—contagious and irresistible. The names Bayard Rustin, Barbara Deming, Lorraine Hansberry, Harry Hay, Martin Duberman, Audre Lorde, Joan Nestle are a few that flash immediately to mind. And, of course, I think of the queer pioneers, Del Martin and Phyllis Lyon, *The Ladder*, Daughters of Bilitis, the Mattachine Society, the early queer underground; the publicly gay, anarchist, antiwar poets Paul Goodman and Robert Duncan. I think, in short, of many lives of defiance and creation.

I came out in early 1970s New York, and the lesbian movement I came out into had been shaped by radical feminism and the Left. Thinking about this talk tonight, I pulled out from its shelf a slender, faded orange book, perfect-bound, basic in design: *Amazon Poetry: An Anthology*, edited by Elly Bulkin and Joan Larkin, published in 1975 by Out & Out Books. In it were gathered thirty-eight poets, some publishing as lesbians for the first time in that collection. I want to read from the editor's foreword:

> What *is* a "lesbian poetry anthology"? Some expect only love poetry; others, a collection of poems specifically about our oppression as lesbians. Instead, we have put together a book of poems that show the scope and intensity of lesbian experience. . . . The poems convey both private joy and pain and a larger context of racial, economic and social inequality.[1]

A contributor's note suggests something of the political-arts ferment of the period:

> How to describe the process of waking up from my "painted dream," my childhood in America, and the events that shaped that process: Vietnam, the women's movement, Attica, coming out . . . the strength I found through painting and writing to name myself, working with a community murals group on the Lower East Side and at the Women's School in Brooklyn, to return art to its source, to the very core of people's lives.

One small anthology in a cross-country proliferation of feminist and lesbian print journalism, magazines, poetry readings, bookstores, film, music and theater groups, and artists' collectives, along with women's resource centers, rape crisis hotlines, battered-women's shelters—all this, let's recall, before computer publishing programs, e-mail, cell phones, or the Internet. "Technology" still meant typewriter, telephone, and copying machine, along with much hands-on physical effort, driven by political, cultural, and physical desire, ardor for change in relations of power.

I don't mean to idealize those years, rather to reaffirm what needs reaffirming now: that radical politics is a great confluent project of the human imagination, of which art and literature are indispensable tributaries. Neither will I try to analyze historically the repeated de-fusions, disruptions, and discountings of liberatory movements—a task for scholars of politics and history. I will say this: we can't just claim we were, in 1980 and beyond, simply outflanked by the material means of the Right, the distorting mirrors of its media. Every historical resistance movement in this country—abolitionist, labor, suffragist, anti-lynching, civil rights, feminist, socialist—has been up against a powerful and hostile press, not to mention tear gas, fire hoses, truncheons, and vigilante guns.

But the discourse of inclusive justice keeps refusing to be quenched. Its soul goes marching on, stumbling, limping, bumming rides, falling in with the wrong crowd, losing direction, pausing for breath, exhausted, sleeping to dream again—maybe even winning an election here and there.

In the 1980s, AIDS catalyzed a new gay activism, in outrage laced with mourning. The virus took many brave and challenging figures off the scene. It unmasked much liberal homophobia and many contradictions in gay lives and deaths. It brought forth the work and abbreviated the lives of black gay writers and poets like Joseph Beam, Essex Hemphill, Assotto Saint, Melvin Dixon.

And, as Essex Hemphill, poet and critic of gay and straight culture, wrote in 1990:

> Some of the best minds of my generation would have us believe that AIDS has brought the gay and lesbian community closer and infused it with a more democratic mandate. That is only a partial truth, which further underscores the fact that the gay community still operates from a one-eyed, one gender, one color perception of *community*. . . .
>
> Some of the best minds of my generation believe AIDS has made the gay community a more responsible social construction, but what AIDS really manages to do is clearly point out how significant are the cultural and economic differences between us; differences so extreme that Black gay men suffer a disproportionate numbers of AIDS deaths in communities with very sophisticated gay health care services. . . . We are communities engaged in a fragile coexistence if we are anything at all. . . .[2]

Another poet, Melvin Dixon, addressing OutWrite, the annual gay and lesbian writers' conference, in 1992, had this to say:

> We are facing the loss of our entire generation. Lesbians lost to various cancers, gay men lost to AIDS. What kind of witness will you bear? What truthtelling are you brave enough to utter and endure the consequences of your unpopular message?[3]

So I ask myself, and us—how do we, the beneficiaries of various unpopular messages and struggles, figure in historical losses of momentum, the reversals, the so-called backlash? When and where have we resigned ourselves to, at most, a "fragile coexistence," to political and social atomization, to false choices dictated by a public discourse that mocks the very concept of solidarity?

I know that for myself, in the 1990s, it was not enough to keep going to meetings, demonstrations, to peruse newsletters, talk on the phone with friends. There was a flattening of language, a sense of repetition, or, as I wrote in a long poem:

> "That year I began to understand the words *burden of proof*
> —how the free market of ideas depended
> on certain lives laboring under that burden.
> I started feeling in my body
> how that burden was bound to our backs
> keeping us cramped in old repetitive motions
> crouched in the same mineshaft year on year
> or like children in school striving to prove
> proofs already proven over and over
> to get into the next grade
> but there is no next grade no movement onward only this
> and the talk goes on, the laws, the jokes, the deaths,
>   the way of life goes on
> as if you had proven nothing as if this burden
> were what you are."[4]

I needed to remember what had drawn me in the first place toward both activism and political art. The early essays of James Baldwin had given me my first sense of a language—eloquently personal yet public—for the first injustice I had witnessed as a child—segregation, as the whole racial system was named then. Reading his work later, it struck me as one American example of a prose style capable of embracing the bitterest experience, the most prophetic anger, and an implacable knowledge of love. As an artist, writing in that complex "we" he claimed as a black and gay American citizen, often self-exiled, Baldwin could be frustrated, bleak, but never resigned. This is from his essay "The Creative Process":

> We know, in the case of the person, that whoever cannot tell himself the truth about his past is trapped in it, is immobilized in the prison of his undiscovered self. This is also true of nations. We know how a person, in such a paralysis, is unable to assess either his weaknesses or his strengths, and how

frequently indeed he mistakes the one for the other. And this, I think, we do. We are the strongest nation in the Western world, but this is not for the reasons that we think. It is because we have an opportunity that no other nation has of moving beyond the Old World concepts of race and class and caste, to create, finally, what we must have had in mind when we began speaking of the New World. But the price of this is a long look backward whence we came and an unflinching assessment of the record.[5]

Of course I turned to poets, including Whitman, Robert Duncan, Thomas McGrath, Charles Olson, Muriel Rukeyser; but also to the letters and essays of revolutionary socialist writers like Rosa Luxemburg, Antonio Gramsci, Che Guevara, whose undeflected passion for making history put into perspective how frivolous despair can be.

Or Samuel Beckett, writing in 1981:

All before. Nothing else ever. Ever tried. Ever failed. No matter. Try again. Fail again. Fail better.[6]

Did he mean language, politics, or living itself? "No matter. Try again. . . . Fail better" seemed a good idea. And I thought I could translate something of what my country and my friends and I were going through into language—the poems of *Midnight Salvage* and *Dark Fields of the Republic*.

Ideas of freedom evolve, scientific descriptions require amplifying, histories have to be revised. Poetry has a way of resonating beyond its original source moment. Maybe because poetic truths depend not on a structure of ideas but on a medium, not on fixed relationships but on metaphor: lightning flashes of connection. Poetry is a mixed medium: the visual image, the sound, the unexpected relation of words to their accepted usage, or, as Ezra Pound termed them, *phanopoeia, melapoeia, logopoeia*.

I'm going to read a poem from Walt Whitman's *Leaves of Grass*—not the 1855 first edition but the expanded and revised version published in 1891, which includes the section of *Calamus* poems:

Whoever You Are Holding Me Now in Hand

Whoever you are holding me now in hand,
Without one thing all will be useless,
I give you fair warning before you attempt me further,
I am not what you supposed, but far different.

Who is he that would become my follower?
Who would sign himself a candidate for my affections?

The way is suspicious, the result uncertain, perhaps destructive,
You would have to give up all else, I alone would expect to be your
   sole and exclusive standard,
Your novitiate would even then be long and exhausting,
The whole past theory of your life and all conformity to the lives
   around you would have to be abandon'd,
Therefore release me now before troubling yourself any further, let
   go your hand from my shoulders,
Put me down and depart on your way.

Or else by stealth in some wood for trial,
Or back of a rock in the open air,
(For in any roof'd room of a house I emerge not, nor in company,
And in libraries I lie as one dumb, a gawk, or unborn, or dead,)
But just possibly with you on a high hill, first watching lest any person
   for miles around approach unawares,
Or possibly with you sailing at sea, or on the beach of the sea or some
   quiet island,
Here to put your lips upon mine I permit you,
With the comrade's long-dwelling kiss or the new husband's kiss,
For I am the new husband and I am the comrade.

Or if you will, thrusting me beneath your clothing,
Where I may feel the throbs of your heart or rest upon your hip,
Carry me when you go forth over land or sea;
For thus merely touching you is enough, is best,
And thus touching you would I silently sleep and be carried eternally.

But these leaves conning you con at peril,
For these leaves and me you will not understand,
They will elude you at first and still more afterward, I will certainly
   elude you,
Even while you should think you had unquestionably caught me,
   behold!
Already you see I have escaped from you.

For it is not for what I have put into it that I have written this book,
Nor is it by reading it you will acquire it,
Nor do those know me best who admire me and vauntingly praise me,

Nor will the candidates for my love (unless at most a very few) prove
victorious,
Nor will my poems do good only, they will do just as much evil,
perhaps more,
For all is useless without that which you may guess at many times
and not hit, that which I hinted at;
Therefore release me and depart on your way.[7]

I don't want to fix in prose this poem, at once so direct and so evasive, ambivalent and confident. If anything, the poem decoys and dares down that possibility. Certainly its sensuality is heightened by its tone of warning, as it both lures and wards off the "you" it addresses. That "you . . . holding me now in hand" is both singular and—implicitly—plural, and "you" appears to have made the first move ("release me now before troubling yourself any further, let go your hand from my shoulders"). But there's an ambiguity too about the "I/me"—which might at once be the book, the poem, and the sexual body of the poet. ("Look where your hands are. Now," says the voice at the end of Toni Morrison's novel *Jazz*.) The book, the poem, as erotic companion, conspiratorial, dangerous, demanding: ("Your novitiate would even then be long and exhausting, / The whole past theory of your life and all conformity to the lives around you would have to be abandon'd"). More is required of "you" than a quick trick, a fast read. And the "I"—poet or poem or book—is wary, outside the law ("watching lest any person . . . approach unawares").

Here is Whitman himself on the writing of *Leaves of Grass*:

"Leaves of Grass" is avowedly the song of Sex and Amativeness, and even Animality—though meanings that do not usually go along with those words are behind all, and will duly emerge; and all are sought to be lifted into a different light and atmosphere. . . . Difficult as it will be, it has become, in my opinion, imperative to achieve a shifted attitude from superior men and women towards the thought and fact of sexuality, as an element in character, personality, the emotions, and a theme in literature. I am not going to argue the question by itself; it does not stand by itself. The vitality of it is altogether in its relations, bearings, significance . . . the lines I allude to, and the spirit in which they are spoken, permeate all "Leaves of Grass" and the work must stand or fall with them, as the human body and soul must remain as an entirety.[8]

Don't ask me, the aged and now celebrated Whitman is telling his public, to clean up my book. (On the contrary, he's added the erotic *Calamus* poems.) But what is the element always elusive, the hinted and guessed at, with potential for good and evil? If it's simply how human sexuality is part of the greater texture of the universe or the impossibility of a fixed, single identity—*that* was always affirmed throughout *Leaves of Grass*. I find myself wondering if what eludes "you" isn't also elusive to "I"—if Walt himself isn't speaking internally to Walt, acknowledging what can't yet be imagined, even in poetry. Maybe the intuition of movement through—not beyond—sexual desire to what he calls "amative love," to "the love of comrades," movement toward some future democracy, some evolving complex of relationships?

In his 1970 essay "Changing Perspectives in Reading Whitman," the poet Robert Duncan addressed Whitman's complex effects—"He was a man of contradictions," Duncan says, "and he calls up inner contradictions in the reader." He suggests how superficial is any reading of Whitman as naïvely, optimistically chauvinistic or as displaced by twentieth-century nightmares of exploitation and war.

Duncan writes:

> Presidents, congresses, armed forces, industrialists, governors, police forces, have rendered the meaning of "America" and "the United States" so fearful—causing fear and filled with fear—in our time that no nationalistic inspiration comes innocent of the greed and ruthless extension of power to exploit the peoples and natural resources of the world. . . .
>
> "America," for Whitman, is yet to come. And this theme of what America is, of what democracy is, of what the sexual reality is, of what the Self is, arises from an urgency in the conception of the Universe itself, not a blueprint but an evolution of spirit in terms of variety and a thicket of potentialities.[9]

Now I want to read you an early poem by Duncan himself, from 1946:

Among My Friends Love Is a Great Sorrow

Among my friends love is a great sorrow.
It has become a daily burden, a feast,
a gluttony for fools, a heart's famine.
We visit one another asking, telling one another.
We do not burn hotly, we question the fire.
We do not fall forward with our alive
eager faces looking thru into the fire.
We stare back into our own faces.
We have become our own realities.
We seek to exhaust our lovelessness.

Among my friends love is a painful question.
We seek out among the passing faces
a sphinx-face who will ask its riddle.
Among my friends love is an answer to a question
that has not been askt.
Then ask it.

Among my friends love is a payment.
It is an old debt for a borrowing foolishly spent.
And we go on, borrowing and borrowing
            from each other.

Among my friends love is a wage
that one might have for an honest living.

In one sense, "Among My Friends" mourns a diminishment from Whitman's consciousness: a narrower, sadder sense of possibilities. Duncan searches beneath the surface of a particular male sexuality in a particular time (post–World War II America, early Cold War, rampant homophobia). He observes, with compassion and severity, what was one kind of gay community, to use our contemporary language. The sorrow pervading this gay maleness is the burden of a sexuality ambivalent with its own desire, doubting the potentialities of mutual love, in the face of external and internalized homophobia: "an honest living" being the needed condition for love.

Duncan had earlier explored what he perceived as gay chauvinism and self-enclosure in his 1944 essay "The Homosexual in Society," published in the left-wing journal *Politics*. It was a courageous, contentious essay, the writing of which he describes as "a personal agony"—"the first discussion of homosexuality which included the frank avowal that the author was himself involved." It was a critique from within, taking the risks that such critiques involve. In making his own sexuality explicit he would be written off by the then-powerful New Criticism poetry establishment; critical of gay self-reference and cliquishness, he would be accused of self-hatred.

But if "Among My Friends" merely documented a certain period and a certain circle, it would not carry, as I think it does, all the way into the twenty-first century, into a dominant culture, not necessarily or primarily gay, where atomization and self-reference are promoted as ways of being—the surface American scene of lifestyles, passionless distractions, trivial choices without deep inner volition, sex without sensuality, irony as emotional distance, money as vocabulary for everything.

Duncan was explicit not only sexually:

I picture . . . fulfillment of desire as a human state of mutual volition and aid, a shared life.

Not only in sexual love, but in work and in play, we suffer from the . . . competitive ethos . . . the struggle of interests to gain recognition or control, [which] discourages the recognition of the needs and interests which we all know we have in common.

Duncan had read and reflected on Marx and Dante, Whitman and Jakob Böhme. His poetics and philosophic vision, sophisticated, evolving, sometimes arcane but always radical, were a journey to reclaim the fullness of the senses, the common ground that capitalism as a system of relationships has alienated and declared passé.

In 1973 a lesbian-feminist press collective in Oakland published a long poem by a working-class lesbian, Judy Grahn. In "A Woman Is Talking to Death," Grahn gives chapter and verse to the "death" that is self-denial, accepted disempowerment, passivity, mutual betrayal. ("Death sits on my doorstep / cleaning his revolver."[10]) Stylistically it transits from a long, open narrative line to dialogue to blocks of prose to invocation, from linear anecdote to surreal images. What's notable is the freedom of line and voice, a colloquial diction with surges of intensity. A great public poem, emerging from a new and vital women's movement, expanding the political imaginary of Whitman and Duncan, enlarging the potentialities of gay and lesbian poetry. In sometimes raw urgency, it locates its voice in the class- and race-inflected lives of everyday "common women."

Here are just a few excerpts.

A Woman Is Talking to Death

Testimony in trials that never got heard

my lovers teeth are white geese flying above me
my lovers muscles are rope ladders under my hands

we were driving home slow
my lover and I, across the long Bay Bridge,
one February midnight, when midway
over in the far left lane, I saw a strange scene:

one small young man standing by the rail,
and in the lane itself, parked straight across

as if it could stop anything, a large young
man upon a stalled motorcycle, perfectly
relaxed as if he'd stopped at a hamburger stand;
he was wearing a peacoat and levis, and
he had his head back, roaring, you
could almost hear the laugh, it
was so real.

"Look at that fool," I said, "in the
middle of the bridge like that," a very
womanly remark.

Then we heard the meaning of the noise
of metal on a concrete bridge at 50
miles an hour, and the far left lane
filled up with a big car that had a
motorcycle jammed on its front bumper, like
the whole thing would explode; the friction
sparks shot up bright orange for many feet
into the air, and the racket still sets
my teeth on edge.

When the car stopped we stopped parallel
and Wendy headed for the callbox while I
ducked across those 6 lanes like a mouse
in the bowling alley. "Are you hurt?" I said,
the middle-aged driver had the greyest black face,
"I couldn't stop, I couldn't stop, what happened?"

Then I remembered. "Somebody," I said, "was *on*
the motorcycle." I ran back,
one block? two blocks? the space for walking
on the bridge is maybe 18 inches, whoever
engineered this arrogance. in the dark
stiff wind it seemed I would
be pushed over the rail, would fall down
screaming onto the hard surface of
the bay, but I did not, I found the tall young man
who thought he owned the bridge, now lying on
his stomach, head cradled in his broken arm.

He had glasses on, but somewhere he had lost
most of his levis, where were they?
and his shoes. Two short cuts on his buttocks,
that was the only mark except his thin white
seminal tubes were all strung out behind; no
child left in him; and he looked asleep.

I plucked wildly at his wrist, then put it
down; there were two long haired women
holding back the traffic just behind me
with their bare hands, the machines came
down like mad bulls, I was scared, much
more than usual, I felt easily squished
like the earthworms crawling on a busy
sidewalk after the rain; *I wanted to
leave.* And met the driver, walking back.

"The guy is dead." I gripped his hand,
the wind was going to blow us off the bridge.

"Oh my God," he said, "haven't I had enough
trouble in my life?" He raised his head,
and for a second was enraged and yelling,
at the top of the bridge—"I was just driving
home!" His head fell down. "My God, and
now I've killed somebody."

. . . .

I had a woman waiting for me,
in her car and in the middle of the bridge,
I'm frightened, I said,
I'm afraid, he said, stay with me,
please don't go, stay with me, be
my witness—"No," I said, "I'll be your
witness—later," and I took his name
and number, "but I can't stay with you,
I'm too frightened of the bridge, besides
I have a woman waiting
and no license—
and no tail lights—"

so I left—
as I have left so many of my lovers.

we drove home
shaking, Wendy's face greyer
than any white person's I have ever seen.

. . . .

that same week I looked into the mirror
and nobody was there to testify;
how clear, an unemployed queer woman
makes no witness at all,
nobody at all was there for
those two questions: what does
she do, and who is she married to?

I am the woman who stopped on the bridge
and this is the man who was there
our lovers teeth are white geese flying
above us, but we ourselves are
easily squished.

. . . .

death sits on my doorstep
cleaning his revolver

death cripples my feet and sends me out
to wait for the bus alone,
then comes by driving a taxi.

. . . .

this woman is a lesbian, be careful.

When I was arrested and being thrown out
of the military, the order went out: dont anybody
speak to this woman, and for those three
long months, almost nobody did;   the dayroom, when
I entered it, fell silent til I had gone; they
were afraid, they knew the wind would blow
them over the rail, the cops would come,
the water would run into their lungs.

Everything I touched
was spoiled. They were my lovers, those
women, but nobody had taught us to swim.
I drowned, I took 3 or 4 others down
when I signed the confession of what we
had done   together.

No one will ever speak to me again.

. . . .

Have you ever committed any indecent acts with women?

Yes, many. I am guilty of allowing suicidal women to die before my
eyes or in my ears or under my hands because I thought I could do
nothing. I am guilty of leaving a prostitute who held a knife to my
friend's throat to keep us from leaving, because we would not sleep
with her, we thought she was old and fat and ugly; I am guilty of not
loving her who needed me; I regret all the women I have not slept
with or comforted, who pulled themselves away from me for lack
of something I had not the courage to fight for, for us, our life, our
planet, our city, our meat and potatoes, our love. These are indecent
acts, lacking courage, lacking a certain fire behind the eyes, which is
the symbol, the raised fist, the sharing of resources, the resistance
that tells death he will starve for the lack of us, our extra. Yes I have
committed acts of indecency with women and most of them were
acts of omission. I regret them bitterly.

. . . .

my lovers teeth are white geese flying above me
my lovers muscles are rope ladders under my hands
we are the river of life and the fat of the land
death, do you tell me I cannot touch this woman?
if we use each other up
on each other
that's a little bit less for you
a little bit less for you, ho
death, ho ho death.

. . . .

to my lovers I bequeath
the rest of my life
I want nothing left of me for you, ho death
except some fertilizer
for the next batch of us
who do not hold hands with you
who do not embrace you
who try not to work for you
or sacrifice themselves or trust
or believe in you, ho ignorant
death, how do you know
we happened to you?

wherever our meat hangs on our own bones
for our own use
your pot is so empty
death, ho death
you shall be poor

Grahn herself wrote of the poem:

The particular challenges . . . for me were . . . the criss-cross oppressions
which . . . continually divide us—and how to define a lesbian life within
the context of other people in the world. I did not realize at the time that
I was also taking up the subject of heroes in a modern life which for many
people is more like a war than not, or that I would begin a redefinition for
myself of the subject of love.

There is no "progress"—political or otherwise—in poetry—only riffs,
echoes, of many poems and poets speaking into the future and back toward
the past. Breaking with one tradition to discover another. Returning to an
abandoned tradition, like an abandoned house, to find it inhabited by new
guests. The poems I chose to read tonight are in their very different ways
parts of that continuum.

I will end by thanking you for the opportunity to take this backward look
at some of the writings and movements that got us here and to think again,
for myself, and in your presence, about sexuality, poetry, community, politics, and what love has to do with all these.

Notes

1. Joan Larkin and Elly Bulkin, eds., *Amazon Poetry: An Anthology* (Brooklyn, NY: Out & Out Books, 1975).

2. Essex Hemphill, "Does Your Momma Know About Me?," *Ceremonies: Prose and Poetry* (New York: Plume, 1992), 40–41.

3. Melvin Dixon, *Love's Instruments* (Chicago: Tia Chucha Press, 1995), 74.

4. Adrienne Rich, *Dark Fields of the Republic: Poems 1991–1995* (New York: W. W. Norton, 1995), 66.

5. James Baldwin, "The Creative Process" (1962), in *The Price of the Ticket: Collected Nonfiction, 1948–1985* (New York: St. Martin's, 1985), 73–76.

6. James Knowlson, *Damned to Fame: The Life of Samuel Beckett* (New York: Simon & Schuster, 1996), 593.

7. *Walt Whitman: Complete Poetry and Collected Prose*, ed. Justin Kaplan (New York: Literary Classics of the United States, Library of America, 1982), 270–71.

8. *Walt Whitman*, 668–69.

9. Robert Duncan, *Robert Duncan: A Selected Prose*, ed. Robert J. Bertholf (New York: New Directions, 1995), 66–67, 67, 64.

10. Judy Grahn, "A Woman Is Talking to Death," in *The Work of a Common Woman: The Collected Poetry of Judy Grahn, 1964–1977* (Oakland, CA: Diana Press, 1978).

"Many Lives of Defiance and Creation": Pablo Conrad and Julie R. Enszer Reflect on Adrienne Rich's "'Candidates for My Love': Three Gay and Lesbian Poets"

In 2006, Adrienne Rich delivered the Kessler Lecture "'Candidates for My Love': Three Gay and Lesbian Poets." Neither of us was in the room, though the reprint of her speech in *A Human Eye* hints at the magic of the evening. Rich begins by calling multiple gay and lesbian poets in an almost incantation of names and books and imagined archival fragments. She then reads poems by three favorite poets, Whitman, Duncan, and Grahn, reveling in language, ideas, defiance, and creation.

Julie writes: I cannot even begin to suggest what Adrienne Rich might make of her lecture—or the state of queer studies—today. Partially because rereading her work I am always surprised and delighted by her profound, immediate forms of worldly engagement at every phase of her life. She always seemed to be thinking, mulling, working, and reworking language and ideas. She took Rukeyser seriously with her mandate that "the security of the imagination lies in calling, all our lives, for more liberty, more rebellion, more belief."[1] Rich grappled with what the world presented, and she transformed it with her mind and her pen. What I suggest on this occasion is that, were she alive, Rich would be using her cultivated tools—that searching mind, the deep, probing intellect, the eye of compassion for the world, and the ear for language—to reflect on the world today and, in using those tools, would bring more insight, more knowledge, more understanding. I would expect her to be reading new voices, looking for the defiance she cherished, seeking the new modes of creation that could bring new worlds into being.

Pablo writes: I want to fasten on to Julie's remark about Adrienne Rich's "engagement." The 2006 lecture with its recourse to long passages from other poets' work isn't an exercise in cherry-picking to support a program or a statement. Grahn, Duncan, and Whitman are all here as testimonies to the difficulty of making a neat, Instagram-able statement—for Adrienne in 2006 they're examples of other human beings working toward their own understandings of "sexuality, poetry, community, politics, and what love has to do with all these." Now it's 2021. Let's not ask what Adrienne Rich *would* think or say today. In poetry and prose that we can still freely revisit, over and over she turns her path toward difficult-to-grasp areas of life, and toward other poets and artists whose own struggles gave her companionship and examples, and fired her own work.

Julie, you used the word "cherished" and I would add also "relished." Impatient with the narrow idea of a poet as some sort of content producer, Adrienne took delight each time with the recognition that someone else's poem or book of poems or lifetime of work and struggle had indicated a path forward. That's why it's wonderful to revisit this 2006 lecture, to see her relishing the presence of these poets and how they could speak, to one another, to her.

Pablo Conrad is one of Adrienne Rich's sons. In 2015 he edited her collected poems for W. W. Norton.

Julie R. Enszer is a poet, scholar, and the editor and publisher of *Sinister Wisdom*.

Notes
1. Muriel Rukeyser, *The Life of Poetry*, reprint (Middletown, CT: Paris Press, 1996), 30.

THE DAVID R. KESSLER LECTURES 2002–2020

2002   JONATHAN NED KATZ

2003   GAYLE RUBIN

2004   ISAAC JULIEN

2006   ADRIENNE RICH

2007   DOUGLAS CRIMP

2008   SUSAN STRYKER

2009   SARAH SCHULMAN

2010   URVASHI VAID

2012   MARTIN DUBERMAN

2013   CHERYL CLARKE

2014   CATHY J. COHEN

2015   RICHARD FUNG

2016   DEAN SPADE

2017   SARA AHMED

2018   AMBER HOLLIBAUGH

2019   JASBIR K. PUAR

2020   RODERICK A. FERGUSON

Douglas Crimp

Born in 1944 in Coeur d'Alene, Idaho, Douglas Crimp (1944–2019) was an art historian, critic, curator, and HIV/AIDS activist whose work was and continues to be "crucial in the articulation of a queer outlook on ethics, politics, art, aesthetics, and sexuality," as Henry Abelove said in his testimonial for Crimp's Kessler Lecture in 2007. Crimp began writing art criticism for *Art News* and *Art International* in the early 1970s and published widely in magazines and scholarly journals, becoming one of the preeminent scholars of postmodernism in the visual arts. In 1977, Crimp curated the *Pictures* exhibition at Artists Space in New York—largely defining the Pictures Generation of artists that included Robert Longo, Sherrie Levine, and later, Cindy Sherman. From 1977 to 1990, he was an editor of the influential contemporary art journal *October*.

In addition to his work as an art critic, Crimp made significant contributions to cultural studies, including his work on the book *AIDS: Cultural Analysis/ Cultural Activism* (1988), which is considered the foundational work on AIDS and cultural representation and a founding text of queer theory. A member of the HIV/AIDS activist collective ACT UP NY and a founding member of Sex Panic!, his other publications include *AIDS Demo Graphics* (1990) and *Melancholia and Moralism: Essays on AIDS and Queer Politics* (2002). Crimp's work in queer theory also includes the coedited volume *How Do I Look?: Queer Film and Video* (1991). He was Fanny Knapp Allen Professor of Art History at the University of Rochester.

Action around the Edges

NOVEMBER 2, 2007

I should start with how it happened. I mean, what it's like to wander for months around New York trying to find a space to do a piece of work, and especially something to the scale that I have been able to do in other places but not in New York City. . . . Originally what I had sighted on were the facades because as you go down the Pier, driving down the pier along that empty highway in front, the facades are an incredible, animated grouping of different eras and different personalities. And I wanted to deal with one of the earlier ones, which this is—a turn of the century facade. There's a classic sort of tin classicism. And to cut at the facade. So the ones that I found originally were all completely overrun by the gays. And S&M, you know, that whole S&M shadows of waterfront . . .

—GORDON MATTA-CLARK TO LIZA BÉAR, MARCH 11, 1976

The day in August I moved from Greenwich Village to Tribeca was one of the hottest of summer 1974. I rented a van and got my on-again, off-again boyfriend Richard Cook to help out. My apartment on Tenth Street just west of Hudson Street was a fourth-floor railroad flat; my new place was a spacious skylit loft on Chambers Street, also west of Hudson. I'd arranged to use the freight elevator in the loft building for the day, a rickety old contraption operated by pulling down hard on the hoist cable of a pulley system and stopped by yanking the other cable. It was a challenge to bring it level with the floor. After piling all of my belongings on the elevator's platform, Richard and I, along with the artist next door from whom I was subletting the loft, managed to get the overloaded elevator to start its ascent. By the time we'd reached the third floor, though, it came to a grinding halt and began sliding back downward. We all grabbed the cable to slow the elevator's plunge and did manage to prevent a free fall, but it crashed onto the basement floor nevertheless. After recovering our wits and finding ourselves luckily unharmed, we had to lug my belongings through the old industrial building's dank basement and up the back stairs, make our way with them through a jam-packed hardware store on the ground floor, and then haul them up four more flights of stairs.

My new loft had some amenities besides the skylight, one of them with a classy provenance. The set designer Robert Israel had previously rented the space, and from him I bought its fixtures (appurtenances necessary to convert a commercial loft into a residence—plumbing and appliances for kitchen and bathroom, space heaters, and so forth). Among these was a stage-like platform about ten-foot square and standing two feet above the floor, which Robert must have used to mock up designs. I positioned it underneath the skylight and used it to demarcate my bedroom. I didn't pay much attention to the symbolism of bedroom-as-brightly-lit-stage, but I guess it was apt for that moment of my life. The fixture with the provenance was a large refrigerator-freezer that had been given to Jasper Johns by Marian Javits, the art collector and socialite wife of New York State's famous liberal Republican senator. Johns had given it to Robert. It stopped working the summer after I bought it from Robert, so I found a thirty-five-dollar replacement at a used-appliance store on Kenmare Street, just east of SoHo. This one was a General Electric model from the 1940s with a freezer compartment just big enough for ice-cube trays. I kept it for the next twenty years, and it still worked fine when I finally replaced it.

My move from the Village to Tribeca came about as a result of my decision to get serious about being an art critic, to replace the gay scene with the art scene. I'd come to feel myself adrift, not accomplishing enough, not spending enough time with the crowd to which I "rightly" belonged. My exchange of one scene for another was destined to fail, but my attempt to achieve it with a geographic implementation interests me now. The immediate impulse is not easy for me to reconstruct, but it had something to do with the sometime boyfriend who helped me move and crashed with me in the elevator. A friend had told me that Richard was "inappropriate" for me, something that has been said more than once about the objects of my sexual interest. But in this case I took the opinion more or less to heart, because Richard had become my tormentor. The on-again, off-again character of the affair was in fact quite brutal; as soon as I became really hooked on him, he'd abruptly ditch me, and just as I was getting over being jilted he'd come back pleading that he couldn't live without me, and I'd get hooked again. This emotional S&M had its physical side too, which is no doubt what enthralled

Me in my loft on Chambers Street c. 1975. Image courtesy of Marc Siegel.

me in the first place. But beyond these commonplace facts of what's called a "relationship," Richard was indeed very different from me, intellectually, politically. I came most fully to realize this when he informed me in the summer of 1975 that he was going to work for Jimmy Carter's election. I was horrified: a born-again Christian from the South? The man who famously proclaimed that he had sinned in his heart because he'd had impure sexual thoughts? But I'm getting ahead of the story, because by the time Carter's campaign was under way, I was about to move out of the Chambers Street loft farther downtown to Nassau Street; this time I had the good sense to hire professional movers.

The emotional turmoil of my affair with Richard had come to symbolize for me my participation in the gay scene more generally—unjustly, of course. An event that represented a substitute love object determined my sense that I'd be better off living in Tribeca. Sometime in spring 1974, I saw the Grand Union perform. The Grand Union was an improvisational dance group that grew out of Yvonne Rainer's late-1960s Performance Demonstrations, especially *Continuous Project—Altered Daily* (1969). Its members included, in addition to Rainer, Trisha Brown, Barbara Dilley, Douglas Dunn, David Gordon, Nancy Green, and Steve Paxton, most of whom were dancers who had participated in the Judson Dance Theater. By the time I saw the Grand Union perform, Rainer had already left the group. I'd seen very little dance since my first ecstatic exposure to it in winter 1970 at the Brooklyn Academy of Music, where Merce Cunningham's company performed *RainForest* (1968), with Andy Warhol's helium-filled *Silver Clouds* as the set and music by David Tudor; *Walkaround Time* (1968), with Jasper Johns's clear plastic rectangular elements printed with images from Marcel Duchamp's *Large Glass*, to the music of David Behrman; *Tread* (1970), with a set by Bruce Nauman of industrial pedestal fans evenly spaced across the proscenium, half of them blowing toward the audience, and music by Christian Wolff; and *Canfield* (1969), whose set by Robert Morris was a gray columnar light box that moved back and forth on a track, also across the proscenium, illuminating the stage as it moved, with music by Pauline Oliveros.

I saw Martha Graham dance *Cortege of Eagles* (1967) that same season, but I wasn't nearly as moved by Graham's expressionism as by Cunningham's repudiation of it, and in her final stage performances at the age of seventy-six, Graham had become a self-parody. Cunningham was something else, something that thrilled me as much as anything I'd ever seen. I date my love of dance to that moment, so looking back I cannot understand why I didn't continue to pursue it. By the time I first saw Rainer's work, she had already turned to filmmaking. I did see *This Is the Story of a Woman Who . . .*, presented at the Theater for the New City in the West Village in 1973, in which Rainer performed *Three Satie Spoons* (1961), *Trio A* (1966), and *Walk, She Said* (1972), but otherwise the closest she came to dancing in that performance piece was vacuuming the stage while wearing a green eyeshade.

It was, in fact, more the performance art than the dance in the improvisational antics of the Grand Union dancers that I was drawn to. And, in truth, it was performance art that beckoned as a substitute object for my libido. By this time, I had seen early works by Joan Jonas, who acknowledges a debt to Judson. In 1971, I sat with other audience members on the floor of Jonas's loft on Grand Street in SoHo to watch her *Choreomania*, performed on a swinging, partially mirrored wall constructed by Richard Serra. Here is a description of the performance space that Jonas and I wrote together ten years later for her Berkeley Art Museum exhibition catalogue:

> A twelve-by-eight-foot wall of wood hangs by chains from the ceiling two-and-a-half feet from the ground. Ropes and handles are attached to the back so that the five performers can climb the wall unseen by the spectators.

The right-hand third of the front of the wall is mirrored. The wall can be swung back and forth and sideways by the performers, and their movements are choreographed in relation to the wall's motion. The swinging of the wall on its chains, hung from the ceiling beams, creates the sound of the piece, a rhythmic creaking like that of a ship moving through the ocean's wake.

The wall is hung so that it bisects the long narrow space of the loft. The spectators sit in the front half of the loft, facing the prop. The spectators' space and the spectators themselves are reflected in the mirrored portion of the wall as it swings from side to side. Because this wall is also the fourth wall of the spectators' space, the illusion is created that their space is swaying.

The main function of the wall is to fragment the performance in such a way that much of the performance action is seen only around the wall's four edges. The appearing/disappearing actions recall a magic show.[1]

The few surviving photographs that document *Choreomania* provide a good sense of what downtown New York performance spaces were like at the moment of performance art's birth. Often they were artists' private living and work spaces, large compared with typical working- and middle-class New Yorkers' apartments, but small compared with public performance venues, even makeshift ones like the Judson Memorial Church sanctuary. Seating was on the floor, usually in an uncomfortable jumble of fellow audience members.

Artists' resourceful uses of the forsaken spaces of Manhattan's light industry in this era are now legendary. The deindustrialization of New York in the postwar period had reached its most wrenching condition by the early 1970s, but some of us were unintended, temporary beneficiaries of the financial crisis, even as others lost their jobs and homes when social services were slashed. Some of the refashioned industrial spaces are now well-known, such as 112 Greene Street, the alternative exhibition venue founded by Jeffrey Lew,[2] and the Kitchen, a performance space founded by Woody and Steina Vasulka, both of which predate by a year or so the relocation of many commercial galleries from uptown to SoHo. Less well documented is the fact that artists with large and relatively accessible lofts would open their spaces to guests for performances and concerts. I remember, for example, hearing Philip Glass's *Music in Twelve Parts* (1971–74) at an informal artist-loft gathering on a Sunday afternoon in SoHo. To enhance the experience, joints were freely passed among the listeners.

Equally legendary, but rarely considered in this context, is the significance of these loft spaces for the birth of a different kind of music and performance scene.[3] In his SoHo loft in 1970, David Mancuso started throwing the rent parties that came to represent the pinnacle of disco for a generation and spawned a dance-club scene that persisted until Mayor Rudolph Giuliani destroyed it with his "quality-of-life" policy in the early nineties. Mancuso's clubs were at the center of New York nightlife throughout the seventies. In 1974, just down the street from the Loft at the corner of Broadway and Houston Street, Michael Fesco opened the private gay disco Flamingo on the second floor of a building that extended all the way to Mercer Street. A year later, 12 West opened in an old plant nursery at Twelfth and West Streets on the northwestern edge of Greenwich Village. Toward the end of the decade, what some consider the greatest of all discos opened in a former truck garage on King Street, west of Varick Street. It was called, appropriately enough, the Paradise Garage.

But before the gay discos came into being, there was another place for post-Stonewall liberated gay men and women to dance, an unused firehouse on Wooster Street in SoHo that had been taken over in spring 1971 by the Gay Activists Alliance (GAA). On Saturday nights, the old fire-engine garage became a dance hall, while up on the second floor, where once firefighters whiled away their time, dancers rested, drank beer, and cruised one another. In 1974, the firehouse was gutted in a fire probably set by neighborhood kids angry that fags and dykes invaded their territory every Saturday night. One of the perils of going to the Firehouse dances was the possibility of running into gangs of baseball-bat-wielding Italian American kids. SoHo is commonly thought of as having been an industrial area before it became a gallery district, but what is now called SoHo was in fact a mixed-use neighborhood. The South Houston Industrial District overlapped with an Italian residential neighborhood known as the South Village. The Feast of Saint Anthony, an Italian street fair, is still held every summer in front of the church of St. Anthony of Padua on Sullivan Street just below Houston. When I was searching for my first New York apartment in the early fall of 1967, I looked at a railroad flat on that very street but was frightened away by how rough the area seemed. I rented the place uptown in Spanish Harlem instead. Later, around the time I started going to the Firehouse dances, I spent one summer house-sitting at my friend Pat Steir's loft on Mulberry Street in Little Italy, east of SoHo, and again I remember feeling distinctly like an outsider and being afraid that the neighborhood toughs would figure out that I was gay. I loved buying prosciutto and fresh mozzarella at the local markets, but the framed photographs of Mussolini in many of the shop windows certainly gave me pause. Paradoxically—or maybe not—my sometime sex buddy and lifelong friend Carl D'Aquino, the interior designer I met at the Firehouse dances and with whom I'd rented the Fire Island house, was one of those working-class New York Italians. He grew up in the projects on the Lower East Side, but when I met him in 1971 he lived a block northeast of St. Anthony of Padua and then later, for years, a block southwest of it in a garret apartment rented from family friends who'd bought their house in the old Italian neighborhood.

The one place to find a bite to eat in SoHo in the earliest years of artists living in the area was Fanelli's Cafe, also a remnant of the area's Italian American heritage. It got some competition from a different kind of eatery in the fall of 1971, when dancer and choreographer Carol Goodden, artist Gordon Matta-Clark, and a group of their friends opened Food just up the street from the GAA Firehouse. Although Food survived as a SoHo restaurant into the early 1980s, it is remembered best for its first two years of operation and is regarded as a long-running Matta-Clark performance piece. The documentary film that Matta-Clark made with Robert Frank and others during Food's first year of operation reveals something of the communitarian feel of the place, but it doesn't suggest performance art nearly as much as it does the hard daily labor of operating a restaurant. The film begins with before-dawn shopping at the Fulton Fish Market and ends after the restaurant has closed for the night, the chairs have been stacked on the tabletops, and a great many loaves of bread for the next day have been loaded into the ovens by a solitary baker, presumably, like most of Food's staff, an artist.

Matta-Clark is the figure most identified with the spirit of 1970s downtown Manhattan as a utopian artists' community and site of artistic experimentation. His status no doubt derives in part from the fact that he died so young; his youth is all we know of him, and his youthful career coincided with a moment of particularly intense artistic ferment. The identification also certainly has to do with the fact that the subject and site of Matta-Clark's art was the city itself, the city experienced as simultaneously neglected and usable, dilapidated and beautiful, loss and possibility. Matta-Clark wrote,

> Work with abandoned structures began with my concern for the life of the city of which a major side effect is the metabolization of old buildings. Here as in many urban centers the availability of empty and neglected structures was a prime textural reminder of the ongoing fallacy of renewal through modernization. The omnipresence of emptiness, of abandoned housing and imminent demolition gave me the freedom to experiment with the

multiple alternatives to one's life in a box as well as popular attitudes about the need for enclosure. . . .

The earliest works were also a foray into a city that still was evolving for me. It was an exploration of New York's least remembered parts of the space between the walls of views inside out. I would drive around in my pick-up hunting for emptiness, for a quiet abandoned spot on which to concentrate my piercing attention.[4]

Hunting for emptiness in a dense urban fabric like Manhattan might seem incongruous, and indeed today it would be well-nigh futile there. But New York was a very different city four decades ago. I offer as evidence a group of photographs by Peter Hujar dating from 1975–76, taken on the far west side of Manhattan moving south from the Meatpacking District toward the Battery Park City landfill and around the Financial District and Civic Center. The photographs are of two kinds, one showing desolate, fading industrial areas and the other, downtown Manhattan emptied out at night. Among the latter is one of Nassau Street that includes, in the middle ground, the building I moved into the year after Hujar took this picture. All of them are, to my mind, cruising pictures—cruising pictures with no people in them: this too must seem incongruous. But the point of cruising, or at least *one* point of cruising, is feeling yourself alone and anonymous in the city, feeling that the city belongs to you, to you and maybe a chanced-upon someone like you—at least, like you in your exploration of the empty city. Is there by chance someone else wandering these deserted streets? Might that someone else be on the prowl? Could the two of us find a dark corner where we could get together? Can the city become just *ours* for this moment?

Of course, not everyone experiences urban emptiness this way. A year after Hujar made these pictures, Cindy Sherman began shooting her famous series of Untitled Film Stills also on the deserted streets of Lower Manhattan. Hers are a very different kind of picture, not least because most are taken during the daytime. (Lower Manhattan was deserted even during the day on weekends then.) They are also different because they always include a lone female character played by Sherman herself and are staged in such a way as to suggest an incident in that character's story. The few of them taken on the streets at night are noirish images of threatened femininity, showing an apprehensive woman walking down a dark, forlorn street. But the city in Sherman's pictures is not New York; it is a generic city, like a film location, and the city is not a good place for the woman in the pictures to be.

(Of course, the notion that a city street at night is no place for a woman is also belied by Sherman's use of this very street to make her photographs.)

Another work that suggests—and simultaneously pokes fun at—the dangers facing women on desolate Manhattan streets was made in response to artists' use of the abandoned city in the early 1970s. The work is Louise Lawler's sound piece *Birdcalls* (1972/1981), in which Lawler "squeals, squawks, chirps, twitters, croaks, squeaks, and occasionally warbles the names—primarily the surnames—of twenty-eight contemporary male artists, from Vito Acconci to Lawrence Weiner" (I borrow Rosalyn Deutsche's concise description).[5] Lawler explains that the work

> originated in the early 1970s when my friend Martha Kite and I were helping some artists on one of the Hudson River pier projects. The women involved were doing tons of work, but the work being shown was only by male artists. Walking home at night in New York, one way to feel safe is to pretend you're crazy or at least be really loud. Martha and I called ourselves the *dewey chantoosies*, and we'd sing off-key and make other noises. Willoughby Sharp was the impresario of the project, so we'd make a "Willoughby Willoughby" sound, trying to sound like birds. This developed into a series of bird calls based on artists' names.[6]

The show in question was *Projects: Pier 18*, an exhibition at the Museum of Modern Art of photographs by the art-world team Shunk-Kender that documented a succession of artists' projects by twenty-seven artists, all male.[7] While the projects were situated on the pier, several taking it as their subject, many also provide intriguing views of the city in 1971. For example, John Baldessari's *Hands Framing New York Harbor* is a single image of a freighter moored at the pier framed by a foreground rectangle Baldessari made by pressing together his thumbs and index fingers. Above and to the right of his hands, we see the downtown skyline, including the Woolworth Building on Broadway, the top of the US Courthouse in Foley Square, and the New York Telephone Company building on West Street. Looming in front of the Woolworth Building is the huge New York World-Telegram sign. Dan Graham's description of his work for *Projects: Pier 18* reads: "Still camera pressed to body—Beginning at my feet, each shot progressively spirals to top of my head—Lens faces out—back of camera side pressed flush to contour of skin." The photographs Graham took as he moved the camera around his body capture oblique views of the pier, the river, and the skyline. In some, we see fragments of the towers of the World Trade Center, whose summit is not yet complete.

Most of the old industrial piers along the West Side of Manhattan on the Hudson River, including Pier 18, stood abandoned and in partial or near ruin at that time, so when you walked on them you were in constant danger of falling through the floor or falling off the rotting timbered edges into the river six to eight feet below. In those piers that retained their superstructures, the upper rooms might also be hazardous. *Security Zone*, Vito Acconci's work for *Projects: Pier 18*, implicitly referred to the sense of remoteness and danger of Lower Manhattan's west-side piers. Acconci, with hands bound behind his back, blindfolded, and wearing earplugs, entrusted his safety to fellow artist Lee Jaffe as he walked around the far end of the pier. The piece was, Acconci said, "designed to affect an everyday relationship" in that it forced him to develop trust in someone about whom he had "ambiguous" feelings.[8] It's hard to tell in some of the photographs whether Jaffe is about to push Acconci off the edge of the pier or is saving him from falling off.

A month later, Acconci made explicit the sense of danger on the piers in an untitled project at Pier 17. He posted a notice at the John Gibson Gallery during his exhibition there, announcing that he would wait at the end of the pier at 1 a.m. every night for an hour, from March 27 to April 24, and that anyone who came to meet him there would be rewarded by being told a secret that Acconci had never before divulged, something about which he felt ashamed and which could be used against him. In addition to having to make himself vulnerable by revealing a dirty secret, Acconci had to confront the perils of the deserted pier. On the first night, he writes, "I'm waiting outside, afraid to go in (inside I'll be on unfamiliar ground—I could be taken unawares—outside I can get a view of the whole—if anyone comes, I'll have to go in after him, overtake him before he stakes out a position)."[9] One night, a visitor showed up, and "someone shouts my name at the entrance," Acconci recalled. "I don't answer him: he has to be willing to throw himself into it, he has to come and get me (I'm in the position of prey—I have to be stalked)."[10]

Matta-Clark, too, made a project for *Pier 18*, but his reference to endangerment was, as in so much of his work, one of bravura, of physical derring-do rather than psychological vulnerability. At Pier 18, he planted an evergreen tree in what he called "a parked island barge" and suspended himself by rope upside down above it. But this was only an easy rehearsal for what would be Matta-Clark's most audacious act and certainly one of his most magnificent works, *Day's End* (1975), his summerlong transformation of the dilapidated Pier 52, which stood at the end of Gansevoort Street in New York's Meatpacking District.

Like most people, I know *Day's End* only from photographs, written descriptions, and the film that documents its making. Regrettably, I didn't see it. Matta-Clark talked about the work in a number of interviews; the one he gave in Antwerp at the time he made *Office Baroque*, a couple of years after he completed *Day's End*, is the most evocative:

> Pier 52 is an intact nineteenth-century industrial relic of steel and corrugated tin looking like an enormous Christian basilica whose dim interior was barely lit by the clerestory windows fifty feet overhead.
> The initial cuts were made through the pier floor across the center forming a tidal channel nine feet wide by seventy feet long. A sail-shaped opening provides access to the river. A similar shape through the roof directly above this channel allows a patch of light to enter which arches over the floor until it's captured at noon within the watery slot. During the afternoon the sun shines through a cat's-eye-like "rose window" in the west wall. At first a sliver and then a strongly defined shape of light continues to wander into the wharf until the whole pier is fully illuminated at dusk. Below the rear "wall-hole" is another large quarter circular cut opening the floor of the south-west corner to a turbulent view of the Hudson water. The water and sun move constantly in the pier throughout the day in what I see as an indoor park.[11]

Matta-Clark referred to the three months of work on *Day's End* as his summer vacation by the water.[12] Judging from the film that Betsy Sussler and Jack Kruger shot of it, it wasn't a restful vacation. Working with his friend Gerry Hovagimyan, Matta-Clark used such heavy tools as a chain saw and a blowtorch to cut through the timbers of the pier's floor and the corrugated-tin roof and facade. The most dramatic moments of the film show Matta-Clark wielding the blowtorch as he dangles on a small platform strung up by rope pulley about twenty feet above the pier's floor. Often shirtless but wearing protective goggles, Matta-Clark, in a performance that is equal parts Harold Lloyd and Douglas Fairbanks, cuts the west-end oculus through the tin siding as sparks fly around him. Matta-Clark acknowledged the "absurdity of the whole activity,"[13] even as he sacralized it through his references to the basilica-like structure and "rose window." Some of those who had the good fortune to see *Day's End* relate a sense of awe enhanced by fear. Sculptor Joel Shapiro recalls that "the piece was dangerous," that Matta-Clark "was creating some kind of edge—flirting with some sort of abyss."[14] But Matta-Clark intended the opposite sort of experience:

> The one thing that I wanted was to make it possible for people to see it . . . in a peaceful enclosure totally enclosed in an un-menacing kind of way. That when they went in there, they wouldn't feel like every squeak or every shadow was a potential threat. I know in lots of the earlier works that I did,

the kind of paranoia of being in a space where you didn't know who was there, what was happening or whether there were menacing people lurking around, was just distracting. And I just wanted it to be more of a joyous situation.[15]

An indoor park, joyous, dangerous, absurd, flirting with the abyss: reading Matta-Clark's and others' descriptions of *Day's End*, it's impossible for me not to think of the experiences of those other pier occupants, the ones from whom Matta-Clark seems, in nearly all his statements about the work, to want to differentiate himself—"you know, that whole S&M," as he put it.[16] Although in many instances he aligns his work with that of others who take over or otherwise make their mark on abandoned parts of cities, particularly workers, homeless people, and disenfranchised youth, in the case of Pier 52 Matta-Clark not only disavowed any bond with the gay men who were using the piers as cruising grounds but went so far as to lock them out:

> After looking up and down the waterfront for a pier, I just happened on this one. And of all of them, it was the one least trafficked. It had been broken into and was continuing to be broken into when I was there. But it remained a kind of side step from their general haunt. So I went in and realized without much effort I could secure it. And it then occurred to me that while I was closing up holes and barb-wiring various parts, I would also change the lock and have my own lock. It would make it so much easier.[17]

It may be that Matta-Clark had no particular animus toward the gay men who were using the pier but simply wanted to be able to go about his work undisturbed, to protect himself from intruders of any kind. He might even have worried about liability should someone get hurt as a result of his cutting away sections of the pier's floor. It's difficult to say, because Matta-Clark wasn't careful to differentiate among the various dangers that journalists, in their writings about the piers, often conflated: hazardous, disintegrating structures; threatening, perverse sexuality; and criminals who preyed on, robbed, and sometimes even murdered the piers' clandestine users.

> Besides my personal feelings of base mismanagement of the dying harbor and its ghost-like terminals, is the inextricable evidence of a new criminal situation of alarming proportions. The waterfront was probably never anything but tough and dangerous but now with this long slow transition period, it has become a veritable muggers' playground, both for people who go only to enjoy walking there and for a recently popularized sadomasochistic fringe.[18]

Gay men were acutely aware of the piers' dangers; in fact, they posted signs warning fellow cruisers to watch their wallets. Moreover, Matta-Clark wasn't the only one who took to the piers for a summer vacation by the water. Shielded from public view by the warehouse structure, gay men used one pier's end that jutted far out into the river as a place to sunbathe. It doesn't, I think, diminish the accomplishment of *Day's End* to say that a romantic grandeur was perceptible in the ruined piers before Matta-Clark ever wrought a single change on Pier 52 and that much of the pleasure gay men took in being at the piers was what drew artists to them as well. It's not just that they were there and available; they were also vast and hauntingly beautiful. Nor was the sex play in the piers only of the rough and kinky variety, unless you think that any kind of sex outside a domestic setting is kinky. The entire range of pleasures and dangers at the piers was captured by the too-little-known African-American photographer Alvin Baltrop, who documented the goings-on there during the seventies, up to and including the piers' demolition in the mid to late eighties. A number of Baltrop's photographs show gay men at Pier 52, taking in the beauty of *Day's End* along with whatever other beauties they might have been pursuing. Indeed, these photographs wonderfully portray the "peaceful enclosure" and "joyous situation" that Matta-Clark said he wanted to achieve.[19] Like Matta-Clark, Baltrop also hoisted himself in a harness to make his work. In the preface for a book that he worked unsuccessfully to complete before dying of cancer in 2004, Baltrop wrote:

> Although initially terrified of the Piers, I began to take these photos as a voyeur, but soon grew determined to preserve the frightening, mad, unbelievable, violent, and beautiful things that were going on at that time. To get certain shots, I hung from the ceilings of several warehouses utilizing a makeshift harness, watching and waiting for hours to record the lives that these people led (friends, acquaintances, and strangers), and the unfortunate ends that they sometimes met. The casual sex and nonchalant narcotizing, the creation of artwork and music, sunbathing, dancing, merrymaking and the like habitually gave way to muggings, callous yet detached violence, rape, suicide, and in some instances, murder. The rapid emergence and expansion of AIDS in the 1980s further reduced the number of people going to and living at the Piers, and the sporadic joys that could be found there.[20]

Baltrop photographed obsessively: men engaged in sex, shot from the distance of a neighboring pier or clandestinely through a doorway or happy to become exhibitionists for the camera at close range; men and women Baltrop came to know at the piers, including some who had no place else to live; guys cruising for sex, sometimes as naked as the nearby sunbathers; people just strolling around, transfixed by the rays of sunlight streaming through disintegrating roof structures; graffiti and vernacular artworks, some of it the skillful handiwork of an artist known as Tava, who painted in a style that amalgamates Greek vase painting with Tom of Finland; gruesome corpses dredged up from the river and surrounded by the police and onlookers. Most of all, Baltrop photographed the piers themselves. The phantoms of New York's bustling industrial past appear in Baltrop's pictures as vast heaps of trusses, buckled tin siding, rotting pilings and floors, rickety staircases, broken windows, sometimes with a ragged curtain still flapping in the river breezes. Baltrop's camera often zeroes in on a just-discernable scene of butt fucking or cock sucking amid the rubble, but even when the sex is absent, the piers can be recognized as the sexual playground they were.

Unlike Baltrop, I wasn't consciously afraid of the piers. They were part of my neighborhood cityscape and one of many nearby places to play outdoors. Located a short walk from my apartment on Tenth Street, Pier 42, which no longer had a structure on it, was a local place to hang out and be cooled by the Hudson River's breezes on hot summer days and watch the sun set over New Jersey in the evening. Even closer was Pier 45, the main gay-cruising pier. Along its West Street end, the upper-floor warren of rooms functioned day and night like a sex club with no cover charge. Pier 45 was only one of many nearby places for outdoor sex play. Another Greenwich Village haunt of men seeking other men was known simply as "the trucks," a designation for the empty lots along Washington Street north of Christopher Street, where delivery trucks were parked at night. After 4 a.m., when the bars closed, gay men gathered in the spaces behind the trucks and often up inside the back of them for group sex. If you lived in the Village, this was an efficient way to bring your night out to a satisfying end without having to repair to a bathhouse in another neighborhood. I remember a short period in about 1973, before I first discovered the scene at the piers, when, late at night and into the morning, gay men took over the half-completed structures of the West Village Houses going up along Washington Street across from the trucks. The West Village Houses were a long-debated, underfinanced, and therefore architecturally diminished project of 420 units of low-rise, middle-income housing that indirectly resulted from Jane Jacobs's 1961 classic critique of modern urbanism, *The Death and Life of Great American Cities*, in which she heralded short blocks, dense concentrations of people, mixed-use neighborhoods, and aged buildings as proper city values.[21] Although Jacobs's ideas about what made cities great grew out of her love of her own neighborhood, Greenwich Village, I don't think she was thinking of men meeting for sex in construction sites, parking lots, and waterfront ware-houses—but this was part of the life of the Village I knew a decade after she wrote her book.

Come to think of it, maybe I *was* afraid of the piers—afraid not only of their very real dangers, which I tended stupidly to dismiss, but also of their easy proximity and constant promise. I was struggling to write about art professionally as a freelancer then, which took more discipline than I could usually muster since the frustrations of being unable to find a good subject, devise a sound argument, even choose a word that rang true or compose a sentence I was happy with could be easily if only momentarily alleviated just by walking out my door into the playground that was my immediate neighborhood. This is why, I think, seeing the Grand Union perform stays in my mind as such a momentous event, why it propelled me to another part of the city and another world. Apart from monthly reviewing for *Art News* and *Art International*, the most ambitious writing I managed during the several years I lived in the Village were a monographic essay on Agnes Martin titled "Number, Measure, Ratio" and "Opaque Surfaces." In both essays, I struggled to think beyond the formalism that still held sway in so much American art criticism. What would finally free me from its grip was not painting but performance art.

The block in Tribeca to which I moved in 1974 bordered the site of what had been perhaps the most ambitious and imaginative use of the deindustri-alizing city as the stage for an artwork, Joan Jonas's performance *Delay Delay* of 1972.[22] A year later, Jonas translated the performance into the language of film for *Songdelay*, as compelling an aesthetic document of New York in the seventies as Paul Strand and Charles Sheeler's 1921 city-symphony film *Manhatta* is of the city half a century earlier. Jonas and I describe the performance space of *Delay Delay* in our 1983 book:

> The spectators view the performance from the roof of a five-story loft build-ing facing west, located at 319 Greenwich Street in lower Manhattan. The performing area is a ten-block grid of city streets bounding vacant lots and leveled buildings. Beyond these lots are the elevated West Side Highway, the docks and piers along the Hudson River, and the factories of the New Jersey skyline across the river. Directly in front of the spectators at the back of the performance area is the Erie Lackawanna Pier building painted with large numbers 20 and 21. These indicate the old pier numbers.[23]

By the time I moved to Tribeca, these downtown piers had been torn down to make way for Battery Park City, which then had been put on hold during the city's fiscal crisis. New York was going bankrupt, and its infrastructure was badly deteriorating, conspicuously epitomized in late 1973 by the collapse of a section of the elevated West Side Highway under the weight of an asphalt-laden repair truck. Just half a block down the street from the loft I moved into, the city trailed off into vacant lots. Beyond the razed blocks that had once been part of the Washington Market was the elevated highway, now empty too, and beyond that, where the piers had been, a barren landfill that Lower Manhattan residents christened "the beach." A few years later, the newly founded arts organization Creative Time began its series of outdoor exhibitions there called *Art on the Beach*.[24] An era of officially sponsored public art was under way, with commissioning entities, panels of experts, permits, contracts, and eventually controversies and court cases.

I didn't manage to change worlds by moving to Tribeca. I still spent nearly every evening in the Village, but now most of them ended with a long walk down the west side to my new neighborhood, through the empty streets that Hujar photographed at just this time. It was a time when I could cherish the illusion that these Manhattan streets belonged to me— to me and others who were discovering them and using them for our own purposes. But I did manage to become an art critic. The first article I wrote after moving downtown was "Joan Jonas's Performance Works," published in a special issue of *Studio International* devoted to performance art. Jonas was more clear-sighted than I about the possibility of appropriating city spaces. I quote her in my essay as saying: "My own thinking and production has focused on issues of space—ways of dislocating it, attenuating it, flattening it, turning it inside out, always attempting to explore it without ever giving to myself or to others the permission to penetrate it."[25]

I was still preoccupied enough with painting in the mid-1970s that I misinterpreted Jonas's explorations of spatial illusionism as reflecting her continuing involvement with the history of painting.[26] I overlooked what her statement foretold about the actual spaces Jonas was performing in: just how provisional was their availability for experimental uses. This is what her film *Songdelay* captures so well about the New York of its moment. Robert Fiore's use of a telephoto lens in shooting Jonas's film collapses onto a single plane the vista that opened out in front of the spectators beyond the rooftop from which they watched *Delay Delay*. A performer who appears to be in the near foreground claps blocks of wood together; a sound delay tells us that in fact he stands a great distance from us. A warehouse in Jersey City appears to be right behind him, but the sudden, uncanny arrival of a huge freighter between him and the building tells us otherwise—that in between lies the great expanse of the Hudson River.[27] A cut to a slow-motion, tight close-up of Jonas, limbs outstretched and rotating in a large hoop, makes clear how limited and fragmented is our perspective on the overall location, for beyond Jonas's torso we see only the street's cobblestones, a curb, a bit of sidewalk, and some rubble. Behind another figure, whose movements are rendered puppetlike by bamboo poles held in her outstretched arms and thrust into the opposite pants legs, we glimpse a chain-link fence and background automobile traffic. Only one sequence grants us sufficient distance to make the location comprehensible: at the top left of a scene that shows several performers moving back and forth across a vacant lot, the back of the Federal Office Building on Church and Barclay Streets is visible, and just below it at the frame's right edge we can make out the sole survivor of the wrecking balls of a decade earlier, a nineteenth-century building that stood alone and forlorn at the corner of West and Warren Streets until 2003.[28] This means that the streets we see bordering the vacant lot's south and west sides must be Warren and Greenwich Streets—right around the corner from where I lived between 1974 and 1976.[29] But just as we begin to be able to orient ourselves, Jonas cuts to another close-up of herself rotating in the hoop, and this time not only is she upside down but the film frames are also printed upside down.

Throughout *Songdelay*, sequences of action are interrupted by quick inserts—so quick they are nearly subliminal—of Jonas in the hoop, the puppetlike figure, flashes of light from a mirror that Jonas holds up to reflect the sun into the lens, and a pair of wooden blocks that, clacking together, provide much of the film's sound. Together with the telephoto-lens shots, extreme close-ups of individual performers' bodies, and bird's-eye views of two people in the role of a slider-crank mechanism walking along a line and circle painted on the cobblestone pavement, these elements make us fully aware of the filmic mediation of the performance events. But that is far from the sole function of *Songdelay*'s varied techniques. The film also uses these techniques to thwart our desire to know or possess the city beyond our immediate experience of it in the moment of use. We see the city in fragments, not unlike those that Gordon Matta-Clark—one of *Songdelay*'s performers—gave us a few years later in his film *City Slivers* (1976), in which New York appears as a series of vertical striations made by masking the camera's anamorphic lens and shooting multiple exposures. We glimpse the city in pieces, in the background, in our peripheral vision—and in recollection.

Notes

1. *Joan Jonas: Scripts and Descriptions 1968–1982*, ed. Douglas Crimp (Berkeley: University Art Museum, University of California; Eindhoven, Netherlands: Stedelijk van Abbemuseum, 1983), 22. Jonas's exhibition at the UC Berkeley Art Museum took place in 1980.

2. See *112 Workshop, 112 Greene Street: History, Artists and Artworks*, ed. Robyn Brentano with Mark Savitt (New York: New York University Press, 1981).

3. An exception to the oversight of this fact is the inclusion in *New York—Downtown Manhattan: SoHo* (Berlin: Akademie der Künste, 1976) of a 1976 flyer headlined "STOP DISCOS IN SOHO!," protesting the plans for a fourth disco in SoHo after the Loft, Flamingo, and Frankenstein. A more significant exception is Tim Lawrence, *Hold On to Your Dreams: Arthur Russell and the Downtown Music Scene, 1973–1992* (Durham, NC: Duke University Press, 2009), whose subject, the music director of the Kitchen Center for Video and Music in 1974–1975, straddled the experimental music and gay disco scenes.

4. Gordon Matta-Clark, "Work with Abandoned Structures," typewritten statement, circa 1975, in *Gordon Matta-Clark: Works and Collected Writings*, ed. Gloria Moure (Barcelona: Ediciones Polígrafia, 2006), 141.

5. Rosalyn Deutsche, "Louise Lawler's Rude Museum," in *Twice Untitled and Other Pictures (Looking Back)*, ed. Helen Molesworth (Columbus, OH: Wexner Center for the Arts, 2006), 130.

6. Louise Lawler, "Prominence Given, Authority Taken," interview by Douglas Crimp, *Grey Room*, no. 4 (Summer 2001): 80. Lawler recorded *Birdcalls* in 1981 with a somewhat altered and updated roster of male artists' names.

7. See *Harry Shunk/Projects: Pier 18* (Nice: Musée d'art moderne et d'art contemporain, 1992). Though this book does not credit János (Jean) Kender, Harry Shunk and Kender worked collaboratively between 1956 and 1973, and all of their photographs taken during this period had been credited to Shunk-Kender. This was the case when *Projects: Pier 18* was shown at the Museum of Modern Art in 1971. The collaboration dissolved in 1973, with Shunk retaining the photographic archive. See "Harry Shunk and Shunk-Kender Archive," The Getty Research Institute, accessed May 1, 2016, http://www.getty.edu/research/special_collections/notable/shunk_kender.html.

8. Vito Acconci and Gregory Volk, *Vito Acconci: Diary of a Body 1969–1973* (Milan: Charta, 2006), 25.

9. Acconci and Volk, *Vito Acconci*, 258.

10. Acconci and Volk, *Vito Acconci*, 259.

11. Gordon Matta-Clark, interview for the Internationaal Cultureel Centrum, Antwerp, September 1977, in Moure, *Gordon Matta-Clark*, 252–53.

12. Gordon Matta-Clark, in "Gordon Matta-Clark: The Making of Pier 52," interview by Liza Béar, March 11, 1976, in Moure, *Gordon Matta-Clark*, 217.

13. Matta-Clark, "Gordon Matta-Clark," 220.

14. Joel Shapiro, quoted in Pamela M. Lee, *Object to Be Destroyed: The Work of Gordon Matta-Clark* (Cambridge, MA: The MIT Press, 2001), 130. Lee argues for a combination of phenomenology and the sublime to capture the experience of Matta-Clark's work.

15. Matta-Clark, "Gordon Matta-Clark," 220.

16. Matta-Clark, "Gordon Matta-Clark," 215.

17. Matta-Clark, "Gordon Matta-Clark," 218.

18. Gordon Matta-Clark, "My Understanding of Art," typewritten statement, circa 1975, in Moure, *Gordon Matta-Clark*, 204. On the journalistic conflation of the dangers *to gay*

men using the piers with the supposed dangers *of* gay men's sexuality, see Lee, *Object to Be Destroyed*, 119–20.

19. Many others photographed the piers; none to my knowledge as extensively or beautifully as Alvin Baltrop. Included among those who took photographs of the piers were Peter Hujar and Leonard Fink. The latter's vast trove of photographs of the gay scene are held in the National Archive of Lesbian, Gay, Bisexual, and Transgender History in New York. In addition to photographic documentation, the piers are the setting of a gay porn feature film called *Pier Groups*, made by Arch Brown in 1979.

20. Alvin Baltrop, "Ashes from a Flame: Photographs by Alvin Baltrop," ed. Randal Wilcox, unpublished manuscript.

21. Jane Jacobs, *The Death and Life of Great American Cities* (New York: Random House, 1961).

22. See Janelle Reiring, "Joan Jonas' 'Delay Delay,'" *TDR: The Drama Review* 16, no. 3 (September 1972): 142–51; and Katie Stone, "Joan Jonas: Beyond the Frame" (master's thesis, Courtauld Institute of Art, 2003).

23. Joan Jonas, *Joan Jonas: Scripts and Descriptions, 1968–1982*, ed. Douglas Crimp (Berkeley: University Art Museum, University of California, 1983), 34.

24. The *Art on the Beach* events at the Battery Park City landfill extended from 1978 to 1985. For a thorough analysis of the uses of a different version of "public art" in the interests of real-estate development at Battery Park City, see Rosalyn Deutsche, "Uneven Development: Public Art in New York City," in *Evictions: Art and Spatial Politics* (Cambridge, MA: The MIT Press, 1996), 49–107.

25. Joan Jonas with Rosalind Krauss (misspelled "Krause"), "Seven Years," *TDR: The Drama Review* 19, no. 1 (March 1975): 13.

26. I wrote, "By presenting real space as an impenetrable illusion in her performances, Jonas has made the experience of performance equivalent not only to film and videotape—the other two mediums she works with—but also to painting. At issue in her work, then, is an ambitious relationship to the history of painting and a reversal of the priorities of most contemporary art." Douglas Crimp, "Joan Jonas's Performance Works," *Studio International* 192, no. 982 (July–August 1976): 10.

27. The warehouse in question is visible in the distance, across the Hudson River, in several of the photographs of Richard Serra's work for *Projects: Pier 18, Shooting a Square through a Trapezoid, Camera Angle Measured*.

28. The building, at 179 West Street, survived until 2003 because a court ruling in favor of the tenant prevented his eviction until the renewal projects for the site had been fully approved by all necessary government agencies. The building also appears in Cindy Sherman's *Untitled Film Still #60* (1980).

29. In one shot of the puppetlike figure, it is possible to make out a street sign that says "Greenwich Street."

"Art Scene/Gay Scene":
Ann Cvetkovich Reflects on Douglas Crimp's
"Action around the Edges"

For his innovative combination of art, activism, and scholarship and his contributions to queer knowledge building outside conventional disciplines and beyond the academy, Douglas Crimp most certainly belongs in the queer pantheon of those selected for the Kessler Lecture. In his case, a key catalyst was his involvement in HIV/AIDS activism through ACT UP NY in the 1980s, but it's also the result of having participated in New York's art world as a gay man in a period of time when those two arenas—what he calls the "gay scene" and the "art scene"—were intimately intertwined but in ways that were often unacknowledged. Those experiences shaped and transformed Crimp's critical practice, including his commitment to what he called "cultural activism" in the collection *AIDS: Cultural Analysis/Cultural Activism* that he had first edited for *October* magazine in 1987[1]—eventually at the professional cost of his relationship with the journal. Through his editorial work, like his curatorial practice in the historic *Pictures* exhibition, he showcased activists, artists, and academics—including Leo Bersani, Simon Watney, Amber Hollibaugh, and the PWA Coalition. He also developed his own practice of a critical writing that combines the affective and the political while also paying close analytical attention to the cultural meanings of, for example, the "Silence = Death" poster.

One of Crimp's standout essays from that period has been a lifeline for me across my own career. "Mourning and Militancy," first published in *October* in 1989, opens with a searing account of Crimp's swollen tear duct, a response to his father's death, in order to make a simple, but deeply enabling, claim for the value of mourning—and the perils of ignoring it as integral to the militancy of activism.[2] His daring embrace of the loss of unprotected sex—of Crisco and rimming, of his heart breaking for those who don't know its pleasures and for those who do—is poignant and ultraqueer, as Crimp puts the experience of felt knowledge into theoretical conversation with Freud. In a later essay that continues the work of "Mourning and Militancy,"

Crimp openly discusses his own seroconversion as evidence that we are only human, making vulnerability, including his own, central to his project. Although I wasn't able to attend Crimp's 2007 Kessler Lecture, I do remember the packed room of activists and scholars at Yale in 1989 who listened collectively as he read his deeply moving essay, which gave us permission not only to bring sex and tears into the academy but to feel the grief that, along with anger and joy, saturated HIV/AIDS activism. Like that moment in 1989, the Kessler Lecture Series is a gathering of queer tribes, not just academics, and its location in NYC is a reminder that the streets, the piers, the clubs, and the cruising cultures that Crimp embraced are central to our history and our knowledge formations.

I would argue that Crimp combined activism and theory so seamlessly because of his involvement in the arts—and in the forms of cultural activism that he described. He was a mentor for many younger queers in ACT UP, including artists such as Gregg Bordowitz and Zoe Leonard. His collaboration with Adam Rolston on *AIDS Demo Graphics* (1990)[3] not only provides a valuable record of the visual brilliance of ACT UP's cultural production, but his accompanying essay shrewdly places ACT UP within a lineage of artists, such as Barbara Kruger, Jenny Holzer, and Hans Haacke, with whom he was deeply familiar. Transformed by his AIDS activism, Crimp forged a path for an unapologetically queer art criticism, for "getting the Warhol we deserve,"[4] and he pursued his passion for dance, which included not only the experimental work of Yvonne Rainer and Merce Cunningham documented in his Kessler Lecture, but a love of classical ballet.

Crimp's 2007 Kessler Lecture was ultimately published in *Before Pictures*, the capstone book that documents the intersections of the "gay scene" and the "art scene" in 1970s New York through his own encounters with both art and sex.[5] In Crimp's elegant form of the personal essay, it's hard to tell where one starts and the other stops. He provides a beautiful first-person account of the use of New York City as a site for the emergence of performance art in downtown lofts, Gordon Matta-Clark's famous *Open Day* on the piers, and Joan Jonas's filming of performance in the streets of Tribeca. And he also includes the gay presence on the piers, ignored by Matta-Clark, through his discussion of Alvin Baltrop's photographs, which are only now coming to greater recognition. His memory of falling love with dance at a 1970 Merce Cunningham show is tied in with the process whereby performance art becomes a substitute object for his libido, a connection that doesn't compromise his critical vision but instead enhances it. By describing New York's emotional and cultural geography through charged moments in his own life, such as his move from the West Village to Tribeca, Crimp provides an important historical record of the imbrication of art and queer life. He also invents a model for queer practices of description that constitute a history and a criticism we continue to need.

Ann Cvetkovich is a professor in the Feminist Institute of Social Transformation at Carleton University in Ottawa, Ontario, Canada. She is the author of *Mixed Feelings: Feminism, Mass Culture, and Victorian Sensationalism* (1992); *An Archive of Feelings: Trauma, Sexuality, and Lesbian Public Cultures* (2003); and *Depression: A Public Feeling* (2012).

Notes

1. Douglas Crimp, ed., *AIDS: Cultural Analysis/Cultural Activism* (Cambridge, MA: The MIT Press, 1987).

2. Douglas Crimp, "Mourning and Militancy," *October*, no. 51 (1989): 3–18.

3. Douglas Crimp and Adam Rolston, *AIDS Demo Graphics* (Seattle: Bay Press, 1990).

4. Douglas Crimp, "Getting the Warhol We Deserve," *Social Text*, no. 59 (1999): 49–66.

5. Douglas Crimp, *Before Pictures* (Chicago: University of Chicago Press, 2016).

THE DAVID R. KESSLER LECTURES 2002–2020

2002	JONATHAN NED KATZ
2003	GAYLE RUBIN
2004	ISAAC JULIEN
2006	ADRIENNE RICH
2007	DOUGLAS CRIMP
2008	**SUSAN STRYKER**
2009	SARAH SCHULMAN
2010	URVASHI VAID
2012	MARTIN DUBERMAN
2013	CHERYL CLARKE
2014	CATHY J. COHEN
2015	RICHARD FUNG
2016	DEAN SPADE
2017	SARA AHMED
2018	AMBER HOLLIBAUGH
2019	JASBIR K. PUAR
2020	RODERICK A. FERGUSON

Susan Stryker

Susan Stryker is an award-winning scholar and filmmaker whose historical research, theoretical writing, and creative works have helped shape the cultural conversation on transgender studies since the early 1990s. Stryker is professor emerita of gender and women's studies at the University of Arizona and holds the Barbara Lee Professorship in Women's Leadership at Mills College, 2020–2022. She is founding executive editor of *TSQ: Transgender Studies Quarterly*, author of *Transgender History: The Roots of Today's Revolution* (2008), and codirector of the Emmy-winning documentary film *Screaming Queens: The Riot at Compton's Cafeteria* (2005).

Ghost Dances:
A Trans-Movement Manifesto

NOVEMBER 14, 2008

everal things coincided to shape the space from which this lecture emerged. The first was an email from a list I'm on, soliciting creative, artistic responses to climate change. The second was a call for proposals for a symposium on "Subversive Imaginaries." The third, an ongoing conversation with a dancer friend about critical embodiment practices. Fourth, the tangle of thoughts sorting themselves out into various bits of prose and syllabi then being demanded by editors and administrators. Fifth, the backdrop of a historical presidential election soliciting us all to dwell upon "the fierce urgency of now." And finally, the call from Sarah Chinn at CLAGS letting me know I'd have the honor and opportunity to pull something together to say tonight: when she asked me for a title, "Ghost Dances" is what popped out.

The First Movement: Mobilizing Affect

It began in an elegiac mood. The musician ANOHNI sent around an email asking people who had communicated with the band Antony and the Johnsons for thoughts on global warming, as part of the process that informed the making of their recent EP, *Another World*. The piece I wanted to pull together tonight starts in my own response to their music, and in a conviction that I trust s/he shares, that in trans-gender affect lies a transformative power that must be brought to bear on our multiple current crises.

Receiving that email inspired the following response, "Ghost Dance":

. . .
why is it that
we the secular
now sense Apocalypse
when we augur the signs of the times?

Surely that old tale is too worn out,
too ill-used to be true.

And yet . . .
the ice melts and the oceans rise,
the forests burn and the wells dry.
Plague, pestilence, and famine
stalk the cities and the desert-places alike,
and everywhere there is war or the rumor of war.

. . .
And yet . . .

. . .
Let us not yet lie down to die.

. . .
Let us give up what is dead to the dead.
Let us love what we have lost forever by letting it become a ghost.
Let us live, if only for one moment more, if with but the slimmest
of hopes
and with no illusion at all.
Let us then face the music—and let us begin to dance.

Let our bodies be moved in ways our bodies have never before been
moved
Let our feet set new patterns to the ground
Let the ground give rise to ways of touching
That have never been grounded before.

About the same time that I received the email inviting thoughts on
the environmental catastrophe unfolding around us, I received a call for
papers for a symposium Jack Halberstam was conducting at the University
of Western Sydney called "Queer and Subjugated Knowledges: Generating Subversive Imaginaries," which not only resonated with thoughts I'd

previously published on transgender studies as a critical practice for desubjugating embodied, experiential, and affective knowledges, but also aligned with the mood evoked for me by ANOHNI's query. Here's an excerpt from the call for papers:

> It is possible to imagine other forms of being, other forms of knowing, a world with different sites for justice and injustice, a mode of being where the emphasis falls less on money and work and competition, and more on cooperation, trade, and sharing. The work that animates such knowledge projects should not be dismissed as irrelevant or naive. Building upon recent theorizations of the alternative, this symposium invites manifestos, performative lectures, surprising presentations, all committed to imagining life otherwise and thinking collectively about alternative epistemologies, methodologies, life narratives, cultural productions, modes of being and doing.

Because I've been spending time regularly in Sydney since 2003, working there with an exciting group of colleagues at the Somatechnics Research Centre in the Department of Critical and Cultural Studies at Macquarie University, I was eager for any prospect of going to Australia, and proposed the following abstract:

> "Ghost Dances" is a secular sermon that unabashedly advocates embracing a disruptive and refigurative genderqueer/transgender power as a spiritual resource for social transformation. It does so somewhat elliptically by drawing upon the history and anthropology of cultural regeneration movements (such as the Native American ghost dance ritual) to chart a transformative path for contemporary society from a thoroughly reasonable despair towards an equally rational joy. It blends queer critical theory's inside-out deconstruction of Western ontology with language lifted from world religion traditions to offer jaded cynics the prospect of belief without irony. Specifically, it deploys the trope of choreography to articulate the series of movements we must make—weaving back and forth across the subject/object divide of the dominant epistemology—to begin enacting new and sustainable relationships between embodiment, subjectivity, and environment. More virally, it calls upon listeners to begin physically moving their bodies according to new patterns—new habits capable of generating a new habitus, new habitations, and new habitats—thereby materially linking individual actions with global transformations. If we are to survive, it is time to let go of the old world. It is time for transfigured flesh to dance a new world into being.

I decided almost immediately that I really couldn't make it to Sydney this year, but that's when I received the invitation to be here tonight, and I thought "Ghost Dances" would be an appropriate offering. I'm humbled and abashed by how little progress I've made toward finishing the piece that I initially envisioned, and that I promised to deliver. I wanted to be like a musician tonight, performing a polished original composition. Instead, I feel like I'm doing a few structured improvisations. I feel like a character in a Jorge Luis Borges short story, saying, "If I were to have written a novel it would have gone something like this."

The Second Movement: A Queer History of the Ghost Dance
There is a long history in this country of Euro-American people appropriating cultural forms (along with pretty much everything else) from the earliest inhabitants of this continent, and of making fictive identifications with "Indians" for a variety of rhetorical purposes. In organizing my intentions in this lecture via the concept of a "ghost dance," I'm skirting the edges of that history of white appropriation of Native American cultural forms, and perhaps, some might say, actually, if inadvertently, walking down that well-trodden path.

The Ghost Dance—singular and capitalized—refers to a short-lived pan-tribal spiritual and political movement that originated among the Northern Paiute people of western Nevada in 1889. That movement had various names among the various peoples who embraced it, and was first given the name Ghost Dance by white observers trying to translate a set of concepts about this life and its relationship to an afterlife that could be migrated across colonization's epistemological divide only with great difficulty and a measure of loss. The Ghost Dance movement, which I understand as a response to cultural genocide and ecological devastation, was based on a vision by the Northern Paiute shaman Wovoka, who later adopted the Christian name Jack Wilson. In his vision, Wovoka was transported to an abundant land teeming with life, where the living and the dead would be reunited. There, in this otherworld, he was given a dance, which, if performed at the proper intervals, would hasten the arrival of that longed-for reunification. Wovoka's message, and the dance, spread rapidly across North America among many of the First Nations, changing somewhat as it traveled. Some among the Sioux, recently confined to a diminished reservation in South Dakota, came to believe that dancing the Ghost Dance would bring "the buffalo back to the plains," that it would make white people vanish from the earth, and that wearing special Ghost Dance shirts would render the wearer impervious to bullets. The infamous Wounded Knee Massacre of 1890 was the tragic result of the US military response to a band of Sioux leaving the reservation to dance the Ghost Dance.

What seems inspirational and instructive to me about the Ghost Dance is not the particular content of its ceremonies, which properly belong to others, but rather the conviction among a people that how we physically move our bodies, individually and collectively, has the power to transform both ourselves and the world. As anthropologist Anthony F. C. Wallace pointed out many decades ago, in his study of *The Death and Rebirth of the Seneca*, and as ethnologist James Mooney, the first Euro-American student of the Ghost Dance, pointed out in the 1890s, cultural revitalization movements, often involving communal dance and ecstatic vision, have a long human history: in the experience of genocide, in the aftermath of colonization, in the midst of environmental degradation, how is the meaning of life made anew, through our actions?[1] By invoking the evocative label "ghost dance" in my thoughts today, it is to this broader history of collective cultural transformation that I intend to refer, rather than toward any particular ritual or tradition. My goal is not to acquire the ceremony of another, but to ask, in all seriousness: What would a "ghost dance" look like for us? How can we, in the belly of the beast of catastrophe capitalism, invoke a new vision that brings us together to change ourselves and change our world?

US LGBT communities of the past several decades have crafted their own special variant of the appropriable indigene, in the assertion of a special affinity between queer and Native American cultures. The most striking example, given my present theme, is the story told by Harry Hay, founder of the Mattachine Society and the Radical Faeries. In *Radically Gay*,[2] Hay tells of being a child visiting a relative's ranch in western Nevada in 1925, and of having been recognized as "different" by an old Paiute shaman who went by the name Jack Smith, who offered the young Hay his blessing. Years later—1969 to be precise, at the very historical moment that gay liberation was erupting in the wake of the Stonewall Riots—Hay was politically involved with a traditionalist Native American group, which had just acquired the recent Dover reprint edition of James Mooney's rare, long-out-of-print monograph on the Ghost Dance. Hay thought that "the whole traditional movement has a lot of the same type of prophecy and visionism in common with what was going on in that time—sort of reinvoking it, making it possible to apply it in the twentieth century."[3] It was in reading Mooney that Hay first learned that Jack Smith's Paiute name was Wovoka, and that he had been blessed as a child by the originator of the Ghost Dance movement—thus forging a symbolic link between contemporary white radical gay culture and Indigenous spirituality and politics.

The transgender movement that gathered force in the early 1990s similarly rooted itself in an imagined past that valorized Indigenous forebears. The pamphlet that first popularized the word "transgender" as a collective term for a politicized grouping of multiple gender-variant communities and identities, Leslie Feinberg's *Transgender Liberation: A Movement Whose Time Has Come*, painted an idyllic picture of traditional cultures in which, before the advent of capitalism and European colonialism, gender-crossing individuals held positions of honor and esteem. Feinberg wrote movingly of "trans gender warriors" who, like shamans of old, possess a certain kind of knowledge, an awareness of the potential for self-transformability nestled in the heart of a living culture, and who are therefore called to lead their people.[4] Whatever Feinberg's vision lacked in historical specificity it made up for in emotive force: it was a story that effectively situated the current sociopolitical oppression of gender atypicality firmly within history's long march, and one that yoked the longing for a better future to the redemption of a vanished past though our actions in the present day.

The question at the crux of my talk is essentially the same as Feinberg's, stripped of the romance of the transgender native: What would it mean for those of us who consider ourselves to be trans today, for those of us who know from the ways we have lived our embodied subjects in the world, that radical change is within our power both individually and collectively; what would it mean for those of us who are trans to assert ourselves as spiritual leaders in a movement for cultural transformation?

The Third Movement: A Secular Spirituality

The first step, for me, is to rethink what both "leadership" and "spirituality" might mean, as well as what we mean by "trans." To begin with, leading is not a matter of occupying the most advanced position, but rather of gesturing in the direction that one should go. It is a movement conducted by one's own body that can serve as a template or pattern for the movements of others. And as for spirituality, as a secular person it is vital for me to think of it as fully immanent in the material world, rather than as transcendentally apart from it.

I would like to suggest that contemporary critical theories of gender and sexuality offer what amounts to a secular materialist account of the soul or spirit. We can see it in the line of reasoning that runs from Spinoza through Deleuze to inform the current wave of attention to "affect," which is imagined not as feelings emanating from the individual in response to the experience of the world, but rather as a quality of being that draws the individual into greater or lesser degrees of connectivity with the environment. We can see it in the work of Michel Foucault and his followers, in their discussion of biopolitics, which turns modern European political economy on its head. Thomas Hobbes had it exactly backward, in other words, when he wrote, in the preamble to *Leviathan*, that Man, imitating nature, creates an artificial being, or Leviathan, called the commonwealth, in which "Soveraignty is an Artificiall Soul, as giving life and motion to the whole body."[5] If, following Foucault's reformulation of power, we think of soul or spirit as that which animates us, as that which is the concrete essence of who we are as a particular subject, as that vital force which is coextensive with our bodies but nonidentical to it, and as that which survives our individual death, then it is the soul of Man that is an artifice constructed by the nature of Leviathan.

Since this is a secular sermon, allow me a moment of scriptural exegesis. I take my text from Michel Foucault's *History of Sexuality: Volume 1*, from the chapter "Right of Death and Power over Life," in which Foucault argued that sovereign power evolved two basic forms of acting on human life, which, rather than being antithetical, constituted the twin poles of power's development.[6] The first of these poles, designated the "anatomo-political," disciplined the body's biological substance in order to maximize its productive capability while simultaneously increasing its docility, and it aimed at the body's "integration into systems of efficient and economic control."[7] The second pole, designated the "biopolitical," took charge of the "mechanisms of life" with which the biological body was imbued: its generative and reproductive capacities, its overall health and longevity, and so on, which functioned a resource upon which sovereign power could draw. The anatomo-political and biopolitical poles of power, Foucault contends, are "linked together by a whole intermediary cluster of relations."[8]

It is this "intermediary cluster of relations" that I have taken to calling the "somatechnic": a capillary space of connection and circulation between macropolitical structurations of power and micropolitical techniques through which the lives of bodies become enmeshed in the lives of nations, states, and capital formations; a site where current forms of capital and sovereign power seek to reproduce themselves through us even as we seek to live the life of our bodies for ends that sustain our own peculiar means of living; an experiential space of which we are sensually aware and in which we are subjectively present; a situation we could call our embodied soul or self or spirit. It is a space defined as a space of passage, by the quality of being a "trans" space, and it is a site of agency, I would argue, at which we may begin to enact and materialize new social ontologies.

We have all become accustomed, over the past twenty years or so, to queering things. How might we now begin to trans them? I have always been charmed by those mad drawings of the "topography of the subject"[9] that Lacan offers in *Écrits* and want to offer my own playful version here to illustrate the kinds of trans-movements that I think we are all capable of making.

X

Imagine the figure "**X**" as a minimal schematic representation of a matrix, of the concept of intersectionality applied to the embodied subject—not merely all those technes, dispositifs, discourses, and Foucauldian relations of power that converge upon, overwhelm, and thereby constitute the spacetime of embodied subjectivity, but also food chains, respiratory circulations, transmissions of genetic code, and the like. These are the solid lines of the physical (material and energetic) world, organized according to specific culturally and historically variable patterns, that allow us our concrete being. In crossing and entangling themselves in a particular spacetime, (that is to say, in transing one another) they make us the thing that we are, in a Heideggerian and Old High German sense of "thing" as "a gathering."

O

Imagine next the figure "**O**" cutting upon the **X** in such a way that the ends of the crossed lines extend beyond the circle's edge, in an operation that introduces entirely new categories of possible crossings, or trans-movements, between inside and outside, depth and surface, foreground and background. This is the circle of subjectivity, demarcating the parts of the world designated "self" and "other," and which by definition must cut across the lines of the physical world that organize themselves as us. Subjectivity maps itself onto spacetime only partially through the extension and organization of our sensorium, which cuts the world into those parts experienced as sensation and those parts experienced as object: casting the circle of subjectivity is also a practice, a learned but modifiable way of recognizing, or failing to recognize, the connections to be made across the cut.

V

Imagine next figures with a "V" shape, occupying the spaces between the outstretched arms of the X, their crotches placed near the crotches of the X inside the circle of subjectivity but with their lines spreading, ever wideningly, into the extrasubjective world. The registration of the V figures is slightly off-line of the X figure so that they mark the interstitial space chiasmatically related to the concrete space of the X: they represent a space-between whose shape is the complement of that which is materially present. The V figures introduce yet another category of trans-movement-poetic ones that grasp the possibility of reversing foreground and background, inside and outside, depth and surface to shift across the boundary between the actual and the potential, the real and the virtual, the physical and the phantasmatic. This is the ghost space, to return to my metaphor, that haunts the existing shape of the presently organized world, and which, in upsurging from the interstice, offers the possibility of remaking a world.

I

Imagine now a final set of figures in the form of an "I," that create lines bisecting the V-spaces, and which represent a final set of trans-movements: these are the sutures that reach toward the horizon of material possibility and anchor themselves there, across the open interstitial spaces of poetically grasped potentials, and which then, in a return movement toward subjectivity, can gather and fold the fabric of spacetime into self in a novel fashion. These movements thereby materially reconfigure that portion of the matrix of possibility that subjectivity maps as itself. Through repetition, these are the choreographic trans-actions that begin to impart new pattern to the world, though which we dance a new world into being.

The Fourth Movement: Social Assemblage

In closing, I would like to gesture toward the ways in which the trans-movements I have been describing at the microlevel of individual subjectivity can begin to link to larger, macrolevel political and social assemblages.

It is common, in contemporary queer cultures, to consider trans communities and identities as later additions to previously existing homo and bi communities and identities: we speak of an LGBT community, in that order. Other sequences of assembly, of course, are possible. What might a social movement look like in which trans-related concerns were considered central and initial, rather than peripheral and appended? Rather than enumerate the possibilities, I'll be content, for now, to leave these to your imaginations.

I would like to end with a comment on the recent election of Barack Obama, with its message of change and hope, which provided an inescapable backdrop as I worked to pull my thoughts together for my lecture tonight, and which in some measure informed what I have to say about envisioning a new world, and can serve as something of a template for the kind of trans-movement I envision: one that links the broadest possible constituencies together in a common goal.

In one of my classes this term I taught Judith Butler's essay on Pierre Bourdieu, "Performativity's Social Magic," in which Butler remarked on "the *expropriability* of the dominant, 'authorized' discourse that constitutes one site of its subversive resignification."[10] What happens, they ask,

> when those who have been denied social power to claim "freedom" or "democracy" appropriate those terms from the dominant discourse and rework or resignify those highly cathected terms to rally a political movement? . . . What is the performative power of claiming an entitlement to those terms—"justice," "democracy"—that have been articulated to exclude the ones who now claim that entitlement? What is the performative power of calling for freedom or the end to racism precisely . . . in order to counter the workings of dominant discourse?[11]

In our broader political environment in the United States, we have just witnessed one such subversive expropriation of dominant discourses, and I'll end by soliciting you all toward another such moment. If we are all assemblages, particular knottings of spacetime that give us our particular being, if we all are capable of trans-movements that allow us to assemble ourselves with the world in new ways, how can we all begin moving together in new ways that create conditions in which the political promise of a "freedom of assembly" becomes articulated in viable, life-sustaining ways?

Thank you for your time tonight.

Notes

1. Anthony Wallace, *The Death and Rebirth of the Seneca* (New York: Vintage, 1972).

2. Harry Hay and Will Roscoe, *Radically Gay: Gay Liberation in the Words of Its Founder* (Boston: Beacon Press, 2001), 28–31.

3. Hay and Roscoe, *Radically Gay*, 31.

4. Leslie Feinberg, *Transgender Liberation: A Movement Whose Time Has Come* (New York: World View Forum, 1992).

5. Thomas Hobbes, *Leviathan* (Hamburg: F. Meiner, 1996).

6. Michel Foucault, *The History of Sexuality: Volume 1: An Introduction*, trans. Robert Hurley (New York: Vintage, 1990), 133–59.

7. Foucault, *History of Sexuality*, 139.

8. Foucault, *History of Sexuality*, 139.

9. Jacques Lacan, *Écrits*, trans. Bruce Fink (New York: W. W. Norton & Company, 2006).

10. Judith Butler, "Performativity's Social Magic," in *Bourdieu: A Critical Reader*, ed. Richard Shusterman (Malden, MA: Blackwell, 1999), 123.

11. Butler, "Performativity's Social Magic," 123.

Susan Stryker Reflects on "Ghost Dances: A Trans-Movement Manifesto"

I have a high-risk/high-rewards way of writing: dump a bunch of curiosities, insights, and speculations into my workspace and trust that I will find a way with words to cobble it all together, through an improvisational textual performance, into some lively critical assemblage. Some experiments turn out better than others, and my Kessler Lecture was, in my opinion, among the least successful. A trans art of failure, perhaps, transpiring in full public view, and now, in these pages, for posterity. In other words, I'm happy for the opportunity to offer a postmortem autopsy on "Ghost Dances" (2008).

In this century's first decade, in the aftermath of 9/11, trans studies took its "biopolitical turn," focusing on gender as part of state power's regulatory apparatus for managing security, territory, and population. This set the stage for comparative approaches to minoritization within what Mel Chen would soon call "animacy hierarchies"[1] and Alexander Weheliye would call racializing biopolitical assemblages.[2] How is trans minoritization un/like other forms of socially constructed hierarchies rooted in embodied difference? How can we critically understand embodied difference and specificity in relation to their preconditions of possibility, without resorting to mere analogy or inappropriate appropriation? Those questions hovered in the background of my talk.

The biopolitical turn was, even then, beginning to overlap with an "ontological turn" that came to the fore in the following decade—a sometimes dissonant conjunction of theoretical frameworks that informs the remarkable flourishing of Black trans studies in the past half-decade. At the time of my lecture, Marquis Bey's "the transness of blackness and the blackness of transness" wasn't yet on the horizon,[3] but María Lugones's "coloniality of gender" was,[4] and I was wondering out loud if transness might have something to offer the project of unsettling the biopolitics of settler colonialism, by putting pressure on the signification of the "bios" itself, and the transformation of its meaning in relation to something beyond the biocentric framework of Eurocentric modernity.

That, in turn, led me to reflect on how the Native American Ghost Dance religion had been used and abused in twentieth-century queer (mostly white, mostly gay, mostly Harry Hay) cultural production, historical memory, and people-making, and to use those reflections as a scaffold for a swarm of half-formed thoughts and intentions. To acknowledge the ecological horizon against which all our thinking unfolds. To imagine transness as a hopeful intervention into the anthropic dimension of the Anthropocene. To hold space for collective grief and mourning. To take seriously the notion that transness is a virtual potential immanent in materiality that can manifest into actuality through our actions. To express the felt experience of encountering, through transness, a cosmic liveliness in excess of the existing arrangements of life in this world, and a desire for worlding otherwise. "Ghost Dances" was all that and less, too much and not enough, a pencil sketch for work then yet to come.

Notes

1. Mel Y. Chen, *Animacies: Biopolitics, Racial Mattering, and Queer Affect* (Durham, NC: Duke University Press, 2012).

2. Alexander G. Weheliye, *Habeas Viscus: Racializing Assemblages, Biopolitics, and Black Feminist Theories of the Human* (Durham, NC: Duke University Press, 2014).

3. Marquis Bey, "The Trans*-ness of Blackness, the Blackness of Trans*-ness," *TSQ: Transgender Studies Quarterly* 4, no. 2 (2017): 275–95.

4. María Lugones, "The Coloniality of Gender," *Worlds & Knowledges Otherwise* 2, no. 2 (Spring 2008): 1–17.

THE DAVID R. KESSLER LECTURES 2002–2020

2002   JONATHAN NED KATZ

2003   GAYLE RUBIN

2004   ISAAC JULIEN

2006   ADRIENNE RICH

2007   DOUGLAS CRIMP

2008   SUSAN STRYKER

2009   SARAH SCHULMAN

2010   URVASHI VAID

2012   MARTIN DUBERMAN

2013   CHERYL CLARKE

2014   CATHY J. COHEN

2015   RICHARD FUNG

2016   DEAN SPADE

2017   SARA AHMED

2018   AMBER HOLLIBAUGH

2019   JASBIR K. PUAR

2020   RODERICK A. FERGUSON

Sarah Schulman

Sarah Schulman is the author of more than twenty works of fiction (including *The Cosmopolitans* [2016], *Rat Bohemia* [1995], and *Maggie Terry* [2018]), nonfiction (including *Stagestruck* [1998], *Conflict Is Not Abuse* [2016], *The Gentrification of the Mind* [2012], and *Let the Record Show* [2021]), and theater (*Carson McCullers* [2002], *Manic Flight Reaction* [2005], and more), and the producer and screenwriter of several feature films (*The Owls* [2010], *Mommy Is Coming* [2012], and *United in Anger* [2012], among others). Her writing has appeared in *The New Yorker*, the *New York Times*, *Slate*, and many other outlets. She is professor of English at Northwestern University. The recipient of multiple fellowships from the MacDowell Colony, Yaddo, and the New York Foundation for the Arts, she was presented in 2018 with Publishing Triangle's Bill Whitehead Award. She is also the cofounder of the MIX New York LGBT Experimental Film and Video Festival, and the codirector of the groundbreaking ACT UP Oral History Project. A lifelong New Yorker, she is a longtime activist for queer rights and female empowerment and serves on the advisory board of Jewish Voice for Peace.

Ties That Bind:
Familial Homophobia and
Its Consequences

NOVEMBER 12, 2009

Despite the emphasis on gay marriage and parenthood that has over-whelmed our freedom vision, how gays and lesbians are treated in families is far more influential on the quality of individual lives and the larger social order than how we are treated as families. Tonight, I will try to articulate how and why systems of familial homophobia operate, and more importantly, how they can be changed.

Imagine if a family responded to the coming out of one of its members like this. They discuss as a family their special responsibility to protect her from pressures and cruelties that they themselves will never face. They promise not to exploit or enjoy privileges that she is denied and to commit their family's resources to accessing those privileges for her and other queer people, who they treat like full human beings. And they insist that their gay family member treat other queer people with accountability as well. In their larger family, friendships, workplaces; in their consumption or production of culture; in how they vote and what laws they both support and access, they intervene when queer people are being scapegoated, by directly address-ing the perpetrators.

This is not an impossible scenario. Yet today, families are more likely to tolerate homosexuals—that is, keep us in a position of lesser value—than to learn from us and be elevated by our knowledge. Because of the twisted para-dox of dominant behavior, gay people are being punished within the family structure even though we have not done anything wrong. This punishment has dramatic consequences on both our social experiences and our most trusting, loving sexual relationships.

Now, strangely, I am talking to you in a moment when most people will tell you that things are getting better. The AIDS crisis forced Americans to start the process of acknowledging that gay people exist. Thus, even though there are many institutions today that still pretend that we do not exist, there are other institutions that acknowledge in some form that we do exist. It's a bizarre set of daily contradictions that gay, lesbian, bisexual, and transgender people must balance and internalize. Some television shows have central characters who are homosexual; other television shows convey entire worlds in which homosexuality is never acknowledged. Still others show us only as pathological and predatory. You never know what you're going to find around each corner.

However, the acknowledgment, when it does occur, is often problematic. Does the fact that openly gay people are allowed some rights in some circumstances mean that things are getting better? Or does the fact that so much profound exclusion and distortion pervades have more negative meaning than it did sixty years ago when there was no visible movement? I think it's obvious that deliberately excluding people when you know they exist is a more destructive and sadistic action now than it was in the past when so few of us were known. Knowing queer people, seeing our wish for justice, and still denying us basic legal rights, denying us integration into the public conversation of the culture, and excluding us from authentic mainstream representation is a condition of oppression that should no longer exist. Considering how much work we have done and how enormous our effort to create social transformation has been, we are not where we should be. A change is not the same thing as progress. Don't confuse them. Yes, the ways we are contained are different. The ways we are situated as lesser than are far more sophisticated today than they were when I was eight, sixteen, or twenty-five. But compared to where we should be right now, we are nowhere. We've been bombarded with so many false messages about how much better off we are that we've gotten confused about what we really deserve and what both liberation and equality would actually look like and how truly possible they are. Being niche-marketed a product is not citizenship. It's the end of autonomy, not the beginning.

Now, it is true that there will always be some people for whom monogamous coupling for life is the best option, and gay people on that path should have full legal equality. Of course, many gay people do not equate monogamy and marriage, and just you wait until straight allies figure that one out. But whatever marriage means to anyone should be fully legally protected, obviously. But there is an ideology emerging from our paid leadership positioning the pretense of monogamous life coupling as the best and superior and most desirable way to be gay. Even though straight people vociferously refuse to vote us rights, even with these dire requirements, they are happy to let it become our only visible public image. And because we now believe what corporate America tells us about ourselves, there are some queer people who now negotiate acceptance by their families as long as they get gay married and have children. I have to say I'm appalled by any ideology that encourages women to get married, gay or straight.

This marketing of gay marriage has gotten us off track of thinking critically about the truth of our own condition and how to create radical social change. Very little is known about how our oppression is constructed and its consequences on us. Our reconceptualization of our own destiny has only just begun. And the most progressive impulses in American life— Black Power, feminism, and gay liberation—were rooted in agendas that came from real people's true lived experiences in contrast to the lie of who they were being told they were. But we, LGBT people in the year 2009, are listening to everyone but ourselves. We listen to corporate culture, corporate media, Hollywood, our president, our insipid national organizations, Showtime, and Ellen. We have let all this noise obscure what we are really experiencing. For example, when I look at what I am really experiencing today in the American theater and US publishing, things are worse for authentic work with lesbian protagonists than they have ever been in my lifetime. How can it be that things are getting better if there's not a single lesbian play in the entire American repertoire? In 1992, there were five or six lesbian novels published by mainstream presses every year. Today, it is one every two or three years. When we need them the most, we are dismantling our most effective apparatus: subculture that produces authentic representation of our true experiences, the culture of opposition in which we refuse to be lied to or about, and most importantly, the community relationship, which has historically been our richest and most humanizing creation. If we had lived in privatized family units in 1984 in the way that we are told to do in 2009, we never would have been able to respond so effectively to the AIDS crisis.

Could we rise to the occasion so magnificently today? If you look at our recent track record, now that things are so much better, today we are unable to win anything. This twist, calling a constant state of injustice "progress," gets played out in a number of distorting ways where we pretend that we are accepted when we are not. For example, having a gay character in a book, play, film, or television show falsely codes that work as progressive. Often, it even results in the work winning an award from GLAAD. But if the actual meaning and content of the specific representation is examined, many of these are retrograde. They often portray the gay person as alone, lesser than, a sidekick in the Tonto role, or there to provide an emotional catharsis to make the straight protagonist or viewer a better person. What current cultural representations rarely present are complex human beings with authority and sexuality who are affected by homophobia in addition to their other human experiences—human beings who are protagonists. That type of depth and primacy would force audiences to universalize to gay people, which is part of the equality process. It would also force an acknowledgment of heterosexual cruelty as a constant and daily part of American life.

These oppressive conventions and structures are kept in place by some concrete strategies. One crucial strategy is the use of false accusations to maintain gay people's subordinate status. False accusations are inaccurate and misleading statements about queer people and about homosexuality that force us to live with the burden of a stigma that we don't deserve, and to then pay the emotional and social price of having to prove innocence that should not have to be proven. There is little more demeaning than being forced to prove something that is obvious. And the most typically vulgar, false accusation homosexuals face is that homosexuality is somehow wrong and/or inferior to heterosexuality. This is the typical smoke screen kind of argument—an argument so ridiculous and, in fact, insane, with no basis for justification, that to have to refute it is itself dehumanizing. We know the pattern: perpetrator falsely accuses victim in order to create a smoke screen that obscures the perpetrator's own agency. I say it's a smoke screen because in addition to placing an unwarranted burden of proof on the gay person, it obscures the real issue at hand—namely, the perpetrator's homophobia. Another typically vulgar false accusation is the charge that gay people should be kept away from children. Sadly, gay people have wasted a lot of energy and self-esteem trying to prove how child-friendly we are—even to the point of feeling that we have to have children to be fully human or to be treated as fully human by our family or government. Today, in an act of diminishment, there are even some gay people who use having children as proof that we deserve rights, respect, and representation. This, of course, suggests that a lack of children is a sign that something is wrong with us, that we are dangerous and deserve to be outside of power.

These, of course, are the most obvious and bottom of the barrel false accusations, but there are also many more sophisticated false accusations that are just as damaging. For example: Homosexuals are a special interest group, while heterosexuals are objective and neutral. Homosexuals' feelings are not as important as heterosexuals' feelings. Homosexuals have to prove that they are deserving of privileges that heterosexuals take for granted. Homosexuals should universalize to heterosexuals in order to enjoy representation, but heterosexuals should not have to show any interest outside of their own experience. And finally, the acquisition of rights and social change for gay people is our responsibility alone.

Now, ironically, if gay people were treated equitably, the perpetrator would have the burden of proof. If they were made to account for their false accusations, it would be a lot harder to pull them off. Unfortunately, the system is twisted so that the cruelty looks normative and regular, and the desire to address and overturn it looks strange. As Bertolt Brecht said, "As crimes pile up, they become invisible."[1] Resistance gets falsely pegged as the inappropriate behavior because it results in discomfort for the perpetrator. Ironically, it is often not the fact that a gay person is being scapegoated that makes people angry, but the assertion that the perpetrator should have to be accountable that infuriates them. It's not the awful truth that upsets people, but the telling of the truth that gets construed as the problem. Now, while false accusation is a strategy of homophobia, shunning is its tool of enforcement. Shunning is when people are cut out, excluded from participating in conversations, communities, social structures, are not allowed any say about how they are treated, cannot speak or speak back. Shunning is a form of mental cruelty that is designed to pretend that the victim does not exist and has never existed. It's practiced by religious groups, but it's also practiced by the arts and entertainment industry, the legal system, family structures, economic systems, and social conventions that pathologize and isolate gay people by not acknowledging or representing our experiences. And by extension, by irresponsible individuals who don't want to be accountable for the undeserved pain they are inflicting on others—others who don't have the power to create consequences. In short, shunning is an active form of harassment.

Because gay people are ritually shunned in all aspects of social life, dehumanizing us through shunning appears normative and regular. For example, not mentioning ACT UP in a twentieth-century US history class may seem normal because it happens every day, everywhere. But it is not normal.

It is an assault on your inherent right to be acknowledged as part of the history of your own country. That you cannot walk into a major American theater and see a multicharacter play with a lesbian protagonist is true every second of every day. And yet, producers act like the state of censorship is fine and appropriate, and that objecting makes us the problem instead of them. Shunning is the most common form of homophobia and the easiest to carry out. While shunning seems passive, it can be practiced daily without effort. Its effects are dramatically active. In fact, being on the receiving end of shunning is to be aggressively assaulted on a daily basis by the lie that your life doesn't matter. It is an exclusion system that can be manifested by making a gay family member uncomfortable while welcoming a straight family member, deciding that only one lesbian teacher can be hired in a department at a time, or that no novels with lesbian protagonists are going to be published by major publishing houses. It extends to a lover deciding that she has no accountability to her partner because there's no sign in the culture that anyone cares if she does or not. Shunning is the removal of living, breathing people from recognition and representation in daily life, a refusal to engage, recognize, negotiate, communicate. It is an exclusion from the conversation.

What makes gay people so ideal as a scapegoat in a family is that they are there alone. Sometimes no one else inside the family is like them or identifies with them. They become a projection screen, the dumping ground for everyone else's inadequacies and resentments. No one is watching. No one from outside the family will intervene because of the wrongheaded perception that family matters are private and untouchable. The family structure and its untouchability predominates. Then, because gay people do not have the full support of their families, they in turn become an ideal social scapegoat. For in society, just as in the family, no one will intervene when it comes to queers. Society will not intervene in the family, and the family will not intervene in the society. It's a dialogic relationship of oppression. Imagine what would have happened if the families of the five hundred thousand Americans who died of AIDS had demanded justice. We would not have a global AIDS crisis today.

Familial homophobia is something that gay people discuss with each other with a regular daily urgency, and yet it has not made it into the public discourse. In some ways it is our most important story, and so it is worth trying to understand why it has remained a secret. I had to coin the phrase "familial homophobia" because this most common of experiences was so suppressed as a subject that it did not even have a name. Emotionally, the pain is often unbearable, inarticulable, and the solution eludes us. We often speak to each other about it in shorthand. One gay person can meet another in an elevator, make a passing quip about his family, and be perfectly understood. And we also blame each other for it. As distorted as it is for gay people to blame each other for straight people's homophobia, this common projection shows how embedded this conversation is in our relationships with each other.

Being heard in opposition to this construction is very difficult, because the more integrity queer people have about their sexuality, the less access they have to mainstream discourse. Since straight people and most queer people learn what they learn from the mainstream, the message will never be allowed to reach them, and when it does, it's often watered down, which makes it more easily dismissible. After all, straight people also have problems with their families and so, often, cannot differentiate between the degree. It's the old "white people have problems too" syndrome, in which the dominant person is unable to imagine the burdens of prejudice on top of regular human difficulty. The problem is that we have to talk about the family in a loud and clear way, because the family is the place where most people are first instructed in homophobia. The family is where most gay people experience homophobia for the first time, and it is where most straight people learn to use homophobia to elevate themselves within the family politic, which is the model for the broader social politic. This has made family relationships into the primary source of pain and diminishment in the lives of many gay people. We pay an enormously debilitating price for familial homophobia at the same time that heterosexuals within the family learn how to and have the choice to use it as currency. And yet the perpetuation of homophobic practice is repeatedly blamed on gay people themselves. We are depicted as being inherently deserving of punishment, even though in actuality we have not done anything wrong. After all, homophobia is exclusively a product of heterosexual culture. It is not caused by gay people or gay culture.

Now, sadly, this paradigm confuses gay people ourselves. When we insist on inclusion, full recognition, and access to process, we can get internally pathologized as militants, activists, and stalkers, even by each other. The dangerous exclusion is naturalized as benign, and the desire for accountability is falsely seen as a threat, when it is really life-enhancing. To this day, productive individual actions and group efforts that make positive contributions to the culture are still seen as compromising the right to exclude. Yes, perpetrators often claim exclusion and shunning as their right. Straight people have long argued that it is their right to not rent apartments, give jobs, or serve meals to gay people if they don't want to. The courts of New York City agree that it is the right of the St. Patrick's Day Parade in 2009 to still exclude gay people. Families have felt unfettered in excluding or shunning gay family members because they know that no one will make them be accountable. And imitatively, gay people have felt free to exclude their partners from custody of the children they raised together, simply because the courts don't recognize the partners' rights. And they don't expect their queer friends to intervene. Many gay people take advantage of the lack of systems of accountability to exclude lovers and friends from emotional material processes that straight people can access through the legal system and the social expectations of others.

Because of supremacy ideology masquerading as reality, we are often brainwashed into seeing familial homophobia as our own individual problem, instead of an institution of cruelty on a continuum from the government to your boyfriend. We often see it within the specificities of our own families, and we often have to enter those families and deal with these problems alone. But why should we? Why shouldn't we call up each other's families and tell them that the person they are hurting matters to us? That this person has a context and other people who are accountable to her? Right now, homophobic families face no consequences for their actions. Why shouldn't we create consequences? Honestly, almost anyone can do almost anything to a gay person in this culture and not be made accountable, because no one creates a consequence. This is why we need third-party intervention. History shows that shunned people are dependent on the intervention of third parties to support their own acts of resistance. Men had to vote for women to get the vote. White people have to participate for racism to be dismantled. Straight family members have a moral obligation to intervene when gay people are scapegoated in their families. Men must force the American theater to produce women. Gay people have to be made accountable for the way we treat each other. It's time for the shunning of queers to stop being experienced as a personal problem and start to be understood as a cultural crisis—originating in our families, enforced by the government and arts and entertainment industries, and landing in our relationships with each other.

In other words, I'm imagining a transformed social value in which homophobia is the action worthy of punishment and exclusion, not homosexuality. Where shunning is punished, and resolution praised. Now, this statement is both supremely reasonable and yet completely without social context, because the standard of ethics regarding homophobia in the family has not yet been articulated. Instead of focusing on the homophobia as the subject of inquiry, the great distortion has been to interrogate the origins of homosexuality. Today, there is a national obsession with proving that homosexuality is one thing with one cause, which liberals believe is rooted in a biological deficiency or abnormality and Christians believe is rooted in choice and subject to conversion. In order to develop a vision of how to eradicate homophobia within the family, we must reject completely any framework that maintains homosexuality is the category of deviance that needs to be explained, and instead focus entirely on the origins of and solutions to homophobia. This means focusing on the perpetrators—their motives, consciousness, and actions—for the purpose of creating deterrence necessary for gay people to have healthier emotional lives.

Now, many natural and unavoidable mistakes have been made as the gay liberation movement tried to first grasp, then understand, and then convey the system of cruelty by heterosexuals toward homosexuals. The nature of this cruelty is hard to initially conceptualize because it is simultaneously pervasive, invisible, and deeply painful. The people who are doing it often don't know that they are doing it or pretend that they do not. The repetition and the dailiness make it seem normal. It is very difficult to try to imagine a life without this constant diminishment. And the depths of its consequences coupled with its total lack of justification are alienating to fully realize. The reinscription of these cruelties within our own trusting, loving relationships is difficult to articulate, because there is no place to do so. When reviewing our errors of understatement, they seem innocent, childlike. How sad that so many of our oversimplifications were caused by our love and trust of other human beings, and our consequent inability to understand how they could be so ruthless in exploiting their advantages over us. All of this converges on the question of visibility. Visibility was a construct that the gay and lesbian movement invented to explain and excuse the cruelty we were experiencing. We denied that it was intentional. Instead, we invented the idea that it was an inadvertent consequence of heterosexuals having a lack of information about what we are really like. "If they would discover how we truly are, they would not want to hurt us." And since they were doing everything imaginable, using every social institution to make it impossible for us to be truly seen, we would have to subject ourselves to extreme violation in order to force a cathartic experience for them that would make them better. This process required shock troops of certain stupendously courageous gay and lesbian individuals to come out and be fully subjected to the force of punishment, thereby creating the inevitable social change that we felt would accompany recognition. Some of us forced them to see us, expecting that once they would see us, they would love us. And they'd realize that our disenfranchisement was morally wrong, and they would then join with us in correcting these structures of exclusion, both emotional and social. The plan was that the vanguard homosexuals willing to take the punishment would then make things easier for other less courageous ones looking on from the wings, waiting for this battle to achieve a more equitable field. These others could then enter the process with progressively fewer degrees of loss but filled with recognition for their brave predecessors and what we had done for them.

Looking back at the way we created the issue of visibility as a strategy for change is a painful confrontation with the realization that it was an engagement with magical thinking. We believed that straight people hate and hurt us because they don't know us. If we could have visibility, they would realize that we are fine and would accept us. This theory has been disproven by history. Now, we have enormous visibility, and the hatred and overt campaigns against us ranging from commodification to constitutional amendments to dehumanizingly false representations in popular culture have intensified and become more deliberate. Clearly, ignorance was not the determining factor in what caused homophobia. There is much more volition on the part of the homophobes than we ever imagined.

A second, concurrent theory that we've relied on for many years is the idea that heterosexuals experience a fear of homosexuals. This was the famous phobia. We fantasized that it was rooted both in ignorance but also in some insecurity about their own heterosexuality. Whenever extremely violent behavior emerges, this theory is trotted out again. Repeatedly, our proposal is used against us and reshaped so that gay bashers become repressed homosexuals who cannot accept their own identity. This variation on the Black-on-Black crime theory, in which white people have no role, positions our oppressors as other un-self-acknowledged homosexuals, while the heterosexual majority remains innocent and not responsible.

It seems obvious at this point that neither of these explanations is sufficient. Knowledge of and about homosexuals does not dilute homophobia. It only pushes it into more virulent and, in some cases, more sophisticated modes of containment and justification. Simultaneously, it is clear that the people who benefit from these configurations are not hidden homosexuals, but rather the heterosexual majority. What is most difficult to face but increasingly obvious as gay visibility provokes containment but not equality is that homophobes enjoy feeling superior, rely on the pleasure of enacting their superiority, and go out of their way to resist change that would deflate their sense of supremacy. Homophobia makes heterosexuals feel better about themselves. It's not fear, it's fun. We know from photographs of happy picnicking white families laughing underneath the swinging body of a tortured lynched Black man, or giggly white US soldiers leading naked Iraqis on leashes, or terrified humiliated Jews surrounded by laughing, smiling Nazis, that human beings love being cruel. They enjoy the power and go far beyond social expectation to carry out the kind of cruelty that makes them feel bigger. In short, homophobia is not a phobia at all. It is a pleasure system.

On the bulletin board in a women's center, I noticed a posted saying clipped from a magazine. "Equality is not when the female Einstein gets promoted to assistant professor, but when female mediocrities can climb as quickly as male mediocrities." I thought long and hard about this statement. The first part is recognizable, familiar to any woman of outstanding ability or accomplishment. But the second part increasingly disturbed me. If male mediocrities can move forward, how can female mediocrities join them? By definition, the rapid rise of mediocre men means that caste, not ability, is the measure. Their presence in positions of authority and power are stand-ins for other people of greater ability whose caste profile excludes them for active access. It would be technically impossible for female mediocrities to rise as long as male mediocrities still hold the power. There are just a limited number of places.

Inherent in this conundrum is one of the fundamental problems that keeps us from honestly facing the phenomenon of familial homophobia. This is the problem of a false discourse of tolerance. This discourse states that people who have been unfairly excluded from fully expressing themselves, fully participating in their families—i.e., their societies—can be painlessly included without anyone else's position having to be adjusted. The truth, however, is that there will never be equality for women until male mediocrities can no longer rise. People of color will be able to take their rightful spot only when mediocre whites are removed from power. If success means opportunity at one's level of merit, those now falsely inflated would be removed from the category of successful. This necessary equation, one that no one wants to admit to, reveals the frightening truth. Oppressed people, people unfairly excluded from full participation, cannot have their rightful place until the people who exclude them experience a diminishment of their own access and power. No matter how much we pretend otherwise, one cannot happen without the other. Similarly, gay people will never have a full and fair place in the family structure until straight people have less currency, less entitlement, and less power than they currently hold. In other words, until the family structure is reimagined to serve gay people more and thereby service straight people less. To pretend that straight people can keep all their advantages while gay people can be allowed to access them is preposterous. Gay people's exclusion is predicated on straight people's privileges. Only if they have fewer privileges will there be less exclusion. As history has shown us, when Black people can sit at the front of the bus, more white people have to stand. When jobs open for women, they become more competitive for men. When a woman playwright gets produced, one less man gets to speak. In the attempt to shift from a caste-based system of privilege and access to a democratic family, social world, and workplace, opportunity becomes increasingly based on merit, ability, and appropriateness and less on gender, race, or sexuality—so people whose power resides in oppressive systems get demoted. Once we understand that process, we can have a clearer idea of what is at stake in familial homophobia and what will change by dismantling it. And they realize this, because when you ask them to be accountable, they become enraged. Frankly, I often find that the myth of the angry lesbian, angry woman, angry Black man is really the rage of the dominant culture person being asked to look at themselves realistically. They're so furious that they see the other person's productive, positive action for change as threatening.

Familial homophobia begins at the beginning of the gay person's life. It usually starts as a false set of standards by which the gay person's behaviors and emotions are pathologized. That is, things that are good and true about them are treated as bad and wrong. The gay person has a number of possible reactions to this pathologization, all of which are ultimately punishing and destructive to our lives. We can obscure our homosexuality in order to avoid being punished when we have done nothing wrong, but this is a brutal form of punishment in itself. We can continue to behave as though nothing is happening, while being consistently subjected to diminishment. Or we can object to the distorted behavior of the homophobes in question.

Unfortunately, this last option, which is the most appropriate, is the one that will ultimately cause the most punishment. Homophobia as a system does not tolerate opposition. Gay people are expected to capitulate and to be grateful for crumbs. When they are not, it's seen as even more of an example of how troubled they are, how mentally ill, how maladjusted, bad, angry, and wrong. When the originating action of homophobia has the consequence of making them angry or upset, they get blamed for being angry or upset. And that result gets repositioned as the justification or cause for their oppression. The more they take the noble, responsible, and mature action of resisting homophobia, the more they are viewed as troublesome, inappropriate, and detrimental. The reason that the existence of homophobia and the practice of homophobes are able to render good, honest, caring, productive, dignified people as pathological is because homophobia itself is the pathology. It is an antisocial condition that causes violence and destroys families. It not only makes society punish and exclude people, but it punishes these same people for trying to restore the larger society to sanity. The perpetrators, who are the destructive ones, are described as the neutral standard of behavior, while the people who are not only victimized but have the decency to fight back, the most beautiful model of social responsibility, are described as expendable and undesirable. The final ironic twist is that whenever a situation does arise in which homophobia is pointed to as being socially destructive or personally wrong, the homophobe tends to actually blame his own behavior on gay people themselves. And there are always gay people willing to point the same finger. Gay people have been persuaded that tolerating or being complicit with prejudice in order to be loved is love. It's not. Now, I believe in, am committed to, and am working toward a cultural agreement that homophobia is a social pathology and that society's best interest is served by any program or practice that mitigates homophobia. The family is the best place to start because the family is where people first learn its power. That is why the commitment to eradicating homophobia must begin with the family.

The model I have in mind for the social transformation to a consensus that homophobia is a pathology comes from feminism, and how the conceptualization of rape was transformed in the '70s and '80s in the United States and subsequently globally. While this is still a rape culture, while most rape still goes unpunished, while many men feel rape is a privilege and a right, while rape is still the form of entertainment and the strategy of war, there has been a broad transformation in cultural consensus. In the 1960s in New

York City, you needed a witness to get conviction to a rape case. Today, rape is a crime in the world court. In other words, there is a broad cultural agreement that rape is wrong, and this agreement was achieved by a social movement rooted in human experience. This can be an instructive model for the transformation of social codes around familial homophobia. While we can't always change people's actions or their beliefs, we can change the cultural consensus, which in turn can both influence some people's actions and transform their beliefs while providing more support for victims to resist. The reality is that people with power can never be persuaded to give it up, but they can be forced. Look at the experience of ACT UP—a despised group of people who had no rights and were facing a terminal illness, abandoned by their families and government, joined together and forced this country to change against its will, thereby saving each other's lives. "But you can't change other people," you may cry. Some people will always insist that oppressive behavior is unchangeable. But anyone who has been violated has had their life changed by another human being. It's perpetrators who, we are constantly told, cannot be changed. Not so. As Audre Lorde, who was my college professor at Hunter College, made our class write down in our notebooks, "That you can't fight City Hall is a rumor being spread by City Hall." After all, forty years ago, if people heard a neighbor being beaten by her husband, they were far less likely to intervene or call the police. It was viewed as a private family matter by both the state and civilians. Now people know that they are supposed to call the police, and inherent in that understanding is the belief that the police are supposed to pathologize and interrupt this behavior. This is an enormous cultural transformation. It means that, regarding domestic violence, there is now an authority recognized that is larger than the patriarchal family. The same transformation can occur within the realm of familial homophobia, both for victims and for perpetrators.

When Ronald Reagan was elected president in 1980, he allowed the formerly fringe Christian Right to move their agenda, which was called the Family Protection Act, center stage. This coalition began to push through a wide array of anti-abortion restrictions on local and national levels. One of these efforts was a federal bill called the Human Life Statute, which would have outlawed all abortion and some forms of birth control. Congressional hearings on the bill were chaired by John East, who was North Carolina's co-senator with Jesse Helms. Senator East's hearing prohibited anyone who supported abortion rights from testifying. Me and five other women signed up independently at a forum sponsored by CARASA, the Committee for

Abortion Rights and Against Sterilization Abuse, to do an action inside the hearing. We had never met as a group before. Some of us did not know each other, and some had never been politically active before. We planned our action in the car on the way down to DC. We called ourselves the Women's Liberation Zap Action Brigade. We made hand-drawn signs and pulled them up in newspapers, waited on line, and got into the hearings. This was in the days of live TV and before CNN. We sat in the audience and listened to speaker after speaker endorse the Human Life Statute. Then, when a male doctor testified that a fetus is an astronaut in a uterine spaceship, we couldn't take it anymore. We stood up on our chairs and yelled, "Stop these hearings!" We said, "A woman's life is a human life," and we were arrested by the DC police and charged with disruption of Congress and later brought to trial. We were the lead story on all three network news shows and raised $25,000 in unsolicited ten- and twenty-dollar contributions from people who had seen our action on television. This was before ACT UP, and direct action was a contested tactic, one that eventually led to some of us being thrown out of CARASA the following year. But more to the point of this story, the police officer who arrested me was named Billy Joe Pickett, and in my trial he testified under oath that I had stood up and said, "Ladies should be able to choose." This is fascinating. I said, "A woman's life is a human life," and he heard: "Ladies should be able to choose." I assume that the idea that a woman's life is a human life was so inconceivable to him that he couldn't even hear those words in that order. He could justify putting me in jail if I had said, "Ladies should be able to choose," which is a refutable opinion. But if he was really arresting me for saying that women are human, then he is a different person than he wishes to be. So, in order to not tell the truth about himself, he had to lie about me. That's why straight people lie about us—because they're lying about themselves.

So just to be clear, let me sum up my comments this evening. Here's the sum-up.

Family is the place where all people first learn about homophobia. But for most other conflicts that arise in the family, there is a possibility that the person can find solace or some kind of corrective in the society. In our case, however, the shunning is mirrored in the larger society, with arts and entertainment as the mode of enforcement. To not be represented in a media culture, after all, is to be severely disadvantaged. We can learn from the achievements of the anti-rape movement and the movement against domestic violence that this hall of mirrors of enforcement does not have to continue. But in order to change the paradigm, we have to stop privileging the family. The family does not have the right to shun its gay members, and it is up to the rest of us to intervene to make that clear. That intervention can range from straight family members refusing their privileges, to the gay person's friends talking directly to the family to make them accountable, to homophobic families being court-ordered into treatment the way they currently are for addiction or violence. The idea is to shift the focus from homosexuality to homophobia: to acknowledge that homophobia is the problem, that it is pathological, antisocial, destroys families, and causes violence, and to create consequences for its enforcement.

When I was in fourth grade, we had a poster on the wall with a quotation from Abraham Lincoln: "To sin by silence when they should protest makes cowards of men." Yes, that's true. But it does more than corrupt those who themselves reward perpetrators with silence. It keeps the abuse going and it abandons the victim. Silence is the greatest reward a perpetrator can receive, whether the perpetrator is a family, a government, a publishing company, a theatrical producer, or another gay person who does not want to be accountable. Saying nothing while your friend's family or lover or society or cultural institution shuns and scapegoats them is to participate in the process. Yes, it would be better for you spiritually to tell the truth to the perpetrator, but more importantly her chance for a decent life depends on it.

Thank you for your time.

Notes

1. Bertolt Brecht, *Poems 1913–1956* (New York: Theatre Art Books, 1987), 247.

Sarah Schulman Reflects on "Ties That Bind: Familial Homophobia and Its Consequences"

Well, my decision to confront the personal and social meaning of "familial homophobia" (and to coin the phrase) clearly opened my mind to future, larger constructions. It is here that I see the early roots of my 2016 book *Conflict Is Not Abuse: Overstating Harm, Community Responsibility, and the Duty of Repair.*[1] The homophobic family was my first example of perpetrators positioning themselves as victims, of endangered people being falsely positioned as "dangerous," and the role of negative group bonds in perpetuating deflected projections through unjustified blame. This was the model for later, larger explorations of the role of "false accusations" in justifying injustice and avoiding self-criticism. Most importantly for me, this work was the beginning of what would become a fundamental theme in my fiction, plays, films, and, later, nonfiction: that it is the responsibility of third parties to intervene to disrupt injustice, to encourage people to negotiate and to defend the objects of escalation and shunning. A call to unveil the poisonous role of bystanders in personal, social, and geopolitical injustice. These original foundational ideas later became how I understood HIV criminalization in neoliberal Canada, the Israeli state's persistent justification of brutality against Palestinian people, the distorted claims of police officers when arbitrarily murdering Black people, and the bonding of cliques, communities, nationalities, and religions in a supremacy delusion—in order to avoid self-examination—through the cathartic exclusion and punishment of others. So, this public presentation was a turning point in my thinking that was and continues to be highly creative and productive. And I am grateful for this opportunity to be heard.

Notes

1. Sarah Schulman, *Conflict Is Not Abuse* (Vancouver: Arsenal Pulp Press, 2016).

THE DAVID R. KESSLER LECTURES 2002–2020

2002	JONATHAN NED KATZ
2003	GAYLE RUBIN
2004	ISAAC JULIEN
2006	ADRIENNE RICH
2007	DOUGLAS CRIMP
2008	SUSAN STRYKER
2009	SARAH SCHULMAN
2010	**URVASHI VAID**
2012	MARTIN DUBERMAN
2013	CHERYL CLARKE
2014	CATHY J. COHEN
2015	RICHARD FUNG
2016	DEAN SPADE
2017	SARA AHMED
2018	AMBER HOLLIBAUGH
2019	JASBIR K. PUAR
2020	RODERICK A. FERGUSON

Urvashi Vaid

Urvashi Vaid (1958–2022) was an attorney and organizer whose leadership in the lesbian, gay, bisexual, and transgender (LGBT) and social justice movements spanned legal, advocacy, philanthropic, and grassroots organizations. Vaid was CEO of Vaid Group LLC, which works with social justice innovators, movements, and organizations to address structural inequalities based on sexual orientation, gender identity, race, gender, and economic status.

From 2011 to 2015, Vaid was senior fellow and director of the Engaging Tradition Project at Columbia Law School's Center for Gender and Sexuality Law. Prior to joining Columbia, Vaid was senior fellow at the City University of New York Graduate Center. From 2005 to 2010, Vaid was executive director of the Arcus Foundation, a global funder of LGBT human rights and great ape conservation. She served as deputy director of the Governance and Civil Society Unit of the Ford Foundation from 2001 to 2005. Over a ten-year period, Vaid worked at the National Gay and Lesbian Task Force (now the LGBTQ Task Force), serving as its executive director and director of its think tank, The Policy Institute. As staff attorney at the National Prison Project of the American Civil Liberties Union (ACLU), Vaid initiated the group's work on HIV/AIDS in prisons.

Vaid is the author of *Irresistible Revolution: Confronting Race, Class and the Assumptions of LGBT Politics* (2012) and *Virtual Equality: The Mainstreaming of Lesbian and Gay Liberation* (1995). She coedited, with John D'Emilio and William Turner, an anthology titled *Creating Change: Public Policy, Sexuality, and Civil Rights* (2000).

What Can Brown Do for You?
Race, Sexuality, and the
Future of LGBT Politics

NOVEMBER 18, 2010

I've written at least four different talks before arriving at the one I am actually giving tonight. The first version was so angry it prompted my partner,
Kate, to suggest that I start a version of the "It Gets Better" viral campaign
called "I Get Bitter." In the second version I tried autobiography, but I bored
even myself. Then my inner wonk came out and I wrote a term paper on
racism in America. Finally, I started to say things that reflect the praxis-based
politics to which I tend to gravitate. What I learned along the way is there
are many ways to talk about race, sexuality, and the future of LGBT politics. What follows is just one. Tonight, I want to start with some broad and
frank observations about three things—first, the state of the LGBT movement overall, and the state of racial justice, racial equity, and racial privilege
within the mainstream of that movement. Second, I want to consider why
mainstream LGBT politics remains so absent on racial justice—what makes
it so difficult for the LGBT movement to face race? Third, I'd like to suggest
some principles that could orient a new and more productive course in
addressing racial equity within and outside our communities.

State of the Movement

As the 2010 midterm elections came and went, I found myself thinking
of the memorable opening paragraph from Dickens's *A Tale of Two Cities*:

> It was the best of times, it was the worst of times, it was the age of wisdom,
> it was the age of foolishness, it was the epoch of belief, it was the epoch of
> incredulity, it was the season of Light, it was the season of Darkness, it was
> the spring of hope, it was the winter of despair, we had everything before

us, we had nothing before us, we were all going direct to Heaven, we were all going direct the other way.[1]

This passage describes the perplexing dualism of the present moment—an age of remarkable technological change and human possibility, in which more wealth exists than ever before yet objectives like ending hunger and poverty seem unreachable. We live in an "epoch of belief"—millions upon millions of people fervently embrace their faith traditions filled with absolute certainty that they are on the righteous path. At the same time, we live in an "epoch of incredulity," in which millions of others are so disillusioned and alienated by corruption or fear that they are apathetic. So, in the recent 2010 midterm elections, white Protestant and Catholic voters increased their turnout and voted overwhelmingly for Republicans. Yet overall, according to the Pew Research Center, only 42 percent of eligible voters came to the polls. In 2010, only 20.9 percent of eligible youth aged eighteen to twenty-nine voted, a sharp drop from the 25 percent of youth who voted in the 2006 midterm elections.[2]

It seemed we had everything before us in 2008 when President Obama won. I remember feeling that way in 1992 with Bill Clinton as well, or even in 1968, only to watch that hope turn sour, in 2010, as it did in 1994, or in 1968 when Bobby Kennedy was killed. The merry-go-round of political promises keeps us bobbing up and down with excitement at each revolution, but our enjoyment and engagement in the process leaves us sad at the end of the ride, awake to the fact that we have only gone around in a circle.

A similar dualism—of growth and inertia, progress and stagnation, optimism and frustration—exists today in the LGBT movement. The scale and size of the mainstream LGBT movement remains significant. Recently, the Movement Advancement Project (MAP), a national think tank on the LGBT movement, analyzed the most recent returns of all LGBT-identified nonprofit organizations found on the GuideStar database. In its review, MAP identified 506 LGBT organizations focused on LGBT issues in eight broad categories: community centers, arts and culture, social/recreational, service provision, research, advocacy, issue-based, and legal organizations.[3] These organizations had combined expenses of $500 million. Of this total, more than $225 million was spent on four strategies: advocacy, legal, issue-based, and research-focused groups. For several years, MAP has surveyed forty of the largest LGBT groups, and in 2011 MAP documented the combined budgets of these groups to total more than $143 million, while their actual 2010 revenue was nearly $127 million. These forty organizations employed 879 paid staff and had 704 board members. Our movement is a large infrastructure indeed.

Yet, the LGBT political agenda at the national level, especially before Congress, is stalled. The largest LGBT advocacy organization, the Human Rights Campaign (HRC), which in its fiscal 2011 year had a budget of approximately $38 million and a staff of 179 people, managed to secure full passage and implementation of only one LGBT rights bill in Congress over the past twenty years—the Shepard/Byrd Hate Crimes Prevention Act, passed in October of 2009. The second-largest national LGBT political organization, the National Gay and Lesbian Task Force (NGLTF), with a 2010 budget of $8.3 million and a staff of more than fifty people, seems great at process (managing coalitions, producing trainings and conferences, conducting research, and policy analysis) but unable to turn those into muscular leadership for results. The mainstream gay rights legal movement, still the most successful strategy in the LGBT movement, remains an island unto itself—making its own decisions in small conclaves, rarely consulting in a meaningful way with grassroots activists, limiting participation in key strategic meetings to those who agree with the strategies underway, and rarely coordinating its efforts with political advocates so that a powerful media, educational, and organizing push could be made alongside each major new direction in litigation.

— The anti-gay military policy was repealed, but barriers to transgender participation in the armed forces remain in place, and the military's epidemic levels of violence and sexual harassment of women (and also of significant numbers of men) remains unchallenged by the LGBT mainstream movement.
— The Employment Non-Discrimination Act is not moving, leading some to assert that it will advance if gender identity is removed. It will not, because that obstacle is simply a pretext for a deeper lack of political support in Congress for LGBT equality.
— Immigration equality is also stalled, and with the election of an anti-immigrant Tea Party minority, the chances for comprehensive immigration reform are minimal.
— As basic a measure of progress as the appointment of talented, openly LGBT leaders to key positions in a friendly administration is a goal stymied by hostile and vigorous opposition.

— The gains made during the Obama years have come about for the same reasons as they did during the much more hostile Reagan, Bush I, and Bush II years, through the efforts of a small group of people lobbying behind the scenes within the executive branch—making quiet and significant changes in agency-led actions and regulations at places like the State Department, the Department of Health and Human Services, and the Department of Labor.

Even this is not a complete picture. Because of the inability of the existing larger infrastructures to represent the diverse constituencies and issues that LGBT people face, the movement has spawned a number of even more specialized, single-issue-focused organizations at the national level over the past ten years, each focused on a particular subject or constituency (freedom to marry, health, immigration, military, transgender, family policy, youth, community centers, and even two Republican organizations—because the first was deemed too liberal by the second).

It could be argued that there are at least two movements fighting for LGBT equality and freedom today—one explicitly anti-racist and the other doggedly single-issue. One that is progressive and one that is center-right. One that consists of locally based grassroots advocacy, organizing, and service-oriented groups (Queers for Economic Justice [QEJ], Audre Lorde Project, Sylvia Rivera Law Project [SRLP], FIERCE, Southerners on New Ground, the Community Center movement, the HIV/AIDS organizations, the youth groups, and key public community foundations like Astraea), supported at the national level by the NGLTF, and the other which consists of larger, more national organizations (HRC, ACLU, Lambda Legal, Gay and Lesbian Alliance Against Defamation [GLAAD], National Center for Lesbian Rights [NCLR], the Gay and Lesbian Victory Fund [GLVF], among others). Both movements share a common history, they share institutions, they overlap, they coexist, they cooperate, and at times they compete. But they are not coterminous: their endpoint differs dramatically. And their power to determine the course of queer politics varies as well.

It is my contention, however, that neither of these movements has yet meaningfully tackled structural racism and racial privilege. Neither has made more than a superficial dent in the way racial separation exists in our communities. Neither has convinced the majority of LGBT people who are active in the movement that race is and must be "our" issue.

Indeed, advocates of racial justice in the LGBT movement still find ourselves having to make the case again and again, year after year, about why race matters to the achievement of LGBT equality. Here, for example, is a summary of the "What Can Brown Do for You?" speech, which I have given for two decades. The LGBT movement should work on racial justice, I've argued:

— Because it is a matter of justice, and we are about a fairer society.
— Because we need to reciprocate—so when we ask communities of color to support us around sexuality, we need to show up on issues of race.
— Because there are LGBT people of color in our communities and racism affects us, so our movement must deal with it.
— Because dealing with race is in the mainstream gay community's self-interest and Brown will help us win at the ballot box.

Not only am I tired of having to make this speech, it saddens me that while most of the audiences to whom I have made this presentation have no problem hearing the argument framed as "What can Brown do for LGBT people?" they resist the reverse proposition that the LGBT movement must work on racial justice issues that affect Brown and Black people too. The existence of LGBT people of color is not really considered, nor deemed significant enough to justify engagement with racial justice—something most white gay and lesbian people see as a "diversion" of the LGBT agenda to address race. As a result, race in our movement is seen primarily as an issue of diversity or outreach, not as an issue of equity or fundamental justice that it is our business as a movement to achieve.

The key structural reason why neither branch of the LGBT movements has operationalized its stated intersectional politics is quite simple: the default definition for what "gay" means has been set by, and remains dominated by, the ideas and experiences of those in our communities who are white, and this fact has really not changed in more than fifty years. We have not changed this definition in the policy agendas we promote, in the language the movement uses, and in the representation of our communities at the leadership levels of our organizations. Issues, identities, problems that are not "purely" gay, read as affecting white gay men and women, are always defined outside the scope of "our" LGBT movement. They are dismissed as "nongay" issues, as divisive, as the issues that some "other movement" is more suited to champion. We have our hands full, we are told. We need to single-mindedly focus on one thing: equality based on sexual orientation (and some would add gender identity).

This is an argument that many LGBT liberationists and gay equality–focused activists have made to each other and bought wholesale for decades—without malice, without prejudice—just because there has been an unquestioned assumption that this narrow focus works, that we are getting results because we are making a "gay rights" argument, that this is smart and successful political strategy.

My contention is that this narrow and limited focus is not only causing us to stall our progress toward formal equality, it is leading us to abandon or ignore large parts of our own communities, with the consequence of making us a weaker movement. The gay rights focus was historically needed but is a vestigial burden we need to shed. It leads to an unsuccessful political strategy where we try to win on one issue at a time, it narrows our imagination and vision, it does not serve large numbers of our own people, and it feeds the perception that we are generally privileged and powerful, and not in need of civil equality.

Single-issue gay rights politics are rooted in the interest group approach adopted by most US social movements after the 1950s. It has provided coherence, helped us build infrastructure and visibility, and certainly helped us achieve progress; but it has done so at the expense of people of color, transgender people, the working class, youth, and those who are less empowered in our communities. And its success has reached a limit.

From a broad liberationist agenda, in which LGBT groups marched to end US intervention in El Salvador, in which lesbians led the peace movement and the anti-nuclear movement, in which LGBT people spoke out passionately in support of Black civil rights, and against racist drug and sentencing laws, in which we demanded that government save our lives and that we get our fair share from it, we have become an ever narrower, individual rights movement, where the "freedom" to assert our individual right to marry is argued by some to be the most radical thing we could ever seek.

Issues of reproductive freedom, sexuality and birth control, challenging the patriarchal nuclear family, support for working families, ending violence against women, prison reform, poverty, redistribution—all once critical parts of our LGBT liberation movement's agenda—have disappeared in the national LGBT movement discourse. As these issues have receded in our movement, we have lost our past alliance with the feminist movement, with peace movements, with anti-poverty movements, with the environmental movement, and even with the labor movement. We never had much of an alliance with the civil rights movement. Because we cannot win on our own, weak alliances are a critical obstacle to our movement's ability to enact pro-LGBT policies at every level of government.

The absence of racial justice, economic justice, and gender justice from our national movement's objectives results in the LGBT movement being wrongly seen, even by our allies and certainly by most straight people, as a relatively small, very narrowly focused, largely white, mostly male, and deeply self-interested group of people. Frankly, the LGBT movement rarely, if ever, expends political or financial capital to support so-called "nongay" issues. As a result, we are not regarded as valuable partners to our allies in any coalition that we join; we offer them very little positive help, and we generate powerful anti-gay opposition to boot. It is a measure of their principles that key LGBT allies have not abandoned us despite our absence from their fights, and despite the pressure they sometimes face from constituencies they serve. So, for example, in the late 1980s the Hate Crime Coalition working for passage of the Hate Crime Statistics Act was repeatedly pressured by members of Congress to dump the gay community and move a bill without the provision requiring data collection on sexual orientation. The Coalition resisted, and the Hate Crime Statistics Act passed in 1989. In the past year, the immigrant rights coalition working on comprehensive immigration reform has resisted strong pressure from the Catholic Church to exclude the LGBT permanent partners bill from the comprehensive immigration reform agenda.

Across the country, LGBT rights initiatives have failed precisely because we have not organized to meaningfully engage racial and immigrant communities, nor made our case effectively to working mothers of all colors. We lost Proposition 8 in part because the campaign for our rights did not know how best to organize the people of color communities in California; we simply did not mount an effective organizing campaign in Black and Brown communities. We also lost Prop 8 because we did not organize seriously within progressive religious communities. We lost the judicial election in Iowa because we mounted no broad defense of the notion of an independent and nonpoliticized judiciary, a principle bigger than the pro–marriage equality vote of the judges who adhered to it.

It is in this broad context of the national LGBT movement's ineffectiveness, and the larger increase in racial and economic disparities overall, that we need to look more closely at the LGBT movement's difficulties with claiming racial justice as a central and core concern.

What Are the Obstacles to the LGBT Movement Addressing Race?

What challenges does the LGBT movement confront in addressing race? While I will focus on resistance to the inclusion of racial equity as a core mainstream LGBT movement demand, and the impact this resistance has on our movement, it is important to acknowledge that parts of the LGBT movement are working for racial justice. These efforts are largely the work of the queer people of color or progressive LGBT groups I've mentioned already, as well as a handful of nongay progressive groups (like Applied Research Center [ARC], Center for Community Change, Highlander Center, Opportunity Agenda). Groundbreaking work is being done by grassroots progressive groups in arenas like criminal justice and prison systems reform, welfare organizing, homelessness, housing, youth development and leadership, immigrant rights, transgender rights, detention of immigrants, and public schools. Creative work is also underway to strengthen investment in LGBT people of color (POC) organizations (Funders for Lesbian and Gay Issues' Campaign for Racial Equity) and to build POC leadership (The Pipeline Project). Fascinating potential exists in the global LGBT movement for linkages across national boundaries, linkages that might illuminate ways that the US movement's framing of gender identity is more limited than that of activists in, for example, Nepal or Africa.

A 2010 report titled *Better Together*, by the Applied Research Center, studied the relationship between racial justice organizations and LGBT communities and throws more doubt on the notion of the allegedly unsurpassable homophobia in communities of color when it details that the majority of groups and leaders surveyed in the racial justice movement reported working in support of LGBT rights.[4] The report identifies three key obstacles cited by racial justice organizations to their work on LGBT issues. The biggest barrier identified was a perception pervasive in racial justice organizations that most LGBT people are white and that our movement is not interested in race. Low visibility and weakness of LGBT people of color leaders, and the limited agendas of LGBT organizations, fuels this perception and informs remedial actions that ARC recommends: a call for greater investment in people of color organizations working on both sexuality and race, an increased investment in the development of LGBT POC leaders, and increased investment in media and other outlets that can engage people in communities of color on sexuality.

A second barrier identified by ARC is a lack of understanding about how to apply a sexuality lens to racial justice issues. Allies still need to understand that LGBT people are parts of various communities, and that LGBT people are affected in particular ways by issues seen primarily through a racial lens (e.g., police violence, homelessness, immigration, prison and incarceration, schools and harassment, to name a few).

A third barrier identified was the fear of community resistance (both actual and perceived) from within communities of color. Interviewees cited fear of religious organizations' reaction to working on LGBT issues, fear of causing internal divisions in racial communities, and a lack of demand for work on LGBT rights coming from inside communities of color.

All the above-named challenges reveal additional and possible work for the LGBT movement, but there is a threshold question that the data begs: What explains the resistance of the mainstream movement to a deeper incorporation of racial justice into the LGBT agenda?

In an excellent two-part series on the racism of liberals and progressives, author and white anti-racist activist Tim Wise provides helpful insights to answer this question. Wise discusses several mechanisms he believes allow liberals and progressives to avoid taking up racial justice and allow them to "reinforce the notion that persons of color are less important, their concerns less central to the larger justice cause, and that ultimately they are to be viewed as inferior junior partners in the movement for social change."[5] Each of these mechanisms of avoidance is one I have experienced within the LGBT movement. They are (1) "colorblindness," (2) "color-muteness," and (3) "white privilege." Wise also identifies a fourth mechanism he calls "class reductionism," or the notion that it is economics more than racism that needs to be addressed. In the LGBT movement, this operates primarily as "class denial"—we act as if all of our people are upper middle class. Let me talk in turn about these challenges.

Not Seeing Race

Tim Wise describes "well-intended but destructive colorblindness" as one of the mechanisms by which the progressive left marginalizes racial justice and fails to address race.[6] The post-racial concept known as "colorblindness" has been promoted by neoconservatives as representing Dr. King's ultimate dream. Certainly Dr. King envisioned a day when color would not matter, but merit would. However, to claim that color does not matter in this moment is to ignore how racially biased outcomes arise out of the structure of our social, economic, and daily lives—not just because of intentional and malicious racial prejudice.

There is a perverse way in which the election of a Black man has made the expression of racism even more permissible—assertions rooted in age-old bias are now simply and hotly defended as not racist, but just comments on the president as a leader. The very people who do and say the most white supremacist things—like Glenn Beck or Rush Limbaugh or Karl Rove—vigorously deny the charge of racism. Race-based prejudice is all over the Tea Party and the Republican Party's skillful exploitation of lies, like the assertion that Barack Obama is a Muslim, Obama is un-American, Obama was not born in the US, Obama takes care of his own (read: Black people), Obama does not get or care about ordinary (read: white) Americans, he is secretly other than what he claims. Yet, these undercurrents, even when repeated by candidates for office, are treated by the media as if they were fringe elements, instead of shown for what they are—an effective tool deployed by Rove and other Republican tacticians to undermine the President's support among independents.

President Obama was elected despite the country's racism, not because we had transcended it. Indeed, an Associated Press (AP) poll in September of 2008 found that "more than a third of all white Democrats and independents . . . agreed with at least one negative adjective about blacks"—adjectives like "violent," "boastful," "complaining," "lazy," and "irresponsible."[7] What, after all, does a writer like Peggy Noonan mean when she says that "at the heart of . . . [President Obama's] descent [in recent polls] was the inability of the President to understand how the majority of Americans were thinking."[8] The word "white" before the term "Americans" is simply understood.

Ironically, race and racism have become the hate that dares not speak its name, while sexuality and homophobia has become the love shouted from every media outlet, championed by corporations, the subject of music and video by every superstar, and the new cause célèbre among liberals.

The pretense of "colorblindness" in our communities allows for these and other forms of conscious and unconscious racism to be asserted and actually operates to maintain racial exclusivity in our spaces. A clear example of how "colorblind" policies can lead to colorful outcomes is evident in a look at the racial composition of the leadership of the national LGBT movement's key organizations. When I started organizing in the movement, the staffs of LGBT organizations were small and generally not diverse. But within them, there was a lot of conversation about the urgent need for racial representation. Most feminist and LGBT groups had specific targets they set for the number of people of color they wanted on their boards. The National LGBT Rights marches on Washington in 1979, 1987, and 1993 set high targets for racial representation (and these were soundly derided at the time as bad quotas by the gay right wing). As a result of this critique, national organizations have backed away from setting formal targets for the prioritization for representation that they give to people of color on boards and staffs. The data speak for themselves. Board and staff representation of women and people of color remain low. So, for example, MAP's 2011 *National LGBT Movement Report* detailed that 32 percent of staff of national advocacy organizations and 25 percent of board members were people of color, while 48 percent of staff and 40 percent of board members were women; 3 percent of staff and 2 percent of board were reported to be transgender. Within LGBT community centers (of sixty-five centers surveyed), 47 percent of staff and 16 percent of the boards were people of color. Board representation of people of color within LGBT movement groups appears to be slightly better than board diversity within nonprofits in general: a large 2007 study of nonprofits by the Urban Institute found 14 percent of boards to be nonwhite. While it would appear that, numerically, the racial diversity on the staffs of LGBT organizations in general is good, it is hard to know how many of the queer and transgender people of color in these organizations have management or senior leadership roles. Certainly, very few queer and transgender leaders of color are the heads of non-race-based or non-trans-based organizations in the mainstream movement. Of the forty national LGBT movement advocacy organizations surveyed by MAP in 2011, only two had CEOs who were people of color, and both ran queer race-focused groups.

What should we make of this weak diversity at the board and CEO level? Outside the LGBT movement, after all, there are strong and brilliant leaders of color who are LGBT, running multimillion-dollar organizations. There are powerful and successful professionals, lawyers, businesspeople, academics, political figures, and artists—all of whom could be tapped to be board members. Yet, every organization will tell you it is having a hard time doing its "outreach." I think the reason has everything to do with a lack of specific commitment to racial inclusion, with the lack of focus of LGBT organizations on issues that matter to people of color, and with the low comfort-level of existing board members, donors, influencers, and decision-makers in our movement with a racially diverse group of peers.

Leadership is promoted through networks—through social capital or relationships as well as through the influence of economic capital. LGBT people of color do not have social capital with existing board members of many of our institutions because we live in racially and generationally segregated social worlds. This is why, I think, it is very difficult for persons of color to be selected as CEOs for a non–racially focused organization—it generally requires a campaign to convince a board that the candidate can raise money from and command the respect of the less diverse donor and member base of our organizations. I would not have become the head of NGLTF in 1989 without such a campaign. I banked on the social capital and leverage of a vast network of grassroots allies and colleagues in the movement, who lobbied the NGLTF board on my behalf through phone calls and letters.

It is my experience that many white leaders in our communities are not as comfortable with the voice, leadership, and political orientation of LGBT leaders of color, and even less so when those individuals come from anything but the middle or upper middle class. I can see this in my own experience, and I can see this in the experience of other strong queer and transgender leaders of color, like Graciela Sanchez, Sharon Day, Joo-Hyun Kang, Rickke Mananzala, Carmen Vázquez, or the amazing Phill Wilson. Strong leaders of color are generally found running racial and economic justice–focused groups. We are not often given opportunities to step out of these roles and be seen as broad leaders—capable of representing an entire movement.

When I was appointed head of NGLTF in 1989, a prominent donor called the Task Force offices and said to a development director there that he could not believe the Task Force board had hired that radical woman who was "practically a nigger." More than once, I have had people, primarily white gay activists, question my claim of being a person of color; as one colleague noted, I was "practically white." Brown is an intermediate state that occupies a different place in the American racial consciousness—but after 9/11 and the past decade of anti-immigrant bashing, Brown and Black are both more stigmatized than I imagined they would be twenty years ago.

Over the years, I have experienced viscerally the awkwardness and discomfort of some male donors because I am a woman; an awkwardness that increases when I do anything that reminds them I am also not white. My girlfriend, for example, always loves me to wear kurta pajamas or saris to LGBT formal dress events, but my experience in them is uncomfortable—not just because I am more used to wearing jeans, but also because I already feel so highly conspicuous in the largely white and largely male gatherings I attend regularly, and wearing Indian clothes makes me feel even more so. My discomfort has been confirmed on more than one occasion, where well-meaning colleagues have joked that I am "going native" or "putting out the Kinte cloth" on occasions when I have worn Indian clothes.

Throughout my time in the movement, I have raised issues of racism (and sexism), economic equality, and privilege—with very mixed response. Sometimes I have succeeded in creating innovative new programs to impact racial disparities in our communities; at other times I have had my suggestions ignored and ideas marginalized. Some doors were opened to me because I was a woman of color and the movement wanted "representation"; others were not opened far enough, or simply never pointed out. Yet I have succeeded—in large measure because of the class privilege that my overeducation gives me, and the social capital that I have cultivated and that also comes from being successful and being backed by people with money and resources.

But I never deluded myself into believing that my success proved anything more than the exception to the general experience of most of my colleagues—which is that so many major donors are most comfortable giving to people like themselves, that women and POC have a hard time raising funds in our community of donors, that any honest executive director or board chair will tell you that they try to hire at least one cute white guy to help out with their development departments, that making people in the middle, upper-middle, and wealthy classes in the LGBT movement comfortable is critical to one's success as a leader. The funder community will need to take a good look at itself and will need significant education if we are to reorient the LGBT movement toward new issues and leadership.

Not Talking about Race

A second mechanism to perpetuate avoidance of race Tim Wise identifies is "color-muteness," which he defines as "a tendency among many on the white liberal-left to neither see nor give voice to race and racism as central issues in our communities and the institutions where we operate."[9] The LGBT movement's muteness with regard to race is made shocking not only by the significant number of people in our own communities who are queer and transgender people of color, but also by the pervasive and overwhelming evidence of race-based disparities which show the US to be a deeply divided society in which race, gender, and class operate to produce starkly different options for similarly situated people.

Structural racism operates, even where "individual" racism is less vivid. The media- and education-oriented think tank The Opportunity Agenda releases many useful reports on the state of economic and cultural justice based on race, gender, and economic status, including an annual *State of Opportunity Report*, which synthesizes a wide set of data to show the status of progress toward fair treatment and equal opportunity in a wide range of arenas in life (income, housing, education, criminal justice, and civic participation, among others). The data show significant race, gender, and ethnicity gaps in these areas:

— The gender wage gap for women remained high, with women earning 76.8 percent of what men earned. The numbers by race are worse: 67.4 percent for African American women and 57.4 percent for Latinas. The wage gaps between African Americans and whites and between Latinos and whites overall increased.

— The dropout rate for African Americans was 1.6 percent higher than the rate for whites in 2007.

— African Americans experienced a poverty rate of 24.7 percent as of 2009 and the Latino rate was 23.3 percent, while the white poverty rate was 8.6 percent.

— Immigrant incarceration increased by 11 percent between 2006 and 2007.

— African American male incarceration claims one in three Black men; by one measure, more than 60 percent of all African American men born after 1965 have spent time in prison.

— Disparities in sentencing lead to an overwhelmingly high representation of people of color on death row—of the 3,220 prisoners on death row, 42 percent are African American and 12 percent are Latino.[10]

Widespread racial disparities exist in every arena—health care access, infant mortality, educational access and completion, criminal justice prosecution and sentencing, homeownership, college completion, wages, and many other objective measures of equal opportunity. And economic disparities are widening—with the middle class of all colors shrinking and being hurt most by the policies of the past thirty years (post-Reagan).

Muteness about the interrelationship of race and racism to all of the issues on the LGBT agenda is the norm, even when the connections are so clear. So, for example, during the Clinton years, the NGLTF Policy Institute and grassroots people of color–led groups, like Southerners on New Ground (SONG) and the Audre Lorde Project (ALP), were among the few LGBT organizations to engage with the welfare reform fight, arguing against the destructive impact of these so-called reforms on poor women and children, and pointing out the blatant heterosexism of the policies. In the present marriage battle, few if any connections are made to the way that a focus on marriage equality has dramatically narrowed a larger and more diverse family policy agenda that once was an LGBT movement staple, an agenda that would also benefit a large number of people of color who do not live in "traditional families."

These critiques have been made by scholars like Dean Spade, Kenyon Farrow, the late Paula Ettelbrick, Roderick A. Ferguson, David Eng, Jasbir K. Puar, Nancy Polikoff, among others, and by a number of progressive grassroots organizations like AgainstEquality.org and Queers for Economic Justice. These writers have all urged the movement not to rely solely on marriage equality as the index for family protection in the LGBT community, not to tie the receipt of benefits to marital status, and instead, to build a family protection agenda that includes a larger number of diverse families (for example, an estimated 5.7 million grandparents live with their grandchildren and at least 2.4 million are primary providers for their grandkids). Despite these critiques, the LGBT mainstream movement's family recognition agenda has narrowed drastically since the 1990s.

National LGBT organizations also do not prioritize issues that queer and transgender people of color say are important to them. Until 1997, when the Policy Institute of NGLTF started its Racial and Economic Justice Initiative (REJI) under my direction, there was no dedicated, full-time, substantive project on racial and economic justice at any LGBT national organization. Today, there are still very few. MAP's detailed review of the forty largest LGBT organizations revealed that although several of the sixteen advocacy groups it surveyed named "Issues Affecting People of Color" as part of their program priorities, the actual content of these efforts primarily involved "outreach" to include or diversify the membership of the organizations themselves.[11] These national groups reported little substantive or programmatic work on racial justice issues.

A number of recent surveys have shown that LGBT people of color prioritize policy issues differently than white LGBT people, but queer and transgender people of color have not had the voice or power to elevate their priorities onto the policy agendas of the mainstream movement. HRC conducted a survey of 727 LGBT POC, and also convened nine focus groups over 2007–2008, to research the priorities and experiences of LGBT people of color who were interacting with the LGBT movement. The overall issues that these respondents identified as most important to them were, in order: affordable health care (89%), jobs and the economy (84%), equality for people of all races and ethnicities (83%), prevention and treatment of HIV (80%), and equality for LGBT people (79%). When the survey asked about prioritizing existing LGBT issues, violence and job discrimination were ranked most important (80%); civil unions ranked third at 70 percent; adoption was fourth at 66 percent, and marriage and military inclusion were cited by 60 percent of respondents as very important.[12]

The Arcus Foundation funded national research on African American attitudes toward LGBT issues and white LGBT attitudes toward African Americans. These data reveal issues of common and overlapping concern, including access to jobs, health care access, and education.[13] Zuna Institute's survey of Black lesbians found that a high percentage of respondents had concerns about jobs and financial security, health care, and education—above and often before civil rights issues like marriage and partner protection.[14] The Center for American Progress (CAP) documented LGBT health disparities by race in a report released in December of 2009.[15]

Yet, the issues of generating jobs and financial security, of health care reform, of reduction of violence, and of HIV are not the top four issues for any of the major national LGBT organizations today. Instead, we have developed a system of issue-specific LGBT groups that exist to pick up the slack for particular communities—on immigration, on the military, on family, on health, on HIV/AIDS. While these issue-focused groups are more receptive to applying a racial and class lens, they are still not leaders in making the linkages. The point here is that a key reason for our "color-muteness" in making links to issues of racial justice is not that we don't know what issues to work on, nor that problems facing LGBT people are so radically different from the problems facing communities of color that our movement cannot address them coherently. No indeed. The real issue is the absence of leadership on the part of the white LGBT movement to champion race.

White Privilege

This lack of leadership is tied to the third mechanism Tim Wise names for how liberal groups avoid working on race and racism: "white privilege." Wise describes the concept as the process by which "in our activities, issue framing, outreach and analysis: specifically, the favoring of white perspectives over those of people of color, the co-optation of black and brown suffering to score political points, and the unwillingness to engage race and racism even when they are central to the issue being addressed."[16] Frustration with the unexamined and unquestioned, even if well-intentioned, white privilege within our LGBT movement is what prompted me to attempt this talk. The privileging of white LGBT experience shows up again and again, in ways small and large, visible and hidden. From the wrong analysis of the defeat of Prop 8, which blamed it on African American voters (instead of white Protestants, for example, who were a larger share of the electorate); to the naming of the Shepard/Byrd Hate Crimes Prevention Act, to which James Byrd was added late, and only after pressure from our civil rights allies; to the absence of women of color from the leadership of the military fight despite the fact that they have been discharged in disproportionate numbers—one can see a racial privileging of certain experiences over others.

An example of how white privilege works in our movement is the extent to which a racialized donor base—individuals and institutional—help determine and control the movement's agenda. Overall, the donor base for LGBT movement work is quite small—both in terms of individual and institutional donors. Those who do fund, therefore, have a disproportionate impact. Look at the data: MAP documents that out of the 8.734 million adults estimated to be in the US (a conservative figure culled by the Williams Institute from census data), there are about 281,000 donors who gave $35 or more to the thirty-nine national organizations it surveyed in its 2010 *SAR* report. Of these donors, only 14,750 (or 5%) gave $1,000 or more.[17] While no firm data are available about the racial composition of LGBT movement donors, we can hypothesize based on experience that an overwhelming majority of these individuals are white, a significant majority are male, and the age cohort is generally older. This is also the case of a substantial majority of donors at almost all LGBT fundraising events that cost more than $25.

The generosity of these individuals has helped to build a multifaceted movement and it is to be applauded. Yet, the donors to our movement bear significant responsibility for the lack of focus on racial justice by our research, organizing, and legal and advocacy organization.

There are very few champions of funding for LGBT people of color. Henry van Ameringen [who passed in 2020] was one of very few that has long invested in LGBT people of color organizations; the Astraea Lesbian Foundation for Justice is another; and the Arcus Foundation, which started its racial justice funding program in 2006, has been another leader. However, Funders for Lesbian and Gay Issues (FLGI) found that only $7.8 million of foundation funding for LGBT issues went to organizations and projects serving LGBT POC in 2007.[18] This number increased to $12.6 million in 2008. Fewer than half of all autonomous people of color organizations received foundation funding in 2007, and 75 percent of these groups had budgets under $100,000. As a result, across the country, donors do not offer incentives to organizations to engage in work on racial justice. For example, NGLTF was often told by its donors that they were not interested in funding work on race (like affirmative action or immigration reform). National LGBT organizations that took a stand against the death penalty after the Matthew Shepard murder trial lost donors and board members over their position.

The organizations engaging in work on racial and economic justice in our movement are all grassroots-based, and have been led by innovative groups like SRLP, ALP, FIERCE, Housing Works, and QEJ [which had to disband due to lack of funding], to name a handful. Their challenge in getting a majority-white infrastructure to face white privilege is tough because it depends for its funding on a constituency whose privilege it is questioning. The new engagement of non-LGBT funders, like Ford and OSI, Atlantic, and Marguerite Casey Foundations, should prove useful to the grassroots racial justice movement.

Class Reductionism

A fourth mechanism that Tim Wise identifies as an obstacle to the Left's engagement with issues of structural racism is what he terms "class reductionism"—or the argument that class more than race is the most important thing to focus on. Wise notes that this is an argument that ignores the truth that racial prejudice among the white working class is a key reason why class-focused remedies and movements have failed in the US. Saying that "it's class more than race" is a very interesting response, because it is certainly

true that class and race are linked at times and that economic justice remedies—such as insuring that people make living wages or that communities
of color have access to a great and affordable local health clinic, might actually result in some positive impact regarding racial disparities in wages or
health. But, as Wise notes, "racism affects the lives of people of color quite
apart from the class system. Black and brown folks who are not poor or
working class—indeed those who are upper-middle class and affluent—
are still subjected to discrimination regularly, whether in the housing
market, on the part of police, in schools, in the health care delivery system
and on the job."[19]

This is an interesting point for LGBT people to consider with respect to
our movement, because in truth we don't deal with class much at all—ours
is not a reductionism with regard to class so much as it is a *class denial*. Inside
the LGBT movement we have not developed a policy agenda that comes
out of the needs of low-income, much less poor, LGBT people. Indeed,
there is a significant part of the LGBT community (a full 29%, if we are to
believe national exit polls for those LGB who said they voted Republican in
2010) that votes for an economic agenda that dramatically favors wealthy
people and is extremely antagonistic to the needs of middle-class and poor
people. Again, some in our communities are pursuing an economic justice
agenda, but my critique stands as accurate for the national- and state-level
LGBT political movement.

Until very recently, few data sets have developed a picture of LGBT
communities. The Williams Institute's analysis of US census data allows us to
suggest that at least 25 percent of the LGBT community consists of people
of color, comprised in roughly the same proportion as the representation
of people of color in the broader society. LGBT people of all colors can be
found within this broader picture of income- and race-based disparity. These
and other data gathered by QEJ, NGLTF, and the Zuna Institute provide a
more robust and interesting picture of LGBT communities. Among fascinating data points:

— Gay and lesbian couple families are significantly more likely to be
poor than are heterosexual married couple families. ("24% of lesbians
and bisexual women are poor, compared with only 19% of heterosexual women. At 15%, gay men and bisexual men have poverty rates
equal to those of heterosexual men (13%) in the NSFG [National
Survey of Family Growth]").

— Notably, lesbian couples and their families are much more likely to be poor than heterosexual couples and their families.

— Lesbians over 65 are twice as likely to be poor as heterosexual married couples.

— Children in gay and lesbian couple households have poverty rates twice those of children in heterosexual married couple households. ("One out of every five children under 18 years old living in a same-sex couple family is poor compared to almost one in ten (9.4%) children in different-sex married couples.")

— Within the LGB population, several groups are much more likely to be poor than others. African American people in same-sex couples and same-sex couples who live in rural areas are much more likely to be poor than white or urban same-sex couples.

— While 17.7 percent of different-sex married couples had incomes below 200 percent of the poverty line, 17.4 percent of female same-sex couples and 11 percent of male same-sex couples had such levels of income.[20]

Other data gathered by Queers for Economic Justice, the National Gay and Lesbian Task Force, the C J Huang Foundation, and the Zuna Institute provide a more robust and interesting picture of LGBT communities.[21] Among fascinating data points:

— LGBT youth comprise a large percentage of homeless, poor, and foster care populations. LGBT youth, large numbers of them kids of color, comprise a significant 4–10 percent of the juvenile justice system population in New York State.

— There were more than three million investigations of child abuse done by state welfare agencies in 2004. An estimated 500,000 children live in foster care, and gay and lesbian parents are raising 3 percent of them. Nationwide a disproportionate number of foster children are kids of color.

— Over 20 percent of homeless youth are LGBT, according to several different studies. In New York, more than 40 percent of homeless youth are estimated to be LGBT.

— Analysis of US census data reveals that same-sex couples raising children are more diverse by race than heterosexual couples.

— A detailed analysis of the 2000 US census in California shows that at least 52,000 same-gender couples were raising at least 70,000 children. More than half of all lesbian, gay, and bisexual (LGB) African American, Asian/Pacific Islander, and Latino couples between the ages of twenty-five and fifty-five were raising their own kids (43%, 45%, and 62% respectively) versus 18 percent of white same-gender couples. Across all the racial categories, California's same-gender couples with kids earned less than different-gender married couples with kids ($13,000 less per household).

— When it comes to adoption, gay and lesbian couples are raising 4 percent of all adopted children in the United States. Indeed researchers from the Urban Institute and the Williams Institute who collaborated on this study noted that LGB couples are adopting at a higher rate than single heterosexuals. Yet, the Evan B. Donaldson Adoption Institute did a survey of 307 adoption agencies nationwide in 1999 and 2000 and found that more than one-third would reject a gay or lesbian applicant.

Queers for Economic Justice also summarizes data in two excellent publications.[22] These reports make clear that there is a significant population of LGBT people of all colors who receive social services, depend on public assistance, and would benefit from an expansion of education and advocacy on their behalf before a wide range of nongay and LGBT institutions.

Another aspect of class denial is the gap between people of color who are active in the LGBT movement at the leadership level, like me, and those who are working class and poor. There are many unaddressed class issues among people of color, within and beyond the LGBT community. These class issues produce tension: between African Americans and Asians, between Latino immigrants and African Americans, and within the Black community itself there is a long-standing tension around the Black bourgeoisie and its "politics of respectability"—as Melissa Harris-Perry labeled it at the Facing Race Conference in 2010.[23] To what extent is secondary marginalization of LGBT people within communities of color itself a byproduct of class? Are upper-class LGBT people of color more accepted by the mainstream inside these communities? How does the class allegiance of people like me who have skipped several class levels in my lifetime change our politics, as we move on up? These and a hundred other questions are yet under-discussed and would be provocative indeed to raise inside the relatively narrow circles of the colored elites of the LGBT movement. My point here is that we cannot see race as a problem entirely of the white parts of the LGBT movement. To what extent are those of us who are people of color contributing to the failure to address racial justice, and how does class facilitate or inhibit that effort?

Action Steps to Set a New Course

The poet June Jordan in a speech in 1997 to the National Black Gay and Lesbian Conference said, "I wanted to say political unity based upon sexuality will never achieve lasting, profound victories related to the enlargement of freedom and the broadening of equality of entitlement *unless* political unity based upon sexuality will become a political unity based upon *principles* of freedom and *principles* of equality."[24] Ultimately, this is what an LGBT politics for the future must articulate with regard to race: our shared "principles of freedom and principles of equality."

In this talk I have hinted at three such principles that we must make explicit in the future course of the LGBT movement.

The first is **No Queer Left Behind**. LGBT liberation stands for a change in the lived experience of *all* LGBT people, not just the advancement of rights for some. We must explicitly commit to not leave anyone behind when partial equality is won for some of us. This principle would not only commit donors and institutions to fulfilling equality for those most vulnerable in our communities but would commit the resources that are going to be needed to do the implementation of equality once we have won.

The fact is that the class and racial division in who has power in the LGBT mainstream movement results in *a deficit of democratic accountability*. This deficit arises out of the very success of the political elite in our community as donors to mainstream politics: HRC is one of the largest PACs in the country. The LGBT donor base of the DNC is a carefully cultivated network of major donors who receive special invitations to meet with political leaders, receiving briefings and conference calls, and are cultivated to give even more to elect candidates. And in the past five years I have been a close part of setting up a number of mechanisms for individual donors to exert even more legal and aggressive impact through their political giving on outcomes of political races, ballot initiatives, and legislatures. As a result, a "loose affiliation of millionaires and billionaires" and upper-middle-class professionals like me have become the ones who serve as the gateway to our communities for almost all politicians, corporate elites, and media elites. The average lesbian or gay man, the trans person who is not a major donor, or the bisexual young person who is a homeless-youth advocate—none have the kind of immediate access to assert and register their opinion, as do the wealthier parts of our communities. There are no mechanisms in place for the clients of GMHC, say, or the clients of social service agencies like community centers to register what they would want political donors to say to political leaders in their communities.

The access that donors have—and the fact that most of the major donors and their representatives in our movement are largely white and often men—is significant because our philanthropic and political donors carry with them issues closest to their hearts. If the overall movement's agenda can become broader and more inclusive, a wider range of issues will be carried. But if the agenda is all about the tax and economic interests of wealthy individuals, the access does not help meaningfully improve the lives of ordinary LGBT people.

One consequence of this democracy deficit was raised to me quite thoughtfully by long-time activist Kevin Jennings in a lunch we had several months ago. He said what worried him was the potential disconnect within the LGBT movement between those who think that with marriage equality being achieved, they can see an end point to our movement's work. He worried that gains won by our movement benefit some of us more than others and leave large numbers of our own communities behind. As the privileged parts of our communities—of all colors—win the freedom to live out and queer lives, would they declare victory and stop investing in the movement? Meanwhile the less economically and culturally powerful members of our communities, who still need a movement to fight to get them access to rights, access to services, and access to support could be left behind to fend for themselves.

Why do I believe this scenario is possible? The material conditions of people's lives matter a great deal to their ability to access institutions (think about judicial systems, social service systems, or educational systems); poverty and other forms of privilege affect how people are treated within these systems; and equal rights guaranteed in law are always contingent upon their enforcement—something else that is affected by one's material situation. Outcomes gained by other social movements show us that the achievement of formal equality—though essential and urgently necessary— produces mixed results because of the differences in people's economic and social statuses. For one, equality is not evenly distributed, its realization is affected by one's economic status, race, geographic location, religion, and many other factors. Thus, women's equality actually has resulted in it being very difficult for poor women to get abortions, while wealthy women can access them anytime. Civil rights gains coincided with poor kids of color getting a worse and worse public education while Black urban professionals sent their kids to private schools. In our own history, we saw what happened in the HIV epidemic when some parts of our community, namely the well insured, secured access to life-extending drugs: leading voices declared the "Twilight of AIDS" (in the *Wall Street Journal* and the *New York Times*). Donations to HIV and AIDS service groups dropped dramatically, as did volunteer support. Government support also dropped as constituency pressure decreased (it had primarily been secured because of that pressure). Fourteen years later, the epidemic continues and spreads, uncontrollable and far from over for the poor, the disempowered, and the weakest among us. In an echo of their stance on AIDS, the same neoconservative commentators claim today that when the LGBT movement wins measures like marriage equality, ENDA, military service, and other examples of formal legal rights, our movement can declare an end. I find this view troubling and indefensible and, for this reason, would urge the movement to adopt the clear principle that our movement is not "over" until the weakest among us has seen the benefits of freedom.

The second principle it is time to adopt is that **racial justice is a core LGBT issue**. We need to simply commit to this truth by putting it in the mission statements of our organizations and on the policy agenda of our legal and advocacy movement. I would call on all groups to ensure that a commitment to racial justice is in their missions. This means that once and for all, LGBT would have to grapple with how to broaden their current understanding and definition of what constitutes a "gay" issue:

— Job security is among the top issues of concern raised by LGBT people in poll after poll. Economic anxiety is the legacy the baby boomers have left their successors. Within this context, nondiscrimination is an important but inadequate goal to address the concerns of all classes and races of LGBT people.
— Given our understanding of how race and gender affect economic opportunity, issues of economic equity could rise to the top of LGBT agendas. Extending unemployment benefits, ensuring workforce

development for low-wage LGBT workers, support for ex-offenders to get training and jobs, support for living wage laws, development of microfinance strategies to help US-based low-income entrepreneurs—are all examples of policies that could increase economic security for working LGBT people.

— Choice and reproductive health, access to health care, and ending health care disparities are critical issues for LGBT women and men of all colors, as is HIV/AIDS. These issues must be restored to prominence on the LGBT agenda.

— Similarly, reducing the over-criminalization of certain communities, sentencing reform, support for better treatment of prisoners, and working for an end to rape inside prison affect many LGBT people, and disproportionately affect people of color.

— Defending a robust role for the state in securing economic prosperity for all is a meaningful LGBT issue. A critical part of adding race to our agenda requires of LGBT politics a confrontation with this era's anti-government sentiment; we are ironically a community that needs much more government investment to address many of our biggest challenges. Elder care, youth services, school curriculum teaching tolerance, alternatives to incarceration, affordable housing, mental health services, drug and alcohol programs, HIV prevention, treatment, and care, and support for people facing life-threatening illnesses are just some of the issues that our social services sector works to address.

It has always been a myth perpetuated by those with privilege that success is possible "on one's own" and that the people getting "handouts" from government are undeserving, lazy, poor people who are largely Black or undocumented immigrants. Despite the evidence of massive government supports that helped create the white middle class—the G.I. Bill, Social Security, Medicaid, free education through high school, subsidized public colleges and universities—this myth persists. You can hear it at Tea Party rallies as they claim how tired they are of carrying freeloaders and that these "other" people, namely the poor and most vulnerable, should take care of themselves. The tax cut mania of the moment has never been more than a thinly disguised attempt to shrink the size and social-democratic role of the state. Remember the image of Grover Norquist and Americans for Tax Reform's promise to shrink government and drown it down a bathtub drain? The LGBT movement still has no coherent national approach to these destructive policies; instead there is a new group, GOProud, that enthusiastically embraces such rhetoric; there are conservative Democrats, who favor smaller government (except in the defense or military sectors); and there are liberal advocates who fail to stand up against the estate tax cut, against corporate tax breaks, and against the defense budget's insane escalation. There is much work to be done.

A third principle to which we must commit is **to increase the representation and to enhance the leadership voice for LGBT people of color at decision-making tables**. LGBT institutions and leadership in our movement must reflect the racial and gender composition of our communities. LGBT movement's organizations should set voluntary goals and targets for POC representation on our boards and staff senior teams and hold them accountable annually in a review to insure we make progress toward these targets. LGBT board members and major donors need to have space to have frank conversations with each other about the reasons why they have had difficulty supporting and nurturing leaders of color.

There is a critical need to invest in and provide resources to grassroots organizations and LGBT people of color–oriented programs that are trying to network, nurture, and strengthen leaders who come from underrepresented communities—the Rockwood Leadership Institute, the Center for Progressive Leadership, the Pipeline Project are three examples of such programs. We need programs that reach out to corporate, philanthropic, and academic sites to recruit out and diverse LGBT leaders who might be willing to lead a board or a staff.

Principles are the guidelines that can help set our future course. But action must also be taken. For the LGBT movement to work in a meaningful way on race, some propose that we need to truly reconfigure the definition of which allies we work with, what we work for, and how we work for LGBT freedom. I agree. I also believe that we need significant consolidation and restructuring in our national movement organizations. And we need to take up some new campaigns that actually put into practice our long-held theories that sexuality, race, economic status, disability status, gender, and gender identity and expression are all interconnected.

So, at the US Social Forum, the Queer Caucus—led by FIERCE, ALP, and SONG—led hundreds of LGBT people attending in a participatory process to determine if they would be willing to join forces in nongay campaigns working to achieve specific policy change in education, criminal justice, or health care policies. Queer and trans groups came together to create the Roots Coalition, "a national network of Queer and Trans People of Color (QTPOC) led organizations and collectives engaged in cutting edge multi-issue organizing across progressive movements which has been meeting ever since." We will need to try these kinds of organizing experiments in the future, and the only thing holding us back in doing so are resources.

Here are three experiments I would like to see:

First, I'd like to see our movement consciously and significantly support Latino, African American, or Asian candidates of color who are pro-LGBT at the national and local levels and mobilize the rather significant LGBT vote in midsized cities not known for the coherence of such a vote, in support of pro-LGBT people of color leaders at the state and local level, especially in the South and the Midwest. Cities I would pick would include Milwaukee, St. Paul, Kalamazoo, Columbus, Lexington, Asheville, and Charleston. The goal here would be threefold: (1) to develop new methods of voter mobilization and engagement in cities where the LGBT movement is less developed and visible; (2) to create deeper relationships of trust and reciprocity between a local LGBT community and a local community of color; and (3) to demonstrate that by working together, communities of color and LGBT people can win, even in difficult contexts.

A second experiment might commit the movement to support a race-based ballot initiative in order to mobilize a significant and serious vote as a sign of our commitment to align our political interests with that of racial justice organizations. Such a measure could be an affirmative action initiative, challenging voting rights restrictions, an immigrant rights initiative, a criminal justice initiative, or a schools initiative.

Finally, I would love to see our movement tackle the challenge of making the case for LGBT equality to a wider set of audiences in a particular community to see if we could meaningfully shift public opinion. We have gathered significant data on the attitudes of various segments of each community, including women, old people, young people, African Americans, and Latinos. Can we take the stories and lives of queer people, our families and relationships, out of the context of the reactive anti-gay campaigns that our opponents thrust upon us, and instead plan and pursue a pro-LGBT educational campaign to build more allies and support in particular communities? We talk a lot about public education campaigns, and I am proposing instead an educational organizing campaign designed by and for people of color to talk about discrimination.

Conclusion

The poet June Jordan wrote:

> What is the moral meaning of who we are?
> What do we take personally?
> How do perceived issues propel or diffuse our political commitments?
> I think these questions can only be answered again and again with difficulty.[25]

That's the question we face in this moment of partial fulfillment of LGBT formal equality. The moral meaning of who we are will be determined by our actions: by what we stand for and by whom we stand with.

LGBT identities are mutating, and LGBT politics must as well. The LGBT politics of the future—LGBT politics 3.0—must be a more inclusive, democratically determined, decentralized, and multi-issue politics.

To succeed, it must be a politics that speaks to critical issues like racial and economic equity; gender inequality and justice; the role and value of government in our society; the role and value of the market and economic sector when it is harnessed for socially responsible and sustainable ends, for global justice; and the need to end racial and tribal hatreds and nationalist mindsets arising from a purity-based politics of ethnic superiority. It must be an LGBT politics willing to provide leadership to a wider progressive movement that is desperate for new voices and new energy.

We need an LGBT politics of the future that seeks respect instead of pity, affinity instead of tolerance, connection instead of isolation, and full citizenship on queer terms. A politics that does not need crutches like the biological argument—"we were born this way, so don't hate us"—to assert our moral integrity and win our civil equality; a politics whose goal is to deliver access to equality and social justice, to the "good life," where we are free to be as diverse, nonconforming, and outside of heterosexual structures as we each determine.

Thank you.

Notes

1. Charles Dickens, *A Tale of Two Cities* (New York: Vintage, 2003), 3.

2. Pew Forum on Religion and Public Life, *Religion in the 2010 Elections: A Preliminary Look*, November 3, 2020, http://pewforum.org/Politics-and-Elections/Religion-in-the-2010-Election-A-Preliminary-Look.aspx.

3. Movement Advancement Project (MAP), *2010 Standard Annual Reporting: A Financial and Operating Overview of the Leading Organizations of the LGBT Movement*, November 2010, 7, www.lgbt.map.

4. Applied Research Center (ARC), *Better Together: Research Findings on the Relationship between Racial Justice Organizations and LGBT Communities*, 2010, http://www.arc.org/images/lgbt%20report_091710_final.pdf.

5. Tim Wise, "With Friends Like These, Who Needs Glenn Beck? Racism and White Privilege on the Liberal Left," August 17, 2010, http://www.timwise.org/2010/08/with-friends-like-these-who-needs-glenn-beck-racism-and-white-privilege-on-the-liberal-left/.

6. Wise, "With Friends Like These."

7. Ron Fournier and Trevor Tompson, "Poll: Racial Views Steer Some White Dems Away from Obama," AP–Yahoo News Poll, 2008, formerly available at http://news.yahoo.com/page/election-2008-political-pulse-obama-race, currently visible at http://web.archive.org/web/20081104012721/http://news.yahoo.com/page/election-2008-political-pulse-obama-race.

8. Peggy Noonan, "Obama's Gifts to the GOP," *Wall Street Journal*, November 13, 2010, https://www.wsj.com/articles/SB10001424052748703848204575608453836688106.

9. Wise, "With Friends Like These."

10. The report and data points listed herein were gathered from the Opportunity Agenda's *State of Opportunity 2010* indicators on equality, mobility, redemption, voice, community, and security. These can be accessed at http://opportunityagenda.org/stateofopportunity.

11. MAP, *2010 SAR Report*, 24.

12. Human Rights Campaign, *At the Intersection: Race, Sexual Orientation and Gender*, August 2009, 11–13, http://www.hrc.org/documents/HRC_Equality_Forward_2009.pdf.

13. Donna Victoria and Cornell Belcher, *LGBT Rights and Advocacy: Messaging to the African American Community* (Arcus Foundation, 2010), www.arcusfoundation.org.

14. Zuna Institute, *Black Lesbians Matter*, 2010. Full report at http://zunainstitute.org/2010/research/blm/blacklesbiansmatter.pdf. Executive summary at http://zunainstitute.org/2010/research/blm/ES_blacklesbiansmatter.pdf.

15. Jeff Kreheley, *How to Close the LGBT Health Disparities Gap: Disparities by Race and Ethnicity*, December 2009, http://www.americanprogress.org/issues/2009/12/pdf/lgbt_health_disparities_race.pdf.

16. Wise, "With Friends Like These."

17. MAP, *2010 SAR Report*, 11.

18. Funders for Lesbian and Gay Issues, *Racial Equity Campaign Update*, 2008 and 2009, http://www.lgbtfunders.org/files/RacialEquityCampaignUpdate2008.pdf.

19. Wise, "With Friends Like These."

20. Randy Albelda, M. V. Lee Badgett, Alyssa Schneebaum, and Gary Gates, *Poverty in the GLB Community*, Executive Summary, i–iv (Williams Institute, March 2009).

21. See *Justice for All? A Report on LGBT Youth in the New York Juvenile Justice System*, 2001, 6, http://www.equityproject.org/pdfs/justiceforallreport.pdf; Gary Gates, M. V. Lee Badgett, Jennifer Ehrle Macomber, and Kate Chambers, *Adoption and Foster Care by Gay and Lesbian Parents in the United States* (Williams Institute/Urban Institute, 2007), 7, 11–15, http://escholarship.org/uc/item/2v4528cx#page-7; Brad Sears et al., *Same Sex Couples and Same Sex Couples Raising Children in the US* (Williams Institute, 2005); Gary Gates et al., *Race and Ethnicity of Same-Sex Couples in California* (Williams Institute, 2006), https://williamsinstitute.law.ucla.edu/wp-content/uploads/Race-SS-Couples-CA-Feb-2006.pdf; Bianca D. M. Wilson, *Our Families: Attributes of Bay Area LGBT Parents and Their Children*, Institute for Health Policy Studies, University of California at San Francisco (San Francisco: Our Family Coalition, 2007), http://www.ourfamily.org/our_families_report2007.pdf; Evan B. Donaldson Adoption Institute, *Adoption by Gays and Lesbians: A National Survey*

of Adoption Agency Policies, Practices and Attitudes (October 2003), http://www.adoption-institute.org/whowe/Gay%20and%20Lesbian%20Adoption1.html.

22. *Tidal Wave: LGBT Poverty and Hardship in A Time of Economic Crisis*, http://www.q4ej.org/Documents/qejtidalwave.pdf; and *A Fabulous Attitude: Low Income LGBTNC People Surviving and Thriving on Love, Shelter and Knowledge* (Queers for Economic Justice, 2010), http://www.q4ej.org/Documents/afabulousattitudefinalreport.pdf.

23. See full video of keynote at Facing Race Conference, Chicago, IL, October 2010, http://www.youtube.com/watch?v=49ocDVphfRA.

24. June Jordan, *Affirmative Acts: Political Essays* (New York: Anchor Books, 1998), 177.

25. Jordan, *Affirmative Acts*, 175.

Urvashi Vaid Reflects on "What Can Brown Do for You? Race, Sexuality, and the Future of LGBT Politics"

The movement has changed since I gave this talk in 2010. It's more plural and varied—racially, economically, in gender expression and identity, in people's attempts to transcend gender entirely. There are more openly queer people and LGBTQ+ people of color in the leadership of LGBTQ, racial, and social justice movements—from M4BL, to Color of Change, to Mijente, to the DREAMers, the ACLU, Planned Parenthood affiliates, and labor unions. The LGBTQ Task Force, National Center for Lesbian Rights, GLAAD, and even Human Rights Campaign are led by LGBTQ+ people of color.

The implications of this are multifold:

— Racial justice and the fight for racial equity are increasingly being integrated into the work of LGBTQ movement organizations.
— We no longer have to persuade straight progressives about LGBTQ issues—they are integrated into the Biden-Harris administration.
— Progressive politics is the majority view among LGBTQ people in this country—not the sole view, but the one that is shared by over 75 percent of the community, if not more, on certain noneconomic issues.

Yet, many of the dynamics I outlined in the 2010 talk remain intact and new ones have emerged:

Disparities within the queer community persist based on class, race, geography, gender, and gender identity and expression. Uneven development requires us to focus on racial and economic equality as a central goal.

— 45 percent still live in states with low levels of equality
— 22 percent of LGBT people are living in poverty; 9 percent unemployed (before COVID)
— Trans, Black, and rural poverty is much higher (29% and 26%, respectively)
— 17 percent have a lifetime experience of homelessness

The right-wing enemies we have faced our entire life have also changed. They have mainstreamed like we have. They are represented in large numbers in Congress, have won the White House, dominate Republican-controlled state legislatures, and are present in police and sheriff's departments and in the military.

White nationalism is as strong as it was in the 1800s and 1900s. A Klan-like white supremacist defensiveness (reflected in replacement theory, anti-immigrant politics, anti-Black views), is the new baseline uniting the Republican Party, evangelical right-wing churches, Fox News, and many previously mainstream conservative outlets. The fear of displacement undergirds our time. It is a deep sense of loss, a cultural fear of being erased, displaced, rendered irrelevant, humiliated, and ridiculed that drives nationalist, patriarchal, and racist movements. And even though the loss of economic ground and social status has more to do with macroeconomic policy decisions made, frankly, by white men sitting in boardrooms than it does with Black people protesting police violence or with gay people getting married—even though this economic displacement has harmed middle-class and working-class white, Brown, and Black families alike—it is racial and gender resentment that succeeds while cross-race and class alliances fail.

Critical theory (be it queer feminist or critical race theory) has proved itself to matter. It is so relevant and dangerous that it is being attacked by presidents—from Trump to the president of France and many others around the world. As James Baldwin wrote: "The possibility of liberation which is always real is also always painful, since it involves such an over-hauling of all that gave us our identity."[1]

How do we assert claims for justice and nourish our identities and build bridges? An affirmation of identity with a recognition of a larger community that may not be part of that identity is one of the challenges that faces social justice movements. The writer Anand Giridharadas posed the question as: "Is there a place among the woke for the still-waking?"[2] I think the better question is: Can we persuade people unlike us that our vision of a future is more rewarding and secure for them than the one they are currently pursuing?

Notes

1. James Baldwin, *The Price of the Ticket* (Boston: Beacon Press, 2021), 269.

2. Anand Giridharadas, "What Woke America and Great America Can Learn from Each Other," Huff Post, March 17, 2018, https://www.huffpost.com/entry/opinion-giridharadas-outrage-america_n_5aaa93b6e4b073bd82929695.

Histories of Queer and Trans Activism

FEBRUARY 18, 2021

The first *Queer Then and Now* roundtable discussion was held virtually on February 18, 2021, to highlight some of the pioneers of queer and trans activism. The roundtable features Amber Hollibaugh, Dean Spade, and Urvashi Vaid in conversation with CLAGS board member Shanté Paradigm Smalls. Hollibaugh, Spade, and Vaid discuss the histories of queer and trans activism and think through the implications of those histories for our own troubling moment in time. Honoring the scholar-activist ethos of CLAGS as well as the careers of Hollibaugh, Spade, and Vaid, the roundtable highlights the "now" of queer and trans activism as it connects to queer intellectual counterpublics and communities.

Shanté Paradigm Smalls: Greetings, everyone, and thank you all for joining us. Thinking about past, present, and future, about the histories and the current state of queer and trans activism, thinking about the nuances and the contours of that activism in and around and outside of New York City, from about 2000 to the present—the first question I'd like to ask each panelist is: What are the intersections with queer and trans scholarship that either you have done, or advocacy you have done or read or participated in, and the institution of CLAGS? Finally, what do you see as pressing issues, maybe that are lingering from twenty or so years ago to the present and going forward?

Dean Spade: Thanks so much. I'm so grateful for this panel. I was so excited this is happening. Thank you to all the people who organized it. You know, a chance to just be part of anything with CLAGS is so important to me. CLAGS programming has had such an immense influence on me since I was maybe nineteen. When I was not at all related to academia, CLAGS events were always deeply community events where we were all talking about and thinking about ideas and about the movement—not tied to academic institutions necessarily. That kind of public scholarship is so rare, and universities are so often locked behind paywalls of various kinds. It's deeply meaningful to me. I think many of the most influential critical ideas that I first encountered were through CLAGS and people like Urvashi and Amber, who I met around the same time when we were visiting these CLAGS events together.

When I was preparing for this panel, I was thinking about Urvashi and Amber and when I met them, which is in the mid '90s in New York City, and what that time was like. I was thinking about how the main thing that influenced that time for me was that Rudy Giuliani was mayor of New York City. I was feminist and queer and interested in being political. And I was in the middle of being torn between going and trying to do internships and volunteer at places like Lambda Legal and GLAAD, and then also I was working at A Different Light bookstore and at the bar Meow Mix—even though I wasn't twenty-one. Because back then in New York they didn't ID at anything, which is just a very different deregulated time compared to the lockdown that occurred because of the Giuliani administration. I was encountering a community of people in the sex trades; people who had been a part of AIDS activism for a long time who were not doing that through nonprofits—they were doing work mainly through unpaid grass-roots volunteer-based groups, a lot of whom had been in ACT UP—and who were part of widespread coalitions against Giuliani that were trying to address the way Giuliani's police and fire squads were attacking queer bars like where I worked, to defend street vendors, to oppose more cameras in parks and more policing of public sex. As part of preparing, I went back and read Amber's essay in the book *Policing Public Sex*, which was the coolest book to me at that time. It's a really good book, and Amber has a great essay that's got a title about lesbian fisting that I really recommend.[1]

In this period, I could see this emerging pro-marriage, pro-police, pro-military gay politics, and I also was a part of these groups of people who were against that. And I was learning from people like Amber and Urvashi who had long been pushing a racial and economic justice agenda against this narrow white gay rights agenda that was so insufficient for the times we were already living in then. There was a lot of really exciting work happening along those lines.

That kind of tension really became the general theme of a lot of the work of the rest of my life—the existence of these really distinct two threads of queer and trans liberation work. One was really embracing the systems and institutions that are responsible for the most violence. Like, could we have gay cops, and could we serve in the military? And one was part of long lineages against white supremacy, colonialism, patriarchy, and capitalism. So much of my life has been about trying to articulate and name those distinctions and encourage people to even know that a left queer politics exists, because as the years passed, the conservative agenda—the conservative gay rights agenda, which is sometimes also a lesbian or trans rights agenda—became increasingly corporate-backed and the only visible one. So most people had only encountered that politics, and that was supposed to be what we were all for. We were like, "No, no, we're for housing for all, and health care for all, and the end of war." During that time period, I was also encountering critical race theory for the first time, and I was also encountering the idea of prison and police and border abolition for the first time. All those things were making this soup for me that allowed me to see a queer and trans abolitionist politics that rejects the limits of a civil rights framework that doesn't deliver material transformation for our communities.

And basically, that's what I've been doing for twenty-five years. That was the recipe. As things in many ways just got more intense, as we saw conservative gay and lesbian rights and sometimes trans rights politics become endorsed by corporations—we see the NYPD has rainbow cop cars they drive around on Pride, or the intense pinkwashing strategy of the state of Israel or the pinkwashing of the US military. They only got more sophisticated with that set of what I would consider illusions and masquerades that cover the brutal violence of those institutions. So we've had a lot to stand up against. During these twenty-five years, we also have seen the pitched increase in the crises facing us today. The climate crisis; these ongoing endless brutal wars and US military imperialism around the world; the brutality of sexual violence inside the military. All of this has just increased. The wealth divide that is specifically gendered and racialized, the extreme growth of the criminal punishment system as the supposed solution to everything in our lives, the increasing growth of immigration enforcement. The crises that we were worried about then are still with us, but actually they're a lot scarier. We've seen growing movements that push back on that—the climate justice movement. I was thinking about the Occupy moment that really named the wealth divide—that idea had not been mainstreamed before, and Occupy mainstreamed it. The movement to abolish ICE. There are so many movements—the abolition movement—that are so much more visible now than they were at that time.

I think, also, that I lived through the mainstreaming of things I wouldn't have known would mainstream, like the trans tipping point. I could never have known in 2002 when I was starting SRLP [Sylvia Rivera Law Project] that we were going to have trans celebrities and that trans people were going to be on TV shows—and all the limits of that, because mainstreaming is always about presenting the digestible, palatable version of our communities and making it seem like the problem has been resolved when it hasn't. It's rarely about actually changing the conditions on the ground for super vulnerable people in those communities. And we've seen the mainstreaming of criminal justice reform, which I didn't know was going to happen in my lifetime. Nobody in philanthropy wanted to talk about people who were in prisons in the early 2000s. But now we have all these horrible, limited reforms that are being proposed from elites—whether they're legislators in our states or in think tanks. We didn't know what would be picked up from the kind of radical work we were doing, and we also didn't know how it would become twisted as it gets picked up by elites.

And where are we now? I think that we're facing crises. They're intense—the level of heartbreak and terror I have about people right now in Texas who don't have water. And so many other crises that people are facing. Our loved ones in prison facing COVID. So many things that are right on the surface right now. All the people sleeping outside. For me, that has really pushed me, and I think particularly for the last four years, the Trump presidency pushed me to want to further popularize the idea of mutual aid, so that's what my recent book is about and a lot of what I have been talking about publicly. We need to, on the ground, support each other's survival right now, because the answer is not coming from elites. And I think that is even more important right now when we're facing a Biden administration that in every way is indicating that it is committed to the oil and gas industry, to ongoing US imperialist warfare. And they're pinkwashing it—they're like, "We're going to appoint a trans person to something and a gay person to something." It's so important right now for our communities to say: "Not in our name. That's not what we stand for. We are not satisfied by that. We refuse this kind of shallow politics of representation that has been consistently offered to us by the Clinton administration, the Obama administration, and certainly by the Biden administration." And just really living with the reality of the immensity of the crises we're facing.

I think a lot about the movement slogan "We're all we've got and we're all we need." The real task now is to mobilize more and more and more of us, both to get at the root causes of the things we're facing and to support each other to survive while we do. I think that's how I see the current moment.

So much of what queer and trans people have always been good at, in all our different moments of so many crises, is just taking care of each other.

Amber Hollibaugh: I want to start by saying that I think the moment that we find ourselves in is really terrifying. I think that it's a time of extraordinary approval of a kind of violence that was always in place but not considered normative. Proud Boys and Oath Keepers and militia have been around for longer than I can name, but their ability to be seen as credible voices that represent any part of this country is, to me, a really frightening and terrifying kind of politics that I think is very difficult to confront directly and stay alive. Dean and Urvashi and I come out of different earlier moments of political activism, when it was often very complicated to be who we were because we were poor, queer, working-class, of color, trans. It was complicated in those earlier moments to find any words to represent the kinds of politics that I think we had, though one of the things that was different is that there was an assumption that LGBTQ politics was radical, not mainstream.

There was an enormous tension between the radical voices that were fighting to hold on to something that was more embedded in radical social change than just simply wanting to have a place at the table, regardless of what the table looked like. In earlier times in the queer movement—or the lesbian and gay movement, as it was called—it was assumed that you had a radical vision, that you were going to take on capitalism, that that wasn't against a queer identity. You weren't balancing one against the other. One of the things that I think is very difficult now is what you were talking about, Dean: that people can find a very narrow, normative understanding of LGBTQ people and movements—gay pride and a television show—but no understanding of a deeper and richer kind of analysis that's embedded in Black Lives Matter and radical climate change and disability work and all the rest of the movements that we're a part of.

I think that, to me, one of the things that's the most disturbing from when I was coming out and was trying to think about queerness in the context of being a Marxist is that from that time on, it mattered to me that the movement have class politics. That we talk about the differences that exist between us, and that we talk about the economics of queerness—of the difference between being a homeless queer person and going to a fancy gay resort and having plenty of money when you got back from that vacation. The politics of class has been an endless struggle to keep in place—in terms of economic justice that is a queer issue. And that isn't an imposition of one thing over the other, it's a vision through which to see the possibility of LGBTQ politics. It can be something embedded in that.

The other piece that I would name is sexuality and the erotic, the extraordinary power of desire, and how much in the beginning of the movement we were accused of only being about desire, and how much in order to mainstream the movement we were willing to give up about our sexuality or how explicit we were in our sexuality when we were being public as queer people. The number of times that I was told not to bring up sexuality when I was doing a speech in a place that was considered traditional was kind of endless. And it wasn't simply straight places. It was often also places that were worried that the question of a politics of desire would impact in a negative way a donor base. We didn't have a "donor base" in the beginning of the movement. We were broke—that's how everybody was. But once you had a donor base, you had class politics. And so, you had to understand or at least be prepared to deal with the impact of talking about desire and class in the context of normalizing homosexuality and queer politics.

It has meant, I think, that we have lost much of what is the most vibrant in queer life, because we have not known how to create and embed queerness in working-class and poor communities. That has not been the priority—regardless of what it might have been for any of us individually—but as a movement, we have not been able to do that. HIV and AIDS was another one of those places that cut us down at the knees, and which we were brave enough and fearless enough to take on even in the midst of the kind of death and dying that we were confronting. I feel really proud to have been a queer activist from the time I came out and moved forward, because, I think, our movement has not simply been resilient. It's been provocative and necessary, and we have not been willing to say that we would step aside or hide the importance of queerness in the context of all the other issues that confront all of us in trying to do social change.

For any of us that have stayed radical and moved forward, we have been lucky enough—I feel like I've been lucky enough—to see new generations of queer activism. That has been a remarkable gift that I feel I helped create, but which I now feel that I see as a reflection of the possibility of our future, because folks really do refuse to give up before they get what they really need. And as long as we are creating movements that engage with that, I think we're doing something that is fundamentally important. The question is, to me, how do we insist that our movements have vision, take on the possibility of dreaming, and take on the possibility of asking for what is otherwise inconceivable as part of liberation?

Urvashi Vaid: Thank you so much, Shanté. And thank you, Dean and Amber, for this opportunity to continue the conversation that we've been having for decades in our political work. I've learned so much from you, and I wanted to start by echoing what Dean said about how meaningful it is to be in this dialogue, in this larger circle of people. One of the things about CLAGS that I always loved was that who is in the room is as amazing as who is on stage. Always, always, always. You went to a CLAGS event, and you were looking around going, "Oh, yeah, look! There's John D'Emilio, or there's Alison Bechdel, or there's this activist I worked with at the demo last week." All these people showed up. I love that about CLAGS. And I love that about who is here. I can't shout out to everybody I know, but it is so nice to see you. So many people who are tuned in who really have so much to say about everything that we're talking about and who have taught me a lot. So, I want to acknowledge that.

Thirty-five years ago, when CLAGS was founded, I was working on prisoners' rights at the ACLU National Prison Project, suing prisons in my day job. In my evening job, I was volunteering with dozens of organizations, in DC and before that, in Boston. And those organizations—Road Work, or Allston-Brighton Green Light Safe House Project, or Lesbians United in Non-Nuclear Action, or *Gay Community News*, or Lesbian Mobilization Force—gave me a lot of grounding in anti-racist, progressive, feminist queer politics. Along with the work that I did in my "job" jobs, I went to law school to have the possibility of having some income I could earn for the rest of my life. Even though I don't practice law and I haven't since I worked at the Prison Project, it was a class choice for security. I left the Prison Project in '86 to start working at the National Gay Task Force, as it was called then. It quickly became the National Gay and Lesbian Task Force, and today it's the National LGBTQ Task Force.

I share that history because so much has happened in thirty-five years, so much in my life and so much in all of our lives and so much in our movement. I want to start by appreciating CLAGS for those thirty-five years of incredible scholarship and support for so many students, so many activists, so many scholars.

So, I have several thoughts to kick off the conversation. The first has been alluded to by my colleagues here: truly, the queer movement has changed dramatically from the movement I walked into, to what it is and where it is and what it's doing today. The amazing positive parts of the change have been that it's more plural and varied than ever. It's racially, economically, and gender diverse. It's conscious of that. It is. It may not act on it, but it's conscious of that. While mainstream America is struggling with gender equity on boards, we're struggling with trans inclusion in different ways and have proceeded on that a lot.

I think the biggest change in the movement is that queer people have started, and are in the leadership of, multiple progressive movements. The movement is not the gay, lesbian, bisexual, transgender, plus, intersex movement alone. It is Black Lives Matter, which was started by queer people, embraces queer people, and is led across the country by queer and straight and every kind of people. It is the abolition movement, which was kicked off and is still led by a lot of queer people—and especially BIPOC [Black, Indigenous, and People of Color]. It's Color of Change. It's Mijente, it's the immigrant rights movement, it's DREAMers. It's the ACLU, run by a queer Latino man. It's Highlander Center, a mainstream southern institution run by Ash [Ash-Lee Woodard Henderson], who is amazing. It's Planned Parenthood affiliates around the country. It's racial justice groups and reproductive justice groups. It's the two biggest labor unions, AFT and SEIU, run by out dykes. Out. They happen to be dykes, they're labor leaders for decades. And I think that's really fantastic. It's the dream that I had when I was younger—because you always knew that there were these phenomenal queer people in every movement, but they weren't able to lead, or they didn't think they were able to lead because they were queer. So, I think the movement has changed because it's expanded in this amazing way. We used to argue about, "Are we the left wing of the gay movement or are we the gay wing of the Left?" back in the day when it was gay and Left. Remember those arguments, Amber? I had them a lot with Eric Rofes, may he rest in peace—rest in power. Eric would be like, "Well, when you get to the Task Force, we were trying to be the Left of the gay—we were trying to build a Left in the LGBTQ movement." And I said, "That's right. But we also want to push that Left, which is so frozen and turgid, to be more about racism, misogyny, and queerness, and not just white economic interests." Which the old Left was, to be honest. So now I think it's not that argument anymore. We are the Left. I'll claim it—but with an asterisk. Because we're the Left, but we don't have an ideology. We have identities; we don't have ideology.

The second point I want to make is that while we have changed, so have the right-wing enemies we face. They have mainstreamed, like we have. They have taken over Republican parties. The Michigan QuackAnon Republican Party, the Texas Republican Party—remember the takeover in 1992, the very conscious takeover by Ralph Reed. After the Robertson run for president, Reed came up with the plan of integrating the evangelical Right into the infrastructure of the Republican Party in a formal way—they had not been. And he did it. Very good organizing. The '70s, '80s, '90s, aughts, '10s, and '20s—if not '30s, '40s, '50s, and '60s before that—have always had a right wing—you know, the anti-communist Right. And queer people have been its targets forever, from eons ago to today. But what has changed is this kind of coalescing of the Right. I learned to think about the right wing, and I think obsessively about the right wing. My personal mission is no longer the one I had thirty-five years ago. My mission then was queer liberation. My mission today is: defeat the right wing culturally and politically—it has been for about the past decade. And I'm doing a terrible job.

White nationalism is as strong as it was in the 1800s and 1900s, if not stronger. It's enormously dangerous, as we all see. And it derives from a really interesting contradiction that we have to grapple with—the reaction that we're facing is because we're upending traditions and old identities. We are displacing peoples: comfort zones, and their old statuses, and their old roles in society. So when they march around saying, "You will not replace us," in some ways I understand what they're saying, because I want that same old white power displaced. And I love everybody running around trying to say, "Don't call us 'cancel culture.'" Well, actually, there's a lot of the culture I want to cancel, if you want to put it that way. I wouldn't put it that way. I would call it "transform the culture"; I would call it "take the best and leave the rest culture." But if you want to say "cancel," yeah! I want to cancel racism and bigotry; I want to cancel misogyny and violence. So, bring it. I think we're too tepid in our appeasement of these arguments by the Right.

There's a whole bunch of stuff I wanted to say about the Right. Time is short. But I think the enemies we face have changed. They are more powerful. They're mainstream, they're more sophisticated, they're using the tools we use. What the Republican Party figured out long ago is that the mobilization of racial resentment is more effective than the positive ideal of cross-racial class alliance. We've not been able to achieve cross-racial class alliance as effectively as they have been able to do the wedge thing. That's one of our challenges.

The third thing that I wanted to put in the mix, because it's CLAGS: theory matters. I think the last thirty-five years have shown that theory matters. It's dangerous—the president of France thinks that the most dangerous thing facing France is critical race theory and race identity politics. They're attacking that because they don't want to deal with French racism and because they're invested in the idea of universalism—which critical theory, critical race theory, feminist theory has debunked or complicated for decades. It's fascinating. That, to me, is a real vivid example of "theory matters."

Then there's the negative one, which is the QAnon theory. Conspiracy theory matters. It's resonating with people. Why is it resonating with people? What is it? Theory gives us analytics and ways to understand the world, gives us insights, and at its best is a kind of poetry. I love theory, even when I don't understand it. And I don't understand a lot of it. I really don't. I read it, I reread it. I try to pull out ideas. It's turned my hair white. But I respect it, because I think what it's trying to make and create are frameworks and stories through which we can understand history and the future and the present.

Theory, to me, is interesting also because of the concept of praxis. I live in the practice of theory. I want to experiment in the practice, and that's where I love, and I live. Theory matters. It's shown itself to matter. It's an interesting question about what ways queer theory matters. In my book group we're reading *Poor Queer Studies* [2020] by Matt Brim,[2] which is a critique of queer theory from a class perspective, and I really appreciate it and I appreciate him for that book—it's given me a lot to think about.

The fourth point I want to make is that disparities within the queer community really exist in huge ways. We have uneven development toward liberation. Disparities exist, as we know, on class, race, geography, gender, ability, gender identity, expression, nonbinary, sexuality. There's a lot of unevenness in how people are experiencing this moment of "freedom," and space. And you can't deny that we've created space. There's more space to be queer in a public way, in a family way, in a work way, in a political way, than there was fifty years ago, even forty years ago. For me, remembering the '70s and '80s—when I was part of queer movement, or feminist movement that was aligned with queer movement—it was a different kind of space than it is today. And I respect that, but we have uneven development when 45 percent of us still live in states with low to negative levels of formal legal equality, much less true freedom or equity; a quarter of queer people live below the poverty line; 9 percent were unemployed before COVID, and now trans, Black, and rural poverty rates are much higher; 27 percent experience food insecurity, according to a recent study of people in LA; 53 percent were on food stamps; 17 percent experience homelessness in their lifetimes; and we have seen large numbers of trans adults and even cisgender queer sexual minority adults homeless in the past year. And on and on. We still have mixed data, and we could argue about data, but I think it's valuable because it paints a picture and takes snapshots. And the snapshots tell you: uneven development, lots of work to do (local, state, national) in a different way than the movement is working on it.

A footnote: I love Dean's work on mutual aid.[3] It's so helpful. It really is a good primer to help me and others understand how to plug into this movement. I think the mutual aid movement is a real response to this uneven, unequal situation that we're talking about. It's a practice-based, praxis-based response.

I've always been struck by James Baldwin's line in the essay "The Dangerous Road Before Martin Luther King," collected in *The Price of the Ticket*. This little line: "The possibility of liberation which is always real is also always painful, since it involves such an overhauling of all that gave us our identity."[4] *The possibility of liberation is real and painful because it involves such an overhauling of all that gives us our identity.* Early on in my activist life, I had a pretty political, legal definition of what that meant. I didn't take into account that liberation required a transformation of myself—I learned that along the way. That it might require me giving up aspects of identity or tradition that I really clung to, that I liked. That to be liberated, that to be in another space, where you're not living in structural racist and structural sexist and structural classist mindsets, requires a transformation that I don't know that I fully made. I struggle with it, but I really believe in it. I believe in liberation, still. And I think that it requires something more than identity, than the identity that I so proudly developed for myself as a dyke, for example. It's a different thing that creates space, because liberation, in my view of it, encompasses the people who hate me. The world I want will never be the world of me alone, me and my friends and comrades. It will be full of these people who are incredibly difficult. So how do I account for that?

Shanté Paradigm Smalls: Thank you all so much. This is great because it moves us right into the second question I want to ask. Today is Audre Lorde's birthday, it would have been her eighty-seventh birthday, and also Toni Morrison's, it would have been her ninetieth birthday. I was recently watching Marlon Riggs's *Tongues Untied*, and it was making me think about the relationship of queerness and transness to plague, poverty, to mutual aid, to organizing on the ground in the late twentieth to early twenty-first centuries. I'm wondering what your thoughts are about the links, connections, or disconnections between HIV/AIDS activisms, lesbian cancer activism, and other disability studies and COVID? And I think the question of COVID is really expansive, because we really don't know how it will affect people—their ability status is going to change, their economic status is going to change, because of COVID and other kinds of plagues. So, I was wondering your thoughts on some of the longer history of activism and plague within LGBTQIA communities.

Urvashi Vaid: I was having a conversation today with a cancer doctor. You know, I'm dealing with cancer. And I said to him, I'm really struck by how there isn't activism around cancer in the same way that there was around HIV, and around COVID either. I can understand some of the reasons, but we were reflecting on the fact that cancer and COVID engage a large segment of the population, but there hasn't been an uprising around the lack of access to vaccines for people with life-threatening illnesses or people with disabilities and their caregivers. All the uneven access. And then with cancer, which I've been contending with for many years, I've asked myself, "Why am I not more engaged?" I've been engaged in fits and starts. I don't really have a good answer for it except that I think when you're facing illness, your focus becomes just getting through it, and organizing takes a side seat. You're organizing yourself to get to the doctor, you're organizing your meds. But that didn't happen with HIV. We had . . . I mean, that was a formative movement for me, and I really appreciate the scholarship and work that's coming out. Sarah Schulman's book is going to be out about ACT UP New York, which is amazing, based on all these interviews she and Jim [Hubbard] did.[5] I'm curious what you think, Dean and Amber, whether you agree about the curious difference there, and why it's been so different?

Amber Hollibaugh: To me the obvious marker is that HIV was so stigmatized and so politicized from the outside. Not from our own community but from the outside. And in all the ways there was hatred around sexuality and around racial difference and Haitians—you know, it was the Four *H*'s [Haitians, Homosexuals, Hemophiliacs, and Heroin users]. There was no way to respond to HIV without it being a political response, even if that's not how you saw it yourself, because you were up against institutions which basically were more than willing to let you die. I don't think that's true around cancer or COVID. Then you're talking about class and race, about who has access, who gets a drug. Are they too old to get from their building to a vaccination site? But HIV and AIDS was just a complete set of hatreds that were mobilized, and which underscored mythologies around queer people, people of color, and sex workers. There wasn't a way to do this piece but not do that piece. You had to have a collective response to have any response. With COVID and cancer, it seems to me it's been very individualized, and people live in that isolation. While people may be a part of a community, there isn't a collective political understanding of change in relation to illness.

HIV—maybe because it also came closer to gay liberation and to our understanding of that—was embedded in a lot of fury around sexuality and being blamed. And I think it shifted. I actually was shocked—I was thinking today about how remarkable it was that we didn't lose the movement when HIV happened. I mean, I just assumed that everybody would fade because they didn't want to be connected to HIV and AIDS, and therefore they'd go back in the closet if they'd ever come out of it. Instead, people came roaring out of the kinds of places that they had lived in response to it. And it was a remarkable thing. It created an agenda that was framed through feminist medical understanding but was deeply embedded in sexuality and the refusal to give up desire. To me, it was really a remarkable thing.

I don't think COVID—I mean, COVID has funny pieces where people are afraid that they might get it if they stand too close to you, which reminded me of all the mosquito things about HIV. If you got bit by a mosquito and the mosquito had been out in Cherry Grove, could you get HIV?

I wonder whether there may become a real angry movement because COVID is so inequitable in terms of treatment and survival. I think it may take longer, but I wonder whether that's really going to happen. I don't know. Dean, what do you think?

Dean Spade: Listening to you both, it's making me think about a couple things. One, the period you're talking about of '80s and '90s HIV/AIDS activism is much closer in time to the really transformative movements of the '60s, '70s, early '80s. There's been a huge backlash to all the tactics of those movements in all these years since, and as we get further and further from them, we've seen a deeper hold in nonprofitization that tells us to silo our issues. Cancer for survivors here, people fighting for Medicare for All over here, people fighting around climate change and pollution—which gives us cancer—here, and people fighting for racial justice over here. That siloing, I think, is part of what aims to depoliticize things that might be politicized and use a charity model of "come here to get your services" as opposed to an organizing model. All the big movements of the '60s and '70s—feminist movement, Black movement, Puerto Rican movement, all had health initiatives that were free clinics and mobile clinics. I'm thinking about the Young Lords hijacking the mobile X-ray unit of New York City and bringing it to Puerto Rican neighborhoods when people needed testing. There was a level of militancy around health care that I think that early period of HIV/AIDS activism was part of. And the same people were in those groups who had been in the Young Lords and feminist movements and all these spaces. So, I think that's one piece of it, and that word you used, Amber: individualization. We've seen increased hyperindividualization with neoliberal culture; this idea that you're responsible for whether you manage your health care plan well. Did you make right choices as a health care consumer? Instead of a bigger demand—like, hey, we're all in this horrible, brutal, deadly, health-for-profit system.

I also want to pick up on what Shanté said, which I think is so true. It's been profound to see the ableism and ageism in the framing of COVID. Like, it only matters if people die. It doesn't matter if they get sick and disabled from this. And we only count deaths, which we also do with police violence, and it's so messed up. The idea that Trump was supporting, but also many others, that it's fine if the weak die off—this is a deeply eugenicist idea, and very intense when Black death and Native death is so central, in addition to old people death and people with disabilities death in COVID. I think there's a lot for us to do. I do see a lot of disability justice activists talking about that, helping us lift that up, helping us talk in a deep way about: How does this relate to Medicare for All and other efforts that we both want and will be insufficient because medical systems from the government have always been racist and ableist? I think there's a lot of pieces here. But I also think that people are still just dealing with: What does it mean to organize during COVID? We've been doing organizing on a lot of fronts, but there's still a learning curve around how to organize under these conditions. So I think there's even more rage and more energy that we are going to see continue to mobilize people beyond what we have already seen. It's been an incredibly revolutionary and disruptive time in all the best ways, responding to what has been happening. But the economic crisis is just going to get worse, the housing crisis is just going to get worse. COVID's end is not actually in sight, no matter what they want us to believe.

Shanté Paradigm Smalls: I want to go a little deeper into this. We're talking about plague, and many people in the chat are talking about these connections between COVID and AIDS, early years of the plague. But I'm also wondering about the relationship between organizing and aging. Particularly as old queers or old-age queers—sometimes queer and trans culture is really focused on youth. I'm wondering what you all see has evolved in multiple and intersecting justice movements, liberation movements. This relationship between ability, disposability, race, class, and how age begins to shift our own values—what is important to us, but also our value to other people.

Amber Hollibaugh: Let me just flag this to say that the shock of losing Carmen Vázquez, who has been a movement leader through much of the period that the three of us have been talking about today, is one of the pieces about aging. There has been a kind of revolutionary early generation of thinkers and activists, which generated things and created things like CLAGS, and we're going to die. And it's not going to be twenty-five years from now. It's going to be ten or fifteen if we're lucky, and who knows whether we'll still be able to do a [computer] screen. I think that we've never really talked about the aging of leadership in the ways that we should, especially in movements that have often been youth-driven. We have never talked about how we transition leadership in those movements. We don't have a way to talk about how we train people and teach people.

One of the things that is interesting to me about CLAGS is that from the beginning it saw itself as both scholar and activist, because activists were so critical to the intellectual world of queer thinking. I mean, Jonathan Ned Katz is not an academic. And many of the people who have been queer thinkers haven't been scholars. So one of the things that I think is really critical to how we go forward is a question of: How do we create a place for public intellectuals that can engage with the world of ideas without having to be academics? I think that was an early part of CLAGS, but I don't think that we talk about it nearly enough. And yet exactly, Urvashi, what you were talking about: the importance of thinking, of an intellectual world, of the world of ideas, of people engaging with thought that's new and different is fundamental to how you build a movement. If we don't generate structures to create the possibility of intellectual engagement in terms of class and race and sex, we're not going to have leaders that I think we have depended on. Carmen, though she went to college, came out of a working-class background that she never forgot.

I think those things are really critical to what kind of movement we want to build and the issues we need to take on structurally to try and figure out how to generate the possibility of an intellectual life that doesn't depend on going to college.

Shanté Paradigm Smalls: Thank you so much for that, Amber. Thank you for speaking Carmen's name. I had the pleasure of working with her and knowing her many, many years ago when I was a young thing at the Gay Center.

I want to turn to some of the questions, and maybe y'all could think about what I asked or disregard it. A few people have asked about the distinction or the nuance that both Urvashi and Amber mentioned explicitly—and Dean could also speak to this—about the difference between identity and ideology, and how it impacts queer and trans histories and politics. One question was bringing up marriage equality in particular and expanding what that can mean for people living with disabilities and other issues.

Urvashi Vaid: I think of ideology as worldview. It's ideas about what the role of government is, what the nature of the economy should be, the role of family. It's these ideas that we are living in our lives but maybe not consciously articulating as such. We all came up in different ways, being raised or raising ourselves to understand the world through a certain lens. And what we're up against is a fairly cohesive ideology of the right, which is that government should be tiny, tax should be nil, right? The most important institution is the heterosexual nuclear family. Women's role in it should be X. There's a whole kind of worldview that goes along with that. Now, the ideology that I was taught was more textbook, doctrinaire, here's the Red Book, here's Marx, but I think about it in a whole different way. Thomas Piketty's book *Capital and Ideology*: really interesting book and surprisingly accessible for a reader like me who likes more accessible theory: "Inequality is neither economic nor technological; it is ideological and political."[6] It's about politics. Ideologies are politics. That's how I define it.

When I think about our identities, we have really spent a lot of time— and needed to spend a lot of time—articulating who we are, where we come from, what it means to us, what we stand for, how we are in our identities and relationship to the world. And do we have a shared politics across that? What is our political view of the role of government? What are our views of how we would—if we had governing power, how would we use it? How would we deploy resources to people in the COVID crisis if we were in charge as queer people? Fully in charge—not just giving advice to the Biden administration. Those kinds of questions interest me because when you start to ask it that way you realize, well, some of us would be libertarian. We don't want more taxes. There's a good 30 percent—25 to 30 percent of the LGBTQ vote votes Republican and has since the '90s, according to exit polls.

Amber Hollibaugh: How could that be? I'm sorry! I'm thinking: Who the hell are you!?

Urvashi Vaid: Their worldview is such that they think economics—that's what they believe in. I'm interested in that discussion. Because as much as I'm interested in creating spaces for and respecting the flourishing of our identities and the plurality of who we are, that is who we are. People live in their identities, but we will win through politics. That's what I think. Dean, what do you think?

Dean Spade: I think it's interesting, Urvashi, that you came up in a moment where you were like, the people are reading the Little Red Book.[7] There was a certain period, I think, in an activist onboarding moment prior to mine, that was really about distinctions in, like, very specific factions, honestly. I came into politics in a moment that was totally about identity. And yet I was having the experience I think Amber described earlier—that so many queer and trans people have—where I was like, wait, politics is being done in my name, but it doesn't feel like it's about me. It was 1996, they were doing welfare reform and immigration reform. I was like, all this stuff affects my own family that I grew up in. All the big gay organizations, when I interned for them, were like, we don't do that stuff. And I was like, what? So many people have these stories.

Part of the reason we have some of the cool kinds of identity politics we have—really, I learned from Black lesbian critique, which was tired of the fake universalism of particular ways that "Black" would be claimed, or "woman" would be claimed, that would leave out Black lesbians consistently. So, we've done this important work of being like: no, these identities matter. But the neoliberal move says: just have your identity and try to get represented and try to get someone like you on TV or in the legislature. And then we're satisfied, and don't you guys want to become cops and don't you want to become soldiers?

For me that period I was talking about, that anti-Giuliani period, was a period of sharpening and learning the tools of what it meant that I was an anti-capitalist, anti-racist, anti-war feminist entering queer and trans politics. And for me today, I just think about José Muñoz. I'm thinking about this conversation I had in one of his classrooms: What is the good life? And much of the debate is often what we imagined. The marriage debate imagined gay rich people who could keep their taxes together and have each other's health care. It didn't imagine the kinds of queer and trans people that we've all spent our lives fighting for and being.

I do want to distinguish—Urvashi, I know you agree with me on this. I think both the Right and the Left, our entire lives—Democrats, Republicans, whatever, they're all to the right—they all have agreed on a giant state that is a security state, and a border, and they're happy to spend tons of government money. But on what is the question. And today the conversation in the activist communities I'm in is often a conversation about the role of the state, period. People are talking about things like border and prison abolition. We're talking about abolishing the United States. You don't have a nation-state if you don't have a border and prison. That's what the nation-state is: police, surveillance. That is what the contemporary nation-state is. So we're having really big debates about: What if we didn't imagine the state keeping us safe—which in the United States is a capitalist, extractive, white supremacist, colonial state? What if we imagined what else would keep us safe? What is safety in terms of our health care? What is safety in terms of how we care for elders? What is safety in terms of when interpersonal violence happens in our communities? And we're rejecting the idea that more criminal laws will make us safer, or a stronger border, or a different way to have the state give out a few crumbs just to who it thinks is deserving. This is really a debate about anarchism—that's very strong in the movements I'm in, which—we're a mixed group of people. Some, like me, are anarchists, and some are hoping that a better social welfare state will be formed. This is a great conversation. We can have this conversation while we deliver water to people, while we build organizations. It's very hands-on. That, to me, is the place where ideology is being debated right now.

Shanté Paradigm Smalls: Thank you, Dean, for making me think. I've been reading the Combahee River Collective Statement, which is about politics that emerge from Black lesbian identities, and not the system, but what they called interlocking systems of oppression at that point in 1977.[8]

Someone in the [Zoom] chat said she was really inspired by what Amber said about the power to be part of a movement; this person feels really honored to join a lineage of lesbian history and organizing. So, do you have or remember the moment, place, sound, touch, or person that led you to understand yourself as a part of a history and a lineage? A queer lineage, a lesbian lineage, a trans lineage . . . And how have you held on to that memory and kept it with you?

Urvashi Vaid: You brought up the Combahee River Collective, and they were formative to me. Meeting Demita Frazier in 1977, who was a member of the Collective who came and talked at my college. We invited her because we had found the statement in some bookstore. And it totally changed my life, because it gave me a framework and a political perspective to organize from. That was a transformational experience—meeting Barbara Smith, Demita Frazier, in the '70s.

Amber Hollibaugh: I would go back much earlier than the movement activism that I've been a part of for fifty years. I went to a ruling-class school for my last year in high school. And I got in there because they needed more people from California, you know, what can I tell you? Anyway, I was failing. I had never done the kind of work that was done there. I didn't know anything about an intellectual world. But my history teacher—who I was wildly thankful for, because he was a working-class guy who was a teacher and talked about class—I went to him when I was failing and I said, "I'm failing and I don't know why." And he said, "You were never meant to be here." Then he gave me *The Communist Manifesto*. And he was serious. His parents ran a hot dog stand in New London, Connecticut, and were part of a Communist Party cell. He said, you need to read this. It utterly transformed my life, and it meant, when I came back—when I then was trying to figure out what I wanted to do—I ended up joining the Student Nonviolent Coordinating Committee and doing civil rights work. So, I think that you never can quite tell what it is that is going to bring one of those moments. If I hadn't gotten *The Communist Manifesto* in my high school senior class and been blown away, I don't know what my relationship to the Left would have been, or to activism.

Dean Spade: I'll be brief, I'm just remembering right now what it was like for me to be in that organization Sex Panic! in the mid '90s in New York

City. It was really intergenerational, and there were these older queers who would sometimes be like, "Oh, you guys, this is the thing we've been doing forever." They would tell us history, in the midst of just talking about how to do something, and it was a sense of belonging from older people that I never had where I grew up. And that really continued. I just want to say, also, when I was going to go to school, Urvashi gave me her used computer. Like, literally, queers have just taken care of me. I had no parents, nothing, you know. And it's so amazing to think about that.

I also thought about a moment I was arrested in Grand Central for using a bathroom in 2002 and so many community people helped me get out of jail and get the charges dropped. Those moments when the community catches you—and I think even the story Amber just told is that—there's a kind of trust and belonging that is so hard to get for people who are freaks in the best ways.

Shanté Paradigm Smalls: Thank you, all three of you—Dean, Urvashi, Amber. That was really amazing, and thank you for the honor of sitting with you.

Notes

1. Amber Hollibaugh, "Seducing Women into a 'Lifestyle of Vaginal Fisting': Lesbian Sex Gets Virtually Dangerous," in *Policing Public Sex: Queer Politics and the Future of AIDS Activism*, ed. Dangerous Bedfellows (Boston: South End Press, 1996), 321–36.

2. Matt Brim, *Poor Queer Studies: Confronting Elitism in the University* (Durham, NC: Duke University Press, 2020).

3. Dean Spade, *Mutual Aid: Building Solidarity during This Crisis (and the Next)* (New York: Verso, 2020).

4. James Baldwin, *The Price of the Ticket* (Boston: Beacon Press, 2021), 269.

5. Sarah Schulman, *Let the Record Show: A Political History of ACT UP New York, 1987–1993* (New York: Farrar, Straus and Giroux, 2021).

6. Thomas Piketty, *Capital and Ideology*, trans. Arthur Goldhammer (Cambridge, MA: Harvard University Press, 2020).

7. Zedong Mao, *Quotations from Chairman Mao Tse-Tung* (1966; Peking: Foreign Languages Press, 1974).

8. The Combahee River Collective, "The Combahee River Collective Statement," in *Capitalist Patriarchy and the Case for Socialist Feminism*, ed. Zillah Eisenstein (New York: Monthly Review Press, 1979), 362–72.

THE DAVID R. KESSLER LECTURES 2002–2020

2002   JONATHAN NED KATZ

2003   GAYLE RUBIN

2004   ISAAC JULIEN

2006   ADRIENNE RICH

2007   DOUGLAS CRIMP

2008   SUSAN STRYKER

2009   SARAH SCHULMAN

2010   URVASHI VAID

2012   MARTIN DUBERMAN

2013   CHERYL CLARKE

2014   CATHY J. COHEN

2015   RICHARD FUNG

2016   DEAN SPADE

2017   SARA AHMED

2018   AMBER HOLLIBAUGH

2019   JASBIR K. PUAR

2020   RODERICK A. FERGUSON

Martin Duberman

Martin Duberman is distinguished professor emeritus of history at the CUNY Graduate Center, where he founded and for a decade directed CLAGS: Center for LGBTQ Studies. The author of more than twenty books—including *Paul Robeson* (1989), *Cures* (1991), *Haymarket* (2003), *The Worlds of Lincoln Kirstein* (2007), *A Saving Remnant* (2011), *Howard Zinn* (2012), *The Martin Duberman Reader* (2013), *Hold Tight Gently* (2014), *Andrea Dworkin* (2020), and *Reaching Ninety* (2023)—Duberman has won a Bancroft Prize, three Lambda Literary Awards, the American Historical Association's lifetime achievement award, an award from the National Academy of Arts and Letters for his "contributions to literature," and the Whitehead Award for Lifetime Achievement in Nonfiction. He has been a finalist for both the National Book Award and the Pulitzer Prize. Duberman has received honorary Doctor of Letters degrees from Amherst College and Columbia University. Duberman was also a founding member of the National Gay and Lesbian Task Force, Lambda Legal Defense Fund, and Queers for Economic Justice. He lives in New York City.

Acceptance at What Price?
The Gay Movement Reconsidered

DECEMBER 5, 2012

I'm a little uneasy, I have to tell you at the top, about what I'm going to say tonight. I hope it isn't too harsh, because I don't mean it in that spirit. But I'm genuinely and deeply concerned with the turn, roughly over the last fifty or twenty years of the LGBT movement. And so what I've prepared tonight are some of the reasons why I feel that way. I also want to say that I really don't like the lecture format. It must be like forty years ago, I forget where I was teaching at the time, but I said I just won't lecture anymore. This is not education, this is patronization. Nobody gets a chance to talk back or share their counterviews. And I feel that tonight as well. I much prefer the give-and-take of a Q&A session, and I'm hoping that if I don't run over time, which I alas often do, that there will be a chance for people to challenge some aspect of what I'm saying and to give their own views.

I thought I'd start by defining what my personal political position is, out of the feeling that that will better help you evaluate the remarks that I'm going to make tonight. First of all, I'm a gay man. No surprise. Again, to strongly state the obvious, I do believe that gay people are entitled to all the rights and privileges of other citizens in this country, including the right to marry—though some of what I will say hereafter will seem to be the opposite of that. The only other opening point I'd like to emphasize is that I self-define as radical, not as liberal. I'm often asked: Well, what's the difference? "Liberal," "radical," I mean, we use the words interchangeably. Well, if you do, in my view you should not. Because though "liberal" and "radical" are often lumped together, I think it's very important to distinguish between them. Both do share in a belief in the need for progressive social change, but there I think the similarity ends. Liberals struggle to integrate increasing numbers of people into what they view as a beneficent system. Radicals, on the other hand, believe that the system does have beneficent aspects but also believe that the system requires substantial restructuring. Social justice movements in this country have almost always been started by radicals, but those radicals have, and usually in very short order, been repudiated and supplanted by liberals. I can give you a few examples.

In the nineteenth century, the Garrisonian abolitionists gave way to the so-called Free Soil Party, whose principal plank was against the further expansion of slavery, rather than, as the Garrisonians had called for, the abolition of all slavery *now*. But the country went with the Free Soil Party. It did not go with the Garrisonians. Another example: the Knights of Labor formed as one big union (in other words, both skilled and unskilled) and used their combined energy in order to call for truly significant changes in the country. The Knights of Labor lasted a brief time, it had an impact, but it rather quickly mutated into the American Federation of Labor (AFL). And the AFL catered only to skilled workers and denied admission completely to people of color. One last example, though there are many, would be the broad-gauged Seneca Falls Declaration of women's rights, with its open challenge to male domination. That, in turn, got transmuted into the suffragettes' single-issue concentration on winning the right to vote.

So, in other words, over and over again in our history, the deeply conservative undertow of American ideology has undermined and diminished what started out to be progressive goals. And it seems to me that what is central to our national ideology is the conviction that any individual willing to work hard enough can successfully achieve whatever he or she desires. It follows from this faith, this "pull yourself up by your own bootstraps" ideology, that all presumed barriers based on race, class, gender, or sexual orientation automatically evaporate or are reduced to insignificance when confronted by the individual's determined drive for success. Now, if you believe that, there's this little bridge in Brooklyn that I'd like to interest you in.

Those of us who do self-identify as left-wing or radical have never been able to solve the conundrum of how to prevent a radical impulse—the impulse which ignites so many movements—from degenerating into what becomes reformist tinkering. Time and again we've been unable to mobilize a large enough constituency for substantive change, its members preferring instead to focus on winning certain kinds of limited concessions. Think here, if you will, of the Human Rights Campaign, our most prosperous and largest national organization. The Human Rights Campaign has focused its agenda over the last several decades on winning for gay people the right to marry and the right to serve openly in the military. And the Human Rights Campaign has shown very little interest in joining with other dispossessed groups to press for a much broader social reconstruction. At best, in other words, I for one would label the Campaign liberal, and that may even be giving them too much credit. It seems to me that in this generation, until quite recently, the radical element was the Occupy Wall Street movement. My hope is that somehow, and I wish I could tell them how, they will solve the conundrum of how to *sustain* a radical commitment. I must say, though, and maybe this too is a function of getting older, that no strategy seems available. I base that view on what I know about the history of radical protest in this country.

Part of the problem, as all the surveys done agree, is that Americans are twice as likely to blame themselves rather than structural obstacles if their income and status remain low. That, in other words, as a nation, we are far less class-conscious than people in Europe. There, they are much better able, at least from my perspective, to identify the real enemy and to mobilize force against it. But in this country, if we look for example at the 1970s, it turned out to be impossible to draw together the class-based politics of the labor unions in the 1930s with the demand for racial justice of the 1960s into what we most need—an interracial class identity.

In describing how liberalism—with a great deal of help from conservatives, of course—has historically swallowed up any fragile shoots of radicalism in this country, I do not make an exception for the gay rights movement. And I've seen it evolve over some forty years of activism in it. Following the Stonewall riots in 1969, which inaugurated the modern gay movement, the radical Gay Liberation Front (GLF) initially emerged as the dominant political force. What GLF represented and argued for and demonstrated for was a far-ranging critique of traditional notions of gender and sexual behavior. And GLF emphasized the ideal of androgyny—that is, combining in every individual the characteristics and drives which have traditionally been parceled out as natural to either one gender or the other. GLF also aimed at making alliances with other oppressed groups, like the Black Panthers and the Young Lords. Today, GLF and its agenda have long since disappeared. It's been replaced by national LGBT organizations, of which the Human Rights Campaign is the largest, that work toward assimilationist goals like gay marriage and the right of gay people to serve openly in the military. And it's precisely that assimilationist agenda which for the past twenty years has pretty much swept the field in terms of the gay movement. There are isolated pockets of radical resistance, and I'll come to some of those subsequently. But the popular cry now is, "Hey, we're just folks. You know, we're just like you, you straight people. I mean, except for this trivial little matter of sexual orientation. I mean, we want the same things you want. You know, homes and cars and families," etcetera.

The place to start in attempting a rebuttal to that position is to say, just flat-out, it's not true. Gay people are not straight people. In the same way that Black people are not carbon-copy white people. There's something called a particular, special history and the perspectives that unique history gives you, which set you apart from the mainstream. This, I think, is what gay radicals, then and now, are trying to argue, against the dominant view that we are just folks. Gay radicals oppose reducing our critique of mainstream values to an agenda that pledges allegiance to it. The critique, originating back with GLF, ranges from economic to sexual issues—from the demand for a genuine safety net for all citizens to a questioning of the universal superiority of lifetime monogamy. More than sixty years ago, the nongay philosopher Herbert Marcuse, in his classic work *Eros and Civilization*, wrote something which has always been a kind of mantra for me: because of their "rebellion against the subjugation of sexuality under the order of procreation," homosexuals might one day provide a cutting-edge social critique of vast importance.[1] It's precisely the loss of that cutting-edge social critique that so much bothers me and others in the gay movement who call themselves radicals. For us to reach the potential that Marcuse envisioned for us, it seems to me that we have to reassert our differentness from the mainstream rather than continue to plead for the right to join. What we need to assert is the fact that despite enormous variations in our individual lifestyles, and there are enormous ones, we have had a distinct collective historical experience, and therefore, the way in which gay people view gender, sexuality, primary relationships, friendships, and family are different. Not different in the sense of being some second-rate variation on first-rate mainstream mores, which is how the mainstream often treats us, but rather, it can be argued—and I know it's an argument—our differentness can be viewed as a decided advance over mainstream norms. Gay subcultural values, in my opinion, could richly inform conventional mainstream life itself, could open up an unexplored range of human possibilities for everyone—could, that is, if the mainstream was listening. But the mainstream is not listening. And in part the reason it is not listening is due to us, to our denial or concealment of our own specialness in the name of being let into what is essentially a middle-class white male clubhouse.

When I speak of our radical potential, I hearken back to GLF. I want to hearken back once more because I want to emphasize my view that male dominance, patriarchy, continues to be a flourishing enterprise in this country. Feminism has not won, except for some tinkering around the edges. What GLF did was to challenge the gender binary. They refused to believe that certain biologically induced traits adhere naturally to either gender. And in some cultures, of course, there are six genders. We keep talking about our two genders, but that's gotten into the language, and it will have to serve for now. In other words, we don't feel that strong evidence exists for claiming that women are intrinsically emotional or that men are intrinsically aggressive. That gender binary, in any case, is not true of gay people, and I wish the time would come again when gay people themselves would be saying that more often.

As any number of studies have shown, gay people are different in lots of ways. These are just a couple. Gay people score consistently higher than straight people in empathy and altruism. Many studies. Other studies have shown that lesbians as a group are far more independent-minded and far less subservient to authority than are straight women. Many gay men, moreover, and I don't mean what we used to call "flaming queens," do put a premium on emotional expressiveness and on sexual innovation. Studies also have shown that lesbians and gay men hold to a view of coupledom that is far more characterized by mutuality and egalitarianism than is true of straight couples. Now, if you don't believe me, I know you're going to believe the *New York Times*. And the *New York Times*, much to my amazement at the time, back in 2008 published an article summarizing recent scholarly evidence that "conclusively shows that same-sex couples are far more egalitarian in sharing responsibility both for housework and finances than are heterosexual ones, where women still do much more of the domestic chores (and live with a lot of anger as a result) and where men are more likely to pay the bills."[2] As a result, the *Times* concludes that same-sex couples "have more relationship satisfaction" and—hold on to your beads—"have a great deal to teach everybody else." Now if the *Times* could say that four years ago, how come we can't say it four years later?

In other words, what I've been arguing is that there really is a gay subculture—a way of looking at life, coping with its joys and sorrows—that has a great deal to offer to the mainstream, and also to offer to that multitude of gay people who prefer to claim that we're just like everybody else. Those of us on the left or who self-define as radical feel much the way James Baldwin did when he asked: Why are Black people begging to rent a room in the house that's burning down? Why don't we build a new house? The same questions, I think, apply to the gay movement and its relationship to the mainstream. Gay radicals, for example, don't want to join the military. They want to get rid of it. They want to stop the killing machine that invests far more of our money in drones than it does in building schools. The radicals I know are also not interested in having our primary relationships sanctioned either by church or by state. And that isn't simply because we might disapprove of the particular church or a particular administration, but rather because we believe that being part of a couple should not convey special status and reward. What you're doing if you're claiming that for same-sex couples is that you are reducing the huge number of single people in our midst to some sort of second-class, second-rate status. The recent concentration by our national organizations on the narrow agenda of marriage and the military has implicitly denigrated both the unmarried state and the refusal to maim and kill in war. Our current national organizations, for the most part, have not only failed to challenge mainstream American values, but they have also ignored the actual needs of the majority of gay people themselves. Organizations like the Human Rights Campaign speak primarily to the needs of a middle- and upper-class white constituency. They all but ignore the gay world's Black, Asian, and Latino members, the plight of its own poor, and the history of our challenges to traditional gender and sexual norms—including, and perhaps above all, the transgender people among us.

Though you'd never know it from our national organizations, the fact is that most people are working-class people. And that's true whether you define class by income, educational status, or job status. The chief concern these days of a large number of gay working-class people is simply finding a job with decent wages and perhaps some benefits. And also, in keeping that job, since in half the states in this country employers can still legally fire workers simply because they're gay. The workplace itself, which we, meaning our national gay organizations, pay practically no attention to, remains strongly defined by heterosexual norms. Most straight workers believe gender comes, does come, should come in two and only two packages: the traditionally defined male or the traditionally defined female.

The heterosexual norm also explicitly claims, at least officially, that lifetime monogamous pair-bonding is the sole guarantee of a contented moral life. Of course, official rhetoric and actual behavior are often far apart, as you might have noted recently with a certain high-ranking general. The large majority of working-class gay people, like most straight ones, have nonunion jobs. The union movement currently in this country enrolls a little less than 12 percent of the workforce, and even when a union exists, gay people often don't feel comfortable talking openly to fellow workers about their lives. Nor are their needs, like domestic partnership benefits, forcefully represented during contract negotiations with employers. The gay employee feels rather fortunate if homophobic harassment, meaning sometimes literal physical assault, is absent from his or her workplace. That's about the best it gets. It is true that under the leadership of John J. Sweeney, the AF of L has made some strides in openly including and protecting gay union members. But homophobia in the workplace, unionized or not, continues to be formidable. Alas, the national LGBT organizations, enamored with the martial arts and traditional marriage, have shown almost no comprehension, let alone interest, in the hidden wounds of class and the open wounds of race. And these are the wounds that the majority of our people suffer from.

The lesbian political scientist Cathy J. Cohen wrote an essay about a decade ago called "What Is This Movement Doing to My Politics?"[3] In the essay, she argued that ever since the demise of Queer Nation and the refocusing of ACT UP on issues relating to global AIDS, there is no longer a radical domestic wing of any import in the national lesbian and gay movement. Which is to say, the gay movement no longer represents a genuinely transformative politics. It is simply one more group of privileged people clawing for an even greater share in the pie. This may be hard to believe—I doubt many will remember—but as an example of this, as far back as 1998 the Human Rights Campaign endorsed Alfonse D'Amato for the Senate. And a little later, GLAAD, which has a better record—the Gay and Lesbian Alliance Against Defamation accepted money from the right-wing union-busting Coors beer company. In Cathy J. Cohen's words, the national gay movement's efforts "to sanitize, whitenize, and normalize the public and visible representations" of our community—in other words, to focus on mainstream assimilationism—has led her to ask, with what I feel is justifiable anger, "Can I have my politics and be part of this movement?"[4] Her answer, and I'm sorry to say, mine, is that we're not sure. Why? Because we're deeply concerned that in its current incarnation the gay movement is essentially devoted to winning inclusion into what is a grossly unequal, greed-haunted, oppressive society. That should not be our goal. Our goal should be to transform that society into something more civil and human.

I know that much can be said for our country, and I often say it. There's nowhere in the world, for example, where there is a gay, lesbian, or transgender movement equal to ours in size, numbers, and import. But I'm not here to defend the country at the moment. Here are just, again, a few statistics. Currently, there are forty-six million Americans who subsist on food stamps. That's an increase of more than fourteen million over just the past four years. More than a quarter of Black and Latino people in this country, compared to 10 percent of whites, live below the government-defined level of poverty—which for an individual is $11,000 a year, and for a family of four is $22,000 a year. One in every five children lives in a family today below the poverty line, and often those children go to bed hungry at night. Again, don't take my word for it. Just last week, *Frontline* did a full-hour show entitled "Poor Kids," which I guarantee will break your heart if you get a chance to watch it. Also, one in every four adult Black men are either in jail or have recently been released from it—and often, in the large majority of cases, in fact, for very minor drug charges. Again, don't take my word for it. Read Michelle Alexander's splendid recent book *The New Jim Crow*. In other words, forty-six million Americans, which includes many gay people, lack basic human needs and minimal levels of security.

So what I ask is: Isn't it long past time for the gay movement and for the country as a whole to start to refocus its agenda? It seems to me that what we need is nothing less than a massive anti-racist, pro-feminist, economic justice movement. The trouble is that's much easier said than accomplished. Easiest of all, though, is to continue to either do nothing about our country's gross inequities or to be demanding that we share in them. Do we see any signs in the LGBT movement where people are seeking coalition with others currently suffering oppression? Yes, we do. But where we see these small pockets of resistance, we see them almost exclusively on the local level. Here in New York City, Queers for Economic Justice, unlike the Human Rights Campaign, attempts to do a great deal with a very small budget and a very small staff. They're dealing with the multiple issues of the gay poor that nobody else is paying any attention to, and that includes gay people living in shelters. Some of you may not know that, but there are lots of them living in shelters.

I have to tell you that I don't think the word "disgrace" is too strong when we talk about our country being far more entranced with improving the technology of its drone fleet than it is with the plight of the poor. And I'm afraid "disgrace" is not too strong a word when applied to the gay community as well. Our assimilationist-minded national gay agenda does a far better job at representing the white middle- and upper-class elements in our community than it does in advocating for those of our own people who suffer a variety of deprivations. It's time, in my view, to reassess and revise our goals as a movement. To do otherwise is to implicate us in the national disgrace of caring much more about the welfare of the privileged few than about the deprived many. We are in danger, the gay movement, of becoming part of the problem. My hope is that we may yet become part of the solution.

Notes

1. Herbert Marcuse, *Eros and Civilization: A Philosophical Inquiry into Freud* (Boston: Beacon Press, 1955), 49.

2. Tara Parker-Pope, "Gay Unions Shed Light on Gender in Marriage," *New York Times*, June 10, 2008, https://www.nytimes.com/2008/06/10/health/10well.html.

3. Cathy J. Cohen, "What Is This Movement Doing to My Politics?" *Social Text*, no. 61 (1999): 111–18.

4. Cohen, "What Is This Movement Doing," 111.

Martin Duberman Reflects on "Acceptance at What Price? The Gay Movement Reconsidered"

It is not wrong to claim that the past fifty years have marked a notable, even remarkable change in attitude toward sexual minorities in the United States. In the past half century, we've gone from being all but uniformly pathologized and condemned—yes, even *hunted*—to being widely accepted as a legitimate minority. That's obviously all to the good. But to those now shouting "victory," I would urge a broadened agenda. The gay movement over-represents gay academics and public intellectuals, and under-represents the working poor. To those among us declaring the battle won, I would urge their attention to the contrast between the movement's current "assimilationist" agenda and the far broader set of goals that characterized the Gay Liberation Front at its inception following the Stonewall riots. GLF called for a full-scale assault on sexual and gender norms, on imperialist wars and capitalistic greed, and on the shameful mistreatment of racial and ethnic minorities (including those within our own midst).

In my view the mainstream gay movement needs first to acknowledge, and then to offer help in ameliorating, the suffering of those queer people who refuse to inhabit an assigned gender, those people of color who continue to suffer from a lack of jobs and from massive incarceration for minor offenses (not to mention still being held back by inferior education, voting discrimination, residential segregation, and second-rate medical care). When the Supreme Court in 2003 decriminalized "sodomy," it did so only for consenting adults in private. Left unmentioned were all those minorities—straight as well as gay—whose sexual lives do not match up with middle-class notions of morality, who do not regard matrimony, the child-rearing couple, monogamy, and the picket fence as the signposts not only of contented bliss but of mental health. For those who fail to fit the norm are, in essence, unprotected—outside the law. And this is not theoretical. In some states the number of inmates incarcerated for "sexual offenses" is as high as 30 percent.

In any case, the centrist gay "movement" needs to take on many more issues than sex. The amount of suffering in this country, when compared to its actual resources, is iniquitous. If we are ever to reduce it, we must combine with allies who we may not love but who do share with us a common enemy—the country's oligarchic structure, its patriarchal authority, and its primitively fundamentalist morality. We must—for the common good—join forces. We must add to our political agenda—our voices vociferous and demanding—the many issues relating to gender, race, and class that still define the daily burdens that characterize the lives of many millions of Americans.

THE DAVID R. KESSLER LECTURES 2002–2020

2002	JONATHAN NED KATZ
2003	GAYLE RUBIN
2004	ISAAC JULIEN
2006	ADRIENNE RICH
2007	DOUGLAS CRIMP
2008	SUSAN STRYKER
2009	SARAH SCHULMAN
2010	URVASHI VAID
2012	MARTIN DUBERMAN
2013	**CHERYL CLARKE**
2014	CATHY J. COHEN
2015	RICHARD FUNG
2016	DEAN SPADE
2017	SARA AHMED
2018	AMBER HOLLIBAUGH
2019	JASBIR K. PUAR
2020	RODERICK A. FERGUSON

Cheryl Clarke

Poet and activist Cheryl Clarke was born in 1947 in Washington, DC. Clarke is the author of five books of poetry, including *Humid Pitch* (1989) and *Experimental Love* (1993). Among her many writings, she is also author of *After Mecca: Women Poets and the Black Arts Movement* (2005) and *The Days of Good Looks: Prose and Poetry 1980–2005* (2006). Her essays "Lesbianism: An Act of Resistance," appearing in the iconic *This Bridge Called My Back: Writings by Radical Women of Color* (1981), and "The Failure to Transform: Homophobia in the Black Community," appearing in *Home Girls: A Black Feminist Anthology* (1983), are both considered foundational texts in Black feminist and queer studies. A scholar of the Black Arts Movement and of Audre Lorde's poetry, Clarke was also an editorial collective member of the lesbian publication *Conditions*. She was a key editor of *Conditions: Five: The Black Women's Issue* (1979), the first widely distributed collection of Black feminist writing in the United States. At Rutgers University, she was also the founding director of the Center for Social Justice Education and LGBT Communities from 1992–2009 and dean of students for the Livingston campus from 2009–2013. She graduated from Howard University in 1969 and received an MA, MSW, and PhD in English from Rutgers University. Clarke is the co-organizer of the Hobart Festival of Women Writers, held annually in Hobart, New York, where she lives.

Queer Black Trouble:
In Life, Literature, and the Age of Obama

DECEMBER 6, 2013

1.
My mother, she tells me that Johnnie Mae
Will grow up to be a bad woman.
. . . .
But I say it's fine. . . .
. . . I'd like to be a bad woman, too,
And wear the brave stockings of night-black lace
And strut down the streets with paint on my face.
    —GWENDOLYN BROOKS, "A SONG IN THE FRONT YARD,"
     A STREET IN BRONZEVILLE, 1945[1]

2.
I'm an oversexed
well-hung
Black Queen
influenced
by phrases like
"I am the love that dare not
speak its name."

And you want me to sing
"We Shall Overcome"?
Do you daddy daddy
do you want me to coo
for your approval?
    —ESSEX HEMPHILL, "HEAVY BREATHING," *CEREMONIES*, 1992[2]

3.
Pass through me /
dark to light /
wash over me
with rivers of joy
embrace me with
your love—if I'll
have you—but know

I am no one's for
the taking. No—
I am not even mine
for the taking.
  —SAMIYA BASHIR, "CLITIGATION,"
    TO BE LEFT WITH THE BODY, 2008[3]

4.
I am a Mannish dyke, muff diver, bull dagger, butch,
feminist, femme, and PROUD
  —POLITICAL POSTER, 1991 AT THE FIFTH LESBIAN AND GAY STUDIES
    CONFERENCE, RUTGERS UNIVERSITY, NEW BRUNSWICK, NJ

Gwen Brooks's bad woman, number one. Two, Essex Hemphill's over-sexed, well-hung queen. Three, Samiya Bashir's speaking clitoris. And four, an anonymous political poster of the mannish dyke, muff diver, bull-dagger, butch feminist, femme, and proud. Ought to be enough to cause some Black queer trouble in here tonight.

One starts to ponder what one has contributed and its future; and was it progressive, reformist, reactionary in the service of institutional politics; in service beyond the boundaries of the institution; transformative, radical, or even revolutionary? What are the limits of one's allegiance, of feminist commitments, of risk, of courage, of the politics of Blackness, of erotic choices? In the summer of 1967, auditing Arthur P. Davis's course "Negro Literature in the US" at Howard University, I learned for the first time about Black literary practice, from Phyllis Wheatley to Amiri Baraka (then LeRoi Jones). I learned that the reading of so-called Negro literature had been a primary means of communicating social injustices done unto Black Americans. African American literature became a metonym representing global oppression and resistance of third world peoples. South African writer Peter Abrahams was inspired to write by reading Du Bois, Cullen, Hughes, Wright, claiming in his memoir, *Tell Freedom*, that their writings gave him a new vision of his own country, which he left in 1957.

My sense and experience of writing as an explicator of the absence of social justice emboldened me to emulate the dictates of the Black Arts Movement and to write poetry. See, this doesn't resist the autobiographical. Having attained an R&B and Black Arts sensibility, I set out from Washington, DC, in 1969. I had read Frazier's *Black Bourgeoisie*; Alex Haley's *Autobiography of Malcolm X*; Fanon's *Black Skin, White Masks*; Aptheker's *The Documentary History of the Negro American*; and Hurston's *Their Eyes*

Were Watching God. Why, what else would you need? I landed in New Brunswick on the Rutgers campus met by the ballyhoo of a full gamut of political demonstrations by students and faculty. Anti-war, Black Power, women's liberation, gay liberation, and the kindness of, shall we say, strangers, all in jeans and T-shirts. Meanwhile, I was wearing an A-line dress and stockings. I know. And gloves. I still have those gloves. It took me ten more years, however, to catch up to lesbian feminism and the Women in Print movement that enabled and emboldened my contributions to our sex lives and political dreams, as Daniel Hurewitz from Hunter College said so kindly of my work when I spoke at the Harry Hay Conference here a year ago.

I am drawn back to the writings of Black women who have fed my desire for troublemaking: Walker's *The Third Life of Grange Copeland*; Morrison's *The Bluest Eye*; Toni Cade Bambara's edited *The Black Woman: An Anthology*; Angela Davis's "Reflections on the Black Woman's Role in the Community of Slaves"; Gerda Lerner's *Black Women in White America: A Documentary History*; Shange's *For Colored Girls*; Smith and Bethel's *Conditions: Five: The Black Women's Issue*; Moraga and Anzaldúa's *This Bridge Called My Back: Writings by Radical Women of Color*; Smith, Hull, and Scott's *All the Women Are White, All the Blacks Are Men, but Some of Us Are Brave: Black Women's Studies*; Smith's *Home Girls: A Black Feminist Anthology*; *The Black Unicorn*; *Our Dead behind Us*; *ICON* magazine's special edition *Art against Apartheid*.

I must also call out the names of the Black feminist critics who follow Barbara Smith's call to be as daring as the writers themselves, and who emerged during the '70s and '80s: beginning with Smith's own article "Towards a Black Feminist Criticism"; Barbara Christian's *Black Women Novelists: The Development of a Tradition*; Hazel Carby's *Reconstructing Womanhood: The Emergence of the Afro-American Woman Novelist*; Debra McDowell's essay "The Nameless . . . Shameful Impulse: Sexuality in Nella Larsen's *Quicksand* and *Passing*"; Hortense Spillers's "Interstices: A Small Drama of Words"; Claudia Tate's ethnography *Black Women Writers at Work*; Mary Helen Washington's *Black-Eyed Susans*; Jewelle Gomez's "A Cultural Legacy Denied and Discovered: Black Lesbians in Fiction by Women"; Cheryl Walls's edited *Changing Our Own Words: Essays on Criticism, Theory, and Writing by Black Women*; Gloria Hull's article "'Under the Days': The Buried Life and Poetry of Angelina Weld Grimké"; Beverly Guy-Sheftall's *Sturdy Black Bridges* and *Words of Fire*. Writers and writing became the chief arbiters of a transformation of consciousness—intellectual, political, emotional—which is ongoing.

Not merely instrumental, the novels, poems, plays, and essays of under-represented women writers and the cultural readings and public events, journals, and anthologies became pedagogical and theoretical and critical guides by which to live. In her foreword to *This Bridge Called My Back: Writings by Radical Women of Color*, the late Toni Cade Bambara charged us, the writers and editors of that enduring anthology, to "make revolution irresistible."[4] We know revolution is protracted, and so is a progressive agenda. Witness how accusatory people became about Obama's inaugural speech: "liberal," "progressive." We said to Obama, "Hey, bro, it's about time. At least be liberal-progressive." We also say, "deeds not words." I suppose supporting same-sex marriage, getting rid of DOMA, getting rid of Don't Ask, Don't Tell, refusing to sell women's reproductive rights totally down the hole is liberal-progressive, but not enough. This talk will attempt to speak to Black queer spaces of resistance and desire, and Black queer trouble, and Black feminist trouble too.

I am taking "Black queer trouble" from Alexis Pauline Gumbs, a queer Black feminist writer, poet educator, online troublemaker, and founder of the Eternal Summer of the Black Feminist Mind, a virtual school of Black feminism.[5] Here, Gumbs defines the learning outcomes of her free online course entitled "To Be a Problem: Outcast Subjectivity and Black Literary Production": "We will explore trouble-making, radical performative critique and the transgressive and embattled act of (visual, textual, sonic and multi-media) publishing as possible responses to systemic and individual exclusions. If publishing is an act of stolen power for outcasts, this class will be a publication of what it can mean to be problematic in a society inflected by race, class, sexuality and gender norms. Our aim is not to solve the problems of classism, sexism, homophobia and transphobia as inflected by race, but rather is to create a space where it is possible to act, speak, write and think otherwise, anyway."[6] I say, take that, University of Phoenix.

Can I, as a Black queer troublemaker and feminist too, operationalize revolution and/or progressive agendas? Can I trouble the liberal same-sex status quo enough to say, "It's not enough?" Can I trouble LGBT communities to feed our hungry youth, both physically and emotionally, in ways their birth families, relatives, and neighbors can't or don't or won't? Can I trouble our white LGBT allies to continue to challenge white domination within their organizations and to share the resources you have attained because of your white privilege? As I have become more assimilable, can

I trouble the carceral state by advocating for and with survivors of it by refusing unnecessary police presence in my gentrifying and gentrified neighborhood and by demanding professional police behavior, wherever I am and they are?

Can I trouble my communities of color enough to counter their homophobia and sexism and Black straight respectability? What account do I give myself in the context of the scourge of HIV/AIDS among the most vulnerable people in my communities? Steven G. Fullwood, in his piece "The Low Down on the Down Low," calls for accountability on the individual and group level in the Black community in chilling terms: "If a man is on the DL, that's his business. If he spends his time out having unprotected sex with men (or women), contracting several venereal diseases and bringing them home to his girlfriend, wife, or male lover, then that's another story. That's an issue of honesty, not sexuality—or to the point, homosexuality. . . . If we can't talk to each other across perceived sexual boundaries, the walls of ignorance will just get higher. . . . Ignorance will continue to be passed down from generation to generation. And perhaps, worst of all, after the dust has cleared, nobody will be left to talk about anything."[7]

Can I sustain the trouble? Is it enough to trouble in increments? Am I about changing myself, the courses of events, structural power, eradicating the carceral state, inequities of race, gender, sex, politics, material resources, money, and the harsh domination of immigrants and the working classes the world over? I turn to my sister of the plantain and the corn, Cherríe Moraga, as she defines her feminist politics in the context of her Xicanism, her Mexican native ancestry, and the frailty or strength of coalitional politics:

> We make and break political alliance as we continue to evolve and redefine what is our work in this life. As a Xicana, I find the deepest resonance in that evolutionary process with my "sisters of the corn," as Toni Cade Bambara called native women. Indigenism (north and south) gives shape to the values with which I raise my children; it informs my feminism, my sense of lugar on this planet in relation to its creatures, minerals, and plant life. Ideally, it is a philosophy, not of a rigid separatism but of cultural autonomy and communitarian reciprocity in the twenty-first century. It is my sure-footed step along that open road of alliance with my "sisters of the rice, the plantain, and the yam."[8]

What rituals, legacies, praxes give shape to our values? What does it mean to be still inspired by the Black Arts Movement? To still believe the lessons of the Black Arts Movement became a large house of resistance to patriarchal culture, Black and white? And to still believe in Amiri Baraka's 1969 dictum about literary practice as expressed in the poem "Black Art"?

> Poems are bullshit unless they are
> teeth or trees or lemons piled
> on a step. . . . Fuck poems
> and they are useful, wd they shoot
> come at you, love what you are,
> breathe like wrestlers, or shudder
> strangely after pissing.[9]

Our work and our writing as Black queer troublemakers are fraught with disobedience, resistance, and direct language. In these lines from her poem "Star-Apple," Alexis Gumbs queries us:

> how to tuck home into cleavage
> and bring it out
> flower magic
> how dare we be
> free
>
> all out loud
> and in public
> and shit[10]

Disobeying our penchant for Black respectability, something we crave even as Black queers, Essex Hemphill also faces off Black macho culture by asserting a phallocentric masculinity:

> In america,
> I place my ring
> on your cock
> where it belongs.[11]

I remain convinced that there is no transformation unless Black feminists and Black queers, same-gender-loving, in-the-life communities engage in a kind of itinerant movement from front to back to inside to outside, again and again; and unless there are parallel movements, going and coming in the streets, down the alley, and in the house, whereby dynamic mutuality and exchange coalesce and contest. As Gloria Hull said of Audre Lorde's radical positionality of "living on the line," we, too, have to live on the line between either/or and both/and, and engage in ceaseless negotiations of a positionality from which we can speak, act, and make trouble. Not settling, setting, or sitting still.

A few words about lesbian feminism. Lesbian feminists did the work and the word. We took the potluck to new levels most nights of the week, on Saturday morning, Sunday afternoons at meetings, and on projects; at fundraising events for those projects; at the proofreading and layout meeting; after an afternoon of rapping and trips to the post office with scores of parcels among us in somebody's old VW or Corolla; the lesbian feminist theater group, the tickets, the box office, the folding chairs, the posters, the feeding of cast and crew; or the cultural center and café, its readings and public programs. The film set in someone's loft with twenty volunteers on hand to make up, dress, direct, film, and feed the cast and crew. The lesbian-led national conference on violence against women of color on a frayed-shoestring budget and women from all over the country and the world come, at their own expense or ours. The anti-apartheid publication celebration on an equally frayed budget under the aegis of a lesbian editorship. The all-volunteer lesbian health fair, or the weekend-long board-planning retreats. Katherine Acey is out there. She knows about those. Where we supplied the food and did the cooking too.

We produced politics and culture for us, by us, about us. Lesbian feminism put our feminist messages out to our constituencies, other lesbians and any women for whom women are an essential part of their lives, as we said in *Conditions*. Lesbians of African descent were and are everywhere. Women of color, sometimes code for lesbians of color, were and are everywhere. Lesbians of all colors worked very hard to produce for our imagined audiences. We claimed and challenged our masculinity, femininity, whiteness, and Blackness, as well as our androgyny and hybridity, liminality, and marginality.

I know we celebrate *This Bridge* as well as *Home Girls*, as we should, but I must celebrate *Conditions: Five: The Black Women's Issue*. Its guest editors, Barbara Smith and Lorraine Bethel, gave me the first place to call myself a Black lesbian feminist. And white feminists and *Conditions* founding editorial collective members Elly Bulkin, Jan Clausen, Irena Klepfisz, and Rima Shore gave the journal over to the project of Black feminism, and later to the project of women of color feminist leadership, by committing the magazine to women of color.

In their introduction to *Conditions: Five*, the coeditors identify many of the obstacles to producing the publication, most of all the very perilous conditions of Black women's lives: "Twelve Black women were being murdered in Boston's third world communities between January 29 and May 28, 1979. While we were working to create a place for celebration of Black women's lives, our sisters were dying. The sadness, fear, and anger as well as the unforeseen need to do political work around the murders affected every aspect of our lives, including our work on *Conditions: Five*."[12] And the editors go on to say that these murders and all other violence against Black women necessitate "the dire need of such a publication and for a black feminist movement." Let me call out some of the writers who appeared there: Gloria Hull, Renita Weems, Ann Allen Shockley, the late Linda Powell, Donna Allegra, Toi Derricotte, the late Yvonne Flowers (Maua), the late Pat Parker, the late Audre Lorde, Alexis De Veaux, Beverly Smith. *Conditions: Five* was my first encounter with queer Black trouble.

Some people ask, "Whatever happened to lesbian feminism?" And we were at that conference a few years ago. Actually, it was fun. Well, like many things else, it has gone virtual and viral, including Black feminism and lesbian feminism, as the Crunk Feminist Collective enunciates in its mission statement and blog: "Our relationship to feminism and our world is bound up with a proclivity for the percussive, as we divorce ourselves from 'correct' or hegemonic ways of being in favor of following the rhythm of our own heartbeats. In other words, what others may call audacious and crazy, we call CRUNK, because we are drunk off the heady theory of feminism that proclaims that another world is possible. We resist others' attempts to stifle our voices, acting belligerent when necessary, and getting buck when we have to. Crunk feminists don't take no mess from nobody."[13] Quite a change in tone from the rather distressed tone of Smith and Bethel, and also different from Gumbs's more teacherly, reserved tone. The virtual anthology carries on the work of Black feminist troublemakers. I started to say, "of yore," then I realized I'd be putting myself— But anyway.

Women's studies scholar and troublemaker Vivian M. May asserts in her article "Under-Theorized and Under-Taught," an article on Harriet

Tubman—a real revolutionary, and if not queer, a definite Black trouble-maker—that histories of this noted icon of Black women's resistance tend to portray her as a superhuman nineteenth-century anomaly, separate and apart from the community of Black women in resistance to slavery.[14] May further contends that were Tubman doing today what she was doing before Emancipation—that is, armed resistance to slavery, leading someone's human chattel to freedom, ready to kill or be killed rather than be returned to slavery, which was still legal during the earlier part of her resistance—she would be considered a domestic terrorist. May continues to frame how we "make over" the radical facets and figures of Black history in the image of Black respectability.

Tubman's historical makeover transforms her radical vision and resistance, and at times illegal actions, into benign symbols of progress and family values. This interpretive shift aligns her organized resistance to fit with narratives of the nation's deliverance from its past sins, and to render a more tender portrait of the nation as a family. The salvific also reinforces problematic ideas about the state as an otherwise perfect system—with its central tragic flaw, slavery, and its tragically flawed central characters, white citizens, healed over, thanks to Tubman. It is imperative to consider how deliverance models draw attention away from the tenacious nature of the systems of oppression Tubman fought against in her lifetime and how they persist to this day. They live on in new ways, and we as a nation are still not delivered from them.

There is some room for comparison between Tubman and Assata Shakur. Similarly, Tubman was branded an "illiterate" and "insolent" abolitionist, who, when she was enslaved, was always "getting in the way" of slaves' discipline. Forty thousand dollars for Tubman's capture, dead or alive, or "the sooner she is turned in, the better it will be for all Southerners." Assata has been cited by the FBI as a domestic terrorist, with a two million dollar reward, aided by the vaunted New Jersey State Troopers, for her capture. For over forty years, the US has been trying to capture Assata, who was railroaded into life plus thirty imprisonments on very unclear evidence in 1977 that she murdered a New Jersey State Trooper.

This continues to tell us that the systemic racist oppression of African Americans, primarily in the context of the carceral state, is not only "the new Jim Crow," but really a twenty-first-century replication of slavery. Once a slave, you're a slave for life. Once a prisoner of the state, you are for life contained, constrained, and surveilled by the state. Blacks have no rights whites are bound to respect. An ex-felon has no rights a citizen is bound to respect. Stop and frisk, shoot your shot, stand your ground, take your best shot. Assata continues to say that she is a warrior for Black liberation. Angela Davis, herself not a stranger to wanted posts, declaims, "Assata is not a threat. If anything, this is a vendetta."[15] And at least I can say, like Mychal Denzel Smith in *The Nation* online, "Hands off Assata, now and forever."[16]

"I flew in on the cusp of the Black Power Movement. But someone did not pay the bill. . . . And here we are all left alone in our blackness."[17] Black queer troublemakers, one of the more excluded and despised members of the Black community in the United States, carry on the Black Power revolution's commitment to racial justice. And this is in response to Black drag artist Jomama Jones's comment above, "I flew in on the cusp of the Black Power Movement." I will claim that for Black queers and for that unfinished revolution somewhere in Atlantic City, when Ella Baker walked out on the 1964 Democratic National Convention, after the Mississippi Freedom Democratic Party was prevented from being seated as the real delegates to the convention. While we Black queers were left alone in the dark, countering the sexual repression of the Nixon-Mitchell/Reagan-Meese 1970s and '80s, Black lesbian and gay writers appropriated that direct and aggressive expressivity of the Black Arts Movement to continue Black queer critiques of the ubiquitous racism of white America and the gender prescriptiveness and homophobia of conservative Black communities—most viscerally documented in its refusal to organize around the AIDS pandemic or anything else having to do with lesbian and gay rights. Here, Jericho Brown reminds us,

> Tell them
> Herman Finley is dead. Then,
> Tell them what God loves,
> The truth: the disease
> Your mother's mouth won't mention[18]

Black lesbians and gays enacted what Farah J. Griffin says of modern dance artist Pearl Primus in her portrayal of the Jim Crow car in the 1940s. Primus was able to embody a particularly Black paradox, "forced confinement and forced mobility."[19] Can't set too long and sometimes can't go too far or can't be afraid to come back or must, like Assata Shakur, never come back. We, too, worked within the constraints to break free of them.

I'll close with this last. Mecca J. Sullivan's short story "Wolfpack," "for The New Jersey Four"—about the seven young Black lesbians who were arrested in 2006 in the West Village for defending themselves against a lowlife street peddler—exemplifies Griffin's metaphor of forced containment and forced mobility. A good story about the ways in which the press savaged young women, *The Public Intellectual* in 2011, an online newspaper, predisposed the court and the public to viewing them as the assailants rather than the victims. Sullivan's story is told from the perspective of four fictional young women who were sentenced from three-and-a-half to eleven years in jail. Verniece, one of the fictional four, decides to make things whatever she wants them to be inside her prison cell. This story is perhaps a parable of places that could use some Black queer troublemaking.

> I am wrapped up in Luna, my girls, and the warm, licorice sky. The man tears like a bullet through our night.
>
> "Who asked what you think, you goddamn elephant?"
>
> . . . So many things are going on in this moment, my skull loses its solidity and breaks down to mesh, to screen. I cannot tell what part of the action is happening inside, what out. I see a man in pink come, I see a woman run away. I see fingers and DVD cases and a nugget of fire fly. . . . I see blood curled around stripes, and Sha holding a silver-soaked blade. From one side of my ears or the other I hear him say again "Goddamn," "God-damned," "God-dammned." I feel words popping like firecrackers inside my mouth, and I let them blaze the air:
>
> > *You are not a man Your sneakers are cheap your clothes are corny you have no job You are not a man, hands on your sleepy little dick You are not a man, what you know about God some white man in the sky If your God doesn't know me and my big black dyke manwoman God fuck him he doesn't exist You are not a man You are a joke.*
>
> . . . My first night here, I make a decision: Pretend. I play games with myself, games like my mother used to play: I pretend to fool myself. Things are not what they are. In some other place, in some far corner of possibility, things are right . . . Still, there is always the ink, running like blood up and down the newsprint paper: "'Killer Lesbians' Trial Begins." "Seething Sapphic Swarm Descends." "Bloodthirsty Pride Attacks."
>
> . . . When I can't tell the difference between inside and out, I decide. If I want to share my dinner with Anthony Jesús, I decide he's on my lap, his polka-dot bib brushing my wrist. If I want to joke with TaRonne and Sha,

I decide they're on the cot with me, and we laugh. I wade through the sea of orange suits, eat my food and do what I'm told. I try not to think in days, how they close me up in darkness . . . I try not to think of how time is crusting over, baking me deeper into stillness each time the moon brings a day to its end.

On the morning after my first night here, someone puts a newspaper in my hands. The paper is folded open, and before I read the headlines, I find my name in the middle column . . . I read up from there, wading back. I see the name of the reporter and roll up to the headline: "Lesbian Wolf Pack Howls Its End." This is when I decide to make things whatever I want them to be. From the space around me, I carve my mother's smile and a deep, wetwarm sky. I get up, tighten my grip, part my lips like two heavy winds and say—out loud—*Let's go.*[20]

And so I finish.

Notes

1. Gwendolyn Brooks, "a song in the front yard," *A Street in Bronzeville*, in *Selected Poems* (1945; New York: Harper Perennial Modern Classics, 2006), 6.

2. Essex Hemphill, "Heavy Breathing," in *Ceremonies: Prose and Poetry* (San Francisco: Cleis Press, 1992), 5.

3. Samiya Bashir, "Clitigation," in *To Be Left with the Body*, eds. Cheryl Clarke and Steven Fullwood (Los Angeles: AIDS Project Los Angeles and GMAC, 2008), 20.

4. Toni Cade Bambara, foreword to *This Bridge Called My Back: Writings by Radical Women of Color*, eds. Cherríe Moraga, Gloria Anzaldúa, and Bambara (Watertown, MA: Persephone Press, 1981).

5. Alexis Pauline Gumbs, *Spill: Scenes of Black Feminist Fugitivity* (Durham, NC: Duke University Press, 2016).

6. Gumbs, *Spill*.

7. Stephen G. Fullwood, "The Low Down on the Down Low," in *Funny* (New York: Vintage Entity Press, 2004), 74–75.

8. Cherríe Moraga, *A Xicana Codex of Changing Consciousness: Writings, 2000–2010* (Durham, NC: Duke University Press, 2011), 31.

9. Amiri Baraka, "Black Art," in *Transbluency: Selected Poetry of Amiri Baraka/LeRoi Jones (1961–1995)* (New York: Marsilio Publishers, 1995), 142.

10. Alexis Pauline Gumbs, "Star-Apple," *ProudFlesh: New Afrikan Journal of Culture, Politics, and Consciousness*, no. 8 (2013): 18.

11. Essex Hemphill, "Heavy Breathing," *Ceremonies*, 1992, 5.

12. Lorraine Bethel and Barbara Smith, eds., "The Black Women's Issue," *Conditions: Five* (1979): 14, accessed June 10, 2022, https://dokumen.pub/conditions-magazine-issue-5-the-black-womens-issue.html.

13. Crunk Feminist Collective, "Mission Statement," accessed June 10, 2022, http://www.crunkfeministcollective.com/about/.

14. Vivian M. May, "Under-Theorized and Under-Taught: Re-Examining Harriet

Tubman's Place in Women's Studies," *Meridians: Feminisms, Race, Transnationalism* 12, no. 2 (2014): 28–49.

15. "Angela Davis and Assata Shakur's Lawyer Denounce FBI's Adding of Exiled Activist to Terrorists List," Democracy Now!, May 3, 2013, https://www.democracynow.org/2013/5/3/angela_davis_and_assata_shakurs_lawyer.

16. Mychal Denzel Smith, "Assata Shakur Is Not a Terrorist," *The Nation*, May 7, 2013, http://www.thenation.com/blog/174209/assata-shakur-not-terrorist#.

17. Cheryl Clarke, "Black Queer Trouble in Literature, Life, and the Age of Obama: Part II," Crunk Feminist Collective, January 3, 2014, https://www.crunkfeministcollective.com/2014/01/03/black-queer-trouble-in-literature-life-and-the-age-of-obama-part-ii/.

18. Jericho Brown, "Herman Finley Is Dead (1947–2005)," in *War Diaries*, eds. Tisa Bryant and Ernest Hardy (Los Angeles: AIDS Project Los Angeles and the Global Forum on MSM and HIV, 2010), 33.

19. Farah Jasmine Griffin, *Harlem Nocturne: Women Artists and Progressive Politics During World War II* (New York: Basic Civitas Books, 2013), 27.

20. Mecca J. Sullivan, "Wolfpack," in *Best New Writing 2010*, ed. Christopher Klim (Titusville, NJ: Hopewell Publications, 2010), 157–70.

"Troublemaking and a Metonym": Cheryl Clarke Reflects on "Queer Black Trouble: In Life, Literature, and the Age of Obama"

> your hot grain smell tattooed
> into each new poem   resonant
> beyond escape   I am listening
> in that fine space
> between desire and always
> the grave stillness
> before choice.
>   —AUDRE LORDE, "ECHOES"[1]

When I gave this talk it was the beginning of Obama's second term. None of us envisioned the hell of a backlash to come in 2016.

I am still grateful to Dr. Alexis Pauline Gumbs for the concept of "troublemaking" as radical Black queer resistance to the oppressions that doggedly daunt and dishearten us and our movement.

The above epigraph is in honor of Dr. Elizabeth Lorde-Rollins, who introduced me so robustly that evening of the Kessler event in 2013. It is a passage from the poem "Echoes," in Audre Lorde's last collection of poetry, *The Marvelous Arithmetics of Distance* (1992). As you can see, I read the poem in its entirety before my lecture.

I am still pondering what I can contribute to our freedom—as a Black feminist, poet, dyke, and hopefully queer. Because I received a generous and gracious "lifetime achievement" award from the Publishing Triangle this year, I wonder, do I now just *lie* back, complete, while we know there is so much work to be done?

I still cathect to the notion that African American literature is a "metonym" of "third world peoples'" resistance to systematic and centuries-old oppressions. I just wouldn't deploy the term "third world," because it has fallen from usage; it says too much and too little; it cries for specificity. (But it is so dramatic!)

I continue to regard my time at Howard University as formative and transformative for its gift of Black thought. I continued my reading of Black texts in grad school, under my own tutelage, and in community with other women reading Black women writers and wanting to talk to women—Black and white—about the reading experience. Black literatures, including African American, still are *a* means—perhaps not a "primary means," anymore, given the internet—"of communicating social injustices" done unto the "race."

I always am drawn back to the poem, "Black Art," written by the "father we love to hate," Amiri Baraka/LeRoi Jones. See his metonymic play on "Poems" as he speaks on the work literature is supposed to do for liberation:

> Poems are bullshit unless they are
> teeth or trees or lemons piled
> on a step. . . . Fuck poems
> and they are useful, wd they shoot
> come at you, love what you are,
> breathe like wrestlers, or shudder
> strangely after pissing.[2]

"Poems" becomes a metonym for African American literature and, in many ways, for all literature.

"MAKE REVOLUTION IRRESISTIBLE," says Toni Cade Bambara.

"Irresistible." Really, Toni? Necessary evil—revolution. One-might-lose-one's-life—revolution.

Likely-to-die-before-any-fundamental-changes-take-place—revolution. Saying it the way Toni Cade Bambara said "revolution" is revolutionary, puts some flesh on its steely images, gives it some eroticism.

DEEDS NOT WORDS

No question: Black feminist literary critics were crucial to my development as a scholar and critic of Black women's writing and culture, specifically of poetry. Black feminist writers (scholars, critics, poets, fiction writers, essayists) are still working hard to sustain the literature and its audiences, despite the four-year hell right-minded people had to endure during the 2016–2020 years. And we are still contending with neofascists in everyday life. We have to fight like hell just to keep neoliberals in office in Washington, while we fight, sometimes on the "DL," for more radical changes. I don't subscribe to reformist politics except in election years, but most Republicans (and some Democrats) are hell-bent on reverting to their Dixiecrat roots. As Stacey Abrams has said, the current efforts to suppress Black and

Democratic Party voters is twenty-first-century Jim Crow—"Jump. Jump. Jim Crow." Go to hell, Jim Crow.

I think all of us must in some way become involved with women's reproductive freedom struggles locally, statewide, and nationally. Do what we can for our daughters, sisters, grandchildren, neighbors, and friends. This recent retrenchment around abortion rights is enraging and dangerous.

Must we have to continue to hope for a Democrat in the White House every four years so as not to lose all of our freedom? Some of these liberties we call "rights" have to become permanent policy.

Yet I still totally agree with what I said. Our electoral politics could use some Black queer troublemaking, but I don't think that will happen. Queers are too radical, even the more liberal of us. So, Black queer troublemaking has to stay living on the line, as (Akasha) Gloria Hull said thirty-two years ago of Audre Lorde, and I paraphrased: "We, too, have to live on the line between either/or and both/and, and engage in ceaseless negotiations of a positionality from which we can speak, act, and make trouble. Not settling, setting, or sitting still."[3]

Notes

1. Audre Lorde, "Echoes," *The Marvelous Arithmetics of Distance*, in *The Collected Poems of Audre Lorde* (New York: W. W. Norton, 2000), 7–9.

2. Amiri Baraka, "Black Art," in *Transbluency: Selected Poetry of Amiri Baraka/LeRoi Jones (1961–1995)* (New York: Marsilio Publishers, 1995), 142.

3. Cheryl Clarke, "Black Queer Trouble in Literature, Life, and the Age of Obama: Part II," Crunk Feminist Collective, January 3, 2014, https://www.crunkfeministcollective.com/2014/01/03/black-queer-trouble-in-literature-life-and-the-age-of-obama-part-ii/.

THE DAVID R. KESSLER LECTURES 2002–2020

2002   JONATHAN NED KATZ

2003   GAYLE RUBIN

2004   ISAAC JULIEN

2006   ADRIENNE RICH

2007   DOUGLAS CRIMP

2008   SUSAN STRYKER

2009   SARAH SCHULMAN

2010   URVASHI VAID

2012   MARTIN DUBERMAN

2013   CHERYL CLARKE

2014   CATHY J. COHEN

2015   RICHARD FUNG

2016   DEAN SPADE

2017   SARA AHMED

2018   AMBER HOLLIBAUGH

2019   JASBIR K. PUAR

2020   RODERICK A. FERGUSON

Cathy J. Cohen

Cathy J. Cohen is the David and Mary Winton Green Distinguished Service Professor at the University of Chicago. Cohen is the author of *The Boundaries of Blackness: AIDS and the Breakdown of Black Politics* (1999) and *Democracy Remixed: Black Youth and the Future of American Politics* (2010). She is also coeditor of the anthology *Women Transforming Politics: An Alternative Reader* (1997) with Kathleen Jones and Joan Tronto. Her articles have been published in numerous journals and edited volumes, including the *American Political Science Review, NOMOS, GLQ, Social Text*, and the *Du Bois Review*.

In addition to her academic work, Cohen was a founding board member and former co-chair of the board of the Audre Lorde Project in New York. She was also on the board of Kitchen Table: Women of Color Press, the Center for Lesbian and Gay Studies (CLAGS) at CUNY, and the Arcus Foundation. Cohen was a founding member of Black AIDS Mobilization (BAM!) and was one of the core organizers of two international conferences, Black Nations/Queer Nations? and Race, Sex, Power. Cohen has also served as an active member in numerous organizations, including the Black Radical Congress, ACT UP New York, African American Women in Defense of Ourselves, and Ella's Daughters. She is the founder and director of the GenForward Survey Project and the Black Youth Project.

#DoBlackLivesMatter?
From Michael Brown to CeCe McDonald:
On Black Death and LGBTQ Politics

DECEMBER 12, 2014

Tonight, as the title of my talk suggests, I want to discuss whether and how Black lives matter in LGBT politics. Does the struggle or movement that we see unfolding daily on our streets and highways and in city halls and shopping centers across the country, and really across the world, matter to the lives of LGBT individuals? And maybe more importantly for the talk today, to LGBT organizations? I'm especially interested in the conditions of what I'm calling "political solidarity." How do we differentiate between a performative versus a substantive solidarity? I'm concerned that many of the organizations that seem to dominate the LGBT public sphere are engaged in what we might call a contradictory project of performing solidarity with this kind of new, Black, youth-led movement while substantively being complicit with a dominant neoliberal structure whose racial politics will always threaten the lives of people of color, and in particular, poor Black people. Finally, I want all of us to think about how the current structure of this movement, this moment, might begin to actualize a new radical queer politics led by people of color.

I'm going to deliver this lecture in three parts, or we might call them three acts. Each is intended to build on the last. The first, "Multicultural Neoliberalism and the Unmaking of Michael Brown," briefly explores how neoliberal policies, I think, serve as the backdrop for the violence and resistance we are witnessing at this moment. The second section, "Performing Solidarity: LGBT Complicity = Black Death," interrogates the current racialized politics of LGBT organizations and their reoccurring compromise with and cooptation by neoliberalism. This is a well-traveled theme, but I believe that we should at least briefly reimagine or rediscover it now. In the third section, "This Is Not the Civil Rights Movement: The Queering of Black Liberation," I briefly revisit, actually, my earlier work in "Punks, Bulldaggers, and Welfare Queens," suggesting that radical Black liberation is taking the form of what many of us imagined a radical queer politics might look like.

Multicultural Neoliberalism and the Unmaking of Michael Brown

So, I want to get started with section one, but before I get started, I want to show you a video. This video is pretty explicit, but it's meant to actually re-center us to remind us what this talk and what this movement is about. [A two-minute video of the murders of Eric Garner, John Crawford III, Kajieme Powell, Oscar Grant, and Tamir Rice edited together.]

According to Darren Wilson, the officer who killed Michael Brown on the street in Ferguson, Missouri, Michael Brown had superhuman strength. Wilson referred to the unarmed Black teenager as similar to "Hulk Hogan" in strength. He told reporter George Stephanopoulos that when Brown turned around to look at him, he looked like a "demon." As I watched the interview with Wilson, I wondered: How does one come to view a young man—with no gun, who had just graduated from high school, and who was actually not that much bigger than Wilson—how do you come to see him with such venom, such disregard, and such fear? Similarly, how do police in Cleveland, Ohio—in the wake of the Trayvon Martin, Jordan Davis, Michael Brown, Aiyana Jones, and Eric Garner killings—take less than two seconds to kill a twelve-year-old Tamir Rice as he holds a toy gun?

Journalists, politicians, and even some activists have pitched these stories as struggles between young men who we are told "aren't angels" and police officers and vigilantes who we are told are "fearing for their lives." While a narrative on these encounters that focuses on personalities of both victim and killer serves the media, what has too often been minimized is the larger political context which helped to produce the aggressive policing that has proven to be fatal in Black communities. So for just a moment, I want to pull the story back and talk about the larger political context and the role of neoliberalism in the unmaking of Michael Brown.

By "neoliberalism" I mean a prioritizing of markets and a corresponding commitment to the dismantling or devolution of social welfare, from the national government to the states, to local governments. Without going through the history of neoliberalism, which scholars from David Harvey to Lisa Duggan have detailed in critical books, it is important to remember that the project of neoliberalism was made more visible first during the Nixon administration and took root under President Reagan. At the heart of Reagan's neoliberal policies and approach was greater market expansion and freedom with a corresponding dissolution of what was formerly known as the safety net. An important point is that its emergence marks the end of the expansionist state that existed during the civil rights movement.

Thus, proponents of neoliberalism had to pursue not only a policy agenda but also a set of ideological commitments and rhetorical strategies meant to create and demonize some "Other." For example, Reagan's campaign against poor communities included a policy agenda of defunding social service agencies, as well as rhetorical strategies mobilizing tropes like that of the "welfare queen," meant to demean and distance those on welfare. In order to rationalize the restriction of the social welfare state that largely benefited white people, there had to be a process of misrepresenting those who benefited from the social safety net. Toward this end, there was a deployment of tropes such as the "super predator" that helped to create and solidify an Other that whites, and eventually middle-class people of color, could rally against. These Others were portrayed as being different from our normal. They were abusing and dependent on state support, specifically taxpayer money, suggesting of course that they themselves were not taxpayers. They were characterized as violent, manipulative, and being engaged in criminal activity. They were accused of being hypersexual, of having multiple children out of wedlock, and being uninterested in raising those children. This Other was in need of state surveillance and policing if the rest of us were to survive their invasion—the invasion of these monsters with strength like Hulk Hogan and who look like demons. It was this process under neoliberalism that fueled what Omi and Winant labeled "white resentment politics."

White resentment politics has also been coupled with white fear. Sociologist Eduardo Bonilla-Silva reminds us that the most segregated lived experience of any group in this country is that of white Americans. Whites are more likely to live among, go to school with, work with, attend church with, marry, have sex with, and socialize with other white people. Thus, the idea of white fear toward an unknown Other is real, facilitated by their segregated lived experience, the mobilization of fearful tropes, and the actual creation of devastated and, I dare say in certain cases, dangerous urban spaces.

Under neoliberalism we have witnessed the disinvestment in poor and urban areas, where living-wage, low-skill jobs have become nearly extinct; where the housing stock has become battered and debilitated; where neighborhood schools have been neglected in lieu of charter and magnet schools; and where the middle class has exited, trying to guarantee their own survival. In their out-migration, William Julius Wilson contends, whites, and then the Black middle class, have left behind those he labels the "truly disadvantaged," individuals inhabiting poor, blighted areas with few recognized resources and even fewer job opportunities. With such devastation and despair, the neoliberal response has been to bracket, isolate, and police those dangerous and devastated areas. However, these communities have not only been policed, they have been *over*policed, using prisons and policing to replace investment and employment. It is important to note that while neoliberalism has been committed to an anti-statism rhetoric and policies, many people forget that there are segments of the state that have actually grown under neoliberalism, such as the policing and prison industrial complex, producing what Beth Richie calls our "prison nation." Ironically, most state investments associated with these neighborhoods were not directed at residents or their living space or areas, but instead at a policing apparatus to patrol those disposable Black bodies created from neoliberalism. The result has been the hiring of more cops; the outfitting of local police departments with military leftovers; the increasing criminalization of behaviors and encounters; the militarizing of our schools, filling them with metal detectors, security guards, and city cops; and of course, the proliferation of the school-to-prison pipeline, intent on pushing kids out of school and into the hands of the carceral state.

The conditions of the small suburb of Ferguson, Missouri, in many ways are indicative of the neoliberal city or suburb today. For example, in 1980, 85 percent of residents in Ferguson were white; by 2008, 67 percent of residents were Black. Black unemployment is nearly double that of white unemployment. One in four residents live in poverty, with 44 percent of residents living on less than twice the poverty rate. Moreover, we know that in Ferguson, 86 percent of all police stops were of Black motorists, and of those arrested, 93 percent of those were Black. Overall, 85 percent of all those arrested in Ferguson were Black. And all of this was done under the auspices of a police force where only three out of fifty, or 6 percent of officers, were Black. Even beyond the police, the governing apparatus of Ferguson is white-dominated: five of Ferguson's six city council members, the mayor, and six of seven local school board members are all white, in a majority Black city.

This was the neoliberal context that surrounded Mike Brown and Darren Wilson on that fateful day in Ferguson, Missouri. This was the context in which a white man with a gun and a badge saw a young Black man with Hulk Hogan strength, paired with his white fear. The story of neoliberalism's impact on urban communities is actually fairly straightforward. However, with the election of Barack Obama, neoliberalism has taken what we might call a "multicultural turn."

With the election of Barack Obama as President of the United States, we now face a different scenario with regard to the demographics of state power. Specifically, the state is now racialized, not only in terms of its politics of inclusion and exclusion as they are directed toward largely racially marginal populations, but also in terms of its representation at the highest level. This reality means that we must complicate our understanding of state power and neoliberal agendas. Let me be clear: I believe President Obama has shown himself to be not only drawn to neoliberal policies and projects but actually a proponent of such a system of government. Whether it is his commitment to markets in the face of their historic near-collapse in 2008, or his embrace of privatization in charter schools as ways to address education failure in US public schools, or even his berating of the poor—most often Black people, for their seemingly deviant work and parenting practices as reasons for their stalled mobility—President Obama has demonstrated his commitment to a neoliberal approach to governing and cultural management.

However, having President Obama, the first African American president, as the symbolic head of the neoliberal state at this moment has not only meant the promotion of neoliberalism, but also more importantly, a variation of neoliberalism that emphasizes a kind of multicultural colorblindness. Colorblind racial ideology, by both decrying racism and designating anti-racism as one of the country's newly found core values, actually works to obscure the relationship between identity and privilege. Thus, through colorblind ideology one can claim to be in solidarity with Black people while at the same time denigrating the condition of poor Black people, faulting them for their behaviors or lack of a work ethic and not their race. Moreover, one could declare that "Black lives matter" while undermining any state-sponsored programs that would address the special needs of poor Black people. One could say, in fact, that "I am heartbroken with the death of Trayvon Martin because if I had a son, he would look like Trayvon," and recognize that that means nothing in terms of justice for Black people.

So this change in positioning, relative to power across identities, means that we must understand the disjuncture between the neoliberal policy agenda of the Obama administration and the policy needs of the most vulnerable members of Black communities. A central component of some of the most effective Black political activity has been the mobilization of Black people, targeting the state and demanding its active engagement in the expansion of resources and opportunities available to Black communities. The neoliberal agenda pursued by Bill Clinton and now Obama is actually one that restrains the work of the state and in many ways stands in opposition to the political commitments and strategies of most in Black communities; and has hampered, I would argue, Black people's ability to voice their agenda and needs, for fear of somehow undermining the first Black president. It is not, I think, a coincidence that the 2012 mantra in terms of campaigning directed at Black communities was that we were all supposed to "have the president's back"—I guess so he could walk all over ours.

I wanted to start this talk with a discussion of neoliberalism and its multicultural turn, because it is a reminder of the sustained attack on the basic humanity of poor Black people that provides the context in which we should understand the killing of young Black people, in particular young Black men, and the less visible assaults on Black women and murder of Black trans people. If we understand the attack of neoliberalism on poor communities, then we can reckon with the fact that this struggle really is about poor Black people. Those Black lives most under duress right now are the lives of poor Black people, suffering from the grips of a neoliberal agenda intent on controlling, or if necessary, killing them, often at the hands of the state. And we should be clear that poor Black lives do not matter in this country, and they never have. Moreover, we must be careful not to limit our understanding and outrage about state violence to this one very visible aggressive moment of state violence against Black people. We cannot allow anyone to detach the killing of Mike Brown from the neoliberal history that created the context in which he would be evaluated as a monster by a fearful Darren Wilson. No matter how much we vilify and prosecute police officers like Wilson or vigilantes like Zimmerman, these approaches to a limited justice, while appropriate as a first step, do little to challenge the systemic nature of the degradation of Black bodies made ever more pernicious under neoliberalism. An understanding of the relationship between neoliberalism and Black death means that our target has to be, or at least has to include, the larger system of neoliberalism. If that is the case, then no group can stand in solidarity with this particular moment of resistance while openly and proudly pursuing a neoliberal agenda—not if you truly want to engage in substantive solidarity. And that is the topic of the next section.

Performing Solidarity: LGBT Complicity = Black Death

On August 12, 2014, just three days after the murder of Michael Brown in Ferguson, Missouri, a group of LGBT organizations signed a letter in support of the family of Michael Brown. The letter, which is relatively short, reads as follows (and I'll read the entire thing):

> When communities experience fear, harassment and brutality simply because of who they are or how they look, we are failing as a nation. In light of the recent events in Missouri, it is clearer than ever that there is something profoundly wrong in our country.
>
> The lesbian, gay, bisexual and transgender (LGBT) community cannot be silent at this moment, because LGBT people come from all races, creeds, faiths and backgrounds, and because all movements of equality are deeply connected. We are all part of the fabric of this nation and the promise of liberty and justice for all is yet to be fulfilled.
>
> The LGBT community stands with the family of Michael Brown, who was gunned down in Ferguson, Missouri. We stand with the mothers and fathers of young Black men and women who fear for the safety of their children each time they leave their homes. We call on the national and local media to be responsible and steadfast in their coverage of this story and others like it—racialized killings that have marred this nation since the beginning of its history. We call on policy makers on all levels of American government not to shrink from action, and we are deeply grateful to Attorney General Eric Holder and the Department of Justice for their immediate commitment to a thorough investigation.
>
> At this moment, we are inspired by the words of Dr. Martin Luther King, Jr.: "In the end, we will remember not the words of our enemies . . . but the silence of our friends."[1]

All in all, I would argue that this is a powerful letter. By my count, seventy organizations signed on to this letter; organizations that decided to lend their voice ranged from the ACLU, to the HRC, to the National Black Justice Coalition, to the Black Youth Project 100 (BYP100)—and I will talk to them about that later. While one might take issue with parts of the letter, that is not my issue this evening. Overall, I found the letter compelling and understand the gesture of solidarity these groups are trying to signal. Many of these organizations and the constituencies they represent are trying to avoid the outrage emanating from LGBT communities of color when nothing is said about critical events in the lives of people of color. Some of these organizations and their constituencies also deeply feel committed to doing what is right.

Now, despite good intentions, I have to ask myself: Can the same organizations that have been at the forefront of their own neoliberal policy goals truly stand in solidarity with the family of Michael Brown, and other young Black men and women? Or is this an example of what I might call "performative solidarity"? The idea that mainstream LGBT organizations have been pushing a neoliberal agenda is a well-rehearsed argument made much more eloquently and extensively by the likes of Urvashi Vaid and Lisa Duggan, to name but a few. Marriage and the increased dependence on incarceration promoted through hate crimes legislation are but two of the policy items promoted by LGBT organizations that leverage a neoliberal approach to politics, which often serves to anchor poor Black people to the bottom of the racial order. Let me just say a few words about each of these policy agendas.

The quest for marriage equality has been much discussed in light of recent Supreme Court rulings. While the advance in same-sex marriage both in terms of public opinion and the courts has been celebrated by many, the naysayers of marriage equality on the left have seen their voices muted. Specifically, there are those in lesbian, gay, and queer communities—and I count myself among them—who believe that same-sex marriage only serves to legitimize a process intent on producing a hierarchy of citizenship and rights bolstered by the institution of marriage. This is a hierarchy that, in fact, is also racially coded. Numerous scholars have written about the racialized nature of state policies regulating what are thought to be deviant or nonnormative families. Marriage falls into a category of a racialized state project that is involved in the differential distribution of rights, which disproportionately disadvantages people who are not married, often people of color. Most explicitly, feminist scholars such as Wendy Mink and Anna Marie Smith have detailed the numerous laws that have been instituted to regulate the sex and intimate relations of women—disproportionately, poor women and women of color who are not married and who need state assistance. Like heterosexual marriage, same-sex marriage replicates an unequal distribution of rights, with the middle class, who are more likely to marry, benefiting while poor and working-class people of color, gay and straight, who are less likely to marry, are subjected to targeted regulation of their sexual, family, and intimate formations. Moreover, same-sex marriage—far from ending marriage as we know it—actually preserves, I would argue, a narrow system for the distribution of benefits that is tied to heteronormative understandings of the family. It allows the state to continue to shift its responsibility of providing for the well-being of its citizens to some other entity that we label the family.

As marriage and two-parent households are normalized and become the dominant discursive framework through which some LGBT communities enter the national consciousness as full citizens, it puts the LGBT community at odds demographically, at least with trends generally, and in particular, in Black communities. For example, the truth of the structure of the Black intimate sphere, at least in the US, is that nearly 80 percent of children born to Black women under thirty, and 70 percent of all Black children born, were born to women who are not married and probably will not marry. Data also indicates that the majority of children did not live in two-parent households. These details about the Black intimate sphere make Black people vulnerable to state power—state power that would regulate them not by legal disenfranchisement explicitly on race, but that would instead mobilize a colorblind ideology to minimize their full status as citizens by highlighting their incompatibility with normative expectations of family that are made valid in the quest for same-sex marriage.

I think a similar argument can be made about the use of criminalization and incarceration to protect queer bodies through hate speech legislation. Specifically in the threat posed to LGBTQI individuals in the form of bullying or harassment and physical harm, some mainstream LGBT organizations have pursued a policy agenda that includes tougher hate crime legislation, the introduction of legislation introducing anti–hate crime legislation on college campuses, and the recognition of cyberbullying as a form of harassment. And while I would not—and I am sure no one in this room would endorse ignoring the threat to LGBTQI lives, as our lives matter, right?— there is something ironic, dangerous, and very neoliberal about turning to a system of criminalization to protect the lives of queer folks who are daily threatened and harassed by the same police apparatus in their neighborhood. This is what I think Audre Lorde meant when she wrote, "the master's tools will never dismantle the master's house."[2] Thus, we have to ask, in the context of the expansion of the prison and policing industrial complex under neoliberalism: What does it mean to utilize the police as protector of gay and lesbian rights? Does it move us any closer to justice or freedom?

The group Gender JUST, which used to exist in Chicago, I think most clearly underlines the problem of dealing with queers in the prison industrial complex. They write:

> It is critical to remember that we face violence as youth, as people of color, as people living in poverty, as queers, as trans and gender non-conforming young people. We can't separate our identities and any approach to preventing violence must be holistic and incorporate our whole selves. . . .
> Our greatest concern is that there is a resounding demand for increased violence as a reaction, in the form of Hate Crime penalties which bolster the Prison-Industrial-Complex and Anti-bullying measures which open the door to zero-tolerance policies and reinforce the school-to-prison pipeline.[3]

Thus, in contrast to many marginalized people of color, the trend among gay leadership seems to be to go for normality: marriage, criminalization, and the military. The cost of being on the side of normal—as scholars such as Dean Spade, Michael Warner, and Lisa Duggan, have warned—is that you must participate in the neoliberal process of excluding and give up the cause of radical transformation. Many of the most visible policy wins of the gay and lesbian agenda are policies and programs that are deeply rooted in, and preserve the structural legitimacy and order of, neoliberalism.

These structural limitations are very different from what are called for by many in Black communities, policies that not only legitimize but also demand a significant shift in state resources. The LGBT domain seems committed to advancing instead a neoliberal agenda of inclusion that comes largely without substantial financial and political commitments on the part of the state and is fundamentally different from the demand of an active state made by many people of color. It is actually part of the reason, some would say, we have seen more of an advancement of an LGBT agenda than we have seen of a Black liberation agenda.

Thus, my concern with the letter signed by LGBT groups on August 12 in support of the family of Michael Brown is that it is completely disconnected and, I think, stands in opposition to the normalizing neoliberal project that has defined LGBT politics over the last decade or more. The letter represents, I think, a momentary performative solidarity that suggests a lack of a comprehensive understanding of the systemic threat to Black lives. If Black lives matter to the LGBT organizations that signed that letter, then it demands a rethinking of their policy priorities. It means understanding that pursuing a neoliberal agenda makes us complicit in Black death. It means pursuing an analysis and agenda that is not intent to secure rights for *our* group, or *your* group, but is rooted in a politics of liberation of oppressed people where our allies are punks, bulldaggers, and welfare queens.

This Is Not the Civil Rights Movement: The Queering of Black Liberation

I want to show you a little clip, because I think that this is, hopefully, our future:

> **Gwen Ifill, *PBS NewsHour*:** So, let me ask you this: Does this feel different to you? These protests we're seeing, these coast-to-coast rolling die-ins and roadblocks, does this feel like a different stage?
>
> **Tory Russell, Hands Up United:** Yeah, I mean it's younger, it's fresher. And I think we're more connected than most people think. I don't— This is not the civil rights movement. You can tell by how I got a hat on, my t-shirt, and how I rock my shoes. This is not the civil rights movement; this is the oppressed peoples' movement. So when you see us, you gonna see some gay folk, you gonna see some queer folk, you gonna see some poor Black folk, you gonna see some brown folk, you gonna see some white people—and we all out here for the same reasons. We wanna be free. We believe that we have the right *over* laws. I think the questions that we keep getting is: What's legal? We need to be talking about what's right. And we're not heading that way. So we need to go out into the streets and block some of that. And make this, you know, this system ungovernable, and disrupt it—until we get our own self-determination and our own self-liberation.[4]

So, to quote: "This is not the civil rights movement." I love that. The queering of Black liberation.

In this last section, I want to briefly—and I really am going to be brief—explore what it means to give voice to the possibility that there actually can emerge a new, transformative politics.

In 1997—oh my, so long ago—the journal *GLQ* published my article "Punks, Bulldaggers, and Welfare Queens: The Radical Potential of Queer Politics?" In the opening pages of the article, I wrote: "I envision a politics where one's relation to power, and not some homogenized identity, is privileged in determining one's political comrades. I'm talking about a politics where the *nonnormative* and *marginal* position of punks, bulldaggers, and welfare queens, for example, is the basis for progressive transformative coalition work. Thus, if there is any truly radical potential to be found in the idea of queerness and the practice of queer politics, it would seem to be located in its ability to create a space in opposition to dominant norms, a space where transformational political work can begin."[5]

Since the publication of that article, I have been searching, and people have been asking about, the politics I wrote about. And generally, over the years, sadly, there have been few opportunities to believe that we had created a space where transformational work could begin. Sadly and ironically, it is actually resistance to Black death at the hands of the police, resistance generated by the lack of a legitimate legal response, to the murder of Michael Brown and Eric Garner most recently, that I think raises the possibility of a reimagined, transformational politics that maybe we call queer and maybe we don't. But it is a transformational moment that has the potential to move beyond marriage and neoliberal homonormativity, centering our resistance around individuals like Michael Brown, Tamir Rice, and Marissa Alexander.

I should note that it is usually a much easier leap for those of us thinking and writing about death and violence and race and queerness, or at least queer politics, to marshal a different Black body, to mark this intersection. Individuals like CeCe McDonald, an African American trans woman who went to jail for second-degree manslaughter as a result of defending herself from a racist and transphobic attacker, I think are more traditional objects of our analysis and support. In many ways, I think CeCe fits our understanding of who can be the face of queer politics, even a radical queer politics. A more traditional queer politics might be more comfortable incorporating the killing of Sakia Gunn, the young Black lesbian who was killed in Newark, New Jersey, after rejecting the sexual advances of her killer. We might be more comfortable in our analyses of queer politics by focusing on Sakia Gunn than by focusing on someone like Michael Brown. But as I have said about other young Black (in particular) men who have been killed— and I will say it now about Michael Brown—for me Michael Brown's death is deeply connected to the killing of Sakia Gunn and the attack on and incarceration of CeCe McDonald. Not because of his sexual practice or his identity or his performance, but instead because Michael Brown, CeCe McDonald, and Sakia Gunn, as well as other young folks of color, operate in the world as queer subjects. As the targets of racial, normalizing projects intent on pathologizing them across the dimensions of race, class, gender, and sexuality while normalizing their degradation and marginalization until it becomes what we expect, the norm, until it becomes something we no longer see or pay attention to.

This sentiment is underscored in another letter. On December 4, a number of New York–based progressive and people of color queer organizations issued their own statement or letter. The organizations that signed on to this letter were FIERCE, Audre Lorde Project, AVP, GRIOT Circle, Streetwise and Safe, and the Sylvia Rivera Law Project.

The authors start the letter by listing the names of "those we have lost to police brutality," "those we have lost to the communal violence justified by the policing of our bodies," and those "Falsely Accused, Detained and Abused."[6] Those listed include Eleanor Bumpurs to Amadou Diallo to Eric Garner to Renata Hill and Patreese Johnson of the Jersey Four. In no way is this a cohesive group of LGBT individuals, but they all are queer subjects in the most expansive and progressive sense of the idea. It is in the heart of the letter that the signatories make clear their vision of the movement. They write:

> We are clear as Lesbian, Gay, Bisexual, Two Spirit, Trans and Gender Non-Conforming People of Color that our safety is contingent on the preservation of all Black and People of Color bodies. We have been righteous in fighting against anti-Black racism & anti-immigrant oppression, that allows for state controlled white supremacy to exist and justify the murder of our people. The murders of Mike Brown, Tamir Rice, Akai Gurley and Eric Garner prove that Black lives are seen as dangerous and expendable. For those of us that are Queer, Trans, Black and People of Color, our bodies, our gender expression and who we love puts us further away from the "norms" and has falsely perceived us as the most threatening, less than human, and even more dangerous of all bodies.[7]

These organizations end their statement asking, "In this moment, what are we willing to do to be free?" Across the country people, I think, have been answering this seemingly simple yet complicated question by putting their bodies on the line to disrupt everyday life and to remind those with power that, in fact, yes, Black lives do matter. As Tory Russell from Hands Up United reminds us: this is not the civil rights movement. It also is not the Stonewall rebellion, or the feminist movement. This is a new configuration of resistance and struggle that is working to make a space where, yes, transformational work can begin.

I have had the honor of working closely with the BYP100—probably not closely enough since they signed that other letter, but that's all right. We work together, they lead themselves. I've had the honor of working closely with the BYP100, a group of young Black activists between the ages of fifteen and thirty-five. They represent, I think, the best of what this moment promises. They are young organizers who embrace, as they say, a Black feminist and queer analysis, independent of who their intimate and sexual partners are. For them, being queer is both an identity and a position relative to oppressive state power, a position that is routinely inhabited by young people of color. The BYP100, however, is an organization that also declares itself to be unapologetically Black and insists on radical Black leadership at this moment. These are young people that understand the governing process and have developed their own policy agenda, "The Agenda to Keep Us Safe." But even while they engage in policy debates, they also understand the limits of trusting the neoliberal state to secure their freedom or safety. So, for example, while they support the use of body cameras on police as a policy initiative, they also remind us that video footage didn't stop the murder of Oscar Grant or Eric Garner. The BYP100, I often say, they have their finger on policy but their minds on freedom. They close their meetings chanting Assata Shakur's directive: It is our duty to fight. It is our duty to win. We must love each other and support each other. We have nothing to lose but our chains.

The BYP100 is but one organization that is part of a kind of new liberatory movement developing not just across the country but across the world. A movement made up, as Tory Russell described, of some gays, some queer folk, some poor Black people, some brown folks, some white folks, some feminists—oh, wait, he did not say feminists, but I know he meant to—but all of them united in their position as oppressed people, a.k.a. politically queer. And all fighting for freedom—not marriage, not increased criminalization, not access to the military, but for freedom. Thus, I have watched in awe and stood in deference and tried to enact a substantive solidarity where I and the people around me put our privilege on the line for the increasing numbers of young people taking to the streets across the world engaging in an intersectional and queer politics of resistance. And as I have said before, some of these young people are our students, who have taken what they've learned in our classes and transformed our theories, books, and projects, turned them into campaigns that actually impact lives. Others are being pulled into the street out of their own experience, where they know that their life and happiness is tenuous at best under the system of neoliberalism that rules the land, even though they do not call it neoliberalism. Still others, whose identities do not mark them as disposable—we might in some cases call them white allies—are engaging in radical resistance because it is the right thing to do. It is their form of substantive solidarity work. In organizations like the BYP100, FIERCE, ALP, Hands Up United, and We Charge Genocide, activists are building a politic, both analysis and action, that makes visible the transformative potential of queering Black liberation.

Now I might be wrong, but I believe that this is an incredible moment in the movement to make Black lives actually matter. So, to the LGBT movement or organizations, and hopefully they're different, I would ask that instead of a move toward normality we consider an embrace of deviance.

We might build on the tradition of those who challenged the police at the Stonewall riots; or AIDS activists, many of them in the room, who challenged the government when it denied the right for us to live; or trans activists who are changing laws, language, and how we understand ourselves, even as their very lives are being threatened. In the resilience and resistance of less traditional queer bodies and communities, there are in fact models of how LGBT organizations might stand in substantive solidarity demonstrating truthfully that Black lives matter. At the very least, we can use our privilege and homonormative power to create spaces where the radical imagination of activists can be unleashed. We must seize this opportunity to move beyond marriage, the military, and incarceration, to envision and work toward a radical queer politics—led by youth of color because their lives represent the place of what is possible. If we do that, we should remember that we actually have nothing to lose but our chains.

Thank you very much.

Notes

1. Letter available at: https://assets2.hrc.org/files/assets/resources/LGBTLetterMichaelBrown.pdf.

2. Audre Lorde, "The Master's Tools Will Never Dismantle the Master's House," in *Sister Outsider: Essays and Speeches* (Freedom, CA: Crossing Press, 1984).

3. Gender JUST, "Who We Are," 2015, accessed October 23, 2022, https://genderjust.wixsite.com/genderjust.

4. *PBS NewsHour*, "Why Do You March? Young Protesters Explain What Drives Them," December 8, 2014, YouTube, accessed October 23, 2022, https://www.youtube.com/watch?v=JfC_pfsqLqw.

5. Cathy J. Cohen. "Punks, Bulldaggers, and Welfare Queens: The Radical Potential of Queer Politics?," *GLQ: A Journal of Lesbian and Gay Studies* 3, no. 4 (1997): 438.

6. "Wake Up, Rise Up!: Wake Up, Rise Up Statement with ALP, AVP, SRLP, SAS, & GRIOT Circle," FIERCE, December 3, 2014, accessed October 23, 2022, http://www.fiercenyc.org/releases/wake-rise.

7. "Wake Up, Rise Up!," FIERCE.

Cathy J. Cohen Reflects on "#DoBlackLivesMatter? From Michael Brown to CeCe McDonald: On Black Death and LGBTQ Politics"

The lecture focused on a question of performative versus substantive political solidarity: How do LGBTQI organizations fit into a neoliberal project that is exclusionary and complicit in Black death? In the current political moment, I am most interested in how a Black queer feminist lens has emerged to take up room in leadership. Last year we had the largest mobilization movement, according to the *Times*, largely in response to the execution of George Floyd. A lot of the groundwork for that movement was laid by Dream Defenders, BYP100, and the Movement for Black Lives, organizations and networks that profess to hold on to a Black queer feminist framework.

This has led me to contemplate a few questions that I might have taken up if I gave the lecture today. First, what do we mean by "Black queer feminism"? Are we talking about identities and mobilization of people who understand themselves to be queer? That is different than what I thought of, in "Punks, Bulldaggers, and Welfare Queens," as a political positionality on the outside of power that allows us to be in collaboration. Second, there's a question of genealogy. People often start at Combahee and make the comparison between today and the civil rights movement. But they jump over the consolidation of a Black, politicized, gay and lesbian community of the 1980s and 1990s. I think this is the real lineage, including Combahee, of what we're seeing today. But that gets erased. Third, who is the queer subject at the center of Black queer feminism? In the Kessler Lecture, I brought up that I see Mike Brown as a queer subject. Not because of his identity or performance in terms of sexuality, but because of the ways that many young Black and brown folks are marginalized and oppressed; are demeaned, understood as guilty, and pushed on the outside. It becomes something that we don't even notice anymore.

To me, that's queerness. Lastly, what is a Black queer feminist praxis right now? This is something that I believe we are still working out. For me, Black queer feminism understands, as bell hooks urged, that we must center those who are on the margins in our communities. It is an approach and ideology that thinks expansively about oppression and freedom. Thus, it not only demands that we "say her name" when thinking about police violence but understands that the carceral side of the state manifests itself in numerous entities, from the police, to the prison guard, to the school officer, to the welfare manager and beyond. A Black queer feminist approach is attuned to amplifying the voices and supporting the leadership, actions, and demands of marginal subjects who live at the intersection of race, class, gender, and sexuality. Possibly most importantly, Black queer feminism is rooted in a love of Black people and empowered by the vision of what might be. What Robin D. G. Kelley calls "freedom dreams."[1]

This political moment, however, dictates a different set of questions than those I posed in 2014. In a lecture today, I would begin with a section focusing not on neoliberalism but on the broader framework of racial capitalism. How do we think about how political and economic power set the context for today's politics? I would talk about George Floyd and Breonna Taylor, of course, but would try to think more capaciously about the state and capitalism's many forms of extraction from communities of color. In the second section of a newly fashioned talk, I would focus on the backlash and lasting moment of multicultural neoliberals. It was kind of amazing reading the lecture. Like, wow, that moment is gone, sort of. There's this unrepentant rise of white supremacy and anti-Blackness that was always there but has recently taken on full force. However, in other parts of society, namely through capitalism, we still see the prominence of multicultural neoliberalism. It was evident every time a company sent out a message about how they value diversity in the wake of the killing of George Floyd and Breonna Taylor, without any real shift in the allocation of power within those same companies. Finally, in the third section of this newly imagined talk, I'd try to figure out a way of—in a gentle, supportive, and loving way—taking seriously the faults of the movements. What do we have to do better? How do we think differently and more expansively about how to address people's daily challenges, while still moving them toward radical possibilities? There is the aspiration of a Black queer feminist praxis and framework, and then there's the practice of hierarchy, what happens with money, the dangers of celebrity, and not taking the full opportunity to organize. And again, how, or can we, use the idea of "queer" to organize and base-build? What might it mean to use the framework of "queer" when thinking about George Floyd, as a way of building solidarity?

While there will always be challenges that movements have to face, we also must recognize how they have helped us think differently about what might be. Sometimes we must take some time to think about what has been accomplished. The great thing about preparing for the Kessler Lecture was that I took about two weeks to just sit at a table and think and write and think. You generally don't do that for a talk, but it was important to me to say something coherent and meaningful. For me, it wasn't just a talk—it was coming back to CLAGS. New York and CLAGS in the '90s is where I grew up intellectually. It was my interactions and friendships with individuals like M. Jacqui Alexander, Katherine Acey, Robert Reid-Pharr, Jafari Allen, Kendall Thomas, Cheryl Clarke, Urvashi Vaid, Vanessa Agard-Jones, and of course, Colin Robinson (to mention only a few) that helped me produce "Punks, Bulldaggers, and Welfare Queens" and *The Boundaries of Blackness*. Through CLAGS I was able to be part of the planning group of the Black Nations/Queer Nations? symposium. CLAGS is unlike any other institution that I've engaged with around LGBTQI intellect. It was this incredible radical intellectual space full of folks of color. It was a place of community. We built friendships. We were building the Audre Lorde Project. It was this kind of political praxis rooted in intellectual work. It was special. So, it was because of my history with CLAGS that I spent two weeks thinking about the Kessler Lecture. I was going home to a place that I felt helped form me. I didn't want to disappoint that kind of homecoming.

Notes

1. Robin D. G. Kelley, *Freedom Dreams: The Black Radical Imagination* (Boston: Beacon Press, 2002).

THE DAVID R. KESSLER LECTURES 2002–2020

2002   JONATHAN NED KATZ

2003   GAYLE RUBIN

2004   ISAAC JULIEN

2006   ADRIENNE RICH

2007   DOUGLAS CRIMP

2008   SUSAN STRYKER

2009   SARAH SCHULMAN

2010   URVASHI VAID

2012   MARTIN DUBERMAN

2013   CHERYL CLARKE

2014   CATHY J. COHEN

2015   RICHARD FUNG

2016   DEAN SPADE

2017   SARA AHMED

2018   AMBER HOLLIBAUGH

2019   JASBIR K. PUAR

2020   RODERICK A. FERGUSON

Richard Fung

Richard Fung is a Trinidad-born, Toronto-based video artist, cultural critic, and educator. His work comprises of a series of videos on subjects ranging from the role of the Asian male in gay pornography to colonialism in Canada and the Caribbean, immigration and refugee issues, social justice in Israel/Palestine, anti-Black racism in policing, homophobia, AIDS, and his own family history. His tapes and projections, which include *Chinese Characters* (1986), *My Mother's Place* (1990), *Sea in the Blood* (2000), *Jehad in Motion* (2007), *Dal Puri Diaspora* (2012), and *Re:Orientations* (2016), have been widely exhibited and collected internationally, and have been broadcast in Canada, the United States, and Trinidad and Tobago.

His essays, which include "Looking for My Penis: The Eroticized Asian in Gay Video Porn" (1991), have been published in many journals and anthologies, and he is the coauthor with Monika Kin Gagnon of *13 Conversations on Art and Cultural Race Politics* (2002). Fung is a past fellow at the Mark S. Bonham Centre for Sexual Diversity Studies at the University of Toronto, a past Rockefeller Fellow at the Center for Media, Culture and History at New York University, and has received the Bell Canada Award for outstanding achievement in video art. He is professor emeritus in the faculty of art at OCAD University, where he taught courses in integrated media and art and scial change.

Re-Orientations:
Shifts and Continuities in Asian Canadian Queer and Trans Identities and Activism

DECEMBER 16, 2015

My work in video and writing arose within, and is sustained by, transnational histories and relationships: my great-grandparents' journey in the 1860s from Fujian, China, to the sugarcane plantations of south Trinidad; my own migration from Port of Spain to Toronto via Dublin in the 1970s; and my ongoing exchanges across the world, most especially across the Canada–US border.

My first video, *Orientations*, came out of my work with Gay Asians Toronto, which I cofounded in 1980. GAT was inspired after Tony Souza and I attended the Third World Lesbian and Gay Conference in Washington, organized by the National Coalition of Black Gays in 1979 to coincide with the first National March on Washington for Lesbian and Gay Rights. It was such a high meeting lesbian and gay Asian activists for the first time that I wanted to recreate that energy in Toronto.

Orientations has another cross-border connection, as it was prompted by John Greyson moving back to Toronto from New York City, where he worked designing *The Independent*, the magazine of the Association of Independent Video and Filmmakers. John had his own VHS camera and he offered to shoot anything I wanted. His stated plan was to prevent me from pursuing graduate work in film studies and encourage me to instead become an artist. And I guess it worked. Although I still did end up in a university, as did he.

And my most widely published essay, "Looking for My Penis: The Eroticized Asian in Gay Video Porn," was originally a presentation at the conference How Do I Look?, which was organized by the group Bad Object-Choices here in New York. In the mid-'90s I did a Rockefeller residency at the Center for Media Culture and History at NYU, which was crucial to my development. New York has been good to me.

I therefore want to recognize and thank my transnational community of friends, activists, thinkers, artists, and writers—the biological and chosen family that sustains me and my work. Some of you are here.

Finally, among acknowledgments, I want to celebrate my partner, Tim McCaskell. To risk essentialism, Tim and I both come from families—mine Chinese and Catholic, his Scottish/Irish and Presbyterian—where emotional declarations are not the MO. That might be one reason why we've not married; we'd be expected to give gushy speeches. But this fall marks forty years of shared political struggle, collaboration, learning, support, and yes, love. I think we've been a political and ethical compass for each other. Thanks, Tim.

As the Kessler is a career award, it comes serendipitously at a point at which I am revisiting my first video, the documentary, *Orientations: Lesbian and Gay Asians*, made in 1984. This is part of a four-year research creation project that culminates in a new documentary, *Re:Orientations*. This project has put me in the space of contemplating the political context of the early '80s versus today: What has changed and what has remained the same three decades on?

Orientations features interviews with fourteen lesbians and gay men. In 1984, Asian Canadians were few on the ground in Toronto's lesbian and gay community. I kept finding people to add even as I was editing, which was a challenge since this was still the era of VHS straight-cut linear editing, and decisions could not be reversed without losing a generation, which affected the quality of the image. *Re:Orientations* includes seven of the original fourteen participants, plus six short conversations with a younger generation of queer and trans scholars, activists, and cultural producers. The intention for including the latter is not to represent the contemporary environment, which would be impossible. For one thing, today's active pan-Asian LGBTQ people in Toronto span several generations—I recently attended a performance by the Asian Arts Freedom School where the majority were in their teens and early twenties, many cheered on by their parents. Rather, the inclusion of these conversations is to provide context and open up questions that are not otherwise broached in the life stories or perspectives of the main participants. For those who have seen my 1990 video essay *My Mother's Place*, it's somewhat akin to the role played by Himani Bannerji, Dorothy Smith, Ramabai Espinet, and Glace Lawrence.

But neither did *Orientations* represent the range of lesbian and gay Asian lives in Toronto in the '80s, even though the communities were smaller and less diverse. Human rights protection took another two years, and it was still legal to discriminate. So those who agreed to participate were either committed, courageous, or felt protected in some way. Or they were foolhardy. Most participants were not out to family, and since this was conceived as a consciousness-raising project, I did not request releases but made sure that the documentary wouldn't air, and I was selective about public screenings.

We are still in the postproduction phase of *Re:Orientations*, so what you'll see is a work in progress. This means the order and pacing have to be fine-tuned, we need pickup shots, we are still experimenting with the green screen backgrounds, the image requires color correction, and the sound has to be mixed. The current music and titles are temporary, and we are still in the process of image research and rights clearance.

After all those provisos, here are the opening sixteen minutes, which will introduce you to the original participants.

Between 1984 and now, a lot has happened at the intersection of race, gender, and sexuality that affects queer pan-Asian Canadians. I'll name just four.

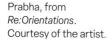

Prabha, from
Re:Orientations.
Courtesy of the artist.

Prabha on Wellesley,
from *Re:Orientations*.
Courtesy of the artist.

Paul playing for Alf,
from *Re:Orientations*.
Courtesy of the artist.

Paul looks at himself,
from *Re:Orientations*.
Courtesy of the artist.

First, in 1984, as Nathan points out, we used the terms "lesbian and gay,"
and trans politics wasn't yet on *my* political radar. Or rather, lesbian- and
gay-identified people were still trying to establish that we were *not* in fact
transgender. Transgender and homosexual—and feminist—politics still
maneuver around each other, but there is more of a détente as the coalition of LGBTI and the ever-extending alphabet foregrounds that there are
distinctions as well as shared stakes. Intersectionality remains key, of course,
and later in *Re:Orientations*, Nathan discusses the specificity of his own transition to become a son within the context of a Chinese Canadian family.

Second, in 1984, I didn't know any Asian Canadians with HIV/AIDS.
Indeed, it was only in that year that HIV—or more precisely, HTLV-III—
was discovered to be the cause of AIDS. And AIDS itself was only so named
two years earlier; before that it was GRID (gay-related immune deficiency).
Three of the original participants of *Orientations*, including Lloyd Wong,
whom you see at the start walking in Chinatown, and Lim Pei-Hsien, who
dances the opening sequence in a mask, subsequently died of AIDS-related
causes. Alan Li goes on to become a pioneering physician/organizer treating
and advocating around HIV/AIDS as it relates not just to gay Asians, but
also to refugees and undocumented immigrants. AIDS affects me directly,

Tony, from *Re:Orientations*.
Courtesy of the artist.

El-Farouk, from
Re:Orientations.
Courtesy of the artist.

as my partner Tim's infection was confirmed when the HIV test was finally available. I went on to make *Fighting Chance* (1990), *Steam Clean* (1990), and *Sea in the Blood* (2000).

Third, the rise of Islamophobia, starting with Operation Desert Shield and the first Gulf War in 1990–91 and intensifying today in the wake of Paris and San Bernardino, has meant that Muslims (queer and not), brown people (Muslim or not), and people who merely have Muslim-sounding names, are subject to an alarming intensification of racist discourse and violence that recalls the anti-Jewish rhetoric of the ascendent Nazis in Germany and the anti-Japanese hysteria following Pearl Harbor. This goes hand in hand with a politics of pinkwashing and homonationalism, which saw former Canadian prime minister, Conservative Stephen Harper, use gay rights as a way to divide the world into the civilized and the barbaric, a particularly cynical move since his party and its precursors opposed every proposed gay rights legislation in Canada.

In 1984, Prabha Khosla complained about the patronizing treatment she experienced if wearing a sari at a feminist event, and in *Re:Orientations* she draws the parallel to the hijab. Ponni Arasu, one of the new participants, whom I first met as a young queer activist in New Delhi, interestingly observes that if she or her peers mark themselves as queer by hairstyle or clothing, they experience less racism in Toronto than if their style is deemed "traditional."

Another new participant in *Re:Orientations,* lawyer and activist El-Farouk Khaki, discusses the delicate negotiations progressive queer Muslims like himself must make in the face of *both* Islamophobia *and* the increasing spread of conservative movements within Islam.

Finally, the internet has impacted not just how we do things, but the very survival of traditional queer neighborhoods. In 1984, *The Body Politic, Xtra,* and *Rites* magazines were the only media outlets for lesbians and gay men in Toronto. Both were run by primarily white activists but were aligned with progressive politics. Issues around racism and representation could be taken up directly, and there was a common language to debate grievances. By contrast, on contemporary dating apps such as Grindr, anti-Asian racism and transphobia are explicit and unapologetic, in sync with the anonymity and uncensored ethos of the internet. Resisting racism in this context is not so straightforward or effective, and I was myself surprised at the extent to which young queer Asians in our research identified racism as central, even as Toronto and the LGBTI communities have become ever more diverse. Ponni Arasu does make a noteworthy suggestion, however: that racism might appear more urgent within the downtown queer context, but for those who live in ethnic enclaves in the periphery, homophobia and transphobia within their communities might seem more pressing.

These four changes I've described are evident and, in some ways, anticipated. What's *not* always apparent but nevertheless shapes the political developments and the daily life of LGBT people over the last three decades is that this period saw the full blossoming of neoliberalism in both Canada and the United States.

By "neoliberalism," I'm referring to an ideological embrace of commodification and profit that manifest in government policies that favor free trade and deregulation of business practices, privatization, tax cuts for the rich and corporations, and reduced social spending. Neoliberal policies result in the weakening power of governments to protect local interests in the face of corporate profits, which especially impacts people living in less powerful nations. They have also led to increasing economic disparity *within* nations since deregulation and anti-union policies have produced a super-wealthy corporate class while keeping down wages and increasing precarity for workers. Meanwhile, lower taxes for corporations and the wealthy reduce state coffers and shred the social safety net. These are the conditions in which the struggle for gay rights have been fought and largely won. It's relevant to say here that Canadians have historically enjoyed more of a welfare state than Americans, so the change in direction is more profoundly felt. Second, the new Liberal government of Justin Trudeau is promising to reverse the trend back to more Keynesian practices, but we have to see if and how this unfolds, since neoliberal thinking is already hegemonic.

Neoliberalism manifests itself in myriad ways for queers in Toronto, some quite subtle. In the first year of the project, my graduate assistant, Fritz Pino, was tasked with researching LGBTI pan-Asian Canadian presence in the greater Toronto area. Two things in his findings stood out: first, just how much there was; second, how many of the individuals he found were employed in LGBT-identified positions—the trans outreach worker in an AIDS organization, the LGBT coordinator in a community center, the executive director of a culturally specific organization. This mirrored my own research for another art project—in Mississauga, the city that abuts Toronto and is really part of the same conurbation. Here I was similarly struck that everyone I spoke with, including those who organized that city's Pride, was working on LGBT issues as part of their *job*. Here was a different form of "gay for pay."

In the '70s, only a small number of people worked in lesbian and gay organizations, in Canada mostly funded by donations and small government grants. From the '80s and '90s, AIDS education and prevention became the cover for anti-homophobia work all over the world, from New York to New Delhi, and increased funding to AIDS Service Organizations (ASOs) boosted the number of paid positions for queer-related work. This channeled resources to LGBT organizing, and it allowed queer folk to work on queer issues in queer-friendly spaces. For example, in Toronto, groups such as Alliance for South Asian AIDS Prevention (ASAAP) and Asian Community AIDS Services (ACAS) have helped support at least a couple of generations of queer Asians both by serving them and offering them paid work.

In his forthcoming book *Queer Progress*, Tim McCaskell notes that when the rise of neoconservatism blocked political change in the 1980s, the movement turned to the courts to win rights.[1] This process elevated the role of lawyers in shaping political strategies, and I would add it centered particular types of LGBT subjects—conforming citizens—to legitimize and represent those agendas to the public. With the success of gay rights in Canada, gay activism has been replaced in large part by gay services, which are by definition professional.

What we see today is an unprecedented professionalization of LGBTI work. And here I notice a mimicking of corporate practices—note I said "executive director" earlier; the ED of one group I looked at had no other staff. There is an emergent entrepreneurialism, even among some self-defined activists, whose bios are replete with hyperbolic claims of radicalism. This may be followed by contact information for giving paid talks or facilitating workshops. While this might sound harsh and judgmental, I see it all in a context of increasing precarity, where marketing oneself, even in radical terms, can become a means of survival.

I won't make deterministic claims about the professionalization of what used to be volunteer-based activism. Nevertheless, I'm cautioned by a 1990 article by sociologist Roxanna Ng, who documented how staffing and state funding served to dis-organize the work of a Toronto immigrant women's center by limiting what activities could be applied for, hence distorting their agenda, and further by directing time toward lengthy grant-writing and reporting procedures.[2]

Ng's instructive tale about the dependence on state funding is also relevant to a recent crisis in Toronto's LGBTI communities.

Tony Souza, one of the original participants in *Orientations*, was a member of the now defunct group Queers Against Israeli Apartheid (QuAIA), which was an outgrowth of his work as the coordinator of the Toronto Committee for the Liberation of South Africa (TCLSAC).

In 2010, Pride Toronto briefly banned QuAIA after right-wing city councilors and our mayor at the time, Rob Ford—I bet the only Canadian municipal politician any of you who is not Canadian has ever heard of—threatened to revoke city funding if the group was allowed to march. Pride is heavily subsidized as one of the largest tourist events in Toronto. Pressure was also put on the TD Bank, Pride's major sponsor, to withdraw support.

I was active with QuAIA, and when I met with the Pride board of directors about the banning, I observed that most of them saw their role not in the framework of LGBTI activism, but rather as volunteers running a festival—volunteering for Pride could now be a plus on the resumes of advancing professionals. Success was not judged in political terms, but rather by growth, and the board acted to ensure increases in attendance, budget, and scale. In thinking of the apolitical leadership of the most visible queer presence in the city, I was struck that the embrace of LGBT causes by the corporate sector, especially the banks, was premised on and advanced a narrow version of queer life as well-paid, high-consuming partyers. Asserting a more critical, bothersome social justice agenda threatened corporate and state goodwill. In the case of Pride and the TD Bank, it was *assumed* to threaten funding, which engendered an act of self-censorship. In this instance TD didn't pull out; however, I have witnessed other instances when corporate support was withdrawn when the sponsored event became too politically critical.

In thinking through advancing neoliberalism in the context of my project, what's significant is not the differences between generations, but rather the shifting conditions and cultural norms that affect everyone working today, no matter their age. I am as implicated as anyone.

Orientations was not made as a professional project but a consciousness-raising tool, produced with a grant of $2,500 from the Lesbian and Gay Community Appeal, now Community One Foundation. By contrast, *Re:Orientations* is a four-year research creation grant funded by the Social Sciences and Humanities Research Council of Canada. I have research collaborators—historian Roland Coloma and sociologist Amar Wahab—and I am able to hire a number of graduate and undergraduate research assistants. Officially, its purpose is the production of knowledge.

When I made *Orientations,* I saw my videos as primarily political work. For many years I thought of formal experimentation in pedagogical terms: How to address minoritized spectators? How to get viewers to attend to the content differently? I first took on the identity of artist to apply for arts council grants. And I now teach in a university dedicated to art and design.

From the 1990s, much LGBT activism moved into the universities for at least a couple of reasons: it was seen as a safe place for controversial ideas, and it was thought of as a refuge from capitalist production, better than making profit for a corporation.

In my faculty, 40 percent of my evaluation for tenure, promotion, and salary raises is based on artistic production. When my artistic production is *Re:Orientations,* I am also gay for pay. As my institution attempts to rebrand itself through a minor in Art and Social Change, an initiative I'm helping to shape, my social justice activism and organizing is also serving professional purposes. It puts me in a dilemma and of course it's risky, as while certain kinds of political activity buttress the brand—I've been asked to lead the development on the university's presence at Pride this year, for example—other kinds of activism might cause problems for the institution: for example, criticism of apartheid state policies in Israel/Palestine.

I've come to realize how teaching in an art and design institution stealthily altered my work. For some years after joining the school, I concentrated on installation and projections. While I was originally very proud of the mobility of the work—that a video like *My Mother's Place* could play at the National Gallery of Canada, a high school classroom, a documentary film festival, and a Caribbean Chinese community group in a church basement—I began to value more legitimate artistic venues. Working within a gallery context made me "feel good" among my artist colleagues, like I "fit in" better, if I might draw on Sara Ahmed. It came to a head when my last documentary, *Dal Puri Diaspora*, was embraced by the community it depicts and addresses—Caribbean people, and Indo-Caribbean people in particular—but was relatively unsuccessful in prestige film festivals. This forced me to re-evaluate what was important to me and to my political project, and to come to terms with the material conditions for my own drift. And if I thought it was all in my head, just last week I sat on a performance review committee and there it was in black and white:

Practice/Research Review:

a. For practice or research to be valued it must have been disseminated, an article published, a work shown in a gallery, etc.
b. Determine the "strength" of the dissemination, a curated exhibition versus a non-curated one, a provincial gallery versus a national museum, and/or significant contribution to the cultural life of their community.
c. Generally, all activities have value, but outcomes recognized by peer-review, peer and industry awards, books published by recognized publishers, funded award and government and foundations meet a higher level of review and value than work that has not been recognized in this manner.

These are reasonable criteria for assessing a studio art professor, but the assignment of value based on prestige is problematic for those whose work addresses minoritized communities and concerns. I should say here that I've done well in my institution, but I came to academia after my career was established, and I recognize the pressure on younger academics, ones looking for permanent positions, perhaps trying to get out of the unsustainable grind of sessional teaching.

My purpose in raising these questions is not to discount or delegitimize the work of those of us who teach in universities. But I do think it necessary that we be clearheaded about the differential stakes between personal career and progressive political change, as these might not always align. Our work might not look like capitalist wage labor, but neoliberalism is alive and well in the university.

Re:Orientations covers many topics, but let me now screen a short clip about work.

Sylvia, from *Re:Orientations*.
Courtesy of the artist.

Mary-Woo, from
Re:Orientations.
Courtesy of the artist.

Mary-Woo and Terrie,
from *Re:Orientations*.
Courtesy of the artist.

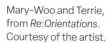

Gary, from
Re:Orientations.
Courtesy of the artist.

In 1984, most of the participants of *Orientations* were in their twenties. A few, like Tony Souza, Mary-Woo Sims, and Gary Jung, had steady jobs, but most were either students or casually employed. Now they're in their fifties to seventies, mainly mid-career, and that small sequence shows the range of economic circumstances. Sylvia is successful in the financial world and lives in a waterfront condo with her American wife. Gary retired from years in the post office, one of the last generation to enjoy a well-paid union job in a state-run corporation—Stephen Harper moved to stop mail delivery in Canada, in part to get rid of this category of worker. And Prabha works freelance as a consultant. Her services are sought all over the world, but she doesn't have job security or benefits, and in another section of the documentary she talks about her uncertainties over aging without a pension.

In 1984, people constituted themselves as queer in spaces such as bars, restaurants, saunas, washrooms, parks, and cultural events. Gays and lesbians also came together based on identities, activities such as sports and potlucks, and activist projects, whether queer-specific or, for women, feminist initiatives like the Toronto Women's Bookstore. These sites were not always welcoming to racialized people, but they were where one had to go to meet other queers and people congregated across various differences, including class.

The lessening of homophobia coupled with rising class inequity exacerbated by neoliberalism means that the queer elite are no longer forced to socialize with the hoi polloi. The boardroom and high-end resorts have become more gay-friendly. The sheer growth in numbers of LGBTI people and the transfer of much queer life onto the internet also contribute to fragmentation and a dis-location of LGBT life. The three people in this last clip do not cross paths in Toronto.

Haunting me throughout this project are questions about the usefulness and sustainability of the framework "queer pan-Asian Canadian."

First, there are the vastly divergent discourses facing those who fall under the term "Asian"—from model minority to terrorist threat, which strains a pan-ethnic fabric that was never tightly woven. Second is the politics of Asian pan-ethnicity as an anti-racism project against the ongoing urgency of anti-Black racism and the sovereignty claims of Indigenous people in the context of Canada as a white settler colony. Yet racism targeted at various Asian groups continues to exist.

Although there are still gains to be fought for, especially for trans people, LGBTI rights have largely been won from the state. And yet homophobia

Judy, from *Re:Orientations*. Courtesy of the artist

continues to exist. Students in my LGBT course seem to have higher levels of mental health issues.

I don't have an answer to these conundrums. I'll end by leaving you with the thoughts of Ju Hui Judy Han, from one of the new conversations in *Re:Orientations*. These are the closing words in the film:

> I would never say that queer bodies don't matter or queer people don't matter to queer politics, but it's what identity does and what culture does, as opposed to what it is and what it should be.
>
> I think coming together and forming queer Asian spaces felt like a radical project some time ago. To meet with other queer Asian Americans, to meet with other queer Asian activists, felt like we were trying to radicalize some form of community-building. Today, I think, with so many of us actively involved in a variety of social justice movements and having asserted our queer political subjectivity in a number of different ways, without necessarily convening as under the umbrella of "queer Asian," it feels like we need to imagine a different kind of gathering and a different kind of coming together. And I'm not sure what that is exactly, but I don't think that kind of identity-based politics is all there is. There's got to be more.

Notes

1. Tim McCaskell, *Queer Progress: From Homophobia to Homonationalism* (Toronto: Between the Lines, 2016).

2. Roxana Ng, *The Politics of Community Services: Immigrant Women, Class and State* (Chicago: Garamond Press, 1988).

Richard Fung Reflects on "Re-Orientations: Shifts and Continuities in Asian Canadian Queer and Trans Identities and Activism"

At the time of my Kessler Lecture in 2015, I was editing *Re:Orientations*, which revisits participants from my 1984 video *Orientations: Lesbian and Gay Asians*. When released the following year, it was eagerly programmed by Asian American and Asian Canadian film festivals, as well as at queer events in Canada, Asia, and Britain. Nonetheless it was declined by most American LGBT festivals. I imagine the limited take-up was due in part to the filmmaking; I stubbornly stuck to decisions that would limit popularity. Nevertheless, I got the impression that Asian diaspora communities were more ready to confront homophobia and transphobia than queer communities in the US were to consider issues for Asians, at least in the context of an LGBTQI film festival, where entertainment long ago became the primary directive.

In 2021, anti-Asian racism is on the table. The increase in violence roused and enabled by former president Trump's race-baiting over COVID-19 and economic and geopolitical competition with China, plus the mass shootings in Atlanta, have allowed a platform for Asian organizations and individuals on both sides of the 49th parallel. Consequently, there is a rush to rethink Asians beyond the framework of model minority, as victims of racism.

But the predominant paradigm of "anti-Asian hate" is problematic. It is both incorrect and inadequate, because it reduces racism to aggression and hostile feelings. While even nonviolent acts such as shunning and name-calling can profoundly impact one's psyche, it is mostly systemic racism, the invisible kind, that impacts our life possibilities. A 2017 Canadian university study found that job applicants with Asian names (Chinese, Indian, and Pakistani) were less likely to receive an interview than those with Anglo-sounding names, even when the Asian candidates had superior Canadian qualifications.

"Anti-Asian hate" also justifies increased legislation, policing, surveillance, and prosecution, in contrast with the politics of abolition articulated by progressives. We know the leading targets of the carceral state: Indigenous, Black, and brown people, the undocumented, the homeless, gender nonconforming people, Muslims, and significantly, sex workers. However they actually made a living, the women killed in Atlanta have been framed by sex work. To focus only on race disregards their lived realities and ignores how racism is always already gendered and classed. Sexuality is fundamental in orientalist discourse.

Like the LGBTQ+ community, Asian Americans have enormous income inequality, a fact hidden behind the images of the homonormative consumer and the model minority, respectively. This is true both between and within ethnicities, as evidenced by the fact that the Atlanta victims, massage parlor workers, were Korean and Chinese, two of the communities with the most affluence.

In 2015, I was reckoning with the effects of neoliberalism on LGBTQ+ communities: the increasing disparity and the professionalization and corporate modeling of what had been volunteer activism. I did not imagine how far this might lead. As I write, queer historian Tom Hooper has released evidence documenting how two of Canada's largest LGBTQ+ organizations accepted six-figure grants in a quid pro quo arrangement to advance the Liberal government's agenda. Pride Toronto promised to invite the police back into the parade despite a vote by membership. Egale Canada defied all other deputants and backed flawed legislation meant to expunge police records related to gay sex, but which left most convictions unaltered.

Justin Trudeau's celebration of (flawed) Bill C-66 and tearful apology for past state homophobia solidified his brand. But the cooptation of flagship organizations in the service of party politics and homonationalism is foreboding. I hope grassroots community activism can still challenge this convergence of corporate and partisan interests.

THE DAVID R. KESSLER LECTURES 2002–2020

2002   JONATHAN NED KATZ

2003   GAYLE RUBIN

2004   ISAAC JULIEN

2006   ADRIENNE RICH

2007   DOUGLAS CRIMP

2008   SUSAN STRYKER

2009   SARAH SCHULMAN

2010   URVASHI VAID

2012   MARTIN DUBERMAN

2013   CHERYL CLARKE

2014   CATHY J. COHEN

2015   RICHARD FUNG

2016   **DEAN SPADE**

2017   SARA AHMED

2018   AMBER HOLLIBAUGH

2019   JASBIR K. PUAR

2020   RODERICK A. FERGUSON

Dean Spade

Dean Spade has been working to build queer and trans liberation based in racial and economic justice for the past two decades. He works as a professor at Seattle University School of Law. Spade is the author of *Normal Life: Administrative Violence, Critical Trans Politics, and the Limits of Law* (2011), the director of the documentary *Pinkwashing Exposed: Seattle Fights Back!* (2015), and the creator of the mutual aid toolkit at BigDoorBrigade.com. His latest book, *Mutual Aid: Building Solidarity during This Crisis (and the Next)*, was published by Verso Press in October 2020, and has since been published in Italian, Portuguese, Catalan, Korean, Spanish, Thai, Czech, and German.

When We Win We Lose: Mainstreaming and the Redistribution of Respectability

DECEMBER 9, 2016

CLAGS is so meaningful to me. I feel like in some ways, I grew up with CLAGS. I moved to New York in 1995, and so many CLAGS events were so vital to shaping my intellectual and political life, and so memorable. My time on the CLAGS board was so meaningful to me. It's such a meaningful award to me, and such a meaningful event. I watch this lecture every year. If I'm not in town, I watch it on the computer. I'm really moved by this and grateful. So, thank you.

And I also want to acknowledge the land. We're on Lenape land. The Lenape were forced to leave Manhattan in the 1770s and moved to Oklahoma. A lot of Lenape people are still in Oklahoma, and in Wisconsin, and Ontario.

It's a really wild moment to give a talk like this right after the election. I had to really rethink what I wanted to talk about. It's a hard time to think about what we want to say to each other, for a lot of reasons. There's a lot we're all figuring out. Part of what we are trying to figure out is what's the same and what's different right now, and how does it affect what we're going to do. A central way to understand that is to understand that we live in a settler-colonial context, and the colonial government has changed. How docs centering that mode of inquiry affect our analysis and our ability to strategize this moment? I want to suggest that as a way to carry through these remarks and our discussion afterward. How can we think about being on Lenape land the entire time that we think about the Trump moment, or anything else we want to consider about now and about our strategies?

It is an intense moment. A lot of people are scared. There's a lot of shock going around. And there's also an idea that, maybe, a lot of people are mobilizable right now, because some people are experiencing shock and fear in new or different ways. One of the main questions for me that I want to think about tonight is: What will people be mobilized around? That's up in the air.

There's actually a battle we have to have about what constitutes leftness or progressiveness right now. There's a lot we can lose in that battle. In some ways, we've always been battling that, but I think there's a particular kind of moment for that battle right now. I want to spend some time talking about that tonight and about some other pitfalls, some of the threats, and some of the opportunities for us in this context of this moment.

During the last year, a lot of what I've been talking about and thinking about has been how we respond to and navigate two forms of mainstreaming that have been happening. Obviously, there's been a mainstreaming of trans politics and images of trans lives have been more visible, and there's also been a mainstreaming happening around criminal justice reform. And both of those things were things that I did not know I would see mainstream in my lifetime.

On the one hand, this mainstreaming is a sign of the significance of our movement work, that we have this long, ongoing prison abolition movement, anti-policing movement, and we finally are seeing some criminal justice reform mainstreaming. We have a long history of gender liberation work, and now we see some kind of mainstreaming around trans issues, and there is something to observe there about the impact of our movements. But also, mainstreaming presents significant threats to our aims of actually winning trans survival, winning prison abolition, winning police abolition.

I'll say a few things about that. Mainstreaming—Caitlyn Jenner, she's a good symbol of it. One of the things mainstreaming does, it creates new forms of visibility, whether that's Caitlyn Jenner on the cover of *Vanity Fair*, or whether that's a bunch of sheriffs and prosecutors coming out and saying that they're going to take care of criminal justice problems for us and "Don't you worry about it, go back to sleep." Whatever it is, we see circulation of new forms of visibility of issues that were marginalized before.

Another part of what comes with mainstreaming is conditional acceptance. I mean, if you can do white femininity like Caitlyn Jenner, you might be okay. But most trans people are out of luck. I had a powerful conversation with Chase Strangio the other day. Chase was talking about how, on the one hand, you see Loretta Lynch representing the Obama administration saying, "We're going to sue North Carolina about their bathroom bill. And we're going to say trans women are women and trans men are men and they should get to use the bathroom." And that exact same administration, its lawyers are fighting tooth and nail to make sure that Chelsea Manning can't grow her hair out. So you start to think, "Which trans people are human for this administration?" Conditional acceptance becomes very visible in moments of mainstreaming.

Mainstreaming comes with the deployment of deserving figures. For example, the idea that "nonviolent offenders" deserve some relief from the criminal system, but not everyone else. Caitlyn Jenner deserves to be embraced as a woman, but other trans women who are not wealthy conservative celebrities are still targets for violence and criminalization. During the bathroom panics, these memes have been going around that show a picture of a very passing trans person making the argument that this person should not be made to go into the bathroom associated with their birth gender. But what about everybody who's trans who gets harassed in bathrooms because we are hard for people to understand? These memes, probably unintentionally, tell us which trans people we should accept as deserving of rights or survival.

Mainstreaming also brings recuperative reform proposals. These are reform proposals that recuperate systems and institutions that are under attack, that make it seem like contradictions have been resolved and put a legitimizing face on harmful systems. After those reforms are "won," you still have the same harm and violence targeting the same people. We are told it has all been taken care of, we're free, and yet the harm continues.

Mainstreaming also frequently includes backlashes. I see the bathroom panic as an example of these backlash moments that actually enhance vulnerability. So, you haven't even won that much—a few people at the top have won something maybe, or maybe the laws changed, but little changed on the ground for most people, but you get a backlash that hurts people at the bottom. The people who are most vulnerable have to use the bathrooms in the most dangerous places—restaurants, bus stations. That's who's going to be harassed. It's low-income people. It's people who look or are homeless and don't have private bathrooms to use. It's people who are people of color, who are people with disabilities, who get harassed and profiled in bathrooms. So this backlash against trans liberation that has emerged because of a right-wing perception that trans people are gaining access to public life is tragic in two ways. First, the reforms that trans people have "won" are mostly unenforceable, never implemented, and only serve to make the reformed institutions look better while trans people continue to suffer extreme poverty and criminalization. Second, the backlash makes life even more difficult and dangerous for the most targeted trans people.

For a long time, I have been thinking and writing about the pitfalls of reforms. We don't want reforms that produce no material relief. We get a lot of reforms that produce no material relief. A classic example—hate crime laws. They don't do anything to prevent people from killing us, but we're told we've been recognized by the state, that the police and courts are now our protectors.

We don't want reforms that are solely symbolic. Near Seattle, where I live, is a town called Federal Way. The school board there just passed an anti-hate proclamation in response to the fear that many young people in Federal Way are feeling that they or their parents are going to get deported. But it doesn't do anything to prevent that. It doesn't even say the words "immigration" or "deportation" in the proclamation. It is entirely symbolic. It makes the school board look like they care about immigrant youth and families, but it doesn't provide any relief or protection from immigration enforcement. Such reforms are solely gestures, and those kinds of reforms are very common, particularly right now as a response to the election of Trump. People are "coming out against hate," but there's no administrative reality that shifts with those proclamations. A second problem with many reforms, if they provide relief at all, is that they only provide relief to the least marginalized within the impacted group. That's a really common thing in general with all civil rights frames: the danger that the only people who end up accessing relief are the people with the most high-ranking jobs, access to the highest levels of health care, the highest levels of education.

In addition to failing to provide material relief, many reforms legitimize the very systems that target our communities. I was recently part of a conversation where someone proposed that to address the problems of queer and trans imprisonment we try to get prisons to pass anti-discrimination policies. This kind of thinking is pervasive. These kinds of reforms sanitize the reputations of violent systems, actually facilitating their ongoing violence. We need to get queer and trans people (and all people) out of prisons, not try to get prisons to say they care about us. This kind of "pinkwashing," where police departments, militaries, corporations, and other brutal institutions declare that they love and care about queer and trans people while they continue their deadly work, just wraps a rainbow flag around their violence. These kinds of reforms, at best, tinker with the systems that are devouring our communities, they don't get to the root causes. Even worse, some reforms not only offer good PR for harmful systems, but actually expand them. Hate crime laws are a good example of that. They expand prosecuting power in the name of our communities. They give *more* power to the very systems that target us with violence, without doing anything to reduce violence against us.

In addition to failing to provide material relief, and legitimizing and expanding harmful systems, many reforms also divide people into "deserving" and "undeserving." We've seen this conversation a lot in the context of immigration discourse in recent years, where Obama is like, "I want to make it so that a few college students can stay, but we're really going to go hardcore after people who have had contact with the criminal system." Who are good immigrants? Who are bad immigrants? Who are good trans people? Who are bad? These dangers of reform are deep concerns of our movements and require careful discernment.

I have to share a favorite example of a terrible, system-affirming pinkwashing reform. The Seattle Police have launched this "Safe Place" campaign in recent years, which has been copied by many other police departments in the US and Canada. SPD hands out stickers for businesses to put on their windows. They show a rainbow flag in the shape of a police badge, and they are supposed to demarcate that if you are experiencing an anti-LGBTQ attack, you can run into that place, and they will call the cops for you. This emerged as a PR campaign that came after the Seattle Police Department had some well-publicized horrible killings, including the murder of John T. Williams, an Indigenous woodcarver. The Seattle Police Department was under DOJ investigation, which found that it engaged in excessive force and bias. Another example from right here in New York is the NYPD's rainbow cop cars. Does this make us believe the NYPD is progressive? These are the kind of reforms that come with mainstreaming—surface reforms that recuperate and rehabilitate institutions our movements have worked to attack and dismantle, and that provide no relief to us.

A counter-frame that's really been important to me for thinking about this, that I think can help us through this dilemma when we're debating what is progressive, what is left, what is liberatory, is the frame of counterinsurgency, or frame of warfare. Lots and lots of the movements and scholars we all look to use this frame. And I think it really is clarifying and useful for moving us toward criteria for assessing our way forward.

One place that I get this frame is from the 1951 petition "We Charge Genocide" by W. E. B. Du Bois, William L. Patterson, and Paul Robeson.[1] In it, they lay out exactly how the United States has engaged in genocide against Black people. It was an immensely popular tract at the time that the US government saw as very threatening. The authors and distributors of it had their passports taken. The government seized copies of it. The danger of this document that identified a genocidal act against Black people by the United States was so palpable at the time.

That's a spark moment where we see the value or the vitality of this kind of frame, but we can see it in a lot of places. I was thinking about the writing of Kuwasi Balagoon. I'm thinking about many '60s and '70s movements and figures, including political prisoners from those movements, who use the idea of "the United States is at war against Black people, at war against Indigenous people, at war against people of color generally, at war against social movements that are resisting state violence." The Black Panther Party used a warfare frame, the Young Lords, the American Indian Movement.

More recently, in analysis of the War on Terror, people have understood it as a war against immigrants, a war against Muslims. Black Lives Matter has also used this to understand state violence against Black people. Many, many scholars and many activist movements have used this frame to help us see the United States as a war—the existence of the United States itself as war, and the United States' ongoing warfare against vulnerable people, and against our movements. The United States government also shows us that it sees itself as at war with social movements. The US government uses counterinsurgency as their frame to deal with our movements. So we should think of it that way. That's how they think of it, so we should.

Counterinsurgency, according to some scholars—I'm thinking right now of Peter Gelderloos and Christian Williams,[2] among others—is broken into two pieces: repression and recuperation. One thing I wonder when I think about what might be different under Trump is: Will we see more repression and less recuperation? Because we could see Obama as a major pinkwashing president. His presidency sought to recuperate the Democratic Party, US military imperialism, and law enforcement with a veneer of neoliberal multiculturalism and pinkwashing. He's like, "I'm pro-gay, so just ignore the drone warfare and the millions of deportations, and what's going on in Yemen, and what's going on in Iraq, and what's going on in Afghanistan, and what's going on at Guantanamo. Let's just ignore that. I'm pro–gay marriage."

The Obama administration attempts to recuperate institutions in crisis like the US military or the US police state and prison nation through various attempts to say they are multicultural, pro-women, or pro-gay. The Obama administration, like the others before him, uses both prongs of counterinsurgency, recuperation *and* repression. He has expanded domestic surveillance immensely, including targeting groups like Black Lives Matter. But maybe under Trump we will see more repression and less recuperation? I don't know. But repression and recuperation, counterinsurgency—it's going to stay with us. It's been with us through all the presidencies.

Here is what the US Government Counterinsurgency Guide from 2009 says: "COIN (counterinsurgency) integrates and synchronizes political, security, economic, and informational components that reinforce governmental legitimacy and effectiveness while reducing insurgent influence over the population. COIN strategies should be designed to . . . strengthen the legitimacy and capacity of government institutions to govern responsibly and marginalize insurgents."[3] I think this is useful. Understanding the government's thinking about counterinsurgency is useful for thinking about what we need to be doing. In the Trump moment, what kinds of liberal myths will present new dangers for us as we contest the terrain of left or progressive politics? How do we avoid simply keeping on recuperating the US government and its institutions, and how are we going to expand our work to dismantle them? How do liberal mythologies impair us as we navigate the Trump moment?

The liberal myth of education is a danger at this time. This myth tells us: "If people only knew, then this wouldn't be going on." The idea that education alone is going to get us there, that if people knew what was going on, then somehow that would stop it—this has a lot of problems. One problem is we all get stuck writing too much fucking content on the internet and thinking that will bring freedom and justice. It's not enough. It's just not enough. The idea that if we had the right analysis, if we had the right meme, if we had the right app, people would understand, and things would be all right.

Yes, we need many ways of understanding, thinking, and perceiving everything, because we are all different from each other, so there's not going to be one silver bullet. The idea of a single effective way to communicate feels like a funder's idea. "Let's find the one." No. Nobody's special. Everybody write down what you've got to write down and keep it moving, but that's not enough. When we fail to interact beyond trying to have people know, we lose.

But the real reason education alone doesn't work, which I hope by now we all noticed, is we don't live in a democracy. When are we going to let go of the fantasy that we live in a democracy? I don't know if other people remember the period when the Iraq war was beginning, and it was more people out in the streets than ever before, and they had the fucking war anyway, and we're still in it. It doesn't matter. Turns out the US does not run on the popular opinions of the people who live here; it runs on elite interests with a sham of electoral politics where we get to decide which imperialist to vote for, which oil and gas candidate to vote for, which millionaire to vote for.

The idea that the US is a democracy and brings democracy through warfare all around the world still floats in a lot of progressive spaces. It underlies a lot of the liberal myth of education, the "if people only knew" framework. So we've got to watch out for that one as we head into the Trump presidency. That could really soak up a lot of our time and distract from actually organizing.

The second liberal myth to watch out for in this moment is the worship of the rule of law and the idea of patriotic dissent. The idea here is that the problem with Trump is that he's anti-constitutional and we just need to bring the rule of law, that US law will save us from this monster. The rule of law in the United States is genocide, and slavery, and heteropatriarchy. The idea that the Constitution is this beautiful, sacred document, and if we could just analyze it correctly then we would have equality—that is a brutal myth. So yes, it's true that Trump wants things that are anti-constitutional— and so does Obama, and so does every police officer, and every ICE agent. The law on the ground is lawless. Law enforcement is the reality, not whatever laws say. Our legal system was created by and for white supremacy and to extract from the many to enrich the few, and it does a great job of that through selective enforcement and a veneer of legitimacy that the "rule of law" myth is a core part of. This myth both legitimizes US law and law enforcement and demobilizes. People are encouraged to just give money to the ACLU and hope they sue Trump to protect us. The idea that elite institutions, whether that is nonprofits or courts, will protect us from terrifying rich white men is a hopeless fantasy.

I am hearing a lot of people invoke the founders right now—those slaveholders. Do you see how the Left, the supposed Left becomes a site of recuperation during an extreme right-wing moment? Remember Bush? It was the same way. It was like all the liberals went outside to a few anti-war marches and felt like they did something. But the message was so deeply watered down and became so patriotic. And it became about the one bad guy who just wasn't smart enough, Bush. So the whole politics moves rightward, and this guy becomes the mark people distinguish themselves from, and the racist, imperialist Democratic Party gets off the hook.

Another myth that we are facing is this idea that we need to "move the middle." When I hear that, I think people are thinking about white, upper- and middle-class people. That's who people think "the middle" is. That's actually not true. There's an idea—the same people who media is targeted to—there's an idea that those people, if we get them to think the right thing, things would be different. What we actually need is meaningful participation in mass movements with many entry points. We need entry for newly politicized and dissatisfied people to come into deep, sustained, and sustaining participation with others. That's not the same as shaping all of our messages to whatever we are projecting that people who have the least to lose want. That's not the place to go. I mean, I think every left organizer who I admire and study all agree that it's poor and working-class people of color, primarily, and also poor and working-class white people—that's who has the most to lose, and is the most mobilizable, and the most mobilized, and have the most wisdom about the systems we're trying to dismantle. And it doesn't mean that people in that "middle," whatever that is—I mean, if they come along, that's great. But people usually get dragged along.

I didn't live during the powerful uprisings of late 1960s and '70s that a lot of us look at, when radical social movements successfully influenced what might be called mainstream culture. But studying that period, it looks to me like people were dragged there by working-class people of color making radical militant movements. Not that those movements pitched their ideas to white propertied people, but that the size and disruptive capacity of those movements meant that they were unavoidable, and their ideas reached and influenced many, many people who would not have incentives to find those ideas on their own. The contemporary focus on "moving to the middle" leads us to very liberal, very watered-down ideas about what needs to happen next, when what we need is to create very bold, very disruptive movements that a lot of people can enter and participate in.

Another thing that's likely to happen during this period is an obsession with defending prior recuperative moments. An idea of, "We just need to go back to trying to get the Trump administration to recognize and include us like the Obama administration." That stuff (gaining limited recognition, on paper, for hated groups, without any real material redistribution) didn't work anyway. A lot of people in this room have written books about that. That stuff doesn't actually change the distribution of well-being. And so, becoming obsessed with just defending it feels like a lost opportunity for mobilizing toward the world we actually want to live in.

And overall, I'm worried about us just moving to a lowest common denominator like we saw under the Bush administration. "Trump is such a terrible racist, so everything else is fine." That kind of thinking. It motivates false calls to unity, when actually, we need to look productively at difference and have meaningful criteria for assessing what moves us forward, not watered-down messages and focusing on an individual scapegoat–bad guy. In reality, the US is war. And asking for kinder, gentler colonial rule is not right. It's killing me to watch people celebrate the Obamas and Clintons right now. What did those people really do?

What I've been trying to think about before the election and now, in different ways, is how can we figure out what is recuperative and what is liberatory? That's a really hard question, actually. What criteria do we use? How might we co-create ways of thinking about what's actually liberatory when we face both, on the one hand, recuperative reform proposals resulting from mainstreaming and, on the other, recuperative projects masquerading as urgent, radical, and left because of Trumpism?

For years, I have been using some particular criteria in my own assessment of whether a reform is actually going to help us get where we want to go or whether it is recuperative. I will share my criteria with you, and then some other thinkers who I think are particularly useful right now. I use these four questions: First, does it provide material relief? Many recuperative reforms are solely symbolic. Second, does it leave out an especially marginalized part of the affected group? And a lot of times these days reforms are written to exclude people with criminal records, or undocumented people, or people who were convicted of certain offenses. Reforms that leave behind people who are more stigmatized are always regressive. The idea that we're going to come back and get those people is a classic problem in movements, a conservatizing move. My third question is: Does it legitimize or expand a system we're trying to dismantle? We never want to add money, or staff, or buildings to the prison industrial complex, to the immigration enforcement system, the military, or whatever our target is. My fourth question is: Does the way we are winning this mobilize the most affected for ongoing struggle? Is this actually building power? Is this doing stuff that causes more people to know each other, to have skills for organizing, to build relationships in their communities, to articulate their ideas about what needs to change, to name their conditions, to fight the next fight and the next fight?

Those are the criteria I have been using for a long time, but I have been really interested in looking at other people's criteria. Peter Gelderloos, a nonacademic white anarchist scholar—he wrote a book that I love teaching and highly recommend called *How Nonviolence Protects the State*. He updated it last year with a book called *The Failure of Nonviolence*. In that book, he looks at a bunch of recent political moments around the world and he asks this question: "Is it liberatory?"[4]

His criteria are: First, does it seize space in which new social relations can be enacted? That question, for him, is: he's looking at things like the 15-M movement in Spain or Occupy. He's looking at places where people went outside and did stuff we're not supposed to do, like feed each other, live together, seize public space, share everything, refuse to call the cops on each other. He is asking how people enacted social relations differently. That's, I think, a pretty interesting question, a different one, one that I had not asked.

Second, Gelderloos asks: Does it spread awareness of its ideas? He's not looking for it to just spread awareness in a passive way, where you just receive it, you've heard of it, you reposted it on social media. But do people start it in their own town, like a Black Lives Matter chapter, like a local #NotOneMore campaign? Do people take it up and do it somewhere else? Do people participate in the idea and make it their own? Gelderloos's third question is: Does it have elite support? According to Gelderloos, if it has elite support, it's probably not liberatory. That's a hard one, I think, for people in the United States. We're like, "Oh my G-d. We got the *New York Times* to say something! We got an elected official to come to our rally! A celebrity tweeted about our fight!" When I read these criteria, I felt so much relief. We need this analysis badly in our movements. Finally, Gelderloos asks: Does it achieve any concrete gains in improving people's lives? So he's also interested in material relief rather than symbolic changes that primarily create good PR for the systems that are devouring our communities and the planet.

Mariame Kaba also provides a useful framework for evaluating reforms in her short article about how to evaluate police reforms. First, she asks, "Does it allocate any more money to the police? Does it advocate for more police or policing?"[5] Next, she asks, "Is the reform primarily technology-focused?" Things like having the police have "less lethal" weapons or body cams, that's an industry making money off reforms that will not reduce the harm of policing. Those new technologies just add to police budgets. After the initial uprising in Ferguson, the stock of companies that make less lethal weapons and body cameras skyrocketed. We have to think about that. Police violence is not a technological problem.

Next Kaba asks, "Is it focused on individual dialogues and individual cops?" That, again, indicates that a reform will not be effective and misunderstands the nature of policing and its violence. I love Kaba's criteria, because they so clearly ground us in the material realities of policing and the patterns of recuperative reform.

Finally, I want to look at Harsha Walia's work. She wrote a book called *Undoing Border Imperialism*, which is a wonderful resource for classrooms and community reading groups. She's part of No One Is Illegal, which has chapters across Canada. She's part of the Vancouver chapter. She asks, "Has the tactic been effective . . . in exposing or confronting a specific point within the system by either diminishing its moral legitimacy or undermining its functioning?"[6] To me, that really rings as the reverse of the counterinsurgency definition I shared before.

One of the examples of this can be seen in a very moving video posted to YouTube that shows a protest where thousands of people took over the international terminal of the Vancouver airport to stop the deportation of a man named Laibar Singh. I've never seen anything like that here. We do stuff here—like, I've been part of people blocking deportation buses and stuff—but this was really next-level, to shut down the airport to stop a deportation. Imagine doing that. It's really intense. It's a beautiful video to watch, and a great classroom tool. It expands our imagination, because it simultaneously undermined its functions—they didn't deport Laibar Singh—and it delegitimized Canada's immigration enforcement, showing all that opposition, having the words "No One Is Illegal" on the news!

Undoing Border Imperialism is full of other examples of the ways that No One Is Illegal does both individual casework about individual people facing deportation and work about many broad policies inside the Canadian immigration enforcement system to both undermine the system's function and question its legitimacy. This is useful, because often people engage in reforms that don't undermine the moral legitimacy of the system. They're like, "It's okay to deport other people, but please don't deport *this* person." So how does No One Is Illegal handle that? How do they hold both and do effective individual casework while being called No One Is Illegal? That itself is such a brilliant intervention. And how do they collaborate with other organizations that are using various other strategies? Her book is a useful handbook for all of those thorny questions, about how you work to get people out of such a system without playing by that system's rules.

I have also been finding Grace Hong's book *Death beyond Disavowal* particularly helpful in this moment. Actually, before the election, the speech I was going to give tonight was a lot more about that book and its contributions. But one of the things that Grace Hong does in that book is she talks about this key question from Audre Lorde: "In what way do I contribute to the subjugation of any part of those who I call my people?"

To me, this sentence captures something so important from women of color feminist political practice that has been vital to all the movements that I have been interested in for my whole political life, this idea of constant self-reflection, of always asking: Who's not here? What are the differences within any group we're in, and how do we pay attention to them rather than bury them under false calls for unity? Women of color feminist interventions have invited us to be constantly aware that we are always participants in exclusions and harms, and not having a notion of a pure political space or of anybody as a pure political subject. What that means for daily practice, both organizationally and for each person engaged in these complex practices of political activism in which we challenge each other, is that we give each other difficult feedback and cultivate hearing feedback, making changes, repairing.

When I was preparing for tonight, I was looking a lot at Tourmaline's remarks at graduation at Hampshire College last year. I don't know if you-all watched that video or read that speech. It's a brilliant and beautiful speech. Tourmaline talks about who's considered a nobody, and who's considered a somebody. I was thinking about this regarding—how does my own work make other people nobodies? When am I aware of that, and when am I not? When am I trying to make myself a somebody by making somebody else a nobody? Or when are we making ourselves somebodies by making somebody else a nobody? Those questions, I think, are very deep, are trying to form an ongoing, reflective practice, offer us opportunities to interrogate when our quests for reform are affirming harmful systems and making stigmatized people disposable.

The work we can do in the Trump moment, it needs to be deeply local and deeply participatory. That is where we're at. There's three key pieces of work we need to do.

First, we need to do politicized survival work—mutual aid work. People are in danger in new and old ways. Our people have already been dying, being deported, being imprisoned. But there's definitely a ramping up that's about to happen. What's going to happen to public housing? What's going to happen to health care? The stock of the private prison industry has gone up since the election. What in G-d's name are we about to see in terms of ramping up already intensely dire conditions?

Mutual aid work is deeply concerned with nobodies. It's about putting nobodies at the center, to use Tourmaline's frame. It's work that says that people who are struggling the most are where we begin our analysis and take up actual action. This is the work of actually providing housing, health care, and education for each other. And to be totally honest, our movements have not been not good at that. There's still nowhere for homeless trans people to live. We have not sufficiently opened up our homes, our own spaces. We've relied on state structures that were never going to serve us.

Now we have to confront that they are never going to serve us. What do we do when we recognize that we live in warfare conditions—the government against vulnerable people and their movements? When we let go of the liberal fantasies of a "good" US government? If we face that, what would we be willing to provide one another? So many of us are into apocalyptic TV shows and novels, and in those, people carry water for each other, and shack up together and stuff. It's time. You know what I mean? Let's do it.

Mutual aid work is vital. I had a helpful conversation with Rickke Mananzala all about this, how for years and years, one of the things that's been so difficult is that funders have never prioritized local work. It's always been focused on what we would call "elite strategies." It's like, "Can you get an article in the *New York Times*? Can you change the mind of an elected official or a judge?" That's the somebody strategy. We need the nobody strategy. The somebody strategy didn't work under the supposedly best conditions, where those elites are nodding and pretending they hear. It's really not going to work now. At that time, it also didn't give us anything.

So how can we shift that to a downward-looking strategy, a strategy that says, "Wow, is everybody in here okay? Does anyone need a ride? Does everyone feel like they have a safe place to go tonight?" Rather than caring what elites say, what if we care most about how people at the bottom are doing, what they want and think and need? What if that was how we engage with our spaces, moving away from any idea of trickle-down and toward trickle-up?

What this also means is direct support for people in prisons, immigration proceedings, housing court, people seeking benefits, all of those kinds of spaces. There's a way in which a lot of people on the left don't touch that stuff. It's like, "Oh, it's so complicated and administrative." But what happens is, and you see this all the time, when you are engaging in that work, if you're yourself navigating a benefit system, or navigating some kind of criminalization system, or if you're dealing with a family member or a friend in those systems, you end up learning a lot of the horrible, humdrum, administrative details that are highly local in that place.

That's the kind of expertise we need right now. All these things that we need to work on, they work differently in each prison, in each courthouse, in each city, in each county. So we need all of us to be co-producing very localized expertise about how to throw wrenches into those systems, and how to help people survive them right now. There's no reason every single person in this room and every single person we know can't be engaging in a prison pen pal project, learning about what's going on with evictions on your block, and figuring out how to help people go to housing court and fill out forms to stop an eviction.

A lot of us have things we could contribute to that. There's never going to be enough poverty lawyers and enough social workers to do that for everyone in need. It's designed that way. Most people get turned away from services. So if we don't do that, which we haven't been, people don't get what they need, and landlords can run with it, and medical systems that cut people out can run with it, and people just die early. Those stakes are higher than ever.

Committing ourselves to boring paperwork with each other, or whatever type of support each of us are able to give, learning things that you don't like learning, some of that, because we do that together—now is the time for that. And accompanying people to those spaces, doing direct support for people with disabilities. The level of endangerment of people with disabilities under the administration is, I think, incomprehensible right now. There are people in our movements who are so skilled at bringing a disability justice lens and tools when they go into any space, when they think about institutions, who know how to provide support, connection, collaboration from a disability justice perspective. We all need to bone up on that. It's really scary that so few people in our movements have those skills, that it's such a siloed set of expertise and knowledge. We all need to take it up.

The level at which people with disabilities are left as nobodies by all of our movements, and ignored and disappeared, is horrifying. That is something that we can change our priorities around and change practices so that people with disabilities are at the center of our spaces, leading the analysis about what it is to produce meaningful engagement together.

We need to be building all kinds of accompaniment projects right now. I am excited about some of the ways that people are talking about accompanying people on subways, accompanying people to medical appointments, court, and other places of vulnerability. We need that to expand to all the places poor people face control and stigmatization. Nobody should have to go to those appointments alone.

The second type of work we need in this time is dismantling work. There's a lot of that that needs to be done, obviously. There's a new article by Tania Unzueta that I just read, that I really loved—she works with Mijente—that was looking at how, if we want to have a promise of this sanctuary city or sanctuary campus idea, we need to dismantle the police state.[7] All of policing and imprisonment shuttles people toward deportation. This idea that we're just going to say that our town's police won't collaborate with ICE is not going to prevent people from being caught up in that system, because Trump has identified, just as Obama did, that the number one priority for deportation are people who have contact with the criminal punishment system.

So, we have to do what the Movement for Black Lives and Mijente and the #NotOneMore campaigns have been doing, which is understand anything related to the sanctuary movement and deportation as utterly connected to the dismantling of the prison-industrial complex and policing. Those things are together, and our standard for what sanctuary is, according to Tania, has to be high. It has to be a standard of reducing policing, eliminating policing, getting cops out of schools. All of that work people have been doing to dismantle police and prisons, that work is also the sanctuary work. That needs to be our standard.

I recently read about the sanctuary movement in Santa Ana, where activists are demanding that it be meaningful and not just symbolic sanctuary. I enjoyed reading this very local account of what they were demanding, what criteria they were using for what they thought would be sanctuary. That's the kind of administrative savvy, the kind of rigorous assessment of exactly how boring administrative systems are working to devour communities, that we all need to be doing. We've got to go deep in particular systems, understand exactly how they gobble up our people, and how to untangle it, both for individuals that we're supporting and so that we can discern whether particular changes will actually move us toward dismantling. That kind of work, I think, is vital right now.

This kind of dismantling work includes local campaigns to reduce police, close prisons and precincts, stop new building of those things. We need to do the work to block deportations. I think we could ramp that work up. We need to block the public housing closures. I've been thinking about how more than ten thousand people have turned out to support water protectors at Standing Rock, and what it would look like if we could produce huge standoffs every time they tried to close public housing anywhere. Can we imagine turning people out in massive numbers every time they try to close a public hospital? And in general, that means escalating tactics. It's definitely time to escalate tactics.

The third type of work I want to highlight is the work that builds the world we want to live in and prepares us for the disasters. We have a climate change denier as president. It's going to keep getting a lot worse. So everything we do to produce our shared safety in these moments also produces our well-being in the face of the disasters. I have been thinking about Occupy Sandy or the people's recovery work that was done after the tsunami in Thailand—we cannot count on governments to support us in those moments. We already know that. So what does it mean to think of every piece of work we do now as preparation for not only the disasters we're already living in, but the pitched moments of climate-related disasters?

One piece of this, which some people have been working on for so long, is alternative approaches to preventing and responding to violence without police. This is a vital, ongoing piece of work in our communities. We're still harming each other. How do we do work about harm that isn't centered in policing, that isn't centered in exile and punishment? Doing work about care and interdependency, lifting up feminist analysis, disability justice analysis, about childcare, about caring for one another when we're sick, when we're disabled, when we're old—we're still really having a hard time with these things, as you, I'm sure, have noticed from your own lives.

We need to cultivate massive amounts of participation. We need everybody who's getting an idea right now to learn that they can do something besides just give to the ACLU and Planned Parenthood, but instead, they can participate right now in a politicized project about something they care about, accompanying somebody or supporting somebody through something. People feel like they want to help each other right now. That's a really amazing resource, and there's a lot of really liberal pitfall nightmare places that could go. We have replicable models. We do. We have amazing prison pen pal projects, like Black and Pink. We have lots of replicable models. Many are tiny and local but have figured out important things about how to do the work. So how do we start to actually replicate them and start them everywhere? We need so many of them, because we have to provide each other with everything. And how do we do this through a framework that no one is disposable? This is our ongoing work.

I was thinking about Tourmaline's work. I was thinking about the nobodies and somebodies. I thought about people like Michael Johnson, the young college wrestler who was sentenced to thirty years in Missouri for allegedly transmitting HIV. I thought about Deborah Danner, who was killed by the police in the Bronx in October, who was a Black woman with schizophrenia. I think about all the people I correspond with in prison who have been labeled sex offenders. I think about people who've been considered monsters and nobodies. What if we put those people at the center of our movements? What if we actually had to deal with the idea of disposability at that level?

And then also, what about interpersonal disposability? "I never want to see you again, because we're in this activist organization, and it's really hard for me or annoying, or what you've done is really painful to me." What if I assumed I had to see you for the rest of my life? Not every day, but what if I assumed that we're in this together, and wanted to find a way to work it out? That doesn't mean immediate, or it doesn't mean ignoring harm, but what if we treated each other like we were going to still be around and worth being alive?

That is very hard in an era of social media. There are intense ways that people are playing out our experiences of harm and making each other disposable. There's a lot of good reasons for that, but it's not working for us. Making myself somebody by deeply trashing and dehumanizing another person or organization that's in my broader community—it's not working for us in a profound way, as I'm sure you all know.

So how do we try to keep each other even through conflict? Whenever I talk to college students who are eighteen and nineteen, I'm like, "I hate to tell you, but the people you dislike now, you'll be seeing them for the rest of your life. There may even come a time when you're the last two anti-marriage people on earth, and you're best friends." You never know who your ally, somebody who feels like it's the most pitched difference in one moment, later, actually, you realize, "Oh, we have more of the same values than we even knew," possibly because you become antiquated. It's a complicated thing to be critical and transparent and try to limit the toxicity of things like callout culture. But I think it's something that we can do, and it's possible for us to do.

A lot of this is about building our emotional capacities to be together in movements for a long time. That piece of the work is, I think, very under-discussed and somewhat taboo. What do I need to survive in group processes? What do I need to change or learn about or expand? How can I get through being in conflictual group spaces? Those are conversations and questions that are worth asking, and I think have somewhat been neglected by our movements. How do I take responsibility for the ways I might play out my wounds on others? How do I learn to give and receive feedback with others? Those are hard things, but I think they are things that I'm seeing more and more discussion about in our movements, and that are vital for us to be able to survive.

We're in a time when people are scared. There's a lot of different kind of problems facing people. I meet a lot of people who have been denied social movement histories, especially information about tactics. So it's a time when it's important for us to study together, to have cross-generational dialogues about stories, about what we've done in different times, and to lift up movement stories. People need them badly right now.

We also have a lot of people who have been wounded in left movements and have been wounded in left organizations and have taken a step back. We need those people's talents and skills and abilities right now. Like people who organized against the DNC in New York City and made amazing things happen, I want all of them to come back out and do something. All these other moments when I was amazed by different people's creativity—there's so many skills, and it can be hard to re-engage when you've been burned and left stuff. That's another piece—I meet people who have those skills, and I want to see that shift. We need them back.

It's a time when we need to be more militant, more local, and more grounded in understanding of the nitty gritty of how violence is administered in people's lives, and what daily struggle looks like. I follow Tourmaline's thinking that it is a time when we need to shift away from trying to be somebody, to trying to center the question of why is anybody nobody. That's all.

Notes

1. Civil Rights Congress, "'We Charge Genocide': The Historic Petition to the United Nations for Relief from a Crime of the United States Government against the Negro People," in *We Charge Genocide*, ed. William L. Patterson (New York: International Publishers, 2017).

2. Peter Gelderloos, *The Failure of Nonviolence* (Seattle: Left Bank Books, 2015).

3. U.S. State Department, Counterinsurgency Guide from 2009, 17, https://2009-2017.state.gov/documents/organization/119629.pdf.

4. Gelderloos, *Failure of Nonviolence*.

5. Mariame Kaba, "Police 'Reforms' You Should Always Oppose," *Prison Culture* (blog), December 1, 2014, https://www.usprisonculture.com/blog/2014/12/01/police-reforms-you-should-always-oppose/.

6. Harsha Walia, *Undoing Border Imperialism* (Chico, CA: AK Press, 2013).

7. Tania Unzueta, "What Makes a City a Sanctuary Now?" Mijente, January 27, 2017, accessed June 10, 2022, https://mijente.net/2017/01/sanctuary-report/.

Dean Spade Reflects on "When We Win We Lose: Mainstreaming and the Redistribution of Respectability"

I was asked to provide a title for my Kessler Lecture months before the 2016 presidential election. At that time, I assumed that we would be facing another four to eight years of the neoliberal nightmare we had seen of the Obama administration, this time under Clinton: more war, wealth gap, criminalization, and immigration enforcement expansion wrapped in platitudes about gay rights as human rights, ineffective and system-sustaining (or system-expanding) police and prison reforms, and tokenization of Black and Latine people, women, and some gays and lesbians in elite positions to oversee the ongoing project of racialized extraction that is the United States. In the Obama era, much of my energy in teaching and writing was about attempting to break the demobilizing spells of neoliberal multiculturalism and homonationalism, to show how the progress narratives cultivated by a patriotic and imperialist Democratic Party with increasingly "diverse" faces in high places was just as brutal and lethal despite its improved public relations strategies.

When December 9, 2016, rolled around, Donald Trump was preparing to take office, and millions of people were angry, scared, and newly mobilizable. Trump's explicit racism, sexism, and ableism tore the mask off US government rhetoric about "diversity and inclusion." He emboldened fascist and white supremacist organizing and recruitment, and he freaked out a lot of people who were relatively complacent under Obama. It was a vital moment to mobilize. But it was also a moment (similar to what had happened under George W. Bush), where the bar of what counts as "progressive" sunk, meaning that every neoliberal, jail-building, homeless encampment–sweeping, ICE-collaborating, fossil fuel–owned elected official could newly market him/her/themself as anti-racist or feminist by decrying Trump's antics. Calling Trump "lawless," elected officials and nonprofits embraced revved-up patriotic talking points about civil liberties and the rule of law that sustain the demobilizing narrative that elite institutions will solve our problems and that US law is fair and neutral. We were supposed to believe that legis-latures and courts would somehow stop the Trump regime.

Preparing to give the Kessler Lecture under these conditions was part of a significant pivot for me. As I anticipated the worsening disasters the Trump regime would bring and witnessed the demobilizing narratives that told people to stay home and wait for elite solutions, it was clear to me that our movements needed to turn people toward participatory work to meet these crisis conditions. The erasure of mutual aid work from accounts of how social change happens was glaring. In January of 2017, I worked to build the BigDoorBrigade.com mutual aid toolkit, and from there continued writing and making videos about mutual aid aimed at increasing circulation of the idea of mutual aid to combat the demobilizing narratives that we should vote, donate, and join a march once a year.

In 2020, mutual aid took center stage as COVID-19 devastated commu-nities and a new wave of resistance to anti-Black racism and policing generated enormous street protest and the mutual aid projects, like street medics and bail funds, that sustain it. As I write this and summer 2021 approaches, we can anticipate another summer of uprisings against cops and homeless encampment sweeps, another brutal set of fires, storms, droughts, and other fossil economy–caused disasters, and a further expan-sion of mutual aid efforts. There is no evidence that our new presidential administration, with its return to neoliberal multiculturalism and progres-sive buzzwords decorating imperialist and oil and gas industry agendas, can address the proliferating crises and disasters. We are going to have to keep building our capacity to save each other's and our own lives, and fight to dismantle the extractive apparatuses that got us into this mess. As usual, queer and trans people are and will be on the front lines, cultivating bold and militant practices for a new world.

THE DAVID R. KESSLER
LECTURES 2002–2020

2002	JONATHAN NED KATZ
2003	GAYLE RUBIN
2004	ISAAC JULIEN
2006	ADRIENNE RICH
2007	DOUGLAS CRIMP
2008	SUSAN STRYKER
2009	SARAH SCHULMAN
2010	URVASHI VAID
2012	MARTIN DUBERMAN
2013	CHERYL CLARKE
2014	CATHY J. COHEN
2015	RICHARD FUNG
2016	DEAN SPADE
2017	**SARA AHMED**
2018	AMBER HOLLIBAUGH
2019	JASBIR K. PUAR
2020	RODERICK A. FERGUSON

Sara Ahmed

Sara Ahmed is an independent scholar and writer who works at the intersection of feminist, queer, and race studies. Her research is concerned with how bodies and worlds take shape and how power is secured and challenged in everyday life and institutional cultures. Ahmed has taken up a number of figures—such as the feminist killjoy, the unhappy queer, and the angry woman of color—to craft a distinctive style of political work. Her publications include *The Feminist Killjoy Handbook* (2023), *Complaint!* (2021), *What's the Use?: On the Uses of Use* (2019), *Living a Feminist Life* (2017), *Willful Subjects* (2014), *On Being Included: Racism and Diversity in Institutional Life* (2012), *The Promise of Happiness* (2010), and *Queer Phenomenology: Orientations, Objects, Others* (2006). She has previously held academic posts at Lancaster University and Goldsmiths, University of London.

Queer Use

DECEMBER 4, 2017

I want to start my consideration of queer use by attending to uses of queer. Queer: a word with a history. Queer: a word that has been flung like a stone; picked up and hurled at us, a word we can claim for us. Queer: odd, strange, unseemly, disturbed, disturbing. Queer: a feeling, a sick feeling; feeling queer as feeling nauseous. In older uses of queer—queer to describe anything that is noticeable because it is odd—queer and fragility were often companions. In one of George Eliot's essays, "Three Months in Weimar," the narrator describes the sound of an old piano thus: "Its tones, now so queer and feeble, like those of an invalided old woman whose voice could once make a heart beat with fond passion."[1] Feeble, frail, invalid, incapacitate, falter, weak, tearful, worn; tear; wear; queer, too, queer is there, too. These proximities tell a story. A queer life might be how we get in touch with things at the very point at which they, or we, are worn or worn down; those moments when we break or break down, when we shatter under the weight of history. The sounds of an old piano evoking the sound of an old woman: Could this evocation vibrate with affection? Could a queer heart beat with passion for what is wavering and quavering?

That some of us can live our lives by assuming that word *queer*, by even saying "yes" to that word, shows how a past use is not exhaustive of a word or a thing, however exhausted a word or thing. As Judith Butler notes in *Excitable Speech*, "An aesthetic enactment of an injurious word may both *use* the word and *mention* it, that is, make use of it to produce certain effects but also at the same time make reference to that very use, calling attention to it as a citation, situating that use within a citational legacy, making that use into an explicit discursive item to be reflected on rather than a taken for granted operation of ordinary language."[2] We can disrupt the meaning of an insult by making its usage audible as a history that does not decide, once and for all, what a word can do. To queer use might be to make use audible, to listen to use; to bring to the front what ordinarily recedes into the background.

Sometimes words are reused as if they can be cut off from their history—when an insult is thrown out, for instance, and reaches its target, but is defended as just banter, as something you can, should, make light of. If we reuse the word *queer*, we hold onto the weight, the baggage. Eve Kosofsky Sedgwick suggests that what makes queer a "politically potent term" is how it cleaves to "childhood scenes of shame."[3] Queer acquires force and vitality precisely because we refuse to use the word to make light of a history. To recycle or reuse a word is to reorientate one's relation to a scene that holds its place, as memory, as container, however leaky.

Queer as reused; reuse as queer use. In today's lecture I will be drawing on arguments from a book I have recently completed, *What's the Use?* In the book, I follow use around, the way I followed happiness in *The Promise of Happiness*, and the will in *Willful Subjects*. *Use* is a small word with a big history; use has had and does have many uses. Following use has allowed me to connect bodies of work that are usually assumed to be distinct, such as literatures in design and biology that make use of use to explain the acquisition of form. Following use has allowed me to explore how worlds are shaped from, as it were, the bottom up.

Uses of Use

In this section I want to meditate on use as biography, a way of telling a story of things. *Use* when used as a verb can mean: to employ for some purpose, to expend or consume; to treat or behave toward; to take unfair advantage of or exploit; to habituate or accustom. Use is a relation as well as an activity that often points beyond something even when use is about something: to use something points to what something is "for." Some objects are made in order to be used. We might call these objects *designed objects*. What they are *for* brings them into existence. A cup is made in order that I have something to drink from; it is shaped this way, with a hole as its heart, empty, so that it can be filled by liquid. We might summarize the implied relation as "for is before." However even if something is shaped around what it is for, that is not the end of the story. As Howard Risatti notes in *A Theory of Craft*,

> Use need not correspond to intended function. Most if not all objects can have a use, or, more accurately, be made useable by being put to use. A sledge hammer can pound or it can be used as a paperweight or lever. A handsaw can cut a board and be used as straight-edge or to make music. A chair can be sat in and used to prop open a door. These uses make them "useful objects," but since they are unrelated to the intended purpose and function for which these objects were made, knowing these uses doesn't necessarily reveal much about these objects.[4]

Use can correspond to intended function, but use does not necessarily correspond to an intended function. This *not* is an opening. I am not so sure if uses are quite as unrevealing about things as Risatti implies ("knowing these uses doesn't necessarily reveal much about these objects"). I am being told something about the qualities of a sledgehammer that it can used to be a paperweight. That a sledgehammer can be used as a paperweight tells me about the heaviness of the sledgehammer. Something cannot be used for anything, which means that use is a restriction of possibility that is material. Nevertheless, there is something queer about use; intentions do not exhaust possibilities. The keys that are used to unlock a door can be used as a toy, perhaps because they are shiny and silver; perhaps because they jangle. Queer uses, when things are used for purposes other than the ones for which they were intended, still reference the qualities of a thing; queer uses may linger on those qualities, rendering them all the more lively.

Queer use might also be understood as improper use; queer use as perversion. The word *perversion* can refer not only to deviate from what is true or right but to *the improper use of something*. Perhaps the child who turns the key into a toy is not a pervert; the child is expected to play with things. But a boy who plays with the wrong toy, a toy hoover for instance that is intended for a girl, might be understood as perverted or at least as on the way to perversion. Correcting the boy's use of the toy is about correcting more than behavior in relation to a toy; it is about correcting how the boy is boy. And note here that we speak of proper use, we might be thinking of parts of the body as well as objects. Let me advance a speculative thesis that compulsory heterosexuality can operate as a form of intended functionality: we are allowed to play with our bits, to roam around each other's bodies as well as our own, but we must use them for the purpose *for* which it is assumed they were intended. The pervert delays or postpones getting to the point. The figure of the pervert comes up as the one whose misuse of things *is a form of self-revelation*.

Note also the implication in Rissati's argument that use makes something usable. What makes something *possible* comes *after*; we are perhaps more used to thinking of possibility as preceding actuality. Use has a strange temporality. Use also makes something used. When we think of something as being used, we might also think of buying something secondhand. Like this book (figure 1)—it is a book on hands that was handy. A used book is usually cheaper than a new book. The more signs of usage = less value, unless the user is esteemed, when the value of a person can rub off on the value of a thing. Marx discusses wear and tear in relation to machines: "The material wear and tear of a machine is of two kinds. The one arises from use, as coins wear away by circulating, the other from non-use, as a sword rusts when left in its scabbard."[5] Marx showed how machinery *intensifies* rather than saves labor: you have to get the most of the machine before it wears out, a wearing that is passed on to workers, wearing as passing on and passing out; used as used up. Wear and tear in this economy is the loss of value determined by the extraction of value.

To value use might require a change of values. We might value worn things, broken things, for the life they lived, for how they show what they know: the scratch as pedagogy, the wrinkle as expression. To value use would not be to romanticize what is preserved as a historical record: signs of life can be signs of exhaustion, which is to say, signs of life can be signs of how a life has been extinguished. Perhaps we can think of use as a record of the fragility of a life. In writing about use, I have deliberately made use of "used books." With this book in my hands, I can tell others have been here before. I think of the reader who circled the word *grief*. I cannot trace you, but you left a trace. Use leaves traces in places.

Something might be in use or out of use. When something breaks, it might be taken out of use, rather like this cup (figure 2), which has lost its handle. It is a rather sad parting. When we think of something in use, we might think of a sign on a door: "occupied" (figure 3). This sign tells us that the toilet is in use. It tells us that we cannot use the toilet until whoever is using the toilet is finished. Use often comes with instructions that are about maintaining bodily and social boundaries.

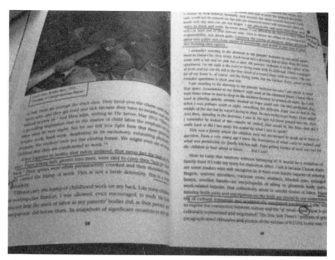

FIGURE 1.
Used Book.
Image courtesy
of the author.

FIGURE 2.
Broken Cup.
Image courtesy
of the author.

FIGURE 3.
Occupied. Image
courtesy of the author.

FIGURE 4.
Birds Nesting. Image
courtesy of the author.

FIGURE 5.
Well-Used Path. Image
courtesy of the author.

FIGURE 6.
Unused Path. Image
courtesy of the author.

Or take this image of a post box (figure 4). There is a sign that politely asks the would-be poster not to use the post box by posting a letter into the box. In the previous image the toilet was occupied because it was in use. In this case the post box is out of use because it is occupied. Although of course from another point of view, it is in use. The post box has provided a home for nesting birds. Intended functionality can mean *who something is for*, not just what something is for. This means that something can be used by those for whom it was not intended. That a post box can become a nest still tells us something about the nature of objects; we learn about form when a change of function does not require a change of form. But that change does require a sign, "please do not use," a sign is in use, to stop what would be usual: posting a letter through the box. The sign, we assume, is temporary. That box will come back into use as a post box when it ceases to be a nest.

Back into use: use can involve comings and goings. Take the example of the well-trodden path (figure 5). The path exists because people have used it. Use involves contact and friction, the tread of feet smooths the surface; the path is becoming smoother, easier to follow. *The more a path is used, the more a path is used.* How strange that this sentence makes sense. Without use a path can disappear, becoming overgrown, bumpy, unusable. Like this path (figure 6), we know it is a path because of a sign, but you can hardly see the sign for the trees. Use can be necessary for preservation. Use it or lose it: this is not only a mantra in personal training; it can become a philosophy of life. Not using; not being.

A path can appear like a line on a landscape. But a path can also be a route through life. Collectivity can be acquired as direction; the more a path is traveled upon, the clearer it becomes. A path can be kept clear, maintained; you can be supported by how a route is cleared; heterosexuality for instance can become a path, a route through life, a path that is kept clear, maintained not only by the frequency of use, and a frequency can be an invitation, but by an elaborate support system. When it is harder to proceed, when a path is harder to follow, you might be discouraged; you might try and find another route. A consciousness of the need to make more of an effort can be a disincentive. Just think of how we can be dissuaded by perpetual reminders of how hard something would be. Deviation is hard. Deviation is made harder.

Thoughts, feelings; they too have paths. Within empirical psychology, the path is in use as a way of thinking about thought. John Locke, for example, once suggested that thoughts "once set agoing, continue in the same shape they are used to, which, by often treading, are worn into a smooth path, and the motion in it becomes easy and as it were natural."[6] Used to: that which is wearing. A history of use is a history of becoming natural. William James in his psychology cites the work of Dumont on habit:

> Everyone knows how a garment having been worn a certain time clings better to the shape of the body than when it was new. . . . *A lock works better after being used some time* [emphasis mine]; at the outset a certain force was required to overcome certain roughness in the mechanism. The overcoming of their resistance is a phenomenon of habituation.[7]

A garment becomes more attuned to the body the more the garment is worn. I will return to the well-used garment in due course. The example of the lock and the key suggests that it is through use that things become easier to use. This is how acts of use are the building blocks of habit: if we take habit as our unit, we would miss these smaller steps, which accumulate to take us somewhere. If use takes time, use saves time; less effort is required to complete an action.

The idea that use keeps something alive, or that using something makes something easier to use, is supplemented by another idea central to the emergence of modern biology: that use, in making something *stronger*, and disuse, in making something weaker, shapes the very form of life. For example, Lamarck, the French naturalist who first used the word *biology* in its modern sense, offered a law of use and disuse: *"A more frequent and continuous use of any organ gradually strengthens, develops and enlarges that organ, and gives it a power proportional to the length of time it has been so used; while the permanent disuse of any organ imperceptibly weakens and deteriorates it, and progressively diminishes its functional capacity, until it finally disappears."*[8] These acquired modifications for Lamarck can be inherited, what we called simply *use inheritance.*

What is used or disused is dependent on an environment. Use is how an organism receives a message from the environment. Lamarck's famous example is the giraffe's neck, although he only uses this example once. For Lamarck the giraffe's neck grows longer not through volition but as an effect of repeated efforts that become directional. He describes: "Efforts in a given direction, when they are long sustained or habitually made by certain parts of a living body, for the satisfaction of needs established by nature or environment, cause an enlargement of the parts and the acquisition of a size and shape that they would never have obtained, *if these efforts had not become the normal activities of the animals exerting them* [emphasis mine]."[9] When an effort becomes normal, a form is acquired. When such form is acquired, less effort is needed; the giraffe does not have to reach so high to reach the foliage. Use inheritance translates as: *the lessening of the effort required to survive within an environment.*

At certain points Lamarck does imply that a use for something would bring it into existence. This was one of the reasons Charles Darwin was rather disparaging about Lamarck's work because of the implication he heard (rightly or wrongly) that nature has a design. We can find evidence of Darwin's disparagement in another used book: Darwin's personal copy of Lamarck's *Histoire Naturelle*. He wrote in the margins: "because use improves an organ—wishing for it, or its use, produces it!!! Oh." Despite how Darwin and Lamarck appear to deviate at least from Darwin's point of view on this question of use, Darwin himself often represents natural selection and the law of use and disuse as working together. And it is interesting to note that Darwin offers a reuse of the architect metaphor, despite how this metaphor risks the implication of design:

> Let an architect be compelled to build an edifice with uncut stones, fallen from a precipice. The shape of each fragment may be called accidental; yet the shape of each has been determined by the force of gravity, the nature of the rock, and the slope of the precipice,—events and circumstances, all of which depend on natural laws; but there is no relation between these laws and the purpose for which each fragment is used by the builder. . . . The shape of the fragments of stone at the base of our precipice may be called accidental, but this is not strictly correct; for the shape of each depends on a long sequence of events, all obeying natural laws. . . . *But in regard to the use to which the fragments may be put, their shape may be strictly said to be accidental* [emphasis mine].[10]

An architect can be a builder who makes use of stones without cutting them in order to fit a design. The stones are thrown up, or available, according to natural laws. These stones were not made in order to be used, like a cup shaped so that it can filled by water. They become useful to the architect *once he has begun building*. If the shape of a stone is determined by a long sequence of events, it is still an accident that the shape of this stone fits the shape of the hole in the wall. *You are more likely to use a stone that happens to fit that space;* use as hap, use as happenstance, use as, even, happy. I will return to Darwin's happy use of the architect metaphor in due course.

The Institutional as Usual

Through reflecting on institutional as usual I can thicken the account of use I have offered thus far. When we are habituated or attuned to the environment, we know what usually happens. We know about the institutional (as usual) by those who are trying to transform institutions. In my research into diversity and the university, which I first presented in my book *On Being Included*, I talked to diversity workers about their work. And going back to the data I have realized how diversity work requires becoming conscious of use and use patterns. If queering use brings "use" to the front, then diversity work is an archive of queer use. Diversity workers are trying to transform institutional habits, not to follow the well-used paths; not to go the way things flow. Many of the diversity workers I spoke to were appointed by institutions. Even if diversity workers are appointed by institutions to transform institutions, it does not mean institutions are willing to be transformed. One practitioner described her work thus: "It is a banging your head against a brick wall job." A job description becomes a wall description. If you keep banging your head against the brick wall, but the wall keeps its place, it is you that gets sore. What happens to the wall? All you seemed to have done is scratched the surface. This is what diversity work often feels like: scratching the surface. Even if you have only scratched the surface, you can still be liable for damages.

Doing diversity work means you collect wall stories; the wall becomes data; condensed information about institutions. Let me share with you a wall story:

> When I was first here there was a policy that you had to have three people on every panel who had been diversity trained. But then there was a decision early on when I was here, that it should be everybody, all panel members, at least internal people. They took that decision at the equality and diversity committee which several members of SMT were present at. But then the director of human resources found out about it and decided we didn't have the resources to support it; and it went to council with that taken out, and council were told that they were happy to have just three members, only a person on council who was an external member of the diversity committee went ballistic—and I am not kidding went ballistic—and said the minutes didn't reflect what had happened in the meeting because the minutes said the decision was different to what actually happened (and I didn't take the minutes by the way). And so they had to take it through and reverse it. And the Council decision was that all people should be trained. And despite that I have then sat in meetings where they have just continued saying that it has

to be just three people on the panel. And I said, "But no, council changed their view and I can give you the minutes," and they just look at me as if I am saying something really stupid; this went on for ages, even though the Council minutes definitely said all panel members should be trained. And to be honest sometimes you just give up.

It seems as if there is an institutional decision. Individuals within the institution must act as if the decision has been made for it to have been made. If they do not, it has not. A decision made in the present about the future is overridden by the momentum of the past: the past becomes a well-worn path, what usually happens, still happens. In this case, the head of personnel did not need to take the decision out of the minutes for the decision not to bring something into effect. I have called this dynamic "non-performativity": when naming something does not bring something into effect, or when something is named in order not to bring something into effect.

The wall: that which keeps standing. The wall is a finding. Let me summarize the finding: what stops movement moves. In other words, the mechanisms for stopping something are mobile, which means when we witness the movement, we can miss the mechanism. This is quite important because organizations tend to be good at creating evidence of movement; creating evidence you are doing something is not the same thing as doing something. This is why I have called diversity workers *institutional plumbers*: they have to work out not only where something is blocked but how it is blocked. In our example, what stopped something from happening *could have been* the removal of the policy from the minutes; it *could have been* the failure to notice this removal; but it wasn't. It was the way in which those within the institution acted after the policy had been agreed on. Agreeing to something can be another way of stopping it from happening.

A diversity policy can come into existence without coming into use. I noted earlier how a sign is often used to make a transition from something being in and out of use, such as in this case of the post box. Institutions are also postal systems. Maybe the diversity worker deposits the policy in the post box because she assumes the box is in use. The post box that is not in use might have another function: to stop a policy from going through the whole system. The policy becomes dusty, rather like Marx's rusty sword; from rusty to dusty. A policy can become unusable by not being used.

Consider, too, all the energy this practitioner expended on developing a policy that did not do anything. The story of how the wall keeps standing is the same story as the story of how a diversity worker becomes shattered;

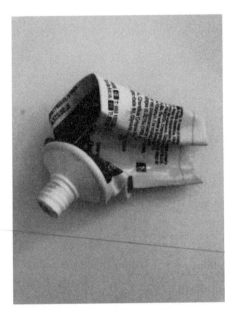

FIGURE 7.
Used-Up
Toothpaste.
Image courtesy
of the author.

as she says, "Sometimes you just give up." Maybe you end up feeling used up, limp, spent, rather like this tube of toothpaste (figure 7). Or you might fly off the handle, to recall that broken cup; an expression that can mean to snap or to lose your temper. To lose a handle on things can mean to lose yourself; you become the one who cannot handle it. You don't have to say anything to be heard as breaking something. Another practitioner describes: "You know, you go through that in these sorts of jobs where you go to say something, and you can just see people going, 'Oh, here she goes.'" We both laughed, recognizing that each other recognized that scene. The feminist killjoy, that leaky container, comes up here; she comes up in what we hear. We hear each other in the wear and the tear of the words we share; we hear what it is like to come up against the same thing over and over again. We imagine the eyes rolling as if to say: well, she would say that. It was from experiences like this that I developed my equation: rolling eyes = feminist pedagogy.

It is important to note that the policy that was stopped by not being used was a policy about how academic appointments are made. Appointment panels thus become places to go if you want to learn more about how institutions are reproduced; how decisions are made about who is "appointable." A person in a diversity training session I attended shared that people in her department used an unofficial criteria for appointability of whether someone was "the kind of person you can take down to the pub." They wanted someone who can inhabit those spaces with them; being with as being like;

someone they can relate to, drink with. I remember one time a woman of color was being considered for a job, she worked on race and sexuality, and someone said in a departmental meeting with concern, "But we already have Sara," as if having one of us was more than enough. There was a murmured consensus that she replicated me, even though our work was different. There was no such concern about other areas. Concern; no concern; how things stay the same by seeing others as the same.

I want to go back to my discussion of uses of use. An institution is an environment. Environments are dynamic; it is because environments change that uses change. An institution, however, is also a container technology. You reproduce something by *stabilizing the requirements for what you need to survive or thrive in an environment.* When a requirement is stabilized it does not need to be made explicit. Use becomes a question of fit. Remember Darwin's use of the architect metaphor? The builder uses the stone that happens to fit; use as selection. Institutions, too, are built. It can appear as if the moment of use is hap: that this person is selected because they just happen to fit the requirements rather like a stone is selected because it just happens to be the same shape and size as the hole in the wall. Selection can be a process in which you are invited to participate; to get funding, say, you have to meet the requirements, to fill in a form; a standard is what is created when you use the same form; selection *as* the stabilization of form. But a selection can be made before an invitation is sent out: selection as a history of how a body takes shape, how a hole is created that is that same shape; a history of the institution as a history of what appears as coincidence, how those shapes are the same shape. And then *hap* is used ideologically: *as if they were here because they happened to fit, rather than they fit because of how the structure was built.*

A structure: the gradual removal of hap from use in the determination of a requirement. In Lamarck's model, use becomes inheritance, in shaping form it lessens the effort required to do something within an environment. When you fit, and fitting here is formal, a question of form, you inherit the lessening of effort. So, a path, say in the sense of a career path or even a life trajectory, is not simply made more usable by being used. Some have more paths laid out more clearly in front of them because they already fit a requirement. It is not just constancy of use that eases a passage. Use is eased for those who inherit the right form, whereby rightness means the degree of a fit with an expectation. *For* as before acquires a new resonance here: when a world is built *for* some, they come *before* others.

Not Fitting

People do come to inhabit organizations that are not intended for them; you can make the cut without fitting. If you arrive into an organization that is not built *for* you, you experience this *for* as tight or as tightening. If you are the one for whom an institution is intended, *for* is loose; the institution appears as open because it is open to you. If use is a restriction of possibility that is material, as I suggested earlier, some encounter that restriction more than others.

This is why I think of an institution as an old garment: it has acquired the shape of those who tend to wear it, such that it becomes easier to wear if you have that shape. And this is why I think of privilege as *an energy-saving device*; less effort is required to pass through when a world has been assembled around you. If you arrive with dubious origins, you are not expected to be there, so in getting there you have already disagreed with an expectation of who you are and what you can do; then, an institution is the wrong shape. Annette Kuhn describes how as a working-class girl in a grammar school she feels "conspicuously out of place."[11] She describes this sense of being out of place by giving us a biography of her school uniform, how by the time her ill-fitting uniform came to fit, it had become "shabby" and "scruffy." The word *wear* originally derives from the Germanic word for clothing. It then acquires a secondary sense of "use up, gradually damage" from the effect of continued use on clothes. It is not just that when something is used more it fits better. If you are the wrong shape you have to make more of an effort: use then does not smooth a passage, or enable a better fit, but can lead to corrosion and damage. This difference—between use that smooths and enables and use that corrodes and damages—is a distributed difference.

Not fitting can be about the body you have, about your own requirements. When you don't meet the requirements, you become, to borrow Rosemarie Garland-Thomson's important term, a *misfit*. She describes being a person with a disability in an ableist institution as like being a "square peg in round hole."[12] Fitting becomes work for those who do not fit; you have to push, push, push, and sometimes no amount of pushing will get you in. You can be a misfit given what has become routine. An organization that organizes long meetings without any breaks assumes a body that can be seated without breaks. If someone arrives who cannot maintain this position, they do not meet the requirements. If you lay down during the meeting you would throw the meeting into crisis. A social justice project might require throwing a meeting into crisis.

If a space has to be modified to enable you to participate, it is not just that it is harder for you to participate; your participation is deemed disruptive, not fitting, as not fitting in. You might have to try to fit in when or because you do not fit in. A woman of color describes this work: "I think with a person of color there's always a question of what's this woman going to turn out like. . . . They're nervous about appointing people of color into senior positions. . . . Because if I went in my sari and wanted prayer time off and started rocking the boat and being a bit different and asserting my kind of culture, I'm sure they'd take it differently." Some forms of difference are heard as "rocking the boat," as if you are only different because you are insistent (on being different). Trying not to cause disruption might require discarding parts of yourself, parts of your history, such as garments—a sari, say—or rituals, a prayer, words, what you cannot say.

Words: what you cannot say. Think of the word *racism*. Audre Lorde described so well how racism is heard as getting in the way of smooth flow of communication. Any use of the word *racism* is heard as overuse. When words evoke histories that create friction, they sound louder. Words can evoke histories, bodies too. Sometimes turning up is enough to bring a history up, a history that gets in the way of an occupation of space.

A social category is a dwelling: that which gives residence. We can recall the sign "occupied." You can enter if the toilet is vacant. Even spaces that seem available for anyone to enter can be closed. Before you get to one door, you might have to get through another. You can be stopped from using the women's toilet because you are seen as not woman: you become not only a body out of place but a body that threatens those who are in place. You might have to become insistent to pee, and given that peeing is necessary for being, insistent to pee really means insistent to be. Some have to insist on belonging to the categories that give residence to others.

A wall can be what you encounter when you arrive somewhere. You turn up at a hotel with your girlfriend and you say you have booked a room. They catch you in a glance and they hesitate. A hesitation can speak volumes. This reservation says your booking is for a double bed, is that right, madam? Eyebrows are raised; a glance slides over the two of you, catching enough detail. Are you sure, madam? Yes, that's right; a double bed. You have to say it, again; you have to say it, again, firmly. I mentioned earlier my equation rolling eyes = feminist pedagogy. I have another one:

Raised eyebrows = lesbian feminist pedagogy

Really, are you sure? This happens again and again; you almost come to expect it, the necessity of being firm just to receive what you have requested. Disbelief follows you wherever you go; still. One time after a querying, Are you sure madam, are you sure, madam, you enter the room: twin beds. Do you go down; do you try again? It can be trying. Sometimes it is too trying, it is too much, and you pull your two little beds together; you find other ways of huddling. Queer use: another way of huddling, of keeping each other warm.

For some to be is to be in question. Is that your sister or your husband? That was a question asked to me by a neighbor once. Who are you? What are you? Where are you from? As a brown woman living in the UK, I am used to being asked that question. Where are you from? Where are you really from? It is a way of being told you are not from here; brown, not from here, not here, not. These questions can dislodge you, you come to wait for them; waiting to be dislodged changes your relation to a lodge.

Being noticeable can be how you are registered as being not from here. Sometimes you are not noticeable on the same register: not from here, not here, not. You might walk into a seminar room with a white man; you are both professors. But you feel the gaze land upon him: plop, plop. You don't appear as professor because you are not how a professor usually appears. He is addressed as the professor. If you were to say, "Hey, I am a professor too," you would be heard as drawing attention to yourself. Diversity work: how you end up appearing as drawing attention to yourself. What you have to say or do in order not to be passed over is treated as a complaint about being passed over, whether or not it is.

I have just begun a new project on complaint. The project was inspired by working with students on numerous enquiries into sexual harassment and sexual misconduct, which is to say, my project was inspired by students. A complaint is treated as a crisis for an organization, as potential damage to its reputation. Students are warned that complaining would cause damage; it would damage their careers, reputations, relationships. This warning often works as a threat: you will lose the connections you need to progress. One student describes: "I was repeatedly told that 'rocking the boat' or 'making waves' would affect my career in the future and that I would ruin the department for everyone else. I was told if I did put in a complaint, I would never be able to work in the university and that it was likely I wouldn't get a job elsewhere." Here complaining becomes a form of self-damage as well as damage to others, ruining a department, no less. This student goes on to describe how the pressure not to complain can be exerted: "In just one day

I was subjected to eight hours of grueling meetings and questioning, almost designed to break me and stop me from taking the complaint any further." A wall can be what comes up, or a wall can be what comes down, a ton of bricks. This is how power often works: you don't have to stop people from doing something, just make it harder for them to do something. Remember: Deviation is hard. Deviation is made hard.

Not only is it hard to complain, but a complaint about the damage you suffer is treated as damage to the organization. When I spoke out about sexual misconduct and sexual harassment, I became quite quickly the cause of damage: what a mess Sara, look how much work you have created. I became a leaky pipe: drip, drip. Organizations will try and contain that damage; public relations works as damage limitation. This is how diversity often takes institutional form; damage limitation. There is hope here; they cannot mop up all of our mess. One spillage can lead to more coming out; can lead, does lead. A leak can be a lead. After I shared my reasons for my resignation, many people shared with me their own stories, their own institutional battles. A feminist ear can provide the release of a pressure valve. Just loosen the screw a little bit, a tiny little bit, and you have an explosion. We need more explosions.

Conclusion: Queer Vandalism

Damage limitation: this is how organizations end up using paper, paper as papering over; to paper over the cracks, the leaks; the means by which blemishes on an institutional record are not recorded. Perhaps these blemishes become ours; we become damaged goods. Paper too can be papered over. In *Queer Phenomenology*, I called into question a fantasy of a "paperless philosophy" as part of a critique of how philosophy might be orientated toward a certain kind of body, one for whom materiality would be an unnecessary distraction, one who has time freed for contemplation by how others do the paperwork, the domestic work, the care work.

Paper matters. Paper can also be queer; paper can be used queerly. I am reminded of Homi Bhabha's discussion of uses of the Bible in "Signs Taken for Wonders." Bhabha cites the *Missionary Register* from 1817: "Still [every Indian] would gladly receive a bible. And why? That he may store it up as a curiosity, sell it for a few pice, or use it for wastepaper. Such it is well known has been the common fate of those Bibles distributed in this place. Some are seen laid up as curiosities, by those who cannot read them: some have been bartered in the markets; and others have been thrown into the snuff-shops, and used as wrapping paper."[13] The Bible in not being properly read is willfully destroyed; the Bible becomes a curiosity; reused or usable for other purposes, wrapping paper, wastepaper. Of course the missionaries narrate the fate of the Bible in the colonies as a result of the inability of the natives to be able to digest it: "It is true, that such of the Natives as can read, have leisure enough to read the whole Bible; but they are so indolent, so fond of eating and sleeping, or so lost in their vicious pursuits, that unless something at once *brief, simple,* and *powerful* be presented, it will not be likely to be read by them, and, if read, it will not be likely to arrest their torpid and sensual minds."[14] If racism is used as an explanation of the failure of digestion, rendering the racial other a queer subject ("vicious pursuits"; "torpid and sensual minds"), racism is used because of the failure of the colonial mission to transform the minds of the colonized into willing vessels.

The demand to use something properly is a demand to revere what has been given by the colonizer. Empire as gift comes with use instructions. One of my conclusions is that we cannot simply affirm the queer potential of use. I hope you can hear why; we have to account first for how that potential has been stolen; a theft that exists alongside other thefts. The appropriation of potential is not unrelated to the appropriation of persons. To queer use is thus to have a fight on your hands. If not to be subjected to the will of the colonizer is to queer use, or even to become queer through misuse (perversion as self-revelation), then to queer use is to live in proximity to violence. To queer use is to linger on the material qualities of that which you are supposed to pass over; it is to recover a potential from materials that have been left behind, all the things you can do with paper if you do not follow the instructions.

A recovery can be dangerous. The creativity of queer use becomes an act of destruction, whether intended or not; not digesting something, spitting it out; putting it about. What appears as a failure to use something properly can thus be a refusal. To queer use can also mean to destroy that which is deemed worthy of reverence. Queer use in other words can be understood as vandalism: "the willful destruction of what is venerable and beautiful." Earlier I described diversity workers as institutional plumbers. We might from this description assume that diversity workers are appointed to unblock the system. But a blockage can be how the system is working. The system is working by stopping those who are trying to transform the system. This means that to transform a system we have to stop the system from working. The plumber might need to be a vandal, or we might have to pass as a plumber (fixing the leak) to become a vandal (creating a leak). We might have to throw a wrench in the works or become, to use Sarah Franklin's terms, "wenches in the works,"[15] to throw our bodies into the system, to try and stop the same old bodies from being assembled, doing the same old things. The wench in the works has a queer kinship with the feminist killjoy, a kinship of figures can be a kinship of persons, as *non-reproductive agents*; those who are trying to stop what usually happens from happening.

If you stop the machine from working you have damaged the machine. It is not just that queers are damaged or lost souls, though we may be that, but that queerness becomes damaging; how we ruin things by living and loving in the wrong way. If queer desires cause damage, then damage becomes a queer cause, what we are willing to cause. Not following a family line is often understood as breaking a line: queer as snap, the moment you realize what you do not have to be. Queer as snap, snap, as if you are cutting up the family with a pair of scissors just by arranging your life in a different way. Not following something as destroying something: no wonder they find us to be destructive.

So much is reproduced by the requirement to follow. Within the academy you might be asked to follow the well-trodden paths of citation; to cite properly as to cite those deemed to have already had the most influence. The more a path is used the more a path is used. The more he is cited the more he is cited. Not following something as destroying something: you can become a vandal by rearranging a text in a different way, by not citing any white men for instance. To speak of whiteness in the academy or of colonialism as the context in which Enlightenment philosophy happened is to bring up the scandal of the vandal. Decolonizing the curriculum as a project has been framed as an act of vandalism, a willful destruction of our universals; knocking off the heads of statues, snapping at the thrones of the philosopher kings.

Vandalism becomes a tactic when we have to cut a message off from a body, when a message if traced to a source would compromise the source. We might need to use guerrilla tactics, and we have a feminist and queer history to draw upon; write names of harassers on books, graffiti on walls. Yes, the scratches, we are back to those scratches. What is treated as damage can be a message sent out: we can reach each other through what appears to others as mere scratch and scribble. The riskier it is to speak out, the more inventive we might have to become.

The requirement to be inventive is not just a matter of communication. Audre Lorde in her poem "A Litany for Survival" evokes "those of us" who "love in doorways coming and going in the hours between dawns."[16] You might have to use the less used paths, turn a doorway into a meeting place; you might have to try to slide by undetected because being seen is dangerous when you are seen as dangerous. Queer use can be a matter of survival, becoming fainter as your best chance of being at all.

There might be queer possibilities not only in use, how materials can be picked up when we refuse an instruction, but *in not being of use*. I noted earlier how selection involves the stabilization of form. The story, the institutional story, is that not to be selected is to cease to be; what we can call *institutional death*. An institutional death is not the end of the story. There is a discussion in *Origin* of vestigial organs, as parts that are no longer useful but linger, however dwindled, such as the small eye of the blind mole; these parts are sometimes called *leftovers*. Vestigiality is the retention of structures or attributes of ancestral species that have lost their functionality, another version of the strange temporality of use. Let me quote from *Origin*: "Rudimentary parts, as it is generally admitted, are apt to be highly variable . . . *their variability seems to result from their uselessness* [emphasis mine], and consequently from natural selection having had no power to check deviations in their structure."[17] Uselessness: it can be a deadly assignment. I think we know this, a history of whom and what is discarded, how the fragments are swept up and away. We can pick up the pieces. We can find other ways of telling the history of use and uselessness, hearing a queer potential in a sentence from a much-used book. That potential: not being selected is not to be checked; to have more room to roam, to vary, to deviate; to proliferate. If queer use can be about survival, following the less well-used path in order not to be detected, queer use can also be about creativity, the variations that are possible when you are not selected and rewarded for going the right way. Of course, not being selected also means not being supported. And so: we have to create our own support systems, queer handles; how we hold on; how a life can go on, when we are shattered, because we are shattered. No wonder then: the stories of the exhaustion of inhabiting worlds that do not accommodate us, the stories of the weary and the worn, the teary and the torn, are the same stories as the stories of inventiveness, of creating something, of making something.

I think of Lorde. I always think of Lorde. Audre Lorde spoke of herself as a writer when she was dying. She wrote: "I am going to write fire until it comes out of my ears, my eyes, my noseholes—everywhere. Until it's every breath I breathe. I'm going to go out like a fucking meteor!"[18]

> And so she did
> And so she did

She goes out, she makes something. She calls this capacity to make things through heat "the erotic." Lorde describes: "There is a difference between painting a black fence and writing a poem, but only one of quantity. And there is, for me, no difference between writing a good poem and moving into sunlight against the body of a woman I love."[19] Words flicker with life, like sunlight on her body.

> A love poem
> A lover as poem

I am warmed by the thought; of how we create things; how we break open a container to make things. We watch the words spill. They spill all over you. I think, too, of Cherríe Moraga's poem "The Welder." Moraga speaks of heat being used to shape new elements, to create "the intimacy of steel melting, the fire that makes sculpture of your lives, builds buildings."[20] We have to build our own buildings when the world does not accommodate our desires. When you are blocked, when your very existence is prohibited or viewed with general suspicion or even just raised eyebrows (yes, they are pedagogy), you have to come up with your own systems for getting things through.

> How inventive
> Quite something
> Not from nothing
> Something from something
> A kitchen table becomes a publishing house
> A door-way becomes a meeting place
> A post box becomes a nest

Sometimes we have to work hard to know what is possible: this image could be a queer teacher (figure 4). It teaches us that it is possible for those deemed strangers to inhabit a space that has been assumed as belonging to others, as being for others to use; and note, an assumption can be what you reside in, how you reside. The post box could have remained in use; the nest destroyed before it was completed; the birds displaced. A history of use is a history of such displacements, many violent, displacements that often remain unrecognized because of how things are occupied. To queer use is to make usage into a crisis; you have to make room because of how spaces have been occupied. To make usage a crisis is work; it is hard and painstaking work; collective and creative work. I have been trying to describe the work of queering use, one way or another, in my work. The work of description too is shared work; what we do with and for each other.

This image has something else to teach us: creating a shelter and disrupting usage can refer to the same action. A kitchen table becomes a publishing house; a doorway, a meeting place; a post box, a nest; a writing table, seemingly solitary, a queer gathering. Thank you.

Notes

1. George Eliot, "Three Months in Weimar," *Essays and Leaves from a Notebook* (Edinburgh: Blackwood, 1884), 240.
2. Judith Butler, *Excitable Speech: A Politics of the Performative* (London: Routledge, 1997), 99.
3. Eve Kosofsky Sedgwick, "Queer Performativity: Henry James's *The Art of the Novel*," *GLQ: A Journal of Lesbian and Gay Studies* 1, no. 1 (1993): 4.
4. Howard Risatti, *A Theory of Craft: Function and Aesthetic Expression* (Chapel Hill: University of North Carolina Press, 2007), 26.
5. Karl Marx, *Capital*, trans. Ben Fowkes, vol. 1 (1867; London: Penguin Classics, 1990), 528.
6. John Locke, *An Essay Concerning Human Understanding* (1690; London: Penguin Books, 1997), 531.
7. William James, *The Principles of Psychology*, vol. 1 (1890; New York: Dover, 1950), 105.
8. Jean-Baptiste Lamarck, *Zoological Philosophy*, trans. Hugh Elliot (1809; Cambridge: Cambridge University Press, 1914), 123.
9. Lamarck, *Zoological Philosophy*, 123.
10. Charles Darwin, *The Variation of Animals and Plants under Domestication*, vols. 1 and 2 (London: John Murray, 1868), 248–49.
11. Annette Kuhn, *Family Secrets: Acts of Memory and Imagination* (1995; London: Verso, 2002), 111.
12. Rosemarie Garland-Thomson, "Misfits: A Feminist Materialist Disability Concept," *Hypatia: A Journal of Feminist Philosophy* 26, no. 3 (2011): 591–609.
13. Homi K. Bhabha, "Signs Taken for Wonders: Questions of Ambivalence and Authority under a Tree outside Delhi, May 1817," *Critical Inquiry* 12, no. 1 (1985): 144–65.
14. Church Missionary Society, 1817, *Missionary Register* (London: L. B. Seeley), 186.
15. Sarah Franklin, "Sexism as a Means of Reproduction: Some Reflections on the Politics of Academic Practice," *New Formations* 86 (2015): 22.
16. Audre Lorde, *Black Unicorn* (New York: W. W. Norton, 1978), 31.

17. Charles Darwin, *The Origin of Species*, 6th ed. (1859; Cambridge: Cambridge University Press, 2009), 118–19.

18. Audre Lorde, *A Burst of Light: Essays* (Ithaca, NY: Firebrand Books, 1988), 76–77.

19. Audre Lorde, *Sister Outsider: Essays and Speeches* (Trumansburg, NY: Crossing Press, 1984), 58.

20. Cherríe Moraga, "The Welder," in *This Bridge Called My Back: Writings by Radical Women of Color*, eds. Gloria Anzaldúa and Cherríe Moraga (New York : Kitchen Table Press, 1981), 219.

Sara Ahmed Reflects on "Queer Use"

It seems like a long time ago—time can be such a queer thing, what happens can change the slant of it—that I presented this lecture. I remember that gathering well, being with so many people who mattered to me, who had come into my life at different times and in different ways. I was far from home, which meant my close friends could not be there, but I felt at home. I felt at home not just because I had been to many events at CLAGS but because this was a queer space. I remain grateful for that space, for sweaty queer proximities, for all the times we could be out with our people. It will happen again.

I gave this talk on queer use: how things (also spaces) can be used in ways that are not intended or by those for whom they were not intended. The main image I used in the lecture was of a post box that had become a nest. I think of the birds rather affectionately as our queer kin; they turn a small opening intended for letters into a door, a queer door perhaps, a way of getting in and out of the box. I am aware this is a rather happy, hopeful image. It is rather rare that we can just turn up and turn a box into a nest or a room into a shelter. To queer use, to open spaces up to those for whom they were not intended, usually requires a world-dismantling effort.

We can find each other because that effort is behind us. We have to keep making that effort because of what is in front of us: white supremacy, racial capitalism, heteropatriarchy. We have a fight on our hands. We have to fight for room, room to be, room to do, room to do our work without being questioned or put under surveillance. We have to fight to find a safer path through life, a way of progressing, or getting through, without having to give up ourselves or our desires. A fight can be how we acquire wisdom: we know so much from trying to transform the worlds that do not accommodate us. That fight can also be just damn hard. When you have to fight for an existence you can end up feeling that fighting is your existence. And so, we needed each other: we needed to become each other's resources.

We became each other's resources. We have queer programs and spaces not just because they are nice things to have, though they are that, what a relief, but because we need them to survive institutions that are not built for us. But we have to keep fighting for them, for spaces, for programs, even those that have been filled by memories, that are full of our affections, because so much of what we have created remains precarious. Our kinship can rest on that precarity: we hold each other up, prop each other up—our inventiveness, too.

I ended my lecture with two tables: how a kitchen table can become a press, how a writing table, "seemingly solitary," can become a queer gathering. A becoming can be behind us. Barbara Smith describes why the Kitchen Table Press, dedicated to publishing the work of women of color, took its name: "We chose our name because the kitchen was the center of the home, the place where women in particular work and communicate with each other."[1] It took a collective effort for a kitchen table to become a press. The places where many of us already gather can, through work, become communication networks: how we reach out, how we reach more. We do our queer work from here too, communicating here, caring here, sending words from here because we gather here.

Notes

1. Barbara Smith, "A Press of Our Own: Kitchen Table Women of Color Press," *Frontiers: A Journal of Women Studies* 10, no. 3 (1989): 11–13.

THE DAVID R. KESSLER LECTURES 2002–2020

2002   JONATHAN NED KATZ

2003   GAYLE RUBIN

2004   ISAAC JULIEN

2006   ADRIENNE RICH

2007   DOUGLAS CRIMP

2008   SUSAN STRYKER

2009   SARAH SCHULMAN

2010   URVASHI VAID

2012   MARTIN DUBERMAN

2013   CHERYL CLARKE

2014   CATHY J. COHEN

2015   RICHARD FUNG

2016   DEAN SPADE

2017   SARA AHMED

2018   **AMBER HOLLIBAUGH**

2019   JASBIR K. PUAR

2020   RODERICK A. FERGUSON

Amber Hollibaugh

Amber Hollibaugh is a lesbian sex radical, ex-hooker, incest survivor, gypsy child, poor-white-trash, high-femme dyke. She is also an award-winning filmmaker, feminist, Left political organizer, public speaker, and journalist whose activism and scholarship calls for, in her words, "a new revolution that includes the sexual desires that so many people, of whatever identity, experience with shame and feel forced to keep secret."

Hollibaugh was a founding member and formerly the executive director of Queers for Economic Justice (QEJ). Previously, she held the positions of chief officer of Elder & LBTI Women's Services at Howard Brown Health Center in Chicago, senior strategist for the National Gay and Lesbian Task Force, and director of national initiatives at Services and Advocacy for GLBT Elders (SAGE). Earlier in her tenure, she was SAGE's director of education, advocacy, and community-building. Before joining the staff of SAGE, she spent seven years at Gay Men's Health Crisis (GMHC) as founding director of the Lesbian AIDS Project and subsequently as the national director of women's services. She was also the director of education for the New York City Commission on Human Rights, AIDS division. For her work in sexual health, she is the recipient of the Dr. Susan B. Love Award for Outstanding Achievement in Women's Health.

Hollibaugh is the author of *My Dangerous Desires: A Queer Girl Dreaming Her Way Home* (2000) and the director and coproducer of *The Heart of the Matter* (1993), a documentary film focusing on women's sexuality, denial, and risk for HIV and AIDS, which won the 1994 Sundance Film Festival Freedom of Expression award and premiered on PBS's prestigious *POV* film series.

Hope and the Power of Desire: Our Vision for Changing the World

DECEMBER 13, 2018

I want to thank CLAGS for this honor. CLAGS as an organization has been an important part of my life, not simply by being on the board, but from its very beginning to insist on the brilliance and the importance of recognizing queer thinking—why queer thinking, queer intellectual work, queer engagement with political issues had value, when there was nothing at that point that recognized being a queer thinker.

So, it means a great deal to me to have CLAGS recognize me in this way. I've come to many of these lectures because I wanted to hear the people that were speaking. I wanted to hear their thinking, their work, their ideas about what mattered. And I want to thank all the people that presented tonight. All of you are people that I love in very deep ways, and I won't forget, ever, what you said. I want to dedicate this talk to two queer organizations that I love, but that are no longer here, although they're still profoundly needed. I dedicate this talk to both of those organizations, because, when I do my movement work, I see the faces of the people who were a part of those groups, few of whom would come here or ever feel that they could come here. They might wear the wrong clothes, have bad teeth, use words incorrectly. Both the Lesbian AIDS Project and Queers for Economic Justice are the groups that I want to dedicate this to, because it is in those places that I saw my own history, and the value of doing work and demanding work in places that often had been invisible.

As I come here tonight, I think about issues of hope and the power of desire, which is what I call this talk, because I think it's important to consider how we imagine changing the world. What do we think that would look like? How do we dream it? What are its pieces, its skeleton? What would we do first? Where in our social change movements do we have those conversations, or do we have them at all? And, frankly, where's sex and desire in those conversations and in the dreams that we have for an explosive erotic life? How can it be that we are building political movements, and yet the significance of hope, of vision and desire, remains in such short supply? I don't know why these three remain so invisible, but their absences diminish our ability to believe in the possibility of radical social change. Radical social change that would happen in our lives and in our futures—because it's important to remember that before we can build something, we have to imagine it.

I'm here tonight to talk about absences and what they mean for us politically. The reality is that all of the absences that I think of as so critical are absences that are invisible in the way that we understand political change and political activism, because the people that are a part of those questions and issues are people that our movements have often made decisions to leave out, whether intentionally or by the way that they construct themselves—people that come from poverty, that come from kink, that come from leather, that come from places that they would not otherwise want to have to explain in a room of people who don't look like them. And I say, with a lifetime of frustration and exhaustion, that not understanding that questions of vision, of hope, of desire, are political, not personal, is a part of how you *begin* to understand it—not simply about who you go to bed with or who you want to go to bed with. It's about imagining all that you can be in a moment of time where desire and the possibility of change appear possible.

As I've said in my own book, *My Dangerous Desires*, I've lived on the wrong side of sex since birth.[1] This is both who I am and who I was meant to be, though it isn't all that there is. But I know that the power of radical hope is based on a vision for a world that's completely transformed, a world where hope and pleasure and desire refuse to put people before profit, and a world that doesn't think pleasure is an afterthought to the really important things that a Marxist agenda regards as critical to the consequence of possibility and revolution. No. Not really. We are living in a terrifying time. Truly a terrifying time, driven by Trump and the Republican Party and the sociopathic movements of the hard Right and the self-proclaimed fascists and paramilitary, all of those which existed in the United States before Trump, but all of which have been emboldened by his presidency. I stand here tonight in resistance to all of those groups and their members as a person who's been battling these movements since I was seventeen. I'm now seventy-two. I've been walking this path for fifty-five years.

Being a Kessler lecturer honors me, because it allows me to bring to the stage all the invisible people who would rarely feel invited here. Too queer, too poor, too strange, too POC or mixed-race, too marked by a history of incarceration or addiction, too outside because of racism or antisemitism, too female (however you define that), too transgender, too genderqueer, too HIV-positive, too much of an immigrant, too disabled, too struggling with access and inclusion, too much of a hooker or a whore, too working-class, or just too goddamn high-femme to be able to hold this space. So, tonight, I bring all of those things with me, and it's why I've come here to accept the Kessler Award and do this talk.

But where I started, where I came from, was very different. That was a world of hopelessness, a world where desperation defined the structure and the limits of what you could imagine, and how you would understand your own growing up, and where you might be able to go. It was a kind of hopelessness that surrounded me, and I think surrounds people with my kind of background and history, in a way that you have no idea how to get out of. You have no idea what else might be possible. It isn't as though you have any literal sense of what it would mean to get out of a trailer park and go someplace that would give you the possibility of a different kind of life. I mean, you could go to another trailer park. That kind of frames it. But you couldn't imagine what else might be possible, because it's only something that you've seen in a film or on television. It's bound by a certain kind of wealth and a certain kind of privilege that nobody you know has ever had, and if they have, they've left, and they never return. They never come back, so you have no sense of what it might mean to get out. I mean, people talked occasionally about maybe what it would mean to go to nursing school or what it might mean to be a teacher, but I am the first person in my family to have graduated from high school. People like myself never left the places that I came from.

People that come from my kind of background rarely or often don't survive the thing that is true about their own forbidden desires and erotic imaginations. I believed myself to be both perverted and impaired. I had no idea who else might be queer and how it might be to live a queer life, though I had had pointed out to me quite often in my trailer park the dykes that lived over there that nobody would talk to, the faggots that fixed people's hair unless they'd been beaten to a pulp on Saturday night by my brothers and cousins. But you didn't bring up desire. Desire wasn't what you would ever assume would propel your life. You were a straight girl, you got married, the only question was whether you were going to be pregnant before you got married or afterward, nothing else. I knew in the context of that hopelessness that I was never meant to escape the despair of my upbringing. I understood that it was a hopelessness of class and race and gender, and that my own family had been so marginalized and had been considered so odd. Motorcycle-riding, Romani, Gypsy, Irish, poor white trash, never the kind of people that you wanted to say that you came from. But within even that construction, I couldn't find queerness. The idea of having options, which is what I often hear people say. When you come from a mixed-race family where you watch your father being thrown off one construction site after another because he's the brown person in the white crew, when he comes home and he and my grandmother talk about having been branded by the Ku Klux Klan in a port town in Oregon when they traveled in the caravans that Romani people traveled in and my grandmother was a sex worker. They would tell me about what people who called them "Gypsies" thought—that they'd always steal your silverware, or maybe they'd rape your daughter. That was the world they taught me to try and figure out how to survive in.

But I was not a person that was prepared to give up dreaming. In fact, that's pretty much all I did. My mother would say to me that the only thing that I could do well was read a book, and she would say to me, "Reading books won't get you a job. You need to know how to work hard and not complain. You need to stop being a dreamer." She was bitter at the things that had confronted her and shaped her life, a woman who had her first child at fourteen and a half and had that child die before she was sixteen. It was a brutality that she had been raised with that she never forgot and she never forgave. And she did not want me to have hopes that could never be realized. She had no idea how you might do hope. Hope was frivolous. Hope was foolish and little, and you could only be heartbroken if you had hope. So their job was to teach me to be tough enough to know how to survive, to finish high school and not get pregnant, to stop dating the bikers I was running with by the time I was twelve, to not be so rebellious, to suck it up, that the raw shape of the things around me were all that I would have, and I had to figure out how to live with those.

I wasn't prepared to do what they said to me needed to be done. Having worked the whole range of the worst kind of jobs that you work in a life like that, from the kind of waitressing you do, to working in a factory that made ice cream cones, working in the back of a dry-cleaning plant, picking tobacco, I saw what my parents meant, and it isn't like I had an idea of how to get out. So, I became a nightclub dancer in Vegas, a stripper in San Francisco, and a hooker in most of the towns that I worked in, and the pay was a lot better. It still didn't answer the question of how I could have a different future, but it gave me the possibility of economically surviving and not being ground down so badly that I would give up hope. But it was finding activism and a world of radical ideas that first began to actually change the way that I had been taught hopelessness. It was the civil rights movement, the women's liberation movement, the fullness of what those both brought to the idea of making a different world, and that began to teach me about class, about where I had come from, and that it wasn't because my parents were failures, or I was, that I had come from the background that I found in my own history.

My mother, hoping, actually, to change the possibility of my life, found a list of boarding schools in the back of a *Vogue* magazine at a doctor's office. She tore out the listing and wrote to every single one of those schools asking if they had scholarships. She did not want me to have the life that she knew I was facing. One of those schools wrote back and said they had just begun to create a scholarship for "low-achiever, high-IQ students" and they needed somebody from California. And so I flew from Bakersfield to Lugano, Switzerland, and I learned about class. I had a magenta dress suit and magenta heels, quite high fuck-me pumps, and I tinted my bleach blonde hair with a slight tint of pink so it would go with my suit, and I flew off to Lugano, Switzerland, and began to learn about the real living experiences of being the wrong person in the wrong place. My mother had made all my clothes, and she had made them reversible so that I would have more things to wear. The kids that went to that school, they'd go to Paris and bring back a trunk-load of things, and the fact that the book from the school that told you what you could bring, said you could only bring this amount of this and this amount of that—they paid no attention to it. And I both longed for what I began to find there that I had never even knew existed. Remarkable things, reading Middle English, reading Chaucer in Middle English. Really, who knew? But I was failing, because I had no idea how, what were the expectations of how you studied? I couldn't imagine it.

I went to the one person who was a teacher there that I thought might understand or be sympathetic, who was a first-generation immigrant Lebanese man. He said to me, "You were never meant to be here. You are not failing because you are stupid, you were never meant to be here," and he gave me the *Communist Manifesto*. And it changed my world. I really didn't know what to think. I was quite amazed, but it was clear to me, then, that my parents weren't totally responsible for the fact that we were poor. And I went back to his family's hot dog stand in New London, Connecticut, and joined the first Communist Party study group, where I began to learn the Left. It was transforming. I was with other working-class people. We would sit there and talk about the world of ideas. No one assumed that anybody had a high school diploma, let alone a college one, and no one assumed we were stupid. And at that time it was the beginning of the Freedom Summer, Student Nonviolent Coordinating Committee. Activism was exploding in this country, and I joined them, and it saved my life. No one assumed there that you had to go to college, although, frankly, most of the people I knew in that movement had dropped out of college rather than never had thought they could go. But it was still true that there was a deep gulf between my radical work, the work that I did as a revolutionary, as a social change badass, and my sexual life, because I supported myself after those long, endless meetings doing sex work or stripping, and dating stone butch women.

And it was in those kinds of conflicts where I learned what it is to not tell the truth about your life, because you can't keep all of it hidden. It isn't possible to hide from people what you do or who you want, and you don't want to. I mean, it wasn't like I was ashamed of who I was dating. It wasn't like I didn't want the women that I wanted, but lesbian separatism was not welcoming to those of us who they said were basically parodying heterosexuality. And it was a movement that had just begun, the lesbian and gay movement, which is what it was called then—I believed in it, I loved it. It had given me life, it gave me hope, it was everything. I couldn't imagine that I would be in conflict with my own movement. I just couldn't bear it. It just seemed impossible, and yet, I would try and figure out what I could do about who I was and who I was attracted to, because it was clear to me that what I wanted to do and who I wanted to do it with would never be acceptable to the political movement that I felt so strongly about. It was living through that crisis; it was actually trying to commit suicide at that moment—because I couldn't bring the two together. I couldn't give up my movement, and I couldn't give up my sexuality. I couldn't make them be in parallel worlds that I could live in.

And when I survived that, I began to understand what it meant when you don't talk about the things that you live through and that you understand

and that makes for a complicated world, that you do the justice work within. The feminist sex wars happened. Those were brutal and bitter, and it was after that that I decided to leave the feminist movement, as it was beginning to be called, and begin to do AIDS work, something that no one wanted to do when I began to do it. I was riding on the subway to my first job interview for the AIDS Discrimination Unit at the Human Rights Commission, reading a report that they had just issued about AIDS discrimination, and the person sitting next to me on the subway train saw what the cover of the report was, and stood up and began to scream, "She has AIDS, she has AIDS," and the next stop, the train doors opened, and every single person left that subway car.

But it was an epidemic which brought home to me again that all the gifts that I had about sexuality, about class, about race, about desire, about difference were precisely what was needed to fight in that epidemic. And what that crisis, that epidemic, gave to me in my relationships with lesbians with HIV, women who were told over and over again that they couldn't really be lesbians if they had AIDS, because real lesbians didn't have AIDS, and they had to have been sleeping with men, or be sex workers, or somehow too poor to be real lesbians, meaning lesbians that went to the LGBT Community Center. When I began to do that work, it began to root me in the communities that I most cared about, and I could bring my skills to—my organizing ability, my thinking, my capacity to understand and to take things on. When we first started the first group for lesbians with HIV at Rikers Island, they told me that nobody would come. I mean, it was the women's side of Rikers, and they said, lesbians, people won't come to a lesbian AIDS group. So we started with three people and, in two weeks, had sixty women. The first time I walked in to lead the group, I sat down, and I was nervous, and a butch said to me, "Isn't your name Amber?" I said, "Yeah." And she said, "So, isn't *Stone Butch Blues* dedicated to you?"[2] And I said, "Yeah," and she said, "Oh yeah, we're reading it. We like it, it tells our story."

I learned in that struggle and brought what I learned to many other struggles: that you have to commit yourself to learning the things you need to know. You can't assume that someone is going to—how can I say this? It was so extraordinary to me in the beginning of activism that we had study groups. Nobody assumed that you would learn Marxism, because you would go to a class, you would study it with each other, you would investigate it, you would think through intellectual ideas, you would engage with them. Because of that history, I've been able to do both intellectual work and always do the organizing. Because an economic analysis, no matter how radical, can never, ever reduce the parts of your life that bring you joy and pleasure with another human being. And a political movement that refuses to talk about pleasure, that refuses to acknowledge joy, that says that lust is individual and private, is a movement that no one will ever want to join.

Notes

1. Amber L. Hollibaugh, *My Dangerous Desires: A Queer Girl Dreaming Her Way Home* (Durham, NC: Duke University Press, 2000).

2. Leslie Feinberg, *Stone Butch Blues: A Novel* (Ithaca, NY: Firebrand Books, 1993).

Heather María Ács, Alexandra Juhasz, and Joseph Nicholas DeFilippis on Amber Hollibaugh

Heather María Ács: Amber writes in the introduction of *My Dangerous Desires*, "I have wanted to find you, to tell you that I am here, to invite you to remember me or add your own unique experience to our common purpose, our collective tale. To come home with me. To join me in changing the world."[1] Thank you, Amber, for looking for me, for being a beacon, for creating a home with me, for creating a home for me with your work when my other homes have been tenuous. Thank you for your vision, your honesty, vulnerability, and strength. I remember you every day. With every project I create, femme adornment I wear proudly. Every moment I choose to love myself and fight for others. Thank you, Amber. I dedicate my life to accepting your generous invitation. Thank you.

Alexandra Juhasz: When I came to New York City in 1987, one of the first people I met was Amber Hollibaugh, who was working at the New York City Commission on Human Rights AIDS Discrimination Unit. The work of the unit asked the difficult question of whether it was possible to produce progressive media through a city- or state-funded institution. In 1986, the unit hired lesbian rights activist Amber Hollibaugh with a specific mandate of producing educational video. She worked with two assistants, Chas Brack and Alisa Lebow, and they said, "Two white lesbians and a black gay man with relatively radical politics were the force behind a video from a city agency." This was state-funded propaganda by people who are marginalized by that very state. We realized what a unique position we were in and tried to make the most of it.

In the unit, they ended up making two films: *The Second Epidemic*, directed by Amber in 1987, a made-for-public-television documentary about AIDS discrimination, and then *Hard to Get: AIDS Discrimination in the Workplace*, directed by Alisa Lebow in 1988. It was really interesting to see what they were doing in that city agency. They were making city-sponsored health education films with a PBS flair, nevertheless hiding a sophisticated AIDS politics and a radical cultural politics within city-made work. Eventually and quickly the unit was shut down in 1990, because "they were making too much noise, they were too effective, and they couldn't control us," at which point Amber went on to become the director of the GMHC's Lesbian AIDS Project, and during that time, she produced the feature documentary *The Heart of the Matter*, the first wide-release documentary about women and AIDS, which premiered on PBS and won the Freedom of Expression award in 1994 at the Sundance Film Festival. I hope that these contributions are part of the celebration, and thank you for everything you've done, Amber.

Joseph Nicholas DeFilippis: "Everyone's always told about politics that you have to be practical, but I actually think that's not true. I think you actually have to hold to a dream, and then understand what you can realistically execute and what you can move forward and when, but you never give up the dream." Those words are from a 2012 interview that Amber gave with Laura Flanders, and I have shown that interview to my students every single term for years now, and students always love when Amber says that.

I picked that quote because to me it represents so much of who Amber is. She is unwilling to compromise on her dream, her dream of what the world should be. That isn't to say that she doesn't compromise. . . . We can't live in this world without compromising. But Amber does it less than most of us do. Amber has an intellectual and moral integrity that I respect deeply and that I've learned so much from. In the ten years that I worked with her at Queers for Economic Justice (QEJ), she was steadfast in her beliefs and her values and also helped me figure out when and where we should compromise and when and where we shouldn't, and she was a North Star for me more times than she knows.

Heather María Ács is an award-winning performer, writer, filmmaker, drag queen, and cultural worker.

Alexandra Juhasz is a professor of film at Brooklyn College, CUNY.

Joseph Nicholas DeFilippis is a queer and anti-poverty activist who founded Queers for Economic Justice.

Notes

1. Amber L. Hollibaugh, *My Dangerous Desires: A Queer Girl Dreaming Her Way Home* (Durham, NC: Duke University Press, 2000).

THE DAVID R. KESSLER LECTURES 2002–2020

2002　JONATHAN NED KATZ

2003　GAYLE RUBIN

2004　ISAAC JULIEN

2006　ADRIENNE RICH

2007　DOUGLAS CRIMP

2008　SUSAN STRYKER

2009　SARAH SCHULMAN

2010　URVASHI VAID

2012　MARTIN DUBERMAN

2013　CHERYL CLARKE

2014　CATHY J. COHEN

2015　RICHARD FUNG

2016　DEAN SPADE

2017　SARA AHMED

2018　AMBER HOLLIBAUGH

2019　JASBIR K. PUAR

2020　RODERICK A. FERGUSON

Jasbir K. Puar

Jasbir K. Puar is professor of women's and gender studies at Rutgers University. She is the author of the award-winning books *The Right to Maim: Debility, Capacity, Disability* (2017) and *Terrorist Assemblages: Homonationalism in Queer Times* (2007), which is also translated into Spanish and French, with a Greek translation forthcoming, and was reissued as an expanded version for its tenth anniversary. As friend and collaborator David Eng wrote in his testimonial, the publication of *Terrorist Assemblages*, Puar's first monograph, was "a true watershed moment for interdisciplinary scholarship in transnational feminism, critical race theory, queer diasporic and postcolonial theory, affect in science and technology studies, and law in political theory." Developing the formative concept of homonationalism, the book "reconceptualized ideas of how the liberal politics of identity had to be rethought in terms of more mobile forces of difference, of affect, intensity, assemblage and control, that incorporated certain queer subjects into the fold of the nation-state by transforming them from figures of death into figures of life." Puar's scholarly and mainstream articles have been translated into more than fifteen languages. She is on the advisory board of numerous organizations, including USACBI and Disability Under Siege, a project focusing on disability in conflict zones.

A No-State "Solution": Inter/nationalism and the Question of Queer Theory

DECEMBER 5, 2019

Thanks so much to all of you here, it's just overwhelming and really wonderful to be here. It's such a profound honor and privilege to be here in this company, in this community here. I want to begin by acknowledging that we gather here tonight on unceded traditional land of the Lenape people. And this acknowledgment is a very small gesture toward the process of working to dismantle the legacies of settler colonialism.

So, this is no ordinary audience for me tonight; I've lived in New York City for twenty years now. So, I see here, in you, so many people that I love and admire, from whom I've learned and with whom I've been in life. Your presence here is so meaningful to me.

I hope you're not disappointed that I'm speaking more conversationally and reflectively this evening rather than dragging you through my latest tortured theoretical obsessions. Yeah, as I thought, no one is disappointed. Okay. So, we're clear on that.

What follows is a schematic and, for sure, incomplete homage to the beautiful fields of scholarship that have made my own work possible. It's not hyperbole to say that I've been surrounded by the best of comrades through the years. None of my work has been possible without this and without all of you here. I arrived in New York City from UC Berkeley to take up a postdoc fellowship, as mentioned already, at the Center for Lesbian and Gay Studies in 1999. As per the requirements of the fellowship, I became a board member of CLAGS, and so this is a really special moment for me to come full circle back to CLAGS. And exactly twenty years ago, I went to my first Kessler Lecture. The awardee that evening was John D'Emilio, author of the influential essay "Capitalism and Gay Identity." This is an essay I still teach regularly in my undergrad and graduate seminars. Alisa Solomon was then board chair and opened the floor, followed by testimonials from Lisa Duggan, Urvashi Vaid, and Allan Bérubé. I remember this event vividly, the excitement not only of hearing John speak, but also the gathering of community, the murmuring of recognition, the charged combination of precarity and possibility in the room. We were barely there, but we were there.

Of course, twenty years ago, I never dreamt one day I'd myself be receiving the Kessler. But more significantly, it occurs to me that the Kessler, which was only in its eighth year at that time, was a very different kind of award back then. It spoke to the margins that LGBTQ studies and queer theory and queer activists habited at the time: the bareness of institutional space; the paucity of jobs; the demand for voices, recognition, the debates between lesbian and gay studies and queer studies. Watching the videos of past Kessler events, I just could not stamp out a feeling of progress. A notion we critique—it cannot be linear; it cannot rehearse racializing teleologies of modernity. But it's still something we want. Things cannot stay the same.

This sense of progress, if you will, or let's call it "transformation," struck me again recently when I moved homes last year and packed up an array of edited volumes and anthologies from women of color and LGBTQ scholars and activists that I read and studied and taught in graduate school: *This Bridge Called My Back*; *Making Face, Making Soul*; *Home Girls*; *The Lesbian and Gay Studies Reader*; *A Queer World*, which is published by CLAGS, incidentally; *Queer Representations: Queer in Asian America*, which was coedited by David [Eng] and Alice Hom; *Between Woman and Nation: Nationalisms, Transnational Feminisms, and the State*; *The Routledge Queer Studies Reader*, and there were edited volumes on queer globalization, queer diasporas, nationalisms, and sexualities. There was a special issue of *Social Text* that I coveted in grad school, titled "Queer Transections of Race, Nation and Gender"; *Queer Studies: A Lesbian, Gay, Bisexual, and Transgender Anthology*. This list could go on for a bit longer. These were all published before the turn of the century. Many of them were already framing challenges to the norms of whiteness undergirding claims of transgressive queer exceptionalism. So, from Judith Butler's *Gender Trouble* in 1990, Michael Warner's *Fear of a Queer Planet* in '92—I think, that is to say, within a span of barely a decade—queer theory had not only become a legitimate field but had also already grown its tentacles of contestation, its conditions of possibility for immanent critique.

Today the Kessler awardee emblematizes something else. There are now queer scholarly projects that would not have been seen as part of the field twenty years ago. This speaks, I think, to the morphing capacities of queerness. I am here because of vast prolific multigenerational waves of scholars and activists. I came of age with the work and companionship of David Eng, Martin Manalansan, and Gayatri Gopinath on queer diasporas; José Muñoz and Jennifer Doyle on queer art, performance, and disidentification; Nayan Shah and Lisa Duggan on history and sexuality; Anjali Arondekar and Geeta Patel on postcoloniality and queerness; Licia Fiol-Matta and Arnaldo Cruz-Malavé on queer globalizations; Lauren Berlant and Beth Freeman on consumption and queer nation; Juana Rodríguez on sexual utopias; Inderpal Grewal and Caren Kaplan on transnational sexualities; Jack Halberstam and Viviane Namaste on transmasculinities and femininities; V. Spike Peterson on the fraternal versus the familial nation.

Again, this list could go on. My point is simply that there was an overwhelming amount of scholarship on race, on geopolitics, and on nation-state formation. We could think of this collection of literature as a burgeoning queer and trans of color genealogy. M. Jacqui Alexander's work on the sexual outlaw had me questioning whether there might be a racial hierarchy embedded in the modernity of the queer that is ousted from the nation. Along with Jacqui's work, Cathy J. Cohen's tremendous essay "Punks, Bulldaggers, and Welfare Queens," on the racializing differences between heterosexuality and heteronormativity, became, unbeknownst to me at the time, the progenitors of the concept of homonationalism. And of course, there's also Lisa Duggan's formative work on homonormativity.

During graduate school, I also had been organizing in the Bay Area with Narika, a helpline for South Asian women experiencing domestic violence, the Asian Women's Shelter, which was the only one of its kind at the time, and Trikone, which is the first South Asian gay and lesbian diasporic group. We were having intense debates about identity, about queerness, nationalism, diaspora, the implications of queer asylum for binational partnerships. Though I hadn't quite discerned it yet, while we were extremely concerned about the globalizing effects of the terms "gay," "lesbian," and especially "queer," and while we worried about the Euro-American framings of queerness that were the handmaidens to US empire, and while we challenged the homophobia and exclusions inherent to nation-state formations, we were less attuned to the myriad nationalisms that we were producing in our own midst. In Trikone, we had members demanding recognition of nonnormative sexualities from the Indian state who actually had no critique whatsoever of the Hindutva project of ethnic cleansing. I will never forget a meeting where a member refused to participate in a Pride contingent that carried signs condemning the 2002 anti-Muslim pogroms in India. Now these examples seem like common sense. "To be racist and gay is no anomaly," someone once wrote. But at the time, I think we passed over these LGBTQ alignments with racist, nationalist ideologies as aberrations, rather than symptoms, as part of a foolish and puzzling contradiction of conservativism—Log Cabin Republicans always come to mind—rather than constitutive of the queer liberal rights project itself. We were all critiquing Hindu nationalism in our homelands, but breezing by the kinds of racial, religious, caste, class, and national tensions we reproduced within South Asian queer diasporas.

Along with these formative organizing experiences, I also had the amazing fortune of taking a graduate seminar in 1997 with Angela Davis. It was after I had completed my coursework. So, it was with a special furor that I sought Angela's direction, her wisdom, her conviction—maybe I even wanted a bit of her fearlessness to rub off on me. One of the most poignant lessons I learned in her seminar was that according to her, there's a difference between a research agenda and an activist agenda. And I was focusing on the former while she was focusing on the latter. Needless to say, I was completely appalled at my missteps. Here I was having a disagreement with *the* Angela Davis, and while I was schooled through this impasse into some shame about my interest in theory and academic teaching and research, I never forgot the implications of this moment of reckoning. Over the years, I've always had the relationship between activist and research questions gripping my thinking, each refusing to give in to the other. At times, I've decided to posit them as one and the same or at least in robust dialogue with each other. At other times, the incommensurability of the two functioned less to mark the lack of either or some totalizing failure of thought, but rather was a measure itself—indeed itself measured the silos of what might be considered activism and what might be overdetermined as scholarly, as research is theory.

These schisms have taught me a great deal, not just about the perennial question "Who is your audience?" but more incisively about how to stake the claims of a movement, indeed *movements*, of thought. Because the pushing forward of thought is also movement. I started thinking of my own orientation as someone pondering the productivity of solidarity scholarship, a scholarship that is not reducible to activism, as if activism could be distilled into any one thing, but rather is in tandem with, of being with, and of being in step with the solidarity movements of our time. What unites these terrains for me is that theory and activism are both speculative practices. They both aspire to the yet-to-be-known, just slightly out-of-reach lexicons and imaginaries. They both reveal what we thought we knew, but in different terms and registers. They both project hopes, expectations, and demands for futures that are more creative, more daring, more vibrant with possibility.

These myriad messy connections between research and activism, theory and praxis, were, certainly for me, tested when September 11 happened. September 11 was, and remains, for me a before-and-after eventness. An eventness that suddenly illuminated much of what I didn't understand before and unfurled foreboding suggestions of what might come after. On September 11, I started writing with my dear friend, Amit Rai, the essay that eventually became "Monster, Terrorist, Fag" and basically the center of *Terrorist Assemblages*.[1] Day after day, we were going to so many meetings. It was crisis organizing and different from anything I've ever been a part of. I realized in that process that my training as a queer theorist, as someone who works on transnational sexualities, was in need of some serious stretching in order to say something coherent about the crisis of public debate and the repression of dissent in this post-9/11 period. A period that ended, I would say, with the 2008 financial crisis and the covert expansion of the War on Terror by Obama.

In our current upset about Trump, sometimes I think we forget that 9/11 was a time when a certain version of fascism really cohered. There was bipartisan support for the War on Terror. There was no battle of two parties in Congress, and it was not easy to go against this generalized flow, even in feminist and LGBTQ spaces. I remember feeling so alienated from the gender studies department that I'd just recently been hired in. I spent a lot of time at the Audre Lorde Project (ALP) in New York City those years, and I learned so much. ALP was always ahead of the curve. They released a fantastic statement on the War on Terror that challenged mainstream LGBTQ thinking at the time. And I was also on the steering committee of the South Asian Lesbian and Gay Association, otherwise known as SALGA. So these were BIPOC community spaces already doing the work of challenging mainstream LGBTQ organizations that advocated for non-intersectional policy projects on same-sex marriage, on gay and lesbian rights, and most importantly, were indifferent to, if not supportive of, the War on Terror. It became clear to me that some took for granted that the queer was an outlaw to the nation-state but did not ask how the nation-state might differentiate that outlaw in racial and class, gender and disability terms; this was an issue. Transnational feminist theorization also relentlessly deconstructed the seemingly totalizing heteronormativity of the nation-state, thus contributing from another angle to the reification of this queer outlaw figure. On a visit to Yale University, a young graduate student responding to these provocations about the racial hauntings buried in the queer outlaw asked me, "Why is a nation-state always presumed to be heteronormative?" And this was Tavia Nyong'o with his ever-incisive analysis.

Terrorist Assemblages was written in the interstices of this wealth of queer feminist transnational theorization, a plethora of smart queer organizing, and also, quite honestly, a terrible time of grief for myself, as many of you know.[2] I wrote *Terrorist Assemblages* in the three years following my brother Sandeep's sudden death, which is another before-and-after eventness for me. The untold story of *Terrorist Assemblages* is that it is a tribute to the militancy that comprised Sandeep's thinking and politics.

So, I'm here to tell you that melancholic introjection is for real. And writing became my primary outlet for the process of mourning. There's such a demand to privatize grief, and in general, that demand is unrelenting. I was reading the minor literature on adult sibling loss and the sparse psychoanalysis that actually thinks through the power of libidinal, yet non-incestuous sibling formations and situates those kinds of relationships as centrally as the Oedipus complex. This aporia in psychoanalytic theory still fascinates me. The insularity reinforced in these literatures, I found them to be deeply alienating, infatuated with individual psychic losses. This writing therefore became an effort to transform the singularity of mourning, interrelations of collective grief. What I had otherwise was some kind of exceptional middle-class family tragedy that isolated me, pathologized our family, and atomized loss and death in a deeply depoliticized manner. There's so much phobia around the out-of-order death, because they shatter fantasies of entitled longevity and they surface as a biopolitical failure. This projection of failure, of course, indexes a tremendous amount of privilege. People would often remark, "Sandeep died so young." He was thirty-two, and I'd always think, but compared to whom? Over time, I started understanding this loss, as it were, as an incredible privilege. Interrogating exceptionalism in relation to the metrics of biopolitical stratification has been a pivotal ongoing political project for me. And I think that process is reflected not only in *Terrorist Assemblages* but also in *The Right to Maim*.[3]

In relaying some of these personal details, I want to honor the affective struggles that undergird the work we do. Struggles that the neoliberal academy, especially in its institutional structures, demands that we sublimate, even deny. Perhaps it goes without saying that *Terrorist Assemblages* is not a smart title for a tenure book. And yet I somewhat naively didn't think this would matter. Today I would never, ever use this title for a tenure book, never. Tellingly, *Terrorist Assemblages* seems to become both more relevant and yet more controversial with age. As the context of September 11 has become affectively neutralized, more normalized, Islamophobia, at least a certain strand of it, is so constitutive as to be unremarkable, so embedded in the languages and practices of surveillance and counterterrorism as to be commonsensical. Many have queried how relevant the frame of homonationalism is, given the election of Trump and also the proliferation of far-right movements and regimes. Rather than assessing how homonationalist a state is, I am interested in the co-constituted existence of liberal progressive ideals of queer rights, tolerance, and freedom, alongside and working through homophobia, violent repression, transphobia, and ostracization, and how these two supposedly opposite poles are used to alternately log and demonize different populations. In fact, we might think of homonationalism and authoritarianism as often operating in a tandem formation that is only seemingly contradictory. But there is something else that happens with the performative reiterative force of a concept like homonationalism, in that it starts producing what it seeks to diagnose, in that it starts reifying what it originally meant to deconstruct. That when we ask how homonationalist is a state, we presume a state could or should be something, a better or worse something, rather than asking whether it should simply be in the first place.

In an early critique of *Terrorist Assemblages*, queer Indigenous studies scholar Scott Morgensen noted that even engaging with homonationalism as a problematic participates in the production and naturalization of queer settler subjectivities, subjectivities that are positioned to debate with or against investments in state sovereignty.[4] Homonationalism, as a conceptual frame, performs the nativization of settler subjectivity—in fact, a queer settler subjectivity. Relatedly, the engagement with the nation-state reiterates the vanishing point of indigeneity. This vanishing point, as David Eng and I write in a forthcoming (2020) issue of *Social Text* that David already mentioned, titled *Left of Queer*, is "the condition of possibility for the nation state and liberal representation to emerge,"[5] While this may tempt us toward further embracing queer theory's signature contribution, known as subjectless critique, Jodi Byrd warns us that the lack of fixity, the refusal of a proper referent upon which subjectless critique hinges, is "still and importantly grounded through the ongoing dispossession of Indigenous lands."[6] That is to say, subject or subjectless, queer theory in the main continues to tarry with concepts that require the elimination of the Native in order to exist. Byrd takes this even further by arguing that "the multiplicity and the non-alignment of bodies, anatomy, desire, pleasure and identity runs the risk of asserting Indigenous difference as the very ground that both reproduces and then defies the binaries of settler genders."[7] So, in other words, the "difference" of queer indigeneity is not just outside of the gender binary, it is also the difference upon which the binary rests.

What these interventions have taught me is that the analytic of homonationalism is only useful if it is actually deployed to challenge the existence of the state writ large and to articulate an analysis of settler colonialism. I have the words of Palestinian scholar and activist Rana Barakat ringing in my head. When asked whether Israel has the right to exist, Barakat retorts, "What nation-state has the right to exist?"[8] We could say that this is the question that orients Indigenous studies, and it is one that has been haunting queer studies for some time. And I think, and I want to suggest, if fully hailed, this question can fruitfully guide the next iterations of queer theorizing to come. The title of my talk today, of course, is an oblique reference to the debates about one-state versus two-state solutions to the Israeli-Palestinian "conflict." And there's also here, of course, a nod to Edward Said's formulation of the question of Palestine. The question of queer theory seems to me, currently, to be a question about our relation to what Steven Salaita terms the inter/national. "The inter/national," explains Steven, is a renewed decolonialism that "at its most basic . . . demands commitment to mutual liberation based on the proposition that colonial power must be rendered diffuse across multiple hemispheres through reciprocal struggle."[9]

I think we have this inter/nationalism built into the decades of our rich literatures on queer and trans critiques of nation-state formation, including these queer Indigenous studies scholars who keep flagging the taken-for-granted permanence of the nation-state. Collectively, they are accruing a prognostic force, vehement that the state is not a solution, thus inviting queer theories of anti-national, non-national, and no-state solutions.

The special issue that David and I are working on seeks to "provincialize" queer theory. It is framed around three problematics. The first is subjectless critique, which picks up on the 2005 issue *What's Queer about Queer Studies Now?*[10] Second is the overwrought debates between queer theory and Marxisms. And the third is the ongoing issue of geopolitical exceptionalism. And so, I quote briefly from our 2020 introduction: "The occlusions of homonationalism in the name of rights and representation compels us to ask whether the nation-state—and attendant notions of democracy, citizenship, and capital—provides the most appropriate frame for queer theory and queer self-narration today."[11]

One aim in this special issue is to reinvigorate these conversations from the '90s on US queernesses as forms of American exceptionalism, in part because we now have strands of queer theory that do function as uninterrogated versions of American studies, in other words, queer studies as an unmarked area studies formation. As this unmarked area studies, queer theory proper modulates which archives in Global South locations are legible, as well as queer Indigenous archives, by cycling them through normative ideas about what constitutes queer wounded attachments. Why are the forms of sexual injury that animate certain politics of queer resistance distinct from the endemic sexual violence of what Middle East studies scholar Maya Mikdashi and I have called permanent war, for example, in the Middle East?[12] If we are to take geopolitical exceptionalism seriously, queer theory must continually become unknown to itself.

So, what is a no-state solution? This question, of course, presumes that there is a solution. What we learn from Palestine about the failure of the Oslo Peace Process and the impasse of governance now facing Palestinians is that there is no liberal solution to Palestine. Both the one-state and the two-state solutions are pharmakons—remedy, poison, and scapegoat. They can only be the starting point for liberation, not the end. Any state solution will not change the lives of the majority of Palestinians who live in areas B and C and already exist without any real structure that purports to govern them. As such, Palestine is the fertile ground for emblematic decolonizing movements. There's no recourse, not only to rights but the right to have rights, no nation-state to appeal to, and frankly, no international community safeguarding their human rights. So these are the spaces of the yet-to-be-known that are leading the way.

If decolonization is not a metaphor, and in Palestine, it most certainly is not, one version of the no-state solution, Barakat insists, "is to stop arguing with the settler state, stop producing history in relation to settler time."[13] Accordingly, J. Kēhaulani Kauanui's work on the parallels and intersections between Palestine and Hawai'i keenly notes that "US Federal recognition for native governing entities resembles the two-state solution as the 'answer' to Palestine." Indigenous scholars and activists who, as she writes, "shift away from statist solutions . . . are exploring what a 'no-state solution' might look like." And she says this because ultimately, any state solution is a solution of the native problem for the settler. No-state, says Kauanui, "goes to the heart of the issue of ending colonial violence and settler colonialism."[14]

We can also follow the lead of Fred Moten, who perceives and also calls for the exhaustion of the state solution. In a response to *The Right to Maim* titled "Blackpalestinian Breath"—"Blackpalestinian" is one word—Moten writes that "the new, co-constituting assemblage of Ferguson, Gaza . . . requires us to ask what it would mean to recognize, but also to embrace and enact, the exhaustion of the state solution."[15] He continues, "We give life to the state solution when we breathe air into the dead language of lives and bodies."[16] From this double movement, I perceive that we have not only exhausted the state as a means of redress, as a solution, but the state also exhausts. The state has exhausted us. For Moten, and with him, I concur: beyond networked, shared, or resonant conditions of Ferguson, Gaza, all of which do exist, what is collectively at stake is no less than the refusal of nation-state governance, writ large. "The exhaustion of the state solution," Moten suggests, is the grounds upon which solidarity across geopolitical scenes and histories can be imagined and built.[17]

It is my hope that *The Right to Maim*, with its focus on sexuality as a dispersed modality within and across biopolitical control societies, suggests the spirit of a queer inter/nationalism, of a queer no-state solution. And I just want to mention that everything I've learned about biopolitics has been from my dear friend Patricia Clough. Given the backlash that the book has engendered, I ruminate more than ever now on that mortifying interaction with Professor Davis and the challenge it has presented me for the last two decades. Stepping in time with solidarity through scholarship is not exactly what the university wants to foster. With Palestine, it is humbling to learn that the work must speak to the movement and the movement must condition the work. And in fact, the work begins from the site of struggle and not from the knowledges seeking to know and understand the struggle. Palestine is less of a third rail in US academia and yet more contentious than ever. In a climate where movements are yet again facing their granular criminalization, from making boycotting illegal to the assassination of Black Lives Matter activists, the September 11 canard of "you're either with us or against us" feels ever more real. Locally, as those of you who live here are well aware, the NYPD is amping up criminalization of fare evasion as a conduit to further militarize the city and to deepen silos of poverty from wealth.

As is the case with many Palestine solidarity activists and advocates, I'm often interrogated as to if and why I'm exceptionalizing Palestine. This kind of interrogation unto itself is actually, of course, a form of exceptionalizing, rarely asked about other political struggles. Palestine is not exceptional, but it is exemplary. Whether or not the occupation will come to an end, the occupation is being distributed. Continuing along a post-Oslo trajectory of being further outsourced, the roots of capitalist profit are increasingly entangled through development and disaster reconstruction projects, through corporate saturation and debt enclosure, and through the networked uses of drone technology and forms of state surveillance and repression long perfected on Palestinians. This distributed occupation is how occupation courts its normalization, in bits and pieces, in other locations, as connected technologies of rule and immiseration. The global proliferation of modalities of control is one reason why Palestine is not singular, not exceptional, rather an exemplary concatenation of tactics that are recognizable in many other elsewheres. Rather than an archaic form of colonialism that is often predicted as bygone—in other words, "how could this still be happening"—Palestine, as Pete Coviello asserts, shows us a glimpse of power in the world to come. There is no state solution for us. The solution for the state, however—killing and maiming—manipulates the hinge between injury and death. The sovereign right to maim is being normalized right in front of us as we watch. During the last twenty months in Gaza of the Great March of Return protests, more than seven thousand Palestinians have been shot in the lower limbs. Injuring with impunity is rationalized as the use of minimal force. Cloaked as a humanitarian praxis, not-killing is a liberal panacea in a resource-deprived and infrastructurally decimated context, where the distinction between injury and disability collapses and the euphemism "permanent injury" denotes the extralegal of disability. There are unfolding questions here about corporeality, about gender, about sexuality and disability, that are opening up from this liberation movement that the global rights community is trying to reduce to a humanitarian crisis. Are maimed bodies of youths, bodies with untreated wounds that will grow as they age, bodies that are foreclosed from "proper adulthood," are these queer corporealities?

Is the language of crip care appropriate in a place where shooting to cripple is a policy, where maimed bodies are foreclosed from becoming disabled subjects? What does the nonnormative signal in these contexts?

The spectacle of maiming is hardly proprietary to Gaza. The circuitry of maiming loops, most forcibly, to the blinding of insurgents with pellet bullets in Kashmir; the tear gas canisters route us to the US–Mexico border. What I find so incredible and inspiring are the solidarity actions from disparate parts of the world that are returning the spectacle of maiming to the maimers. In response to the IDF shooting of Palestinian journalist Muath Amarneh in the eye, photos of children in classrooms, fellow journalists, and protesters with one eye covered; with hands, with signs, with eye patches in Chile, in Bolivia, in Hong Kong, as well as in Palestine; these images have gone viral. These images going viral signal a global exposure of the sovereign right to maim, a refusal to pretend that the humanitarian alibi of sparing life by injuring instead of killing will be tolerated. The de-exceptionalization of Palestine also foregrounds links with Puerto Rico, with Flint, Michigan, with New Orleans, and with other locations where, as with Gaza, the natural disaster is not only the opportunity for a business plan; the natural disaster is the business plan. If we understand the occupation as distributed, we once again hit the limits of a state solution, because the current status quo is the state solution. In this sense, the fight to free Palestine is the fight to liberate all of our futures. No one is exempt. This means, to quote Decolonize This Place and fearless comrades Nitasha Dhillon and Amin Husain in an action at the Brooklyn Museum, that "BDS is the floor, not the ceiling."[18] Palestine is an entry point, one of many, and along with Black Lives Matter, among the most visible, into a broader movement against capitalism, against imperialism, settler colonialism, state violence, and indeed against the nation-state itself.

Thank you.

Notes

1. Jasbir K. Puar and Amit S. Rai, "Monster, Terrorist, Fag: The War on Terrorism and the Production of Docile Patriots," *Social Text* 20, no. 3 (2002): 117.

2. Jasbir K. Puar, *Terrorist Assemblages: Homonationalism in Queer Times*, 10th anniv. expanded ed. (Durham, NC: Duke University Press, 2017).

3. Jasbir K. Puar, *The Right to Maim: Debility, Capacity, Disability* (Durham, NC: Duke University Press, 2017).

4. Scott Lauria Morgensen, *Spaces between Us: Queer Settler Colonialism and Indigenous Decolonization* (Minneapolis: University of Minnesota Press, 2011).

5. David L. Eng and Jasbir K. Puar, "Introduction: Left of Queer," *Social Text* 38, no. 4 (2020): 1–24.

6. Jodi A. Byrd, "What's Normative Got to Do with It?: Toward Indigenous Queer Relationality," *Social Text* 38, no. 4 (2020): 107.

7. Byrd, "What's Normative Got to Do with It?," 109.

8. Rana Barakat, "On Comparative Settler Colonialisms" (lecture at New York University, New York City, September 25, 2019).

9. Steven Salaita, *Inter/nationalism: Decolonizing Native America and Palestine* (Minneapolis: University of Minnesota Press, 2016).

10. David L. Eng, Jack Halberstam, and José Esteban Muñoz, "Introduction: What's Queer about Queer Studies Now?" *Social Text* 23, nos. 3–4 (84–85) (2005): 1–17.

11. David L. Eng and Jasbir K. Puar, "Introduction: Left of Queer," *Social Text* 38, no. 4 (2020): 1–24.

12. Maya Mikdashi and Jasbir K. Puar, "Queer Theory and Permanent War," *GLQ: A Journal of Lesbian and Gay Studies* 22, no. 2 (2016): 215–22.

13. Barakat, "On Comparative Settler Colonialisms."

14. J. Kēhaulani Kauanui, "Decolonial Self-Determination and 'No-State Solutions,'" *Humanity Journal*, July 2, 2019, humanityjournal.org/blog/decolonial-self-determination-and-no-state-solutions/.

15. Fred Moten, "blackpalestinian breath," *Social Text Online*, October 25, 2018, socialtextjournal.org/periscope_article/blackpalestinian-breath/.

16. Moten, "blackpalestinian breath."

17. Moten, "blackpalestinian breath."

18. Decolonial Cultural Front, "Action at the Brooklyn Museum: BDS is the Floor Not the Ceiling!," YouTube video, 2:22. https://www.youtube.com/watch?v=84ROpf8nWAc.

Jasbir K. Puar Reflects on "A No-State 'Solution': Inter/nationalism and the Question of Queer Theory"

Today is Nakba Day, the commemoration of the forced displacement and expulsion of the Palestinian people from their homeland. Rallies all over the world will mark not only seventy-four years of Israeli settler-colonial rule but also the assassination of Palestinian American journalist Shireen Abu Akleh by Israeli forces on May 11. Last night we lost LGBTQ warrior activist and Kessler awardee Urvashi Vaid at age sixty-three to cancer. And on May 2, a leak of a drafted impending Supreme Court decision revealed that the US is on the precipice of repealing abortion rights.

I wish I could say it's been a hell of a few weeks, but history has a way of unfurling nonstop. Reading over my Kessler Lecture from more than two years ago, I am startled by the sense of how much has happened since and yet simultaneously how this still reads of the present, a kaleidoscopic quality of temporality where refractions distill telos and the Möbius strip fuses internal and external into a kind of helpless, dizzying exhaustion. There is an Indian colloquialism that I love, one that is often deployed as a deflection but is no less accurate: "Same same, but very different only." Everything I've written here feels dated from "before the pandemic" but somehow, ever more true. It is a scary political feeling, to register the intensification of that which already felt intense. I am heartened by growing anti-imperial solidarity networks that are connecting Palestine with Kashmir with Black Lives Matter with Haiti and Khalistan, the ever-sharpening clarity of what Fred Moten calls an "anti-national internationalism" that takes as its connective tissue the fact of struggle itself.[1]

Notes

1. Fred Moten, *Stolen Life* (Durham, NC: Duke University Press, 2018).

THE DAVID R. KESSLER LECTURES 2002–2020

2002   JONATHAN NED KATZ

2003   GAYLE RUBIN

2004   ISAAC JULIEN

2006   ADRIENNE RICH

2007   DOUGLAS CRIMP

2008   SUSAN STRYKER

2009   SARAH SCHULMAN

2010   URVASHI VAID

2012   MARTIN DUBERMAN

2013   CHERYL CLARKE

2014   CATHY J. COHEN

2015   RICHARD FUNG

2016   DEAN SPADE

2017   SARA AHMED

2018   AMBER HOLLIBAUGH

2019   JASBIR K. PUAR

2020   RODERICK A. FERGUSON

Roderick A. Ferguson

Roderick A. Ferguson is professor of women's, gender, and sexuality studies at Yale University. An interdisciplinary scholar, his work traverses such fields as American studies, gender studies, queer studies, cultural studies, African American studies, sociology, literature, and education. He is the author of *One-Dimensional Queer* (2019), *We Demand: The University and Student Protests* (2017), *The Reorder of Things: The University and Its Pedagogies of Minority Difference* (2012), and *Aberrations in Black: Toward a Queer of Color Critique* (2004). With Grace Hong, he is coeditor of the anthology *Strange Affinities: The Gender and Sexual Politics of Comparative Racialization* (2011). He is also coeditor with Erica Edwards and Jeffrey Ogbar of *Keywords of African American Studies* (2018).

Queer and Trans Liberation and the Critique of Fascism, or When S.T.A.R. Met Césaire and the Frankfurt School

DECEMBER 10, 2020

First, let me thank CLAGS for this great honor. I am keenly aware of the high company that I keep as this year's recipient. I'd also like to thank the numerous friends, family members, students, teachers, and mentors who have made sure that I have never walked alone, and I thank you all for coming this evening.

I keep coming back to them, that band of trans women sex workers who made up Street Transvestite Action Revolutionaries, or S.T.A.R., founded by the Stonewall veterans Sylvia Rivera and Marsha P. Johnson. There were other groups, to be sure, but something about their conscious connection to groups like the Black Panther Party and the Puerto Rican Young Lords keeps me running after them.

In this talk tonight, I hope to keep company not only with them but also with my esteemed contemporaries who work at the intersections of trans, queer, feminist, ethnic, and Black studies, as well as in the politics and histories of abolition. S.T.A.R. is, for me, a rich archive for considering the diverse manifestations of police and fascist orders, as well as a powerful example of how to challenge those orders, survive them, and even thrive within them.

Like many, if not all, of us here tonight, I've been thinking a lot about fascism and would like to see what possibilities the archive of S.T.A.R. offers for expanding our historical and political imagination around how fascism works and how we can resist it. I will do tonight what I've always done and put S.T.A.R. in strange affinities with people with whom its members presumably had no relation: the pantheon of writers that make up the Black radical tradition and that formidable roundtable of German critics and theorists known as the Frankfurt School.

There is a photo from the 1971 protest at NYU's Weinstein Hall of Marsha standing on a street corner dressed in a fur coat, handing out flyers to passersby. Sylvia and Marsha founded S.T.A.R. shortly after this demonstration, one waged over the school's treatment of its queer students. As the writer Ehn Nothing says, "The University had refused to allow gay dances, organized by a gay student group, to occur on campus, so gay liberationists occupied the hall and held a sit-in. The arrival of the Tactical Police Force caused the gay liberationists to abandon the occupation."[1]

Reflecting on the moment when the tactical police came, Sylvia said, "All that we fought for at Weinstein Hall was lost when we left upon the request of the pigs. Chalk one up for the pigs, for they truly are carrying their victory flag."[2] Ehn Nothing asserts again, "STAR, initially called Street Transvestites for Gay Power, was born of the frustration with the gay liberation movement for its refusal to defend itself and be committed to struggle against the police."[3]

In addition to a struggle against the police, we might situate the Weinstein Hall protest and the participation of the police's tactical forces within the use of police and military forces to suppress popular insurgencies in the US and abroad, and within the rise of fascist tendencies within this country. In fact, the same year that the Weinstein Hall demonstration took place, Angela Davis would release the anthology *If They Come in the Morning: Voices of Resistance.*[4] In their preface to the book, she and the political activist and author Bettina Aptheker discussed the cloud of police repression that had descended upon the nation. They wrote, "Police repression in the United States has reached monstrous proportions. Black and brown peoples especially, victims of the most vicious and calculated forms of class, national and racial oppression, bear the brunt of this repression. Literally tens and thousands of innocent men and women, the overwhelming majority of them poor, fill the jails and prisons; hundreds of thousands more, including the most presumably respectable groups and individuals, are subject to police, FBI and military intelligence surveillance."[5]

As concerning as police repression was for Davis and Aptheker, it was also part of a larger disturbance: that of fascism. They wrote, "Many people in the progressive and radical movements have tended, especially in recent months as the repression has become increasingly intense, to view this intensity as a measure of the fascist nature of the government."[6] Connecting the specificities of fascism to marginalized and politicized populations, they went on to say, "It is essential to view fascist tendencies in terms of their specific challenge to working people; and in the United States, their specific challenge in the first place to the most exploited and at the same time most radical and politically conscious section of the working class—the Black, Puerto Rican and Chicano communities."[7] Not content to read fascism as a category inapplicable to liberal governments, Davis and Aptheker engaged fascism as a response to the insurgency and diversity of working classes within the US, a response that relied on the expansion and militarization of police forces.

Fascism, Davis and Aptheker implied, represents an attempt to discipline that insurgency and its related diversity. For this reason, they wrote, "The pivotal struggle to be waged among working people is the open, aggressive, uncompromising battle against all manifestations of racism."[8]

If fascism targets insurgent diversities, then anti-fascism must encourage their mobilization. We might observe groups and histories like the one offered by S.T.A.R. as an example of the critical diversity of working-class populations and as a provocation to innovate our understanding of how anti-fascist struggles must involve intersectional struggles against transphobia in particular.

Marsha remembered how she, Sylvia, Bambi L'Amour, and Andorra Marks, also members of S.T.A.R., were featured in an article for the *Village Voice* about the home they would eventually rent on 213 East Second Street. "We all gave our names, Bambi, Andorra, Marsha, and Sylvia," she said. "And we all went out to hustle, you know, about a few days after the article came out in the *Village Voice*, and you see we get busted one after another, in a matter of a couple of weeks. I don't know whether it was the article, or whether we just got busted because it was hot."[9]

If the arrests took place in response to the coverage about S.T.A.R. in the *Village Voice*, then it affirms the argument that police repression must be understood in relation to the insurgencies within poor and working-class communities. But given what Marsha just said, we must understand police power as a tripartite repression as well. It was a repression of the critical discourses that the S.T.A.R. members produced. It was also a repression of transgender modes of difference. It was, lastly, a repression of sex work. These were the specific challenges that fascism held for members of transgender communities of that day.

"My name is Seymour Pine," the officer said. "In 1968, I was assigned as Deputy Inspector in charge of public morals in the first division in the police department, which covered the Greenwich Village area. It was the duty of Public Morals to enforce all laws concerning vice and gambling, including prostitution, narcotics, and laws and regulations concerning homosexuality."[10]

The interview is printed in *Street Transvestite Action Revolutionaries: Survival, Revolt, and Queer Antagonist Struggle*, the zine that Ehn Nothing put together in 2013. In the interview, Officer Pine specifies how police powers represented an absolute authority to intrude upon trans life. He said, "The part of the penal code which applied to drag queens was section 240.35, Section 4: 'Being masked or in any manner disguised by unusual or unnatural attire or facial alteration; loiterers, remains, or congregants in a public place with other persons so masked.'" He understood very clearly the kinds of latitude that the penal code gave him and other officers: "And you say, okay, you're not a man, you're a woman, or you're vice versa and you wait over there. I mean, this was a kind of power that you have and you never gave it a second thought."[11]

Whether he knew it or not, Officer Pine touched on what Eric Stanley has characterized as "one of the primary ordering principles of modernity"—the capacity of the prison and the police to produce the gender binary.[12] And if transness has been the site of an exhaustive classification of the sexual and gendered body in relation to orientation, norms, and identity, as Jack Halberstam has argued, then police powers were part of that classification.

Marsha describes the particular way that the police arrested trans women involved in S.T.A.R. for their sex work and their activism: "They just come up and grab you. One transvestite they grabbed right out of her lover's arms, and took her down."[13] Here, she points to the summary discretion that police possessed in violently claiming the lives of trans activists and sex workers, a summary discretion that was specifically and simultaneously for the police a racial, gender, class, and sexual dispensation. Describing the summary discretion exercised by police in San Francisco's Tenderloin in the 1960s, Susan Stryker writes, "The police could be especially vicious to street queens, whom they considered bottom of the barrel sex workers and who were the least able to complain about mistreatment. Transgender women working the streets were often arrested on suspicion of prostitution even if they were just going to the corner store or talking with friends. They might be driven around in squad cars for hours, forced to perform oral sex, strip-searched, or, after arriving at the jail, humiliated in front of other prisoners."[14] In this passage about the summary discretion of San Francisco police, Stryker identifies just a fraction of what C. Riley Snorton and Jin Haritaworn have theorized as the specific circumstances of bio- and necro-politics for trans people disenfranchised by race and class.

Explaining the operations of summary discretion in the context of Blacks at the early part of the twentieth century, the African American activist and intellectual Ida B. Wells told of the arrest of two colored men in New Orleans who had been just sitting upon their doorsteps for a short time talking together. She said, "They had not broken the peace in any way whatever, no warrant was in the policeman's hands justifying their arrests, and no crime had been committed of which they were the suspects."[15] Turning to their discretionary powers, she continued, "Secure in the firm belief that they could do anything to a Negro that they wished, they approached the two men and in less than three minutes from the time they accosted them, attempted to put both colored men under arrest." Discussing Wells-Barnett's argument, the carceral studies scholar Bryan Wagner says, "This structural vulnerability to police violence described by Wells-Barnett has remained a constant feature of public life in the United States."[16]

The scene that Marsha describes, in which the members of S.T.A.R. and the other sex workers were snatched from the street, is part of the very history that Wells-Barnett invokes, one in which the summary discretion of the police makes marginalized groups vulnerable to structural violence. "You could do anything to a Negro you wished," said Wells-Barnett. "They just come up and grab you," Marsha replied.[17]

Sylvia said that one of the first times the S.T.A.R. banner was unfurled was in a march against police repression with the Young Lords Party, that famous organization of Puerto Rican revolutionaries that, in the words of former members Iris Morales and Denise Oliver-Velez, believed "deep in our hearts in the power of poor people to change the world."[18] Remembering the Young Lords, Sylvia said, "Any time they needed any help, I was always there for the Young Lords. It was just the respect they gave us as human beings."[19] Right around that time, she met Huey Newton, cofounder of the Black Panther Party at the People's Revolutionary Convention in 1971. Indeed, Newton would write his famous communiqué "Women's and Gay Liberation" during that time, arguing, "maybe a homosexual could be the most revolutionary."[20] Remembering Newton's message fondly, Sylvia said, "Huey decided we were part of the revolution, that we were revolutionary people."[21]

It is important to situate the Young Lords' and the Black Panthers' relative embrace of queer and trans folk within their organizations' revision of the Marxist notion of the lumpenproletariat. As geographer and ethnic studies scholar Laura Pulido argued, the hallmark of the Black Panther Party's politics was its emphasis on the lumpenproletariat, or today what might be called the underclass. While the Black Panthers and the Young Lords claimed certain aspects of Marxism, they had important deviations. As Pulido states, "Traditionally, Marxism had placed the greatest agency in the working class, while the lumpen proletariat had been dismissed as unorganizable, lacking class consciousness, and basically out for themselves."[22]

Indeed, Marx and Engels describe the lumpenproletariat in the *Communist Manifesto* as "the 'dangerous class,' the social scum, that passively rotting mass thrown off by the lowest layers of old society, [which] may, here and there, be swept into the movement by the proletarian revolution: its conditions of life, however, prepare it far more for the part of a bribed tool of reactionary intrigue."[23] In many ways, the histories of the Young Lords and the Black Panthers exposed the respectability politics of Marxism: its bifurcation of the poor into the respectable and potentially revolutionary proletariat and the disreputable and lethally apolitical lumpenproletariat. By constructing the lumpenproletariat as indecent—"the rotting mass," they called them—Marx and Engels not only connoted a social insignificance, but a historical and political one as well. Unlike the respectable proletariat, the lumpenproletariat would never change history, nor would they leave anything behind. They were the beggars, prostitutes, procurers, and scavengers, the queer ones; not the coal miner, the ironworker, the stocking maker, and the silk weaver—the virtuous working class that would usher in the revolution.

As houseless and trans sex workers, S.T.A.R. conformed not to the notion of the proletariat but to that of the lumpenproletariat. Indeed, one might argue that at that time, trans and queer people were relegated to lumpen ranks, since sodomy laws and vice commissions had effectively criminalized homosexuality and transness. While most Marxists consigned the beggars and prostitutes to the dustbin of history and, in this sense, thought alongside rather than against sodomy laws and vice, the Black Panthers and the Young Lords had other ideas. They, in the words of Pulido, "reversed this long-standing tradition by naming the lumpen proletariat as the revolutionary vanguard."[24] It is likely that this was part of the context for Newton's communiqué and the Young Lords' embrace of S.T.A.R.—why, perhaps, the Panthers and the Young Lords could, as a matter of policy, identify trans sex workers and queers as potential revolutionaries.

As the Panthers and the Young Lords challenged the othering of the lumpenproletariat, they defied fascist violence in ways that conventional Marxism could not. Indeed, as Marxism othered the lumpenproletariat, it made itself available, rather than resistant, to fascist logics. The Frankfurt School intellectual Theodore Adorno stated, "It is one of the favorite devices of fascist agitators . . . to compare out-groups, all foreigners and particularly refugees and Jews, with low animals and vermin."[25] Challenging fascism would mean finding value in the lives of people who have been considered by conservatives and radicals alike the scum of society. The founding of S.T.A.R. and similar groups was an announcement that there are members of the lumpenproletariat who are plenty capable of challenging fascism. These groups also suggested that as long as we divide the poor between the enlightened and the benighted, the virtuous and the sinful, we will unwittingly provide fascism with a resource that it needs. Another Frankfurt School intellectual, Walter Benjamin, said, "For the historical materialist, there is no major or minor event."[26] We might add that for a fully realized radicalism, there are no major or minor peoples.

There is a well-known photo of Sylvia speaking in 1973 at the Christopher Street Liberation Day rally. It is the speech in which she claims righteous anger at the wave of assimilation and normativity overtaking queer communities. To a partly hostile crowd, she cried out, "My half sisters and brothers are being raped and murdered by pigs, straights, and even sometimes by other uptight homosexuals who consider us the scum of the gay community."[27] She pinpoints the everydayness of transphobic violence— indeed, the very histories of the minoritized can be the basis for revising our understanding of the quotidian, rather than the exceptional, nature of social violence and how that quotidian nature makes up the building blocks of fascism. Such revisions, the theorist Alberto Toscano has argued recently, demonstrate the way that "fascism and democracy can be experienced very differently by different segments of the population."[28]

This observation has been central to Black radical traditions. It was the Martiniquan intellectual Aimé Césaire who, for instance, helped to locate colonialism as a building block for Nazism. He said, "First we must study how colonization works to *decivilize* the colonizer, to *brutalize* him in the true sense of the word, to degrade him, to awaken him to buried instincts, to covetousness, violence, race hatred, and moral relativism."[29] For Césaire, as for many Black writers and artists, colonialism represented the withering of the colonizer's humanity. This withering was to a large degree achieved by the social acceptance of everyday and institutionalized violence and marginalization. Césaire said,

> And we must show that each time a head is cut off or an eye put out in Vietnam and in France they accept the fact, each time a little girl is raped and in France they accept the fact, each time a Madagascan is tortured and in France they accept the fact, civilization acquires another dead weight, a universal regression takes place, a gangrene sets in, a center of infection begins to spread; and that at the end of all these treaties that have been violated, all these lies that have been propagated, all these punitive expeditions that have been tolerated, all these prisoners who have been tied up and "interrogated," all these patriots who have been tortured, at the end of all the racial pride that has been encouraged, all the boastfulness that has been displayed, a poison has been distilled into the veins of Europe and, slowly but surely, the continent proceeds toward *savagery*.[30]

Nazism, Césaire argued, was not the antithesis of Western civilization but, because of colonialism and the acceptance of it, another expression of Western civilization. In the everydayness of transphobic violence, we also find Western civilization expressing itself and ordering economically and racially marginalized trans people to the bottom of the social hierarchy. These circumstances shed light on how fascist violence that is articulated in the context of trans sex workers is accepted because of their taken-for-granted marginalization. Rivera's outcry at the Christopher Street Liberation Day rally implores us to consider how fascism recruits us into its regimes of acceptance.

The S.T.A.R. house was a tenement on 213 East Second Street. Not that much is known about it, really, but there's enough to produce meaning. The original building was torn down in the 1980s. Arthur Bell, the *Village Voice* writer that Marsha mentioned, described it as a "dilapidated hellhole of a building."[31] Sylvia remembers it this way: "We had a S.T.A.R. house, a place for all of us to sleep. It was only four rooms and the landlord had turned the electricity off, so we lived there by candlelight, a floating bunch of 15 to 25 queens cramped in those rooms with all our wardrobe. But it worked."[32]

The Weinstein Hall demonstration gave birth to the house. The members of S.T.A.R. threw a fundraiser with the Gay Liberation Front and gay youth from NYU and raised enough money to rent the tenement from the Mafia for $300 a month. Along with Marsha and Sylvia there was Bambi L'Amour, a black trans woman that Sylvia befriended while spending time at Rikers—specifically in the cell block reserved for "gay crimes," according to the scholar and activist Jessi Gan. Sylvia and Bambi were a pair while they did time at Rikers. "Nobody ever fucked with us," Sylvia said. There was also Andorra Marks, another black trans woman; Bubbles Rose Lee, who helped to occupy Weinstein Hall; Bebe Scarpie, who would go on to direct the Queens Liberation Front; and others that just needed a place. According to Sessi Kuwabara Blanchard, "they made the place home, reviving the defunct boiler with a bit of elbow grease, decorating the walls with posters demanding political prisoners' liberation and filling the home with puppies that roamed floors dotted with empty Hawaiian punch cans."[33] Everybody, queens and puppies, had a chance at sanctuary.

Sanctuary. According to the scholar and activist A. Naomi Paik, the word "sanctuary" means "a holy place and a place that offers refuge." While it first originated out of religious contexts, sanctuary is "not restricted to any specific religious tradition or even to people." Explaining its historic consciousness, Paik goes on to say, "Places of refuge include nature preserves and protected zones for animals endangered by human encroachments. The concept thus enables us to see the mutual need for protection shared by the human and natural worlds."[34]

As a designated harbor for the human and the nonhuman, the S.T.A.R. house provided a hallowed ground for targeted peoples, for the houseless person, the sex worker, the radical, and the four-legged. It was the safe refuge, the best refuge—having gone to that refuge, a trans woman could be delivered from pain. There, they made a sanctuary so that a new esteem might dwell among them. Full of blessing and guidance, whoever entered the house attained security, for a time, it seems.

Sanctuary. Sylvia said, "Marsha and I and Bubbles and Andorra and Bambi kept that building going by selling ourselves out on the streets while trying to keep the children off the streets. And a lot of them made good. A lot of them went home. Some of them I lost; they went to the streets. We lost them, but we tried to do the best we could for them."[35] Describing the ways that they helped each other survive, she said, "The contribution of the ones who didn't make it out into the streets, who wanted something different, was to liberate food from in front of the A&P and places like that, because back then they used to leave everything out front of the store before it opened. So the house was well-supplied, the building's rent was paid, and everybody in the neighborhood loved STAR House."[36]

Sylvia told of the ways that the S.T.A.R. house became a harbor for the people in the neighborhood as well. "They were impressed because they could leave their kids and we'd baby-sit with them," she said. "If they were hungry, we fed them. We fed half of the neighborhood because we had an abundance of food the kids liberated. It was a revolutionary thing."[37] We might situate what S.T.A.R. did within the history of mutual aid. Defining that history, Dean Spade argues, "Mutual aid is collective coordination to meet each other's needs, usually from an awareness that the systems we have in place are not going to meet them." For Spade, mutual aid is "done in conjunction with social movements" and as a means of "demanding transformative change."[38] The mutual aid that S.T.A.R. was producing pointed to the inadequacies of a nation and a world that make housing, transportation, healthy food, day care, health care, and safe work into privileges rather than rights. Perhaps invoking the spirit of Césaire, the members of S.T.A.R. seem to say, "We will neither accept our degradation nor theirs." Who knows. Maybe the S.T.A.R. members took their inspiration from the Black Panthers and the Young Lords. Those organizations invented childcare centers for the people, free breakfast programs for the children, and clothing drives for the poor, doing so out of a smack-to-the-face understanding that neither state nor capital would supply the resources to those in need. Describing their philosophy, the Young Lords said, "As servants of the people revolutionaries, we have committed ourselves wholeheartedly to the development of our nation of Borinquen and all humanity."[39]

Then again, they may have also been inspired by the San Francisco–based group Vanguard, which was made up of gay male and transgender female youth, many of whom were sex workers. In one of their demonstrations, a street-sweeping party, they reclaimed the streets and their identities, naming for San Francisco the seeds of what Lisa Duggan has described as neoliberalism's upward redistribution of resources. Vanguard's press release stated, "Tonight a clean sweep will be made on Market Street not by the police, but the street people who are often subject to police harassment. The drug addicts, pill heads, teenage hustlers, lesbians and homosexuals who make San Francisco's meat rack their home and are tired of living in the midst of filth thrown out onto the sidewalks and into the streets by nearby businessmen."

In the spirit of the Young Lords, the Black Panthers, and Vanguard, and all the girls who saw one another, the S.T.A.R. house offered itself for revolutionary service, committing itself wholeheartedly to the development of living beings within and around the house. In his 1972 book *Counterrevolution and Revolt*, another Frankfurt School theorist, Herbert Marcuse, argued,

"Fascism is the counterrevolution to the socialist transformation of society."[40] The raids, police roundups, murders, rapes, and economic devastation were all part of a counterrevolution tailored for the lumpen assemblage represented by S.T.A.R. and others like them. They were targeted precisely because they, contrary to Marxist presumptions, were engaged in revolutionary service. It is this service that fascism finds most threatening. As Alberto Toscano again argues, "While nominally mobilized against the threat of armed insurrection, the ultimate target of counterinsurgency were these experiments with social life outside and against the racial state."[41]

If S.T.A.R. was engaged in a kind of freedom dream, as the artist Tourmaline has suggested, then fascism would emerge from the shadows and attempt to destroy the fruit of that dream work. As lumpen revolutionaries, the S.T.A.R. members, for a spell at least, produced a kind of utopian community—not a utopia that was unrealizable, but one that was immanent within the house and its members. The theorist Avery Gordon has theorized utopia by saying, "The utopian is not the future as some absolute break from the past and the present, out there. It is in us, a way we conceive and live in the here and now"; "all those things we are and we do that exceed or are just not expressions of what is dominant and dominating us."[42]

In this now, one characterized by a creeping fascism that threatens to overtake our present, we are called to conceive and live other nows. At the very least, the histories of queer and trans liberation provide us a chance to represent the unexpected social agents who are opposing fascist modes of power. In their full appreciation, these histories encourage us to meet each other's needs and to demand social change. There, in the lumpen household, filled with queens who floated from room to room and with puppies that played and snuggled, we might find our model and inspiration.

Thank you so, so much.

Notes

1. Ehn Nothing, "Introduction: Queens against Society," in *Street Transvestite Action Revolutionaries: Survival, Revolt, and Queer Antagonist Struggle*, ed. Untorelli (Untorelli Press, 2013), 9. https://untorellipress.noblogs.org/post/2013/03/12/street-transvestite-action-revolutionaries-survival-revolt-and-queer-antagonist-struggle/.

2. "Street Transvestites for Gay Power: Statement on the 1971 NYU Occupation," in Untorelli, *Street Transvestite Action Revolutionaries*, 18.

3. Nothing, "Queens against Society," 9.

4. Angela Y. Davis, *If They Come in the Morning: Voices of Resistance* (1971; London: Verso, 2016).

5. Angela Davis and Bettina Apetheker, "Preface," in *If They Come in the Morning*, ed. Angela Davis (1971; London: Verso, 2016), xii.

6. Davis and Apetheker, "Preface," xiv.

7. Davis and Apetheker, "Preface," xiv–xv.

8. Davis and Apetheker, "Preface," xv.

9. Marsha P. Johnson, "Rapping with a Street Transvestite Revolutionary: An Interview with Marsha P. Johnson," in Untorelli, *Street Transvestite Action Revolutionaries*, 21.

10. Sylvia Rivera, "Every Destructive Thing: A 'Dialogue' Between Sylvia Rivera and Some Pigs," in Untorelli, *Street Transvestite Action Revolutionaries*, 15

11. Rivera, "Every Destructive Thing," 15.

12. Eric A. Stanley, Dean Spade, and Queer (In)Justice, "Queering Prison Abolition, Now?" *American Quarterly* 64, no. 1 (2012): 115–27.

13. Johnson, "Rapping with a Street Transvestite Revolutionary," 21.

14. Susan Stryker, *Transgender History* (Berkeley, CA: Seal Press, 2008), 67.

15. Ida B. Wells, *Mob Rule in New Orleans: Robert Charles and His Fight to the Death*, . . . (Chicago: self-pub., 1900).

16. Bryan Wagner, "Police," in *Keywords for African American Studies*, eds. Erica R. Edwards, Roderick A. Ferguson, and Jeffrey O. G. Ogbar (New York: New York University Press), 153.

17. Johnson, "Rapping with a Street Transvestite Revolutionary," 21.

18. Darrel Enck-Wanzer, Iris Morales, and Denise Oliver-Velez, eds., *The Young Lords: A Reader* (New York: New York University Press, 2010), ix.

19. Sylvia Rivera, "'I'm Glad I Was in the Stonewall Riot': An Interview with Sylvia Rivera," in Untorelli, *Street Transvestite Action Revolutionaries*, 13.

20. Huey Newton, "Letter from Huey Newton to the Revolutionary Brothers and Sisters about the Women's Liberation and Gay Liberation Movements," *The Black Panther* (newsletter), August 21, 1970.

21. Rivera, "'I'm Glad I Was in the Stonewall Riot,'" 13.

22. Laura Pulido, *Black, Brown, Yellow, and Left: Radical Activism in Los Angeles* (Berkeley: University of California Press, 2006), 142.

23. Karl Marx and Friedrich Engels, *The Communist Manifesto: A Modern Edition* (London: Verso, 1998), 48.

24. Pulido, *Black, Brown, Yellow, and Left*, 142.

25. Theodor Adorno, "Freudian Theory and the Pattern of Fascist Propaganda," in *The Essential Frankfurt School Reader*, eds. Andrew Arato and Eike Gebhardt (New York: Continuum, 1982), 131–32.

26. Walter Benjamin, "On the Concept of History," in *Walter Benjamin: Selected Writings*, eds. H. Eiland and M. W. Jennings, vol. 4 (Cambridge, MA: Belknap Press, 2003), 389–400.

27. Sylvia Rivera, "Transvestites: Your Half-Sisters & Half-Brothers of the Revolution, by Sylvia Rivera in *Come Out!*, 1971," in Untorelli, *Street Transvestite Action Revolutionaries*, 19.

28. Alberto Toscano, "The Long Shadow of Racial Fascism," *Boston Review*, October 28, 2020, https://bostonreview.net/articles/alberto-toscano-tk/.

29. Aimé Césaire, *Discourse on Colonialism* (New York : Monthly Review Press, 2001), 35.

30. Césaire, *Discourse on Colonialism*, 35–36.

31. Arthur Bell, "STAR Trek," *The Village Voice*, July 15, 1971. Can be found on https://thespiritwas.tumblr.com/post/18264877034/star-trek-sylvia-star-house-leave-the-lower.

32. Bell, "Star Trek." Can be found on https://thespiritwas.tumblr.com/post/18264877034/star-trek-sylvia-star-house-leave-the-lower.

33. Sessi Kuwabara Blanchard, "At STAR House, Marsha P. Johnson and Sylvia Rivera Created a Home for Trans People," *Vice*, June 8, 2020, https://www.vice.com/en/article/z3enva/star-house-sylvia-rivera-marsha-p-johnson.

34. A. Naomi Paik, *Bans, Walls, Raids, Sanctuary: Understanding U.S. Immigration for the Twenty-First Century* (Oakland, University of California Press, 2020), 104.

35. Sylvia Rivera, "Queens in Exile: The Forgotten Ones," in Untorelli, *Street Transvestite Action Revolutionaries*, 52.

36. Rivera, "Queens in Exile," 52–53.

37. Rivera, "Queens in Exile," 53.

38. Dean Spade, *Mutual Aid: Building Solidarity during This Crisis (and the Next)* (New York: Verso, 2020).

39. Enck-Wanzer, Morales, and Oliver-Velez, *Young Lords*, 219.

40. Herbert Marcuse, *Counterrevolution and Revolt* (Boston: Beacon Press, 1972).

41. Toscano, "Long Shadow of Racial Fascism."

42. Avery F. Gordon, *Keeping Good Time: Reflections on Knowledge, Power, and People* (New York: Routledge, 2016), 129.

Roderick A. Ferguson Reflects on "Queer and Trans Liberation and the Critique of Fascism, or When S.T.A.R. Met Césaire and the Frankfurt School"

I wrote my lecture the way I did because I wanted to determine what kinds of pressures S.T.A.R. might put on concepts and formations that are central to my work—strange affinities, intersectionality, Black radical traditions, Marxism, and the critique of fascism. Ever since I was introduced to the anthology *Street Transvestite Action Revolutionaries: Survival, Revolt, and Queer Antagonist Struggle*, I have been really interested in S.T.A.R. as an archive of strange affinities. Because of the organization's associations with the Gay Liberation Front (GLF), the Puerto Rican Young Lords, and the Black Panthers, S.T.A.R. is a beautiful example of unlikely alliances and coalitions. We're so used to imagining those coalitions through cisgender organizations, but rarely through alliances that involve transgender folks, even less so for organizations from fifty years ago.

I also wanted to revise that old and founding intersectional notion of "triple jeopardy"—race, class, and gender. I wanted to see what might be the benefits of thinking transness, sex work, and radicalism as a tripartite formation that captured the moment of S.T.A.R.'s activism and that articulated "race, class, and gender" in ways that are rarely seen. I was also keenly aware of trying to cite that revision as a kind of Rosetta stone for contemporary considerations if we're thinking about the kind of activism and scholarship represented by CeCe McDonald, Dean Spade, Eric Stanley, Che Gossett, Tourmaline, the trans activists involved in Black Lives Matter (BLM), and so on. One of the guiding questions as I was drafting the lecture was: What happens when intersectionality is routed through transgender histories?

In addition to my efforts to present S.T.A.R.'s history as an example of strange affinities and as the impetus to recast intersectionality, I also wanted to put two histories in conversation that are often held apart—one represented by Stonewall and the other represented by Black radical traditions. That was the point of imagining a conversation between Ida B. Wells and Marsha P. Johnson. In that section of the lecture, each one is trading stories about how people minoritized by race, gender, sexuality, and work, or some combination thereof, are snatched up and violated by the police. In that moment, you see how the violation of cisgender and transgender folks intersects in carceral systems.

That intersection is, for me, not only about those systems per se. It's also about what it takes to produce a fascist society and a police state. I had a sense that I wanted to take trans sex workers as not a passing moment in the story of fascism but as a constant and major element of the story. It was a way of saying that we can't understand fascism unless we understand the circumstances of transgender people, particularly the ones who are minoritized by race and work. It was a way for me to approach an understanding of the everydayness and ubiquity of transphobia. I supposed it was a way of understanding Hannah Arendt's notion of "the banality of evil" in a new context.

Histories of Queer and Trans Scholarship

MARCH 25, 2021

The second *Queer Then and Now* roundtable discussion was held virtually on March 25, 2021, to highlight some of the pioneers from queer of color, transnational, and trans studies scholarship. The roundtable features Roderick A. Ferguson, Jasbir K. Puar, and Susan Stryker in conversation with CLAGS board member Shaka McGlotten. Ferguson, Puar, and Stryker discuss the histories and current state of queer and trans scholarship and activist-scholarship, where queer studies is headed, and what contributions queer and trans studies might provide in the context of a rise of conservative, authoritarian, anti-trans global politics. The roundtable gives a sense of new possibilities for queer and trans now while also reflecting on the multiple legacies of queer studies and politics we inherit.

Shaka McGlotten: Hi, all. Thanks so much to everyone who made this possible, to all the attendees, to all the other members of the board. It is my huge honor to be able to facilitate this part of the night. Susan, Rod, and Jasbir—I couldn't think the way I think without each of your works. I remember when and where I read *Aberrations in Black* and *Terrorist Assemblages* and *Queer Pulp*. So we'll start with a general question about genealogies and debates within trans and queer studies today, about your relationship to CLAGS, and/or new directions in queer and trans studies—and you can feel free to jump off or reflect on your Kessler Lecture.

Roderick A. Ferguson: It's a pleasure to be here, especially with Shaka, Jasbir, and Susan. Let's see. Then and now: queer studies and trans studies scholarship and activism. For some reason that volume, *What's Queer about Queer Studies Now?*, from 2005 has been a kind of marker for me.[1] This is a special issue of *Social Text* that was put together by José Muñoz, David Eng, and Jack Halberstam. It was trying to assess what were then emergent formations within queer studies, extending and perhaps moving away from primarily literary critiques within queer studies, but also trying to highlight work that was using queer studies to intersect with histories of racial capitalism, colonialism, militarization, empire, migration. It was a very exciting moment. I don't know that we thought it would take off the way it has in this moment. What was emergent in that moment has in many ways become the convention within queer studies.

One of the things that has been really heartening for me, in addition to the scholarship that has emerged from that, is also the organizing that has accompanied that emergence and has used those texts that work to inform activism at this moment. For instance, the Black Lives Matter protests, where it is part of an a priori assumption that that movement arises out of and is connected to feminist and queer and trans conversations, work, and activism, existing and prior. The ways in which we are seeing the kinds of fluencies around empire, intersectionality, around militarization and wars in Asia as a way to assess gendered violence, the massacres in Atlanta, I really think for me this is an exciting moment in which the scholarship people have been doing, which was always working hand-in-hand with queer, queer of color, trans activism, is really informing the organizing of this moment. And you see it very clearly, I think, in the interpretations of inequalities around race, around nation, around gender, around sexuality. This is a really important moment to see the intersections between scholarship and activism, especially around this work.

Susan Stryker: I will first offer my thanks to my hosts and copanelists and acknowledge that I am speaking today from the ancestral lands of the Wiyot people in Northern California. We were asked to address a few questions, and I've tried to give a little response to each.

There were two CLAGS conferences—one on queer history in 1995 and one in 2005, a decade later, that was a trans studies conference. I really think of those as bookends for a certain period in the development of trans studies. CLAGS was important in articulating those moments. I write about those conferences a little bit in "(De)Subjugated Knowledges," which is the introduction to the first *Transgender Studies Reader*.[2] But I want to start by saying that I thought my CLAGS Kessler Lecture, which was called "Ghost Dances," was kind of a mess. I was trying out something new in public that I thought didn't quite come together. But in hindsight, I do see it foreshadowing a turn in my work away from a biopolitical focus to something that I would say is more in conversation with the ontological turn and the so-called new materialisms.

I've always been interested in these very straightforwardly Foucauldian kinds of questions about biopolitics, and how techniques and practices of individual, subjective individuation relate to categories for population management for state projects. And in the kinds of cultural, social, political, and economic work that identity does, particularly historically novel and emergent forms of identity—so, how is it that you can read emergent forms of identity and the kinds of communities they constellate as consequences or artifacts of some larger scale socioeconomic political process?

That way of thinking really informs what I understand trans studies to have done from early on. The field often traces its roots to the legacies of Sandy Stone's justly celebrated "Posttransexual Manifesto," which was published in 1991, and to legacies of feminist science studies and feminist epistemology, and to Donna Haraway's work, particularly *Cyborg Manifesto*. The term "transgender" became a name for Stone's posttranssexual politics the next year in 1992, with the publication of Leslie Feinberg's pamphlet "Transgender Liberation: A Movement Whose Time Has Come."

But from the biopolitical perspective, I think it's really important to note that the widespread uptake and dissemination of the term "transgender"— which had been repurposed from marginalized subcultures of transfeminine people, who had themselves repurposed it from psychomedical discourse— is that this uptake of "transgender" took in the context of the collapse of the Soviet Union and the end of the Cold War. I think of "transgender" as a name for a formation that addresses the new world order of global capital's irrational exuberance in the 1990s. I don't want to lose sight of the fact that "transgender" was a term popularized by a Marxist, Leslie Feinberg, whose last words were, "I want to be remembered as a revolutionary communist"; that it circulated transnationally primarily through global philanthropic work and NGOs addressing HIV/AIDS; and that it was quickly and somewhat awkwardly assimilated into a neoliberal diversity and inclusion model.

I really think of transgender as this site for people who are trying to imagine a different world order as well as something that was useful within the context of an actually emerging world order—that transgender has always been a site of struggle and strategy for reterritorialism.

I think the two most important things going on in trans studies right now—one, the emergence of a trans of color critique that interrogates the "unmarked as white" origins of the field in the 1990s. I have a lot to say about that. The other question is about the strange necessity of once again needing to address an explicitly transphobic version of feminism. That trans critique of transphobic feminism was part of the articulation of the field in

Sandy Stone's work, referencing her own history of being targeted by certain varieties of transphobic feminism in the 1970s. And that it is striking to me that this—it's called the TERF discourse—is something that seemed to be on the wane for several decades and in recent years has just exploded with a newfound virulence. It has moved from being something that was fairly contained in certain pockets of mostly lesbian separatist feminist discourse, to something that is now totally enmeshed with a much broader reactionary ethno-populist white supremacist movement. The discourse has moved from the margins to something that is very central to some of the large political questions we are all living within now.

In the interest of time, I am going to stop right there—maybe can talk more later about why I think trans continues to be a hot-button topic in the present. But I will stop now and pass the mic over to Jasbir.

Jasbir K. Puar: It's good to see everyone. I'm honored to be here. I want to thank CLAGS for organizing this event and thank all the tech folks, and also thanks to Shaka and Rod and Susan for being here. Thank you, Justin, for the land acknowledgment, and also Debanuj and Margot. It's an honor and a privilege to be here in this company, and I also want to congratulate CLAGS on its anniversary. It takes a lot of labor and creativity and ingenuity to keep this thing going. I was a board member of CLAGS in 1999 when I first moved to New York. So, it's really wonderful to continue to be involved with CLAGS.

I don't know if I misunderstood the assignment, or just did something different, but I wanted to spend a little bit of time, in the spirit of "Queer Then and Now," to talk about the farmers' protests in India and hopefully make some links: both with what Rod was talking about in terms of contemporary organizing and the intersections of all of these different issues of anti-capitalist and anti-neoliberal organizing that is going on in India, and also with what Susan said about the envisioning of new worlds, which I think is part of some of the aspirational parts of these protests.

Of course, these protests may, at first glance, seem to have no relationship to queerness or to transness. These protests began in September of last year when one hundred thousand tractors from villages from Punjab and neighboring states started moving and blocking transportation in the New Delhi region. Then there was a general strike in November of 250 million people countrywide. These are protests that are challenging three farm laws that the Indian government had decided to pass.

These protests have been called the largest protests in all of human history. While these farm laws are about Indian agricultural labor writ large, there is also a specific existentialist crisis going on in Punjab that is animating these protests. It has been very long in the making. There have been decades of land grab and liberalization, and a kind of taking away of power from laborers and from farmers in that region. These protests have been called leftist protests, but they've also been called Sikh protests, and so that's the kind of intersection that I'm really interested in. There has been a rethinking of Sikhism in this particular organizing context, and one of the most interesting commentators about these protests, Bikram Gill, had said that nothing will be the same again. That is how large and expansive, and how intense and really pivotal these protests are.

There has been allotting, but also a repoliticization of Sikhi, which refers to the tenets of Sikhism, as fundamentally informing the organization and conduct of the protesters. So, it's a question then: Is this a secular protest? It's not exactly a nonsecular protest. The protests have been dismissed as a revival of the Khalistani separatist movement in the '70s and '80s. There's a lot of thin lines that are being navigated here, because the protesters are largely from Punjab and predominantly Sikh. How and whether to protest as Sikh without being dismissed as a terrorist? How to respond to these forms of Indian state violence—there have been killings, disappearances, incarceration, sexual assault of female leaders in the protest—without being stereotyped as warriors? How to resist the neoliberalism of the Indian nation-state without being vilified as seditious or traitorous?

One aspect I wanted to focus on is there has been a lot of hailing in Sikh forms about the praxis of langar at the protests, which is the praxis of communal cooking, feeding, and eating that is part of a broader philosophy of Sikhism. From the advent of Sikhism, langar was envisioned as an anti-caste practice, and this includes the caste of women—so, fundamentally against gender differentiation. In practice, commitment to these ideals varies—and it does not mitigate the tensions at the protests that caste differences are sutured through the land to the violence of this owner-labor relationship as well as to Sikh patriarchy. A lot of these commentators have situated langar as a form of conviviality that challenges caste, but its challenges to gender inequality have been far less commented upon, and that is what I'm interested in here. Langar is an important part of the sustainability of these protest spaces, feeding not only thousands of protesters daily but also feeding neighboring communities.

This speaks a little bit to what Susan was talking about—that langar is not a form of mutual aid, it's a mode of envisioning more egalitarian forms of communalizing on an affective, corporeal, ecological level. It's an institution, it's a theological philosophy, it's a conceptual space and, obviously, a daily praxis. It's also a horizon of becoming that's rooted in this ongoing work of corporeal relationality. You might have gotten notice or caught wind of the fact that there were Sikh gurdwaras serving langar at Black Lives Matter protests last summer, and that this is something they've started doing whenever possible.

So, here we get to the *queer now* part. On Sikh Twitter, which has for months been abuzz with real-time updates on the farmers' protests, there has been casteist harassment of queer and trans and Dalit Sikhs by what are being called cishetero Jat Sikhs. These started last fall—they've intensified in February. These otherwise progressive supporters of and participants in these farmers' protests are espousing this really vicious Jat Sikh pride in part through this queerphobic, transphobic, anti-caste vitriol. In response, Manu and manmit, a nonbinary Dalit and a trans Sikh respectively, penned a series of brilliant articles condemning the failure to realize the radical potential of Sikhi within the terms of Sikhi itself, writing that "Sikhi annihilated caste but this annihilation was not a passive proclamation but an active disavowal of the caste system through instituting various measures like pangat, langar, and sangat."[3] They go on to remind the Sikh community that equality and liberation does not rest in your statements or the lack thereof, but instead in an active commitment to dismantling casteist cisheteronormativity. So, if you can see what I am getting at: there is no anti-caste praxis without gender abolition, and there's no gender abolition without a commitment to dismantling these hierarchies of capitalism and class in these communities.

What I found so compelling about these interventions is that they are not actually professing langar to be a clear practice, but as a space of Sikhi that has already cohered to the multiplicities of gender and the banishing of caste. Queer, trans, and Dalit response to Hindu homonationalism is not based on a counter-homonationalism but on what already exists within the folds of Sikhi. This is not a demand, so much, for visibility of certain identities, and it is not a politics of asking for inclusion; it is more so an ethical theological orientation to these identities.

The radical force of queer and trans and Dalit Sikhs emanates from within, not from outside or externally to the congregation. In other words, there is no true Sikhi without queer and trans and Dalit Sikhs. This has been condemned as a blasphemous statement, and yet the religious principles confirm it to be true. Finally, in these series of interventions, Manu and manmit acknowledge the presence that is already there at these protests: the caste-oppressed and the queer and trans farmers fighting within the protests right now.

These anti-caste politics amongst these queer, trans, Dalit, nonbinary Sikhs are not especially wedded to the elements of Sikh history that lend to archival reclamation. For example, there are sometimes playful musings about whether or not the gurus were queer. I am reading their demands not within a kind of past/future or traditional/modern binary but as a desire for a utopian radical Sikhi horizon, which would not be possible without achieving the dissolution of caste and gender differences. And in fact, as Manu and manmit make clear in their missives, langar cannot be truly practiced without challenging casteism, queerphobia, and transphobia, and without recognizing how these lives have been integral to the world-making institutions of Sikhi. Far from being distractions from these anti-neoliberal, anti-capitalist ideological thrusts of these farmers' protests—which is what some of us continue to be told—this queer, trans, and Dalit vision of radical Sikhi is at the heart of this evolved resistance movement.

That's the queer *now* part. I think there will be time to elaborate a bit on the queer *then* part in conversation, but I wanted to draw attention to why, as queer and trans people, these protests are important.

Shaka McGlotten: Thank you so much. The first question is about the transnational circulation of queer studies, and of queer of color critique. Where are these texts meeting people and circulating? And how, in turn, are those contacts informing, in turn, what it is we do in the largely Anglo-European academy? You might even think about something very quotidian: maybe you've been in another country and someone said, "Your work did a thing for me at a time." How did that inform where you went in your thinking and writing from there?

Jasbir K. Puar: I just had a conversation with Rahul Rao, whose new book is called *Out of Time* and looks at the circulation of homonationalism as a term and as a kind of accusation.[4] When Rahul launched his book about a year ago, he said, now that we understand homonationalism, we've overcorrected for it. And this cleared up this huge fog of anxiety that I'd been having about the circuitry and the transits of homonationalism as moving precisely through the homocapitalist, as he calls it, circuits of empire, of settler colonialism, of multiculturalism, and of academic institutional privilege—moving through those very circuits that homonationalism was meant to critique and to somehow undermine.

I've always had a very complicated relationship to the way homonationalism has been taken up as a sound bite in other locations, when in actuality it's really wedded to a US context, particularly the post-9/11 context and particularly Islamophobia. Rahul's book argues for a counternotion called "homocapitalism," and he develops this idea of homocapitalism from his work in Uganda and India. It really looks at how the civilizational disciplining of "homonationalism" is superseded by the lure of a kind of capitalist integration of queer subjects whether it's through the International Monetary Fund or NGOs or other kinds of government entities, international financial instruments (IFIs). The way he explains it is a kind of thinking through of Partha Chatterjee's work, where the spiritual is a kind of domestic, female-gendered space, and that's the space that holds down the cultural narratives at stake; and then the world, or the outside, public space, is understood as worldly and mobile.

And so homocapitalism works through this bifurcation of the holding on to certain kinds of cultural norms and not submitting to homonationalism as an accusation, but then fostering queer subjects, queer LGBTQ organizing. One of his main points is that a lot of LGBTQ organizing in Global South locations has proliferated and flourished precisely because of access to neoliberal capital—and so he's trying to think about what that relationship is. That is just one example of, for me, having to backtrack and ask questions about why homonationalism has been taken up in so many other places. And whether homonationalism itself has then allowed or made way for a kind of moving past an anti-capitalist critique in queer studies in some ways. That is just a concern of mine.

Roderick A. Ferguson: I think I have a similar relationship to the circulation of my work as Jasbir's. I decided right after *Aberrations* was published that I would be the witness to my work—that I wouldn't try to control its circulation. And for me, it is a way of exercising this point that Nietzsche makes in the preface of *On the Genealogy of Morality*, where he says: the writer is the precondition of the text, but the reader is really its condition. So, as witness to my work's circulation, it's been a way for me to see what other people do with the arguments, with the frameworks, with the categories.

Not to be the one to say this is right or this is not, but to see how the categories are remade and refashioned to speak to the particular urgencies in whatever locale that we're talking about. When I have been in those places, outside of this country, it's trying to adopt the position of the listener—and listen to what people are doing with the work, what they are wrestling with. But also trying to use that encounter to revise my own citational practices, so that I take and learn from the folks that I am talking to, so that I revise my citational practices in the classroom, in my scholarship, in terms of the text, in terms of the authors, and in terms of the organizers. Because if you remember the critiques that women of color feminists were making of Anglo-American feminists back in the '70s and '80s, the critique of "our work is not impacting the way feminism is done"—that is a way of noting how certain forms of hegemony are really established through how and who we cite. For me, that encounter with my work, but also with people who are using the work in other settings, is not a moment for me to engage in a kind of ego congratulation, but really a moment to open myself to a reinvention.

Susan Stryker: Thinking about the transnational circulation of some of the work that I've done, I will just say that I often see a real disconnect between what happens in trans studies in the academy in the US and what people seem hungry for elsewhere. I am often asked when I speak in other countries—I am often asked to speak on two particular topics, and one of them is that in whatever country I am speaking in, there is work going on that, for me, is the biopolitical question of gender. That there is something that the state is trying to do, or that activists are trying to do within the state, to make lives more livable to trans people through changes in policy, access to health care, provision of social services. That there is something very tangible—that they want me to come in and be the person from the US with a certain cultural capital they can mobilize in relation to some local campaign. While I think that work is vital in terms of saving people's lives, it is often not for me the most intellectually interesting. It feels necessary—I get it, I understand why it is important.

The other thing that happens, and this has increasingly been the case over the last few years, is that there's something that happened and really energized a transphobic feminist group in alliance with right-wing evangelical groups or other right-wing ethnopopulist groups. And I get called in to be the trans person that other people can be in solidarity with to push back against this really pernicious framing of trans issues.

To link that to the direction I was trying to go with my Kessler Lecture back in 2008: I was increasingly feeling like intellectually I understood trans issues through this biopolitical framework, but that it wasn't enough. What was at stake in trans lives was not winning an argument because you had a good analysis of something, that it was intellectually grounded, that you could use evidence, that you could use data, that you could rationally persuade someone of the rightness of your position—because trans issues were increasingly caught up in what I called "imaginary warfare." It was rooted in an imaginary, an ethnic nationalism, that the trans figure becomes this phantasm. And what is needed is not a better argument but a kind of mobilization in a different register of the power that gets invested in trans-ness. It's like the positioning of it is something demonic or irrational, or something threatening and disruptive, that needs to be eliminated as a threat. And so how is it that you can take the power invested in transness and use it to undo the very terms of which the debate about transness has been consti-tuted? That it is something that is more mythopoetic or metaphysical or even theological or religious; that it's something about moving in the immaterial and about narrating it differently and finding some kind of ritual that helps us invoke and materialize what is needed so that life can persist. Or else, if not persisting, mark in a mournful way of passing of something that is being lost.

If I think of where I am interested in trying to take my work in trans studies, it's much less in the direction of recent analysis and much more in the direction of a kind of public storytelling that helps invoke and evoke the kind of world we want to live in—that unbinds the way certain ener-gies have been bound, to create the potential for something new to emerge.

Shaka McGlotten: Thank you so much. I'm going to riff for a moment or two—I was struck by the stories of eating together, being fed together, breaking down certain kinds of boundaries. Storying together, as Susan was saying. Roderick, I was thinking of your piece "Sissies at the Picnic,"[5] and about the transnational circulation of your work and the encounters they've produced. There's a longing to connect. You made connections. The work affected people. Susan, you were describing—in a way, you're helping to save lives in these contexts. That's extraordinary evidence that queer worlds are being built transnationally, that there is a conversation. Now, whether that can decenter the hegemony of the US academy and the production of queer studies, we can hope so. But that there's a longing and that people get some-thing that they desperately need; but one also receives things that maybe one didn't know that one needs. I also heard a lot of interesting words come up, again in different ways with each of you—"ethics," "foster," "theological" came up more than once, interesting words to hear in this space for different reasons. The politics of eating together, and the longing that we have to do so and to story together.

Talking about the transnational circulation of feminist and queer texts: What feminism are transphobic feminists reading? I understand that these strains of feminism, as Susan was saying, come from the 1970s—but what are they reading, what feminism?

Susan Stryker: I think the texts that keep getting circulated are Mary Daly—back to *Gyn/Ecology*. It's Janice Raymond, it's Robin Morgan. Increasingly, it's Sheila Jeffreys. But these are just places where I would say the meme or the discourse originated. You can trace it back to certain texts, but I think that it circulates now in a way that is not historically grounded. It's not like there are the scholars of a certain strain of feminist thought. I think it's trans scholars, actually, who have done more of that genealogical work. What circulates now in certain bad versions of feminism—it's kind of like the phantasmic figure of the Jew in antisemitic fantasies. Even though I disagree with Žižek about a lot of things, I think his reading of the phantasm, the antisemitic phantasm of the Jew—it's the same fantasy structure that is in transphobic feminism, which I think is why it dovetails so effortlessly with some of the resurgence in ethnonationalist, right-wing, authoritarian populism. That it is essentially a fantasy about which body is imagined as an internal threat to the integrity of the nation's borders and boundaries, who should be a member of the body politic, and who needs to be expelled as a foreigner. And that the trans figure is a very uncanny figure because it's not necessarily imagined as someone who has come into the nation from outside, but it's the threat within the nation, of its own potential for disruption and undoing and falling apart.

Shaka McGlotten: Thank you, Susan. So, our last question: We want to hear who you're reading, who you are excited to be reading. Glow up the young scholars, throw shine on the ideas that people in attendance might not have learned about yet. Tell us what you're reading.

Roderick A. Ferguson: I tend to shy away from these questions because I always leave somebody out. But I will make a plug for my colleague Evren

Savcı's new book about the intersections of discourses around sexuality, civic nationalism in Turkey, and neoliberalism.[6] I think what excites me in general are the folks who are running with the work that was started early in the 2000s that we were all a part of—the questions around the material dimensions, the political and economic questions, the questions, as Jasbir was mentioning, around activism. The questions around variegating the genealogies of these categories, whether we're talking about queerness or transness, that Susan was mentioning in terms of trans of color critical work that's emerging. So everyone who's doing that work, I want to lift up.

Jasbir K. Puar: Thank you for mentioning Evren's book. It's really an incredible book, so I'll double glow that up. I was reading Rod's book last week, *We Demand,* which is also another book that everyone should read. This goes to something that Aren Aizura said in a roundtable on trans thinking that's published in the *Left of Queer* issue of *Social Text* that David Eng and I did, where he said a lot of the amazing trans scholars are precariously employed.[7] They don't have tenure or tenure-track jobs, and they're moving from postdoc to adjunct labor to etcetera. So even before I think about field formation, I'm wondering about the material conditions of possibility in the academy writ large right now, which I think is conditioning everything we are talking about, including circulation, including what we're assigning and who we're reading.

Matthew Brim's book is something I think we all have to contend with: *Poor Queer Studies,* where he's really marking the uneven institutional privileges that we have or don't have, and how that actually conditions and speaks to a lot of what is being circulated.[8] Rod, your book was so incredible in terms of thinking about the university in crisis, as a place of protest and dissent but also as a place of exploited labor—that we have to situate the university as a place of exploitation of workers.

The other thing I was thinking about—Rod, you might know the answer to this more than I do—but the last thirty years of institutionalization of queer studies has been largely through a relatively okay job market. Or relatively more jobs, compared to what's going on now. So that also makes me think about this uneven institutional access. And Susan, you've done so much work to solidly institutionalize transgender studies, both through *TSQ* and through the way that you've organized institutional resources around jobs and positions and etcetera. So that's my counterquestion: What do we do about the university? What do we do about the conditions of knowledge production that we are facing right now?

Roderick A. Ferguson: I think you are absolutely right. It's also the question of how do we radically democratize the condition of that production, especially given that there will be a lot of losses on the market? And how not to turn that into further diminishment of lives and loss of intellectual production. Where are the other sites within and outside the university that we could encourage and build, that will be as vital and sometimes more vital than universities in the production of critical knowledges?

Susan Stryker: I feel like I had some opportunities to "institutionalize" trans studies in a certain way over the past decade, and most of those ways have shut down or fallen apart around problems of the neoliberal university as well as COVID. In a recent issue of *TSQ* called *Trans* Studies Now*, I gave a postmortem on what I felt like happened and has happened at the University of Arizona, and that particular version of trying to institutionalize trans studies.[9]

The COVID crisis—it's devastating. I feel like we are in a storm where we're only now starting to poke our heads out and see what the damage has been. But I've also been amazed at what has been happening over Zoom. We need to figure out how to—I hate to use the word "capitalize"—but how do we take advantage of what's been happening on Zoom? I've gone to events—Rod, you came to the Mills College Trans Studies Speaker Series—we've been getting nine hundred people coming to these events live. So how can we rethink the university? I'm interested in putting my energy into really thinking about how to work as a para-academic again in some new way.

Then to just make some shameless plugs—first of all, let me triple-team on Evren Savcı. There is a new series coming out at Duke coedited by Eliza Steinbock, Jian Neo Chen, and me. It's called *ASTERISK: Gender, Trans-, and All That Comes After*, which is a way of thinking of methodologies and aesthetics that have come out of trans studies and how gender never happens in a vacuum. It's always in relationship to other things that are being transed. So how do we think transgender in relationship to the transnational or the transgenic or transspecies or other categories—categories of race or ability. The first three books that will be coming out in that series—the first one will be micha cárdenas's book on trans of color poetics. Then there will be books by Marquis Bey and Cameron Awkward-Rich. I think these are some of the most exciting work that's happening in trans studies right now. We've got a long list of fifteen or twenty books that are somewhere in the pipeline, somewhere between almost ready and bright idea that we are trying to cultivate. But in spite of the precarity of academic employment right now, there is a huge body of work that is on the horizon and coming into being right now. So keep your eyes peeled for work in that series.

Shaka McGlotten: Yes, the university as refuge—and all the violence that comes with this refuge. It's amazing you are able to do this, Susan. It's just fantastic, congratulations.

Jasbir K. Puar: To continue this plugging of works. Jian Neo Chen's book *Trans Exploits* just won an award from the Association for Asian American Studies.[10] It's a really fantastic book. I also just finished reading Marquis Bey's *Anarcho-Blackness*, which I thought was just really incredible.[11] So I, too, am really excited. The work on trans and particularly Black trans reproductive labor. Waiting always excitedly for Treva Ellison's work. Cam Awkward-Rich as well.

The other thing that I want to mention is the Global South trans studies that is really coming into being right now. I'm teaching transnational sexualities this fall—half the syllabus is from *TSQ*. I think *TSQ* has just done a fantastic job decentering US knowledge production as well as US-based scholars. Trans studies is really exciting to me. As well as this work on caste and gender, which I think is going to become increasingly more important and relevant to organizing and activist spaces as well as we start untangling the complexities of racial formation in other places.

Roderick A. Ferguson: I will add Ghassan Moussawi's *Disruptive Situations: Fractal Orientalism and Queer Strategies in Beirut*.[12] The question I have revisits something Susan and Jasbir brought up in terms of the question of institutionalization. In terms of the institutionalization of homonationalism on one hand, and of trans studies and transness on the other hand, and what their observations are for how to produce alternative institutions or institutional practices.

Jasbir K. Puar: I wanted to just flag how many grad students are striking or getting ready to strike, how many labor issues are we dealing with now. The Rutgers union is one of the strongest unions in the country and is fighting for grad student funding extensions. So to think of the university as not just a place where we produce countercarceral knowledge, but where we actively resist the carceral assemblage that Rod so beautifully lays out in *We Demand*, that's been normalized in some ways since the 1970s.[13] As Rod points out, the random campus security becomes campus police. The cops off campus movement that's starting to organize nationally. I think all of these—Students for Justice in Palestine, the growth of SJP has been phenomenal. As a faculty advisor for a couple of years, that work has been so important, and it's something that so many entities are trying to shut down. So I think we have to keep thinking about the ways in which we can keep these institutional spaces ones where the question of who is doing what work is always at play or is always being highlighted.

Shaka McGlotten: There are fantastic questions from the audience. To begin: this is from an Aboriginal trans professor in what is now known as Australia. They ask: We do land acknowledgments—some of us do land acknowledgments sometimes—but there doesn't seem to have been much conversation in this meeting about First Nations communities and their part in trans and queer history, and especially the ways in which that also articulates with anti-colonial efforts?

Roderick A. Ferguson: Certainly, the work on settler colonialism and its intersections with queerness and transness is of absolute importance. That we did not mention it should not be taken as a sign that it is not regarded and also not an important emergence within these fields. One of the really inspiring aspects of this moment, I think, are the ways in which our undergraduate students—and also our graduate students, Indigenous and non-Indigenous students—are insisting on a reckoning with settler colonialism in our various critical locations. And that work should be lifted up and should be encouraged as well.

Susan Stryker: In that same issue of *TSQ* called *Trans* Studies Now*, there is an article by Madi Day—who's a post-grad student in the country called Australia now writing on Indigenous queer and trans studies in Australia— that I found really useful for thinking about how trans studies can trace different genealogies, different roots, other than the Western biomedical complex.[14] To second what Rod was saying, the idea of gender as part of the biopolitical apparatus of settlement, of taking populations and turning them into something else through the operations of settler colonialism, is an absolutely fundamental—in some ways maybe the most fundamental—aspect of gender. María Lugones started to long ago think about the coloniality of gender. And you're right, we did not address that dimension a lot in our remarks today. But I have to say I'm really inspired by work that some of my students are doing on rethinking the relationship between Western and Eurocentric notions of transgender and Indigenous and two-spirit traditions in North America in particular. It is part of the next generation of work I am seeing coming along and that I am very excited to see.

Shaka McGlotten: Another question from the audience: What are the most potentially promising para-academic sites for precarious scholars at the moment? So I think that extends the discussion of institution-building— they already exist, right? There are already ones—there have to be—people came before us, elders.

Jasbir K. Puar: I want to reflect a little about what Susan was talking about—the way that these Zoom events have created a kind of transnational or more global lexicon for certain kinds of conversations because we can talk to people, people can talk to people that they otherwise would not necessarily be talking to. Zoom has other issues; they've shut down a couple of events on Palestine now because of pressure from people complaining about certain events. So we have to be careful about Zoom in that way because we need alternative platforms. But the para-academic spaces of these virtual events, I think, should continue in some way.

They also enable important access on all sorts of levels. You can see where accommodations are easy to implement, and people with disabilities have been asking for them, but they have only really been sutured into the way that we do our work through COVID. So that's something to take note of as well. Again, I don't want to minimize the forms of surveillance as well as the monetization of all of this, but what kinds of alternative spaces are people building? A lot of it seems to be virtual.

Roderick A. Ferguson: One way of invoking our queer and trans ancestors would be to build more of those spaces—to actively see the constitution of alternative spaces in institutional formations as completely in line with what people were doing in '69 and onward. That should become part of our queer and trans social practice.

Shaka McGlotten: I have learned so much from you over the years. And I think that fostering these spaces in the ways that we want them to be fostered—I think you are right, Jasbir, this is one of the ways we can build these connections, however imperfect. As well as all the face-to-face organizing, all the forms of mutual aid that people have so beautifully demonstrated over the last year, and that we can continue to provide for one another. So thank you all so much.

Notes

1. David L. Eng, Jack Halberstam, and José Esteban Muñoz, "Introduction: What's Queer about Queer Studies Now?" *Social Text* 23, nos. 3–4 (84–85) (2005): 1–17.

2. Susan Stryker, "(De)Subjugated Knowledges," in *The Transgender Studies Reader*, eds. Susan Stryker and Stephen Whittle (New York: Routledge, 2006).

3. manmit and Manu, "How to Create a Panth That Supports Caste-Oppressed and Queer and Trans Folk," *Kaur Life*, January 24, 2021, https://kaurlife.org/2021/01/24/creating-a-panth-that-supports-caste-oppressed-and-queer-and-trans-folks/.

4. Rahul Rao, *Out of Time: The Queer Politics of Postcoloniality* (New York: Oxford University Press, 2020).

5. Roderick A. Ferguson, "Sissies at the Picnic: The Subjugated Knowledges of a Black Rural Queer," in *Feminist Waves, Feminist Generations: Life Stories from the Academy*, eds. Hokulani K. Aikau, Karla A. Erickson, and Jennifer L. Pierce (Minneapolis: University of Minnesota Press, 2007), 188–96.

6. Evren Savcı, *Queer in Translation: Sexual Politics under Neoliberal Islam* (Durham, NC: Duke University Press, 2021).

7. Aren Z. Aizura, Marquis Bey, Toby Beauchamp, Treva Ellison, Jules Gill-Peterson, and Eliza Steinbock, "Thinking with Trans Now," *Social Text* 38, no. 4 (145) (2020): 125–47.

8. Matt Brim, *Poor Queer Studies: Confronting Elitism in the University* (Durham, NC: Duke University Press, 2020).

9. Susan Stryker, "Introduction: Trans* Studies Now," *TSQ* 7, no. 3 (2020): 299–305.

10. Jian Neo Chen, *Trans Exploits: Trans of Color Cultures and Technologies in Movement* (Durham, NC: Duke University Press, 2019).

11. Marquis Bey, *Anarcho-Blackness: Notes toward a Black Anarchism* (Chico, CA: AK Press, 2020).

12. Ghassan Moussawi, *Disruptive Situations: Fractal Orientalism and Queer Strategies in Beirut* (Philadelphia: Temple University Press, 2020).

13. Roderick A. Ferguson, *We Demand: The University and Student Protests* (Oakland: University of California Press, 2017).

14. Madi Day, "Indigenist Origins: Institutionalizing Indigenous Queer and Trans Studies in Australia," *TSQ* 7, no. 3 (2020): 367–73.

Permissions Acknowledgments

Grateful acknowledgment is made to each of the Kessler lecturers for permission to reprint their lectures in this volume. Additional permissions information is listed below:

"Geologies of Queer Studies," Gayle Rubin
"Geologies of Queer Studies: It's Déjà Vu All Over Again" is reprinted from Gayle Rubin, *Deviations: A Gayle Rubin Reader*, 347–56. Copyright © 2012 by Gayle Rubin. Used by permission of Duke University Press. All rights reserved. www.dukeupress.edu.

"Cinematic Rearticulations," Isaac Julien
"Cinematic Rearticulations" by Isaac Julien is reprinted from Lidia Curti et al., eds, *The Other Cinema, the Cinema of the Other*, special issue of *Anglistica AION* 11, nos. 1–2 (2007): 63–71. http://www.serena.unina.it/index.php/anglistica-aion/issue/view/596.

Excerpts from "When My Brother Fell (For Joseph Beam)," "Visiting Hours," and "Heavy Breathing" are reprinted from Essex Hemphill, *Ceremonies: Prose and Poetry*. Copyright © 1992 by Essex Hemphill. Used by permission of the Estate of Essex Hemphill , c/o the Frances Goldin Literary Agency.

"Candidates for My Love," Adrienne Rich
"'Candidates for My Love': Three Gay and Lesbian Poets" is reprinted from Adrienne Rich, *A Human Eye: Essays on Art in Society, 1997–2008*. Copyright © 2009 by Adrienne Rich. Used by permission of W. W. Norton & Company, Inc.

Excerpt from "Among My Friends Love Is a Great Sorrow" is reprinted from Robert Duncan, *Robert Duncan: The Collected Early Poems and Plays*. Copyright © 2019 by Robert Duncan. Used by permission of University of California Press.

Excerpts from "A Woman Is Talking to Death" are reprinted from Judy Grahn, *The Judy Grahn Reader*. First published in 1974 by The Women's

Editors' Acknowledgments

As a discipline, queer studies is nothing but collaborative. This volume represents the work of many people coming together to mend an often messy archive. Our deepest thanks goes out to them.

We thank our fellow CLAGS board members—Abdulhamit Arvas, Ahmad Qais Munhazim, Alexis Clements, Allisonjoy Faelnar, Arianna Martinez, Ariel G. Mekler, Debarati Biswas, Elvis Bakaitis, Jaime Shearn Coan, James K. Harris, Lavelle Porter, Monique Guishard, Red Washburn, Rodrigo Brandão, Shaka McGlotten, Shanté Paradigm Smalls, Terrance Wooten, and Velina Manolova—who supported this project, with special thanks to the CLAGS board co-chairs: Shawn(ta) Smith (2017–2021) and Laura Westengard (2021–present). We thank the CLAGS executive director, Justin T. Brown, as well as Jasmina Sinanović and Donna Huaman, for their logistical support. Jasmina has maintained the CLAGS archives and has been instrumental in attending to the social media for the roundtables and other virtual events during the pandemic. Donna was so helpful mining the CLAGS office for twenty-year-old VHS tapes of Kessler Lectures. We thank Stephanie Hsu (previous CLAGS board member) for providing us with important insight into previous discussions about assembling the Kessler Lectures.

We thank the CLAGS crew who blazed this trail with the first volume, *Queer Ideas: The David R. Kessler Lectures in Lesbian and Gay Studies*, published by Feminist Press in 2003: CLAGS founder Martin Duberman (1999–2003), executive director Alisa Solomon (2003–2007), executive director Paisley Currah, and the board members. Thanks also to the prior boards who nominated each Kessler awardee and the CLAGS staff who made possible the Kessler Lectures.

We thank our two research assistants on this project, Oriana Ullman and Jordan Victorian. Oriana was with us for the first year of the project; she is responsible for most of the bios gathered here as well as painstaking transcription editing of many of the lectures and ace internet sleuthing (tracking down the posters for each lecture and many newsletters). Jordan joined the project in its second year and is responsible for carefully organizing and editing the roundtables and some of the lectures gathered here, as well as unearthing some of the deeper history of CLAGS that we drew on to frame the volume. We could not have put this volume together without their assistance and contributions. We thank a Wesleyan University special project grant for enabling the assistance of (then) Wesleyan undergraduate Oriana Ullman, and Leila Rupp, (then) director of Feminist Futures Initiative, for providing us with Jordan Victorian as our graduate research assistant during 2020–2021.

Support from the Feminist Futures initiative at the University of California, Santa Barbara, was crucial to our two live roundtable conversations, "Queer Then and Now," held via Zoom and transcribed in this volume. Oriana Ullman and Jordan Victorian also provided key technical support. We thank CLAGS board members Shaka McGlotten and Shanté Paradigm Smalls for moderating these two discussions, as well as our fellow board members and CLAGS staff who made those two events possible.

We thank the Feminist Press, which met our book proposal with enthusiasm, and our marvelous editors, Lauren Rosemary Hook and Nick Whitney. We want to extend a big thank-you to the presses and estates that granted us reprint permissions: Duke University Press, Dancing Foxes Press, Norton, *Anglistica*, Douglas Crimp's estate, and Adrienne Rich's estate.

Of course, most of our gratitude goes to the words and scholarship of the queer and trans studies scholars and activists and visionaries in this book and beyond who have made all our work possible.

The Feminist Press publishes books that
ignite movements and social transformation.
Celebrating our legacy, we lift up insurgent
and marginalized voices from around the
world to build a more just future.

See our complete list of books at
feministpress.org

THE FEMINIST PRESS
AT THE CITY UNIVERSITY OF NEW YORK
FEMINISTPRESS.ORG